I0094776

Political Disaffection in Contemporary Democracies

Citizens of many democracies are becoming increasingly critical of basic political institutions and detached and disaffected from politics in general.

This new comparative analysis of political disaffection focuses on major democracies throughout Latin America, Asia and Europe. Including comparative chapters as well as longitudinal case studies, this study brings together leading scholars to address three key areas of the current debate:

- The conceptual discussion surrounding political disaffection.
- The factors causing voters to turn away from politics.
- The actual consequences of political disaffection for democracy.

This is a highly relevant topic as representative democracies are coming to face new developments. It deals with the reasons and consequences of the so-called 'democratic deficit' in a systematic way that enables the reader to develop a well-rounded sense of the area and its main debates.

This book is an invaluable resource for all students of Political Science, Sociology, Cultural Studies, and Comparative Politics.

Mariano Torcal is Full Professor in Political Science at the Pompeu Fabra University in Barcelona and National Coordinator of the European Social Survey in Spain. **José Ramón Montero** is Full Professor of Political Science at the Universidad Autónoma de Madrid (UAM) and at the Centro de Estudios Avanzados en Ciencias Sociales, Instituto Juan March, Madrid.

Routledge research in comparative politics

Political Disaffection in Contemporary Democracies

Social capital, institutions, and politics

Edited by Mariano Torcal and José Ramón Montero

Routledge
Taylor & Francis Group

LONDON AND NEW YORK

First published 2006
by Routledge
2 Park Square, Milton Park, Abingdon, Oxon OX14 4RN

Simultaneously published in the USA and Canada
by Routledge
711 Third Avenue, New York, NY 10017

Routledge is an imprint of the Taylor & Francis Group, an informa business

First issued in paperback 2012

© 2006 Mariano Torcal and José Ramón Montero for selection and
editorial matter; individual contributors, their contributions.

Typeset in Baskerville by Wearset Ltd, Boldon, Tyne and Wear

All rights reserved. No part of this book may be reprinted or
reproduced or utilized in any form or by any electronic, mechanical,
or other means, now known or hereafter invented, including
photocopying and recording, or in any information storage or
retrieval system, without permission in writing from the publishers.

British Library Cataloguing in Publication Data
A catalogue record for this book is available from the British Library

Library of Congress Cataloging in Publication Data
A catalog record for this book has been requested

ISBN13: 978-0-415-51138-4 (pbk)
ISBN13: 978-0-415-34066-3 (hbk)
ISBN13: 978-0-203-08618-6 (ebk)

Contents

Figures

Tables

Contributors

Geoffrey Evans is Official Fellow in Politics, Nuffield College, Oxford, and University Professor in the Sociology of Politics. A member of the British Elections Studies team for many years, he has also directed large-scale studies of social and political change in Eastern Europe and Northern Ireland. Joint editor of *Electoral Studies* since 1999, in 2004 he became the founding director of the Centre for Research Methods in the Social Sciences at Oxford. He has published over a hundred articles and chapters on electoral behaviour, comparative political sociology, and related topics. His most recent books are *The End of Class Politics?* (Oxford University Press, 1999) and with Pippa Norris, *Critical Elections* (Sage, 1999).

Richard P. Gunther is Professor of Political Science at the Ohio State University. At Ohio State, he has also served as Director of the West European Studies Program and Director of the Office for International Studies. He is founder and co-chair of the Subcommittee on Southern Europe of the American Council of Learned Societies and the Social Science Research Council. His latest publications are with P. Nikiforos Diamandouros and Hans-Jürgen Puhle, *The Politics of Democratic Consolidation* (The Johns Hopkins University Press, 1995); with Anthony Mughan, *Democracy and the Media* (Cambridge University Press, 2000); with Larry Diamond, *Political Parties and Democracy* (The Johns Hopkins University Press, 2002); with José Ramón Montero and Juan J. Linz, *Political Parties: Old Concepts and New Challenges* (Oxford University Press, 2002); and with José Ramón Montero and Joan Botella, *Democracy in Modern Spain* (Yale University Press, 2004).

Ignacio Lago is an Assistant Professor of the Department of Political Science at University Pompeu Fabra (Barcelona). He has a PhD in political science from the Universidad Autónoma de Madrid. He is also a Doctor-Member at the Juan March Institute (Madrid). His research interests include electoral systems, political behaviour, and political parties and party systems. He has published on these topics in journals such as *Economics and Politics*, *Electoral Studies*, and *Pôle Sud*.

Natalia Letki is a Post-Doctoral Prize Research Fellow at Nuffield College, Oxford. Her research interests focus on the relation of social capital, social trust, civic and political participation, and civic morality to the institutional (political and economic) context in the new and established democracies. She has also studied the influence of screening procedures on democratic consolidation in East-Central Europe. Her most recent publications are 'Socialization for Participation? Trust, Membership and Democratization in East-Central Europe', *Political Research Quarterly* 2004, Vol. 57, No. 4, pp. 665–679; with Geoffrey Evans, 'Endogenizing Social Trust: Democratisation in East-Central Europe', *British Journal of Political Science* 2005, Vol. 35, No. 3, pp. 515–529.

Ola Listhaug is Professor of Political Science at The Norwegian University of Science and Technology. He has published extensively in the fields of political behaviour, comparative politics, and comparative sociology. He has been a visiting scholar at the University of Michigan, the University of Iowa, and the University of North Carolina, Chapel Hill. His involvement in international research projects includes participation in the European Values Study and the Beliefs of Government study of the European Science Foundation. He is also affiliated with the Centre for the Study of Civil War, PRIO, as leader of a research group on Values and Violence. His recent book is with Christopher J. Anderson, André Blais, Shaun Bowler, and Todd Donovan, *Losers' Consent: Elections and Democratic Legitimacy* (Oxford University Press, 2005).

Pedro C. Magalhães is a Researcher at the Social Sciences Institute of the University of Lisbon. He has published on electoral behaviour, political attitudes, opinion polls, and judicial politics. He is one of the executive co-ordinators of the Portuguese Election Study. His most recent books are *Portugal at the Polls: the Legislative Elections of 2002* (Lisbon: ICS, 2004) and *Portugal: Democracy and Politics* (Madrid: Siglo XXI, 2004).

José Ramón Montero is Professor of Political Science at the Universidad Autónoma de Madrid (UAM) and at the Centro de Estudios Avanzados en Ciencias Sociales, Instituto Juan March, Madrid. He has been a member of the Standing Committee for the Social Sciences, European Science Foundation, and is currently a member of the Scientific Advisory Board of the European Social Survey and of the Academia Europea. He is also chairman of the Department of Political Science and International Relations (UAM), vice-president of the Spanish Association of Political Science, and member of the Editorial Committee of the *Revista Española de Ciencia Política*. He has published extensively on electoral behaviour, political parties, and political culture. His publications include *Democracy in Modern Spain* (New Haven: Yale University Press, 2004, with Richard Gunther and Joan Botella); and co-edited with Juan J. Linz, *Crisis y cambio: electores y partidos en la España de los años ochenta* (Madrid: Centro de Estudios Constitucionales, 1986); and with Richard Gunther and Juan J. Linz, *Political Parties: Old Concepts and New Challenges* (Oxford: Oxford University Press, 2002).

Kenneth Newton is Professor of Comparative Politics at the University of Southampton. He has worked at the Universities of Birmingham, Madison-Wisconsin, Oxford, Dundee, Philadelphia and Essex, and was Executive Director of the European Consortium for Political Research 1991–2001. Recent books include, with Ian Budge, *The Politics of the New Europe*, with Budge, McKay, and Crewe, *The New British Politics*; and with van Deth, Maraffi, and Whiteley, *Social Capital and European Democracy* (Routledge, 1999).

Pippa Norris is the McGuire Lecturer in Comparative Politics at the John F. Kennedy School of Government, Harvard University. Her research compares elections and public opinion, gender politics, and political communications. Recent books for Cambridge University Press include *Democratic Phoenix* (2002), *Rising Tide* (with Inglehart, 2003), *Electoral Engineering* (2004), *Sacred and Secular* (with Inglehart, 2004), and *Radical Right* (2005).

Claus Offe is Professor of Political Science, Humboldt University Berlin. He received his doctorate from the University of Frankfurt and his *Habilitation* from the University of Konstanz. He taught at the Universities of Bielefeld and Bremen and served as visiting professor at academic institutions in the United States, Canada, the Netherlands, Austria, Sweden, Italy, and Australia. Recent English language book publications include *Varieties of Transition* (MIT Press, 1996); *Modernity and The State. East and West* (MIT Press, 1996); with Elster, Jon and Ulrich K. Preuss, *Constitutional Design in Post-Communist Societies. Rebuilding the Ship at Sea* (Cambridge University Press, 1998).

Paolo Segatti is Professor of Political Sociology at the University of Milano and member of the ITANES (Italian National Election Study) group, which recently published several collective volumes on the 2001 parliamentary election. His most recent publications include a book with Paolo Bellucci and Marco Maraffi, *PCI, PDS, DS* (2000); a chapter written with G. Sani, 'Anti-party politics and the restructuring of Italian politics' in Gunther, Diamondouros and Puhle, *Parties, Politics, and Democracy in the New Southern Europe* (Johns Hopkins University Press, 2001), and a volume edited with Jean Blondel, *Politics in Italy 2002* (2003).

Mariano Torcal is Associate Professor in Political Science at the Pompeu Fabra University of Barcelona and co-ordinator of the *European Social Survey* in Spain. He has been a visiting professor at the University of

Michigan, the Centro de Estudios Avanzados en Ciencias Sociales, Instituto Juan March, and the Kellogg Institute at Notre Dame. He has published articles in major international journals, and chapters in edited volumes such as *Social Capital and European Democracy* (London: Routledge, 1999), and *Political Parties: Old Concepts and New Challenges* (Oxford University Press, 2002). The American Political Science Association awarded him an 'Honorable Mention for the Gregory M. Leubbert Prize for best article in Comparative Politics of 1997'.

Peter Van Aelst is a member of the Department of Communication Sciences and a researcher in the 'Media, Movements, and Politics' group (M2P) of the University of Antwerp, Belgium. His research focuses on social movements and political communication with special interest in the role of the (new) media.

Jan W. van Deth is Professor of Political Science and International Comparative Social Research at the University of Mannheim. He is a Corresponding Member of the Royal Netherlands Academy of Arts and Sciences and Book Series Editor of the *Studies in European Political Science* of the European Consortium for Political Research (with Thomas Poguntke). He is currently German National Coordinator for the *European Social Survey*. His latest books are with Kenneth Newton *Foundations of Comparative Politics* (Cambridge University Press, 2005), and *Deutschland in Europa* (ed. V. S. Verlag, 2004).

Stefaan Walgrave is Professor of Political Science. Since 1996, he has taught Social Movements and Media at the University of Antwerp (Belgium) and has co-ordinated the 'Media, Movements, and Politics' research group (M2P) in the Department of Political Science. His research interests focus on social movements and on mass media. He has published on social movements, mobilizations, political protest, political participation, green parties, and political communication.

Acknowledgements

Although this section of a book is always brief and academically unchallenging, it is likely to be the most satisfying part of the manuscript for editors. To begin with, because it is usually written when everything has already been sent to the publisher. And second, and more important, because this is a long-awaited opportunity to express gratitude openly to all the people and institutions that one way or another have contributed to making the book possible.

In our case, we share this feeling, common among many editors, with great joy given the length of time that the preparation of this book has taken. Its initial impetus came from Ramón Máiz, Professor of Political Science and, at that time, Dean of the Faculty of Political and Social Science, Universidad de Santiago de Compostela. He is the first person who should receive our expression of gratitude. In the year 2000, the ancient and beautiful city of Santiago de Compostela was declared by the European Union to be the European City of Culture. Taking advantage of this event, Professor Máiz organized a very ambitious programme of conferences and seminars to debate a selection of political and social problems of European democracies. This programme was titled '*Europamundi*', and more officially 'Europe in the World: The Construction of Europe, Democracy, and Globalization'. Like many other scholars, we thought that one of the most challenging problems that European democracies face is related to the persistent and increasing distance that their citizens are taking from the institutions of political representation, from their representatives, and even from politics. We had already been working for several years on this conspicuous reality, which we have (re)named *political disaffection*. Of course, this topic had also been a concern for many other scholars working on problems of contemporary democracies, giving way to a significant number of publications during the 1990s.

Many of us found the arguments and findings of this body of literature inconclusive and in many cases unsatisfactory, so we decided to accept Professor Máiz's kind invitation to organize a seminar in which we might share our intellectual concerns and dissatisfaction with some of the best experts in the field. The seminar took place from 19 to 21 October 2000, and provided us with the immense fortune of working with a number of well-known scholars on the origins, measures, and consequences of political disaffection in contemporary democracies; it also provided the groundwork for the significant contributions that constitute the present volume. In addition, we also enjoyed the active and enlightening participation of Juan J. Linz and José Vilas in the seminar. We want to express our gratitude to them.

Many people of the Universidad de Santiago helped to make the seminar a big success and to make our stay in the city a very pleasant experience. We cannot cite all of them now, but at least we would like to thank Daniel Blanch, José Manuel Rivera (at that time the *Vicerrector* for Cultural Affairs at the Universidad de Santiago), and all the members of the City Consortium in charge of organizing the events of the European Capital of Culture.

Over the years since the onset of this project, we have made an endless number of revisions to the papers originally presented in the seminar. The task of transforming the original papers into the current chapters presented in this volume has been possible thanks to the excellent resources and facilities made available to us in the Center for Advanced Studies in Social Sciences (CEACS) in the Juan March Institute (IJM) in Madrid, and in the Departments of Political and Social Sciences at the Universitat Pompeu Fabra (UPF), Barcelona, and of Political Science and International Relations at the Universidad Autónoma de Madrid (UAM). In these institutions we have also counted on the priceless collaboration of people such as Lorenzo Brusattin, Sunnee Billingsley, and Sara Fernández from the UPF; Paz Fernández, Almudena Knetch, Martha Peach, and Gema Sánchez from the library at the IJM; Justin Byrne, Luis Díaz, Jacqueline de la Fuente, Magdalena Nebreda, and Dolores Vallejo from the CEACS; and Irene Martín and Alberto Sanz from the UAM.

We especially want to express our appreciation to the contributors of this volume. Not only have they prepared excellent scholarly work that enhances the quality of this book, but they have also endured, with endless patience, our long and continuous revisions, changes, suggestions, and delays in the preparation of the final manuscript. We hope they now share our satisfaction with the final result and think that ultimately it has been worth it.

We have been very fortunate in publishing with Routledge. The Routledge staff have always been extremely kind and helpful at all times, from Heidi Bagtazo, the editor of Politics and International Relations, to Grace McInnes and Harriet Brinton, the former and current editorial assistants, to the anonymous reviewers of the manuscript. All of them have been supportive and patient. James Rabson, the production editorial manager in social sciences, and Georgina Boyle, the production editor, have encouraged us with their determination in speeding up the different phases of final production. Alice Sparks has taken care of the copy-editing, dealing with the enormous task of detecting errors and helping to maintain the high scholarly and stylistic standards even while working with pieces produced by scholars from ten different countries. Finally, Jan McIntosh has done an excellent job in preparing the book index.

We finally express our gratitude to the Spanish Ministry of Science and Technology for the support given with the research projects SEC2000-0758-C02-01 and SEC2002-03364, which provided the funding to finish this volume.

Barcelona and Madrid, October 2005,
Mariano Torcal, *Universitat Pompeu Fabra,* and
José Ramón Montero, *Instituto Juan March*
and *Universidad Autónoma de Madrid*

Part I

Introduction

1 Political disaffection in comparative perspective

Mariano Torcal and José Ramón Montero

In the mid-1970s, the problem of government overload became a prominent issue. As the oil crisis made evident to almost everyone, the period of economic growth, security, and prosperity, which had endured since the end of the Second World War, had come to an end. The new catchwords were stagflation and economic decline. It took some time, however, before political elites were willing to readjust welfare state policies and public spending patterns to meet new socio-economic conditions and before Western publics – whose political preferences were shaped during a period of unprecedented wealth and prosperity – were willing to accept them. In this setting, starting from completely different points,[1] Neo-Marxists, Neo-Liberals, and Neo-Conservatives claimed that the inability of democratic governments to cope with the ever increasing economic challenges and contradictory public demands would lead to a major crisis of democratic legitimacy in the Western world (Huntington 1968; O'Connor 1973; Crozier *et al.* 1975; Offe 1984; Habermas 1985).

Only 20 years later, these pessimistic projections had largely disappeared (Kaase and Newton 1995; Klingemann and Fuchs 1995a and 1995b). The enduring stability of existing democracies, the consolidation of the new ones that emerged at the end of the 1970s, and the breakdown of the communist regimes in Central and Eastern Europe were regarded as definitive proof of the superiority of democracy. The debate on the crisis of legitimacy was interpreted by many as outdated or at least as an artefact of gloomy social scientists and media reports. But citizens' attitudes toward democracy and democratic institutions may have not actually changed; and their assessments of politics and politicians may have not improved, either. In many Western polities, symptoms of disengagement with democracy have become a familiar feature of the political landscape, whereas levels of confidence in key political institutions have been suffering a secular decline (Barnes *et al.* 1979; Dalton 1988). Even the third wave of democratization was by no means accompanied by an increase in political confidence (Diamond 1999; Torcal 2002a and 2003). In both old and new democracies, citizens seem to have become even more critical regarding the way democracy works, the performance of political

institutions, and the daily activities of political actors. Democratic governments are thus settled on less solid ground to intervene in the policy
process, other democratic institutions have to deliver their outcomes
through a combination of large indifference and harsh criticism, and the
gap between citizens and their representatives has become increasingly
wider (Lipset and Schneider 1983; Klingemann and Fuchs 1995a and
1995b). In fact, this confidence crisis is taking a permanent form and does
not seem to be tied to a particular situation or related to political scandals,
the evolution of a deteriorating economy, and the frustration of either
general or particular expectations (Dogan 1997; Nye *et al.* 1997). *Critical
democrats, critical citizens,* or *disaffected citizens* have appeared as new figures
in the political arena. They were characterized by an interplay of strong
support for democratic ideals, on the one hand, and a large variety of critical attitudes toward democratic performance, on the other (Hibbing and
Theiss-Morse 1995; Klingemann and Fuchs 1995b; Klingemann 1999;
Norris 1999a; Torcal 2002a and 2003; Dalton 2004). And current democracies have also been qualified, using an old concept coined by di Palma
(1970), as *disaffected democracies* (Pharr and Putnam 2000), implying that
many citizens had redefined their relationships in line with important elements of contemporary democracies such as the political process, the
political institutions, and the political elite, but without questioning the
democratic order.

The questions

Despite the appearance of significant contributions dealing with the comparative presence in some countries of a larger number of those 'disaffected citizens', many questions remain unanswered or require further
research. What should we understand by *political disaffection* and how is this
concept related to old, similar concepts such as political alienation, political cynicism, political apathy, political trust, or political confidence? What
is the existing relationship between political disaffection and democratic
support, or other dimensions of political support? Is political disaffection
merely a result of the differences between expectations and evaluations of
democratic performance and institutional achievements, as the original
theorists of the legitimacy crisis claimed? If that is the case, why do these
attitudes seem immune to the substantial economic and social changes
since the 1980s? On the other hand, is political disaffection more a long
stable process with some cultural roots? If this is the case, what associations does political disaffection have to the allegedly declining trends in
social capital? Are all democracies presenting a more or less similar
picture? And even if political disaffection is such a general phenomenon,
why are there still important differences among Western democracies?
Which are the factors explaining these differences? Are they associated to
some social characteristics, political variables, and institutional settings?

Finally, what are the possible consequences of political disaffection for, say, political participation? To what extent are these new critical and disaffected citizens producing a discernible effect on the functioning of representative democracies?

This collaborative volume attempts to answer some of these questions by analysing a wide range of contemporary democracies either through comparative analyses or with some longitudinal case studies. In this book we set out to examine a cluster of attitudes that are often lumped together under the general label of *political support,* but which we argue should instead be treated as conceptually distinct. We claim that critical attitudes toward politics and representative institutions comprise all together a distinctive attitudinal dimension that should be differentiated from political support. We have labelled it as *political disaffection.* We take it to mean a certain estrangement or detachment from politics and the public sphere, as well as a critical evaluation of their core political institutions, their representatives, and the democratic political process. This attitudinal attribute is characterized by a number of specific symptoms, including a sense of personal inefficacy, cynicism and distrust, lack of confidence in representative institutions and/or the representatives elected, the belief that political elites do not care about the welfare of their citizens, and a general sense of estrangement from both politics and the political processes.

We have required the contributors of this volume to make an effort in trying to measure this concept and distinguish it from other close but different ones such as political alienation, political discontent, or political distrust, and whatever other concepts positively or negatively related with political support, a concept so frequently misused in some of the literature on this topic. We have also suggested that they address questions related to the main explanatory factors of the origin, evolution, and levels of political disaffection in some contemporary democracies. Can a general trend be identified? If the answer is negative, how can we explain the different levels of disaffection over time and place? What are the political factors influencing its evolution? Is it possible to design a comparative model explaining why disaffection is on the increase in some societies but not others? Generally speaking, we propose to answer these questions by steering clear of macro-cultural and sociological approaches (Dalton 1988; Inglehart 1990 and 1997a), searching instead for cross-national *political* explanations (Evans and Whitefield 1995; Whitefield and Evans 1999; Pharr and Putnam 2000).

Finally, we have also proposed to the contributors to this volume an exploration of some of the feasible behavioural consequences of political disaffection. Existing studies have come up with a rather contradictory picture. As described by Lipset and Schneider (1983), the confidence gap was originally considered to have very negative connotations and was identified as one of the major fault lines in contemporary representative democracies. More recently, some scholars have highlighted the more positive consequences that increasing numbers of critical citizens may eventually have on the transformation of their democratic institutions, particularly on the relationship between citizens and their representatives (Dalton 1988 and 1999; Kaase and Newton 1995; Klingemann and Fuchs 1995b; Nye *et al.* 1997; Norris 1999a). But, for other scholars, political disaffection might also be essentially responsible for the widespread estrangement of citizens from politics (especially in new democracies) and for the presence of an uninformed and non-participant citizenship (Montero *et al.* 1997a and 1997b). How to reconcile these two opposing consequences? Is political disaffection responsible for the increasing use of new forms of political participation or is it instead conducive to decreasing political involvement? Given the relevance of disaffection for the relationships between citizens and the state, as well as for the functioning of contemporary democracies, we are extremely interested in exploring some of these consequences and the major political factors associated with them.

Setting the conceptual and theoretical framework

Before briefly previewing each of the contributions to this edited volume, we would first like to trace the common theoretical and methodological framework in which our discussions are rooted. While some of the authors might not fully agree with all the editors' theoretical claims, all their contributions share a common concern with the basic themes we outline in the following few pages.

Political disaffection, support for democracy, and political discontent

Although increasingly used, political disaffection is an undefined term. In a recent and important monographic volume on this topic, Pharr and Putnam (2000) do not offer any definition of the concept; they only provide a list of possible indicators of affection and disaffection. Instead, we would like to contribute in this volume with some conceptual clarifications. Following di Palma (1970: 30), we define political disaffection as *the subjective feeling of powerlessness, cynicism, and lack of confidence in the political process, politicians, and democratic institutions, but with no questioning of the political regime* (see also Torcal 2002a: ch. 3 and 2003: ch. 4; Citrin 1974, and Citrin *et al.* 1975). Political disaffection thus contains two aspects or sub-dimensions that are partly independent. The first comprises a cluster of attitudes related to a general distrust of politics and to the respondent's lack of engagement with the political process. We have called this *political disengagement,* or political disaffection *tout court*. The other sub-dimension consists of beliefs about the lack of responsiveness of political authorities and institutions, and citizens' lack of confidence in the political institutions of their countries. We have named this *institutional disaffection* (see Torcal 2002b). Most of the contributions in this volume have focused on one or both of these dimensions of political disaffection.

It should be noted that this definition of political disaffection differs somewhat from other closely related concepts that are frequently used, often interchangeably, in studies of political support. Moreover, some of these concepts are sometimes measured similarly, resulting in a rather unclear and sometimes confusing conceptual and methodological picture. We maintain here that many of these alternative concepts suggest a state of crisis in the political regime that disaffection does not. Unlike the concept of political alienation, for instance, political disaffection does not imply a crisis of democratic legitimacy. Indeed, many democracies, particularly third wave democracies, show high levels of both democratic support and political disaffection (Torcal 2002a and 2002c). Political disaffection is also independent of support for the democratic regime and has different behavioural consequences (Hibbing and Theiss-Morse 1995; Kavanagh 1997). Support for democracy, or democratic legitimacy, pertains, on the other hand, to citizens' beliefs that democratic politics and representative democratic institutions are the most appropriate (indeed, the only acceptable) framework for government. Democratic legitimacy should be regarded as an ideal type, since no system is fully legitimate in the eyes of each and every citizen (Hertz 1978: 320; Linz 1988: 65). Support for democracy may thus be considered the belief that democracy is the 'only game in town'. This definition also implies that support for the regime should be based on an explicit, or most of the time implicit, comparison with other types of regimes. As Rose and Mishler (1996: 52–53) maintain, 'a democratic regime does not necessarily make the "right" decisions ... nor is there a guarantee that the government will be effective. ... Democracy's claim to superiority is that it is an open system making it possible to learn from mistakes and to correct them through the sanction of voting governments out of office as well as into office'. This definition of democratic support is 'based upon the comparison of different regimes within the experience of those undertaking the evaluation' (Rose and Mishler 1996: 53).

Moreover, as we said before, much of the literature on the democratic crisis was based on the assumption that political alienation, political trust, and all the symptoms of the crisis of confidence in democracy were mainly the result of citizens' dissatisfaction with government performance or, more generally, with general democratic performance. For testing this possibility, we have proposed using the concept of *political discontent*, or the expression of displeasure resulting from the belief that the performance of the government is falling short of the citizens' wishes or expectations (di Palma 1970: 30).[2] In this regard, we have first proposed to the contributors of this volume to somehow test if political disaffection appears to occur regardless of a government's popularity or policies. We suspect, based on previous research (Montero *et al.* 1997a and 1997b; see also Nye *et al.* 1997), that political disaffection has little to do with short-term fluctuations in assessments of the government's actions, its decisions, or its current level of popularity. Evaluations of a particular government can affect political mobilization and, ultimately, lead to electoral defeat (*throw the rascals out*), but they have no impact on political disaffection (Farah *et al.* 1979; Kaase and Marsh 1979). Second, we have also proposed to the contributors of this volume to test the connection between political disaffection and satisfaction with the functioning of democracy,[3] paying special attention to the possibility that an increasing level of disaffection might be due to the frustration of accumulated unfulfilled expectations of democratic performance (Pharr and Putnam 2000).

Interpreting Easton's concept of political support

Much of the literature on mass attitudes toward democracy treats the three sets of attitudes discussed above as if they form part of a single broad cluster of perceptions, evaluations, and beliefs about democratic regimes. In our view, this approach overlooks the crucial differentiation between support for democracy, political discontent, and political disaffection. We believe that the tendency to see these attitudes as forming part of a single continuum stems from the theoretical legacy of David Easton's (1965 and 1975) concept of *political support* and the misinterpretation of his import-ant distinction between diffuse and specific support.

In Easton's systems theory, political systems have inputs and outputs, with inputs taking the form of demands and support. Easton originally coined a dual conceptualization of political support that could account both for evaluations of the authorities' performance (specific support) and of more basic and fundamental aspects of the political system (diffuse support).[4] In his own words, 'support was not all of a piece' (Easton 1975: 437) and its constituent classes could vary independently from each other. Diffuse and specific support have been used as an explanatory conceptual tool for a long time, since Easton first introduced this distinction in the mid-1970s. Scholars were then concerned with the conditions under which members of a political system, who were dissatisfied with policy out-comes, could make a move towards radical political or social change. Especially puzzling was the evidence that even intense manifestations of the first phenomenon did not necessarily lead to the second.[5]

This distinction is an important contribution. Specific support can be object-specific in two ways: first, people are assumed to be capable of being aware of the political authorities working on behalf of the system; second, it takes into account the perceived decisions, policies, actions, utterances, and style of the authorities. In this sense, the members of a political system can perform a rational calculation of whether the authori-ties' actions address their needs and demands. Under such conditions, specific support, which can only exist in societies whose institutions allow authorities to be held accountable for their actions and the resulting consequences, will fluctuate according to people's perceived benefits and satisfactions. Diffuse support instead hinges on the general meaning given to political objects and is defined as a 'reservoir of favourable (or unfavourable) attitudes'.[6] It is more durable than specific support and more resistant to or even independent of sudden epiphenomena such as policy outputs and performance. It refers to the body of favourable attitudes that members of a given political system possess, which allow them to overlook outputs that do not benefit their wants. This support also remains, despite the ups and down in outputs and beneficial performances. While diffuse support may change, it is difficult to weaken when strong and to strengthen when weak. Rooted in early socialization and experience, diffuse support might be generated and fostered independently of the fulfilment of particular needs and demands by the authorities. Yet it can also result from several evaluations of a series of outputs and performances over a long period of time and become the consequence of a series of rational judgements. In short, each political object should instead be addressed alternately or jointly by both diffuse and specific support (Torcal and Brusattin 2003).

Easton's contention that all political objects, including political authorities, might enjoy both specific and diffuse support raises both additional interpretations and operationalization problems.[7] The possibility that all political objects may have diffuse support, combined with Easton's definition of diffuse support discussed above, have led a significant number of scholars to conclude that diffuse support for all political objects of the regime is part of, and sometimes a requirement for, broader diffuse support for the whole political regime. The latest refinements in this direction were offered by Norris (1999b: 9–10) and Dalton (2004: 23–24), who distributed the objects of support (political community, regime principles, regime performance, regime institutions, political actors) along a unidimensional axis ranging from diffuse to specific support. In doing so, each political object is assigned a degree of specificness/diffuseness. Put in these terms, diffuse and specific support no longer represent distinct dimensions to be found in each political object. As a matter of fact, it seems reasonable to conceive positive attitudes toward fundamental principles of a regime (i.e. democratic principles) as a manifestation of diffuse support, although it is more difficult to consider regime institutions and political actors as objects almost exclusively attached to manifestations of specific support (Torcal and Brusattin 2003). This reading of Easton's work is obviously questionable and perhaps unintended, but it has reinforced the highly disputed 'congruence argument'[8] precluded by the more deterministic cultural tradition in which underlying ideological and cultural values define individual preferences for a specific set of institutions, fostering or conditioning support for the whole democratic regime (see also Almond and Verba 1963, and Eckstein 1961). And it has also given birth to an excessively broad concept of democratic support, which empirically works as a sort of umbrella under which different dimensions are not differentiated (see, for example, Dalton 2004: 22).

In this volume, we depart from this unidimensional interpretation of Easton's concept of political support. We use the concept of political disaffection as an important dimension of political support that pertains to essential objects of democratic regimes, but it does not constitute a symptom of the lack of specific or diffuse support for democratic regimes. We also consider the level of political support given to these essential objects of the polity as not necessarily linked to the specific support given to the incumbent authorities and their implemented policies. The elements of political disaffection, such as lack of confidence in institutions, negative evaluations on the responsiveness of political authorities, or low political trust, cannot be considered *a priori* measures of either diffuse or specific support to the whole democratic system or specific support to incumbent democratic authorities. The strength of the relationships between support given to the democratic regime, confidence or trust in the institutions of the democratic regime and the political process, and support to the incumbent authorities remains an empirical question to be explored from a multidimensional perspective.

Cultural vs. rational-culturalist models

The research concerned with the origins and evolution of political disaffection is fully linked to the theoretical discussion about the character of political attitudes being cultural or rational. The recent debate on alternative explanations of political confidence (institutional confidence), one of the elements that constitutes political disaffection, is a good example. This debate has brought to the picture two models on the formation of political attitudes; we might have labelled them as the 'traditional-culturalist' and the 'rational-culturalist' models (Mishler and Rose 2001). The traditional-culturalist model, put forth by Lerner (1958) and to a lesser degree by Almond and Verba (1963), contends that attitudes change slowly because they are cultural traits that depend on long-term processes of socialization tending to be reproduced over time.[9] Rational-culturalists, on the other hand, argue that culture can change quickly as a result of political or economic events, as a consequence of experience or conflicts, and as an outcome of institutional performance evaluation in distinctive institutional settings, as well as through rational adaptation and even adult learning (Lane 1992; Whitefield and Evans 1999; Mishler and Rose 2001).[10]

Testing the traditional-culturalist model: social capital

The most salient cultural explanation of political disaffection is the social capital model. Social capital refers to 'features of social organization, such as trust, norms, and networks' (Putnam 1993: 167). This definition comprises a structural element (including social organizations and networks) and a cultural element (social norms and values of reciprocity and social trust). The pure culturalist model is based on the idea that increased political disaffection is a reflection of the declining trend of social trust. The most prominent advocate of this approach is of course Robert Putnam (1993: 90, and 2000), although other scholars have also contributed to an explicit formulation of the various linkages between social engagement and social trust within citizens' political beliefs. For Norris (1999b: 21–22) and Newton (1999a: 17), for instance, the gist of the social capital argument implies that patterns of social interaction are not only related to citizens' trust in each other, but also to citizens' political confidence.[11] In Newton's (1999b: 179) words, political confidence and social trust are considered to be 'different sides of the same coin'. From this perspective, *political* confidence is at least to some extent a by-product of *social* trust and exogenous to the political system (cf. Mishler and Rose 2001: 31). Thus an important number of scholars make claims about the importance of social trust for democracy insofar as they find an association between social trust and political confidence (Putnam 1993: 111–115; Knack and Keefer 1997; Inglehart 1997b; Newton and Norris 2000; Newton 2001; Paxton 2002; Uslaner 2002: 217–248; Rothstein and Stolle 2003).

But Putnam's concept of social capital not only includes social trust; it also refers to people's embeddedness in social organizations. In line with the Tocquevillean tradition, Putnam defends the idea that membership in organizations is the main source of civicness; participation in voluntary associations is a good way of learning civic attitudes.[12] However, there might also be 'a dark side of civic engagement' (Fiorina 1999), and some social participation may be a source of unsocial capital (Levi 1996; Keane 1998). By the same token, participation in specific types of organizations is claimed to be a means of learning democratic attitudes such as institutional confidence (Stolle and Rochon 1998). This is not just a question of the goals and (the democratic or non-democratic) objectives of the different organizations and associations (van Deth 1997; Beem 1999; della Porta 2000). The distinctive effects of associational involvement on civic attitudes are related to the problem of the 'bridgingness versus bondingness effects' of the organizations (Putnam 2000: 23–24). Therefore, testing the effect of social capital on political disaffection also requires studying the relative effect of membership in different social organizations.

Testing the rational-culturalist model: institutions and politics

In this model, political disaffection is considered 'politically endogenous' or 'rationally based'. It should result from factors such as distinctive institutional settings, institutional performance, political corruption, specific political scandals, macro-economic conditions, and/or frustrated expectations. In this literature, social trust has almost no impact in explaining different levels of political confidence; instead, these distinctive levels are related to particular institutional and political factors. Political disaffection might be contaminated, for instance, by partisan preferences or support for incumbents (Hetherington 1998; Holmberg 1999) or by the 'winner and loser effects' of the elections (Clarke and Acock 1989; Clarke and Kornberg 1989; Clarke 1992; Anderson and Lo Tempio 2002). It could also be the result of egotropic evaluations of the economy or different levels of institutional performance evaluations (Listhaug and Wiberg 1995; Miller and Listhaug 1999; Newton and Norris 2000; della Porta 2000; Mishler and Rose 2001). The unfulfilled expectations linked to the government incapacity to resolve current problems could also be a plausible source of political disaffection (Hardin 2000; Putnam *et al.* 2000) along with a declining macro-economic performance and the rolling back of social welfare policies (Alesina and Wacziarg 2000; Pharr 2000). The presence of specific political scandals might also have contributed to the deterioration of political trust (Lipset and Schneider 1983; Nye 1997; Orren 1997). Finally, and *a sensu contrario*, certain institutional settings that produce greater levels of political pluralism and consensus may also explain higher levels of political trust (Listhaug and Wiberg 1995; Morlino and Tarchi 1996; Anderson and Guillory 1997; Nye and Zelikow 1997; Banducci *et al.* 1999; Dalton 1999; Norris 1999c; Katzenstein 2000).

Reconciling the culturalist and rational-culturalist models

Yet, the cultural and rational arguments that explain different levels of political disaffection might not necessarily be antithetical. An approach informed at the same time by the overlapping of cultural and rational components could be more useful (Wildavsky 1987; Lane 1992). In this volume, these two arguments are not conceptualized as rival explanations. They are depicted as complementary, in which attitudes are more or less stable and appear as a result of both long- and short-term factors, and where the relative importance of these factors is essentially an empirical question. Among the long-term factors, we encouraged contributors to analyse once more the effects of social trust and social connectedness on political disaffection. After recognizing the importance of cultural factors in predicting institutional confidence at the individual level, we also emphasized looking at cross-national political and especially institutional factors to account for individual and cross-national variations in levels of political disaffection. This is in line with other scholars (Evans and White-field 1995; Whitefield and Evans 1999; Katzenstein 2000), and thus supports the approaches that reject macro-sociological and cultural variables to explain such variations in attitudes of political disaffection. Additionally, we have suggested that social trust and political factors such as certain institutional settings or specific political events may interact distinctively in many countries and produce different levels of political disaffection (see, for example, Streeck 1992; Hardin 1996 and 2002; della Porta 2000; King 2000; Newton and Norris 2000; Farrel and Knight 2003).

Furthermore, the recognition of the relative role of social capital in explaining individual and cross-national differences in political disaffection does not preclude a clear defence of the 'culturalist' model. We depart here from the suspicion that political disaffection is not a product of economic and social modernization or of any other culturally deterministic characteristic. We also don't think that political disaffection is the product of an individual's personality, nor the major product of any culturally attitudinal baseline (Newton and Norris 2000). We suggest that individual social connectedness and individual social trust, which depend on a considerable number of national political factors, may be predictors of political disaffection. We might even consider that this relation differs from country to country given the distinctive political past of many contemporary democracies (McAllister 1999; King 2000).

Finally, the argument proclaiming the impact of institutions and politics is not a pure rational-culturalist one either. Analysing the influence of institutions and politics on political disaffection not only portrays the effects produced by short-term fluctuations or some change in the specific institutional settings of a country, but also displays existing differences among country levels due to specific cross-national institutional variations. As we argue, together with some scholars of this volume, the effects of politics and institutions can also be traced in the past by analysing some specific socialization patterns or some specific political experiences. Talking about socialization does not mean that attitudes toward political objects are exogenous or generated outside political life (Mishler and Rose 2001: 34–35). Quite the contrary, the origin of such attitudes must be sought within the realm of politics (Wildavsky 1987: 5; Laitin 1988: 590–591). And this does not necessarily mean that the attitudes that constitute political disaffection remain unchanged during one's lifetime.[13] The fact that they are the product of subjective appraisal and perceptions does not mean that they are not also the result of a 'rational' process of evaluating the political environment and the public institutions, people, or discourses that 'formed' them. Thus, institutions do help to define strategies among the different actors in today's political arena, and also play an important role in shaping their preferences for the present and the future. In other words, political institutions are relatively stable phenomena and their effects can be treated as socialization experiences, leading rational citizens to develop feelings of basic belief or disbelief about the responsiveness and trustworthiness of those institutions (Norris 1999c: 219–220; Torcal 2003: 34–35; see also the chapters by Offe and Magalhães in this volume).

In short, this approach conforms with the so-called 'historical institutionalism', which defends that the institutions of the past give form to the attitudes and preferences of the present.[14] Contrary to what the pure 'cultural approach' defends, historical institutionalism stresses the degree to which 'behavior is not fully strategic but bounded by an individual's worldview ... It tends to see individuals as satisficers, rather than utility maximizers, and to emphasize the degree to which the choice of course of actions depends on the interpretation of a situation rather than on purely instrumental calculation' (Hall and Taylor 1996: 936). However, this does not mean that the attitudes that shape these interpretations in a given political generation cannot also be altered by present political events.

Political disaffection and types of democracies

A final theoretical implication of this volume is that the definition of political disaffection outlined above and its distinctive presence in democracies do not entail any criticism of current representative democracies. Neither are we defending any particular model of democracy or any specific model of citizenship. The implications assigned to the different levels of political disaffection in contemporary democracies should be based on their observable effects on citizens' political behaviour. We proposed that the contributors of this volume explore the possibility that political disaffection does not have the same consequences in all democracies. In fact, political disaffection might influence behaviour in different ways depending on the political context in which it has originated and developed. For instance, Norris (1999d: 270) has suggested that in Western democracies the lack of institutional confidence may have positive consequences for transforming deficient or problematic institutions (see also Kaase and Marsh 1979: 38–40; Dalton 1988: 74–79; Nye *et al.* 1997). Some scholars have even applauded public mistrust, since, according to the Madisonian tradition, wariness and scepticism toward a government and its leaders provide a necessary check on government action and strengthen individual freedom (see Orren 1997; and Hardin 1999).[15] Therefore, and contrary to some previous normative analyses, high levels of political disaffection in a particular country might not necessarily have *a priori* negative connotations. But in other countries political disaffection may be conducive to enlarging the distance between citizens and their representatives, to strengthening political inequalities, and to making institutional or political changes much more difficult. While not producing antidemocratic behaviour, political disaffection may have resulted in greater political apathy throughout all forms of political participation (Torcal

2002c: ch. 9 and 2003: 42–43). In many new democracies, higher levels of political disaffection do not lead to higher levels of non-conventional political actions, but rather to generally low levels of political involvement. Political accountability may also be altered, since political disaffection is associated with lower levels of political information among voters, biased informational sources (Gunther *et al.* forthcoming), and even changes in their use of informational shortcuts. Consequences of political disaffection may therefore vary in different political contexts.

Cases, indicators, and chapters

The selection of cases

This is a study of political disaffection in contemporary democracies. Most of the analyses undertaken in the following pages are comparative. Some chapters (such as Chapter 5 by Jan van Deth and Chapter 8 by Pedro Magalhães) focus on 15 of the former European Union members, including three new democracies with distinctive institutional settings (Greece, Portugal, and Spain). However, some of the theoretical questions presented here require the expansion of the analysis beyond Western Europe. Therefore, we have included in this volume comparative studies dealing solely with new democracies. Geoffrey Evans and Natalia Letki present in Chapter 6 a comparative study of Central and Eastern European democracies, Richard Gunther and José Ramón Montero analyse in Chapter 3 the dimensions of political support in some new democracies of Southern and Eastern Europe and Latin America, and Mariano Torcal and Ignacio Lago explore in Chapter 12 some of the consequences of political disaffection in a selection of new Southern European and Latin American democracies. Some other contributors have expanded their scope by contrasting new democracies of Latin America and Southern Europe with old established democracies of Western Europe, as in the case of Chapter 7, by Mariano Torcal. Finally, Ken Newton contributes in Chapter 4 with an even more ambitious comparison by including contemporary democracies from all over the world.

In this volume there is also space for some very telling case studies. These provide the opportunity to analyse the evolution of political disaffection over time in two different traditional democracies: one from Northern Europe, Norway (by Ola Listhaug in Chapter 9), and another from Italy (by Paolo Segatti in Chapter 10). Whereas Norway, a country belonging to the first democratization wave, displays high levels of political trust for decades despite slow but significant electoral changes, the Italian case, belonging to the second democratization wave, has been characterized by high levels of political disaffection, high support for democracy, and stable electoral behaviour. The latter has also been exposed to recent institutional changes together with important electoral shifts during the 1990s. And in Chapter 11 Pippa Norris, Stefaan Walgrave, and Peter van Aelst analyse the possible mobilizing effects of political disaffection among protesters in Belgium, a country with comparatively significant levels of both political disaffection and protest participation.

Indicators of political disaffection

We have proposed to the contributors two groups of indicators to be used for the concept of political disaffection based on the preceding discussion. The first is *institutional disaffection*. It includes two major groups of indicators. First, institutional confidence measured by confidence in parliaments and other democratic institutions such as political parties; second, assessments of the responsiveness of democratic institutions (for instance, politicians and political representatives) through the indicator of external political efficacy. As for *political disengagement*, we propose to measure this second dimension with indicators such as subjective political interest, political salience or importance of politics in life, and internal political efficacy.

In any case, the selection of these indicators to measure political disaffection has, however, varied among contributors of this volume due to the usual problems of data availability. In the following pages most of the chapters just include indicators to measure institutional disaffection. For instance, in Chapter 8 a scale to measure confidence in a set of institutions of political representation is used, whereas in Chapter 4 the goal was to examine confidence in some particular institutions such as the parliament or the government. There are also chapters that include some indicators of political engagement, the other dimension of political disaffection. For instance, Chapter 5 chooses a selection of items measuring political saliency, while Chapters 3 and 5 focus on subjective political interest and discussion of politics.

Some contributors have selected indicators of both dimensions. This is, for instance, the case in Chapters 9 for Norway and 10 for Italy, which cover the evolution over time of a variety of both dimensions of political disaffection according to internal and external political efficacy, confidence in institutions, and trust in politicians. In Chapters 3 and 7 Gunther and Montero, and Torcal, respectively, have also selected indicators of institutional confidence, political efficacy, interest in politics, and political saliency to analyse comparatively two large sets of countries. In the same vein, Evans and Letki in Chapter 6 have created a scale of disaffection based on seven indicators of internal and external efficacy. This is also the case for Chapters 11 and 12, which are monographically devoted to analysing the effects of political disaffection on citizens' participation and electoral behaviour.

The content of the chapters

In Chapter 2, Claus Offe presents an illuminating discussion of the conceptual problems summarized in this Introduction. His chapter explores the theoretical relevance of the distinction drawn between support for democracy and political disaffection. In so doing, he provides further backing for the theoretical issues focused on in this Introduction, as well as a framework for an improved understanding of the endogeneity problem found in many of the political attitudes under study. Completing the second part of the volume, Gunther and Montero deal in Chapter 3 with the measurement and dimensionality of political support. While various chapters explore problems of the dimensionality and/or measurement of political disaffection, and the existing relationships with other concepts such as support for democracy and political discontent, Gunther and Montero's contribution stands out as they provide extremely convincing empirical evidence for grounding this conceptual discussion. Their chapter also deals with some of the consequences of political disaffection on levels of political intermediation.

In searching for factors that account for the evolution and different levels of disaffection, the contributors to the third part of the volume pay particular attention to the role of social capital. These contributions are dedicated to the discussion of the relationship between social capital and political disaffection. In Chapter 4, Newton provides a broad comparison of a large set of countries to study the relationship between social trust and political disaffection, at both the individual and the country level. Newton claims that, even though there is not a clear difference at the individual level, the relationship observed at the country level is somewhat more significant. Alongside this contribution, van Deth attempts to measure in Chapter 5 the effect of membership in a series of associations and organizations on attitudes of political disaffection. He concludes that this relationship is not very strong, but above all that it is not uniform, depending instead on the type of organizations that individuals belong to. Finally, Evans and Letki explore in Chapter 6 the relationship between social trust and political disaffection in the new democracies of Eastern and Central Europe. They demonstrate the presence of a negative relationship (the more social trust the citizens have, the less they participate in politics or have confidence in political institutions and politicians), a finding the authors attribute to the particular political context of these countries.

In terms of the factors explaining the different levels of disaffection, its evolution, and its relations with other variables, contributors of the fourth part of the volume highlight the decisive role of politics and institutions. For instance, Torcal underlines in Chapter 7 that, despite the higher presence of political disaffection in new democracies, this is not a uniform feature in Southern Europe and the American Southern Cone, as significantly lower levels of political disaffection exist in a number of new democracies such as

Greece, Uruguay, and Chile. Thus, high levels of political disaffection are not a defining characteristic of third wave democracies. Instead, he points to the possibility of some kind of institutional legacy from the non-democratic past and through the most recent tortuous democratization history. In Chapter 8, Magalhães takes a similar path. He argues that the distinctive levels of institutional confidence in the parliament, one of the indicators of political disaffection, may be related to levels of legislative decentralization and the presence of important veto-players. These distinctive historical institutional settings, which have been affecting the level of accountability and representation of Western European democracies, partially explain the different levels of political disaffection observed among countries.

In addition, two chapters deal directly or indirectly with the evolution and levels of political disaffection in distinctively relevant cases studies. In Chapter 9, Listhaug's longitudinal analysis of the Norwegian case demonstrates the absence of any clear trend, as a period of increasing disaffection has been followed by another of decline, denying the existence of a secular cross-national decline in civic attitudes, which is so often argued by culturalists. Oscillations of political disaffection over time in this Scandinavian country are attributed to specific political events and punctuated economic situations. And in Chapter 10 Segatti discusses the trend of political disaffection over 40 years in Italy, and concludes that the weight of a negative political past still influences today's levels of political disaffection among Italians. However, the percentage of disaffected changed dramatically when major political events in the mid-1990s threw the actual working of the political system into question.

The fifth part of this volume is dedicated to the consequences of political disaffection. In Chapter 11, Norris, Walgrave, and van Aelst argue, based on data collected with a very innovative survey technique that allowed for the comparison of party members with civic joiners, that demonstrators are similar to the Belgian population and that, moreover, there is little evidence that Belgian demonstrators are disaffected radicals. Finally, Torcal and Lago explore in Chapter 12 some of the consequences of political disaffection on the nature of representative democracies. In the first section of their chapter they claim that, in many new democracies in Southern Europe and the American Southern Cone, disaffection leads to widespread estrangement from politics and public affairs, which further deepens the breach between representatives and citizens. In the second section, they explore the effect of political disaffection on the distinctive use of informational shortcuts among citizens when they are expressing party preferences.

Notes

1 Despite coming from different or opposed intellectual traditions these authors share, as Weil (1989: 683) has pointed out, the common intellectual reference of Schumpeter's 'overload' and 'collapse' theory.

2 More generally, discontent is a reflection of frustration derived from comparing what one has with what one hopes or expects to have (Gamson 1968: 54); and in political terms, it results from beliefs that the government is unable to deal effectively with problems regarded by citizens as important (Dahl 1971: 144; Morlino and Montero 1995: 234).

3 In fact, satisfaction with democratic functioning is highly related to party preferences, as has been recently discussed by Linde and Ekman (2003).

4 As nicely described by Mishler and Rose (1999: 3), 'Specific support ... is the temporary and relatively ephemeral acceptance or approval that individuals extend to a political object as a result of its satisfaction of their specific demands ... Diffuse support, in contrast, is conceived as a deeper, more enduring, and more generalized political loyalty resulting from early life political socialization. As such it is conceived as immune to short-term inducements, rewards or performance evaluations'.

5 Some authors have even questioned citizens' capacity to distinguish between Easton's diffuse and specific support (Loewenberg 1971; Muller and Jukam 1977; Mishler and Rose 1999).

6 According to Easton (1965: 273), 'members [citizens of the system] are capable of directing *diffuse* support toward the objects of the system. This forms a reservoir of favourable attitudes or goodwill that helps members to accept or tolerate outputs to which they are opposed or the effect of which they see as damaging to their wants'.

7 In some cases, this oversimplification of Easton's work is perhaps unfair, but it is attributed to the fact that his original conceptualization was so vague as to lead invariably to research that is 'ambiguous, confusing and noncumulative' (Kaase 1988: 117).

8 For a classic analysis on the dispute of the congruence argument, see Barry (1970).

9 There are, however, significant disagreements on this interpretation of Almond and Verba's causality model. Lijphart (1989: 47 ff), for instance, maintains that the use of the terms 'independent and dependent variable' does not imply unidirectionality between political culture and the political structure.

10 For discussions of the classical rational-culturalist models and a defence of the argument of the role of institutions in shaping political attitudes, see Barry (1970), Pateman (1971), and Eckstein (1988).

11 It should be noted that these theoretical arguments cannot be seen as a literal translation of the models outlined by any of these authors. Although scholars like Norris and Newton have tried to contribute to the development of the social capital approach into a coherent model, we should not necessarily consider these authors as advocates of the social capital approach.

12 The direction of causality is not immediately evident here. On the one hand, Putnam claims that 'causation flows mainly from joining to trusting' (Putnam 1995b: 666). Newton (1999a: 16–17), however, has argued that causality may be the other way around.

13 Besides Wildavsky (1987), the most serious attempt to combine the two approaches can be found in Mishler and Rose (2001).

14 The difference between 'rational institutionalism' and 'historical institutionalism' is that the former considers institutions essential only as shapers of political strategies, while the latter argues that institutions are responsible for the formation of attitudes and strategies. See Thelen and Steinmo (1992: 7–10) and Hall and Taylor (1996).

15 For a completely different position, see Offe (1999).

Part II

Concepts and dimensions

2 Political disaffection as an outcome of institutional practices?

Some post-Tocquevillean speculations

Claus Offe

In this chapter I proceed as follows. Its first part provides a conceptual map by which we can locate the various symptoms of political *malaise* and disenchantment which beset, as it is widely perceived, political life and political developments even in established liberal democracies (and *a fortiori* in new ones). The second part proposes to invert the chain of causation that is widely used in empirical political science as a model of analysis. Rather than proceeding from opinions to behaviour to institutional viability, I propose here, in an admittedly speculative mode, to proceed in a top-down perspective from institutional patterns to the observable 'enactment' of institutions and the perceived opportunities, incentives, and expectations they inculcate in citizens and finally the opinions, habits, and attitudes people exhibit and which are in turn registered and analysed by the methods of survey research. In the third and final part of the chapter, I propose a taxonomy of the various sorts of 'failure of citizenship' (or deficient modes of its practice) that we encounter within established democracies of the OECD world. I conclude with a few remarks on the hypothetical impact of disaffection upon the liberal democratic regime form.

Dissatisfacion, illegitimacy, disaffection: towards a conceptual map

Eighteenth-century political philosophers believed that there are three forces in the nature of human beings that shape all of social and political life: people have *interests*, *reason*, and *passions*. In other words, they pursue their *advantage* against others, are open to rational *argument* as well as capable of finding and giving comprehensible reasons for what they think and do, and they are emotionally or passionately *attached* to other people, communities, and shared values and life forms. The ('proper', though in no way exclusive) institutional arenas in which these forces or capacities unfold are the market as the sphere of the rational pursuit of interests, the polity as the sphere of reasonable argument, and the community as the sphere of emotional or passionate attachment. But also *within* political life itself, all three of these capacities – the pursuit of interest, the ability to form and to accept rational argument, and the emotional attachment to the political community – all have their role to play.

It seems that this tripartite classification is still useful as a set of conceptual tools suitable for the analysis and understanding of present-day political realities and changes. One of today's central concerns of both political scientists and often also those actively involved in political life is – somewhat paradoxically, it might seem – the issue of the robustness and viability of the liberal democratic regime form. Numerous books and articles that appeared in the 1990s try to make sense of the coincidence in time of two things. First, the *triumph* of the liberal democratic regime form that is *the* major global political event of the fourth quarter of the twentieth century. And second, the democratic *malaise* or *desencanto* that seems to be creeping into many contemporary political and analytical discourses. A guiding question is: How certain can we be that the accomplishments of political modernization and civilization that we have achieved are of a durable nature after the end of state socialist and other authoritarian forms of governance, rather than being susceptible to deformation and decay? What do we make of the numerous symptoms of challenges, crises, malperformance, fragility, and perversions of nascent as well as established liberal democratic regimes and their widely perceived failure to redeem the promises of the liberal democratic regime form? The experience of victory is followed by a sense of deep crisis and uncertainty. Such complaints and concerns often seem to follow a spiral of decay: as the promises and options of the conduct of public policies and their alternatives become unappealing, citizens get bored, frustrated, and disaffected, if not outright cynical about the dealings of the 'political class'. And as citizens become disengaged in political institutions and their operation, there is ever less support and the potential for mobilization that political elites can rely upon. To quote just one prominent voice from the academic world:

> Far from being secure in its foundations and practices, democracy will have to face unprecedented challenges. Its future ... will be increasingly tumultuous, uncertain, and very eventful.... The ability [of democracies] ... to accommodate the growing disaffection of their citizenries will determine the prospects of democracies worldwide.... All [citizens] experience in their daily lives are what Antonio Gramsci called 'morbid symptoms' – a lot of grumbling, dissatisfaction, and suboptimality.
>
> (Schmitter 1995: 15–22)

I understand that the notion of 'disaffection'[1] is widely held to be a promising concept which, if developed into a sharp analytical tool, may help us to assess empirically the extent to which concerns of this sort can in fact be substantiated. It usefully highlights the 'affective' dimension of political life and involvement of citizens in it. 'Disaffection' is clearly the antonym of 'passion', and operationalized as such (Montero *et al.* 1997b: 141). It thus is a welcome component in an effort to 'reactivate', as it were, on the level of sophistication of modern social science the eighteenth-century conceptual triplet of interest–reason–passion into a set of three conceptual tools which, however, are framed in *negative* terms. That is to say and propose: if my interests are being violated, I am left with a sense of *dissatisfaction*; if the reasons given for the worthiness of the political order and its actual practice of governance are not supported and confirmed by autonomous insight, we speak of *illegitimacy*, as experienced as a lack of good and valid reasons in support of what we actually see happening at the level of public policies and the ways they affect 'us'; and if people dissociate themselves from a polity or political community that they experience as being strange, boring, incomprehensible, hostile, or inaccessible, we can speak of *disaffection*.

A similar conceptual structure emerges if we link the three types of political aversion to the three hierarchical levels of political identification and support that David Easton (1965) has famously distinguished. Citizens are tied to the policy outcomes of particular *governments* by their (material as well as ideal) interests and how they perceive them to be affected by a particular set of policies or a party in government; in the negative case, they are frustrated or dissatisfied. They are tied to – or can be rationally convinced to maintain there loyalty towards – the *political regime* such as liberal democracy; failing that, we speak of a condition of delegitimation or illegitimacy. Finally, they are attached by passions (e.g. through patriotism, nationalism, sense of identity, pride, but also chauvinist and xenophobic emotions) to some *political community* as a whole; in the absence of such attachment, we speak of disaffection.

Yet 'political disaffection' is still largely an under-conceptualized term. While the term does play a certain role in some diverse and highly specialized fields of the social sciences and humanities (such as urban studies, curriculum studies, organization studies, gender and race relations, as well as marriage and family therapy), it has been relatively rarely used until recently, beyond the everyday language and *ad hoc* semantics, in political analysis and the study of political behaviour. Here, it has much less of a standing as an established concept than related concepts such as political alienation, political apathy, *anomie*, sense of powerlessness, 'negative social capital', distrust, cynicism, perhaps also 'post-modernism', and the like. The Spanish word of *desencanto* or the German concept of *Politikverdrossenheit* seem to be more widely used in these languages than are their English equivalents, though more often in journalistic accounts of current conditions and developments than in academic ones.[2]

If we speak of political disaffection, I take it to mean a group of phe-nomena that have to do with negative attitudes and behavioural patterns of people towards the universe, their fellow citizens, political life in general, political institutions (above all parties and party elites), and the practice of citizenship (such, as a minimum, voting). As in the use of 'dis-affection' in the above fields of social and educational science studies, dis-affection in politics also refers to the primarily emotional and passionate (rather than cognitive) condition of absence of a 'sense of belonging', not 'feeling at home' in the political community, marginalization, perceived lack of representation, institutionally mediated lack of capability to make one's voice heard, deprivation of political resources, lack of horizontal and vertical trust, profound aversion to the political order, etc.

If these preliminary semantic approximations can serve as a guideline, we can, it seems to me, usefully proceed to develop a typology of the range of phenomena we have in mind; try to assess the interaction between vio-lations of interest, absence of compelling reasons, and negative emotions, also addressing the question of possible cumulative effects; look at trends and patterns of distribution across time, across societies, and across seg-ments of the social structure; explore possible causal antecedents and effects of political disaffection; discuss the question on whether or not these dispositions might involve negative consequences for the robustness of liberal democratic regimes; and, if so, at which level of the social and political system these consequences can be observed and what might even-tually be done about them. All that can of course not possibly be done within the limits of the present chapter.

On democratic legitimacy

'We regard legitimacy as citizens' positive attitudes towards democratic institutions' (Montero *et al.* 1997b: 126). I wish to argue that this is an overly 'thin', or insufficiently demanding, definition of what democratic legitimacy 'is'. It lacks, or at any rate de-emphasizes, one important *antecedent* and one relevant *consequence* of the condition of legitimacy. As to the antecedent, I wish to suggest that the sense of democratic legitimacy does not just depend upon a person's having a positive attitude, but depends (at least in the context of any 'modern' society) upon the argu-ments and *reasons* given for, and accepted as effectively supporting and validating, the democratic regime form and its institutions. For instance, a person could say that 'I hold a positive attitude towards democratic institu-tions because experience tells me that my interests are well served by the operation of these institutions; should this turn out to be no longer true, I will have to reconsider the case'. Or the person could say that, while liberal democracy is definitely not a desirable institutional arrangement of political life, we'll have to stick to it for the time being as its alteration appears currently unfeasible. For this person, democracy is obviously not 'legitimate', but at best a contingently beneficial or useful arrangement, and at worst one that must be accepted for the sake of 'realism'. Similarly, an attitude derived from habituation such as this would positively *not* do as proof of legitimacy: 'I am in favour of democratic institutions because I am used to them and emotionally feel familiar with them'. In contrast, what would be a consistent proof of democratic legitimacy, as held as an attitude by citizens, would be a statement such as the following:

> I hold a positive attitude towards democratic institutions because in societies such as ours there is simply no compelling case that could be made (or that I, at any rate, would be willing to accept from autonomous insight) in support of an *unequal* distribution of political and civil rights; all arguments in support of, say, a privileged right of dynastic, military, authoritarian, ethnocratic, theocratic, racist, or party-monopolistic rulers to make collectively binding decisions are clear non-starters (especially after what the world has seen in the course of the twentieth century). Hence the only argument in support of political authority I, as well as my fellow citizens, are likely to accept is the argument that all those who are supposed to obey the law must have an equal right to participate in the making of the law. And all members of the political elite must be held effectively accountable for what they are doing or fail to do. Furthermore, there is no conceivable good reason permitting the political authorities to dictate or interfere with my freely chosen religious, economic, communicative, or associative preferences.

In short, a liberal democracy is reliably anchored in supportive attitudes of the citizenry only if these attitudes, in their turn, are in fact informed by the kind of arguments for individual liberty and popular sovereignty I have just alluded to.

I am perfectly aware of the fact that modern survey research measures *attitudes and opinions*, not the *modalities of arriving* at and holding fast to these attitudes, nor the reasons supporting opinions at the individual level. But it still seems worthwhile to highlight (for instance, through methods of discourse analysis) the *way* people arrive at (or the basis upon which they hold) attitudes, and what *reasons* they give in their defence. For this genetic aspect of attitudes and opinions is significant for the *function* of legitimacy beliefs (rather than an attitude of opportunistic or 'realist' acceptance). For it is invariably for the sake of the function, or consequences, of legitimacy that we are at all interested in the concept. Following Max Weber, the function of the belief in the legitimacy of a given political order consists in the belief's capacity to *motivate obedience or compliance* on the part of those who hold the belief, even in cases when the decisions to be complied with are contrary to the manifest interests of those called upon to comply. The assumption here is that if my allegiance to the liberal democratic regime form is based upon reasons and autonomous insight, such insight will condition my compliance *even if* such compliance is contrary to my interests (or, for that matter, my emotional attachment or aversion to certain communities and life forms). In other words: only reason- and insight-based, and certainly not to the same extent interest- and passion-based, 'positive attitudes towards democratic institutions' will generate what legitimacy is all about, namely compliance. Thus, legitimacy is not just any positive or supportive 'belief', but a belief specifically *rooted* in certain arguments and principles and, most importantly, a belief *resulting* in certain behavioural outcomes, namely voluntary compliance.[3]

Democracy's triumph

Let me venture the generalization that reasons-based legitimacy (as opposed to situationally contingent acceptance) of the liberal democratic regime form is more firmly entrenched and more widely shared in today's world than it has ever been in history. If this is so, it can be explained as the combined effect of two conjunctures. For one thing, non-democratic regimes which would be able to muster strong arguments in support of themselves have virtually vanished from the scene.[4] Dynastic, theocratic, fascist, state socialist, or military versions of political authoritarianism are clearly on the retreat, though unevenly so and with some transitions to democracy stagnating at the point of defective 'semi-democracy'. For another, the variability of the liberal democratic regime form and the diversity of its present-day incarnations is so great that all conceivable arguments for (and interests in the improvement of) a political order can be accommodated under the broad 'liberal democratic' roof. In short, nobody (not even, say, Mr Milosevic) has a presentable *argument* (as opposed to opposing interests and passions) why democracy (in any of the many versions it allows for) is 'bad' and to be feared in view of its consequences, or why any conceivable alternative regime form should be held to be preferable.[5] At the very least, this rule applies to 'old' democracies, while the argument in new, nascent, and semi-democracies is at best (or rather at worst) that 'our country is not yet quite ripe', given some looming ethnic, religious, or class conflict, for the introduction of a regime form; the long-term unavoidability, however, is conspicuously rarely at issue. With the exception of much of the Islamic world, the issue is when and how, not whether, democracy, including a regime of human and civil rights, is to be adopted, and a democratic transition to be made. When, in the course of the fourth quarter of the twentieth century, the percentage of democracies jumped up from less than 30 to more than 60 per cent of all states, intellectually minimally respectable arguments against the adoption of the democratic regime have virtually vanished.[6]

It is not only the institutional and ideological system of state socialism (as the only 'really existing' alternative political order for a modern society) that has collapsed after 1989. Similarly collapsed have autocratic and military regimes. At any rate, they are in the process of doing so under the impact of international organization, the threat of intervention, policing, and the practices of 'conditionalism', and the international and supranational politics of 'promoting and protecting democracy', as well as the current and often dubious strategies of 'state building' or even 'nation building' from the outside. Where they still exist, non-democratic regimes are put under both internal and external pressure to liberalize. The international embeddedness of regimes has also helped in many cases to invalidate the 'pragmatic' reasons for the reluctance to democratize which is based on the pretext that if 'we' would allow the transition to a liberal democracy 'now', the result would be not liberal democracy, but the collapse or breakup of the state *tout court.* With all the supranational military, political, and economic resources in place, even the 'not yet'-objection (that has taken the place of any outright 'no'-argument) has lost much of its credibility.

Moreover and second, liberal democracy is a regime form that allows for a considerable range of variation. It can be *ethnos*-based and *demos*-based, presidential and parliamentary, centralist or federal, majoritarian and proportional, direct and representative, bicameral or unicameral, with an extended or highly limited bill of rights, with or without a written constitution, with or without constitutional guarantees of social rights, with or without autonomous institutions (such as the central bank or a constitutional court), and so on. Moreover, democracy comes in degrees; it can be 'complete' or defective (or 'delegative'), and its installation can proceed through a revolutionary rupture or a negotiated transition. Thus both the components of 'liberalism' and of 'democracy' allow for a great deal of variation. Given these wide-ranging options, there are hardly any economic, cultural, ethnic, political, or social concerns which could not be suitably built into a specifically designed case of a liberal democratic polity-to-be built, arguably with the exception of religious concerns of a theocratic sort. Also, most conceivable committed anti-democrats would be dissuaded from pursuing (and even voicing) their hopeless ambitions owing to the fact that there is a very slim chance of success in advocating any such anti-democratic political initiative, both because such an initiative would fail to get much support from others and because it would be vigorously resisted by democratically elected authorities, domestically as well as internationally.

Hence the legitimacy of the democratic regime form as such simply does not seem to be the major problem, given the overwhelming weight of reasons supporting it. Virtually nobody has anything resembling a reasonable argument (i.e. having the chance of being endorsed by citizens on the basis of autonomous insight) proposing a political arrangement *other* than what passes for liberal democracy. This is in stark contrast to the intellectual situation of the inter-War period. Liberal democracy has become, and not just in advanced societies, 'commonplace' – the 'only game in town'. This has given rise to the speculation that democratic legitimacy may be in the process of becoming a victim of its own success. The reasons why democracy is 'better' fade away with the evidence, provided on a daily basis, of the conditions prevailing in non-democracies. After its only 'modern' alternative, i.e. state socialism, having made its dramatic disappearance, democrats and political elites of democracies may be deprived of an arguably essential challenge to point out and validate, to themselves as well as to others, the reasons on which democratic legitimacy is based. Thus the absence of a (nearby, seriously 'comparable') synchronic alternative, as well as the fading of diachronic memories and recollections, might eventually contribute to the transformation of a reason-based legitimacy, or rationally motivated support of democracy, into habituation, banalization, and unthinking routine. But it is certainly too early to pursue such gloomy speculations any further here.

But perhaps we must consider high levels of support and enthusiasm and the ensuing strong involvement of citizens with the political process, such involvement being based on emotions, interests, or reasons, something that is an exceptional rather than normal condition of democratic citizenship and its practice. Could it be the case that 'consolidated' (i.e. well-established and no longer precarious) democracies in the course of their 'normal politics' are *generally* not good at engaging the hearts, minds, and interests of citizens? If so, it would follow that in times of normal politics it is to be expected that citizens would mentally withdraw from political life and turn into rather apathetic actors, coolly and selectively watching political events in an emotionally distanced, somewhat bored, and indeed disaffected manner, spending most of their energies on the pursuit of their private lives. Securely established democracies are not good at evoking strong sentiments, visions, and ambitions – and that may well be for the better. As it is formal procedures with uncertain outcomes that make up the essence of democratic political life, it arguably does not provide much opportunity for citizens to get engaged, particularly as in modern democracies individual citizens seem to have less and less a role to play relative to representative collective actors that populate the scenery of political life. In that sense, widespread apathy has been conceived of as a sign of *strength* of democracy, not of weakness, as withdrawal and non-participation is taken to be indicators of consent and diffuse support for the regime and its *modus operandi*.

de Tocqueville: how democratic institutions generated democratic citizens

In his two volumes on *Democracy in America*, Alexis de Tocqueville takes the opposite view. He consistently and repeatedly makes the three-step argument that (i) life in democratic societies does indeed generate disaffected, depoliticized citizens, that (ii) such degeneration is by no means a harmless development, as it facilitates the rise of despotic or tyrannical deformations of democracies and the loss of liberty, which is why he is (iii) intensely interested in the identification of spontaneous rebounds, or endogenous counter-tendencies, that are capable of overcoming and neutralizing such dangerous tendencies. Let me briefly reconstruct the dialectical chain of these three arguments that he develops in either of the two volumes.

Volume I of de Tocqueville's work on American democracy[7] is the account of a proponent of a 'new political science', as the author states in his introduction to volume I (lxxiii). (i) Democracy is defined by the presence of equal political rights of all citizens and the absence of an aristocratic status order, with collective decisions on laws etc. being made by majority rule. (ii) The bad news is that the power of the majority is so overwhelming that 'no sure barrier is established against tyrannical abuses' (307). This leads, at the elite level, to mediocrity and opportunism of people who try to please the majority, with the consequence of a 'singular paucity of distinguished political characters' which is to be explained by the 'ever-increasing activity of the despotism of the majority in the United States' (313). Similarly, at the mass level, this leads to pervasive conformism and a lack of freedom of opinion that is even worse, he claims, than that which prevailed under the Inquisition in Spain (312), with the minorities being urged to desperation (317) by the majoritarian force of opinion.

But then there are also (iii) 'good news',[8] summarily introduced as 'causes which mitigate the tyranny of the majority' (319). These causes include the four countervailing powers of the legal profession and its constitutional role and 'magisterial habits' (321), in particular the educational impact the practice of trial by jury has upon the 'judgment' and 'intelligence' of ordinary people (337); the *mores* which comprise 'the whole moral and intellectual life of a people'; religious institutions and their exclusion from political control, this exclusion being the reason why religion's 'influence is more lasting' (370) than it would be if it were permitted to exercise political control; and, perhaps most importantly for de Tocqueville, what he observes as a learning-on-the-job pattern of forming political culture through endogenous preference-building, rather than through 'book-learning' (377): 'The American learns to know the law by participating in the act of legislation; and he takes a lesson in the forms of government, from governing' (378). Political life itself will inspire the people, de Tocqueville believes, 'with the feelings which it requires in order to govern well' (391).

As to volume II, originally published in 1840, we get the sociological version of the same three-step theory of how (i) 'democracy' causes (ii) damages that (iii) can be corrected. Here, the argument proceeds roughly as follows. (i) The 'democratic age', as he observes it in the United States, is defined by the equality of conditions, i.e. of legal status of all citizens (115). Equality of legal status entails the desire, on the part of each citizen competing with every other citizen, for ever greater equality of outcomes, the 'ardent, insatiable, incessant, invincible' (117) desire for 'living in the same manner' (114). (ii) That concentration on competitive equalization of material gain seduces citizens to forget about their freedom (always understood in the republican sense as the opposite of tyranny). 'If they cannot obtain equality in freedom ... they still call for equality in slavery' (117). Why this is so follows from de Tocqueville's subtle theory of the respective temporal structures of equality and freedom. The good that comes from equality is instantaneous and affects all, whereas the good that comes from freedom is long term and is appreciated only by some (116). As to the negative effects of each, the reverse holds true: equality is a long-term threat, resulting in a slow and imperceptible deformation, while the threat coming from, as it were, 'too much' freedom is perceived as short term of the calm and orderly conduct of business. Given the general human propensity to discount the future, the resulting preference order is obvious: equality > freedom. Yet the equalization drive breeds individualism, egotism, the inclination to dissociate from fellow citizens, which in turn 'saps the virtues of public life' (118), and 'the bond of human affection is relaxed' (119). People become 'indifferent and strangers to one another' (120), and this 'general indifference' (120) applies also to the temporal dimension, as the 'track of generations' is 'effaced' (119). People develop 'the habit of always considering themselves as standing alone', so that everyone ends up being 'entirely confined within the solitude of his own heart' (120). The author presents a long list of character-damaging socialization effects that result from living in an egalitarian and competitive society: their 'feverish ardor' (161) and constant 'anxiety to make a fortune' (167) puts the life of citizens in a mood of 'strange unrest', 'strange melancholy', and even 'disgust of life' (164). Above all, people are profoundly de-politicized: 'they lose sight of the close connexion that exists between the private fortune of each of them and the prosperity of all ... The discharge of political duties appears to them to be a troublesome annoyance, which diverts them from their occupation and business' (167). Such a people will 'ask nothing from its government but the maintenance of order' and is by that token 'already a slave at heart' (168). This syndrome of negative, dissociating effects of egalitarian market society upon people's character invites despotism. 'A despot easily forgives his subjects for not loving him, provided they do not love each other' (123).

But now de Tocqueville points to the way out of this disaster and offers again (iii) a set of good news by claiming a spontaneously operative and experience-based mechanism of self-correction. The citizen 'begins to perceive that he is not so independent of his fellow-men as he had first imagined, and, that in order to obtain their support, he must often lend them his cooperation' (124). This spontaneous solution of the problem of collective action relies on two causal mechanisms: equality leads to interdependence, and interdependence in turn to the widespread practice of 'the art of associating together' (133). The conditions which mediate the latter causal link are several: the 'local freedom' (126) of small communities, the absence of the 'governing power' of a state that 'stands in the way of associations' with the consequence that individuals will be 'losing the notion of combining together' (131), and, most importantly, the religiously inspired (150 ff.) alleged capacity of the Americans, based upon the Christian belief in the 'immortality of the soul' (175), to revise constantly their narrowly conceived notion of individual short-term interest according to the 'principle of interest rightly understood' (145 ff.), leading them to the pursuit of an 'enlightened' egotism (148) and the ultimate fusion of private interest and public virtue: 'It is held as a truth that . . . [man's] private interest is to do good' (145).

Democracy's crisis?

This short excursion into some of the work of, arguably,[9] the greatest political theorist of the nineteenth century should provide us, I believe, with a useful model with the help of which we can shed light on the mass phenomenon of contemporary political disaffection. I take it to be the essence of de Tocqueville's argument and mode of analysis that he puts the habits, *mores*, opinions, etc., in a top-down perspective, as he sees them as generated and inculcated by the practice of the political process itself and the constitutional rules by which it is governed.[10] The argument that I am about to pursue follows this logic of 'on-the-job learning'. It comes in two parts.

For one, I would claim that if we look at the contemporary scholarly literature on social foundations of liberal democracy, we hardly find any analogue to the type of optimistic arguments and evidence that de Tocqueville presented at stage (iii) of his analysis. De Tocqueville had claimed that 'the great privilege of the Americans [as the author's model case of a democratic society, C. O.] . . . consists . . . in their being able to repair the faults they may commit' (I, 268) by virtue of a continuous process of broad self-education through participatory politics. It does not seem easy to make and support a similar empirical claim today,[11] be it concerning the American or any other variant of today's liberal democracy.[12] After all, if it were, we would not be speaking of political disaffection.

The second part of my argument is more ambitious (and presumably more controversial), as it moves from the observation of an academic field just made to an attempt to explain phenomena in the real world. Boldly stated, and using de Tocqueville's core idea of 'inculcation' or 'habituation' as a mechanism of what might be called soft causation, the perspective I wish to suggest is that everything we mean by disaffection is as much a 'fallout' of current institutional practices and experiences as were the civic-republican virtues that de Tocqueville found to be nurtured by the political process of American democracy he observed at his time. The only, though of course all-important, difference is that, in his time, de Tocqueville could see that democracy breeds competent and experienced democrats trained in the arts of self-government and cooperation, whereas we need to understand why today's practice of democracy breeds evidently growing numbers of consistently alienated, uninvolved, and dis-affected cynics who get stuck, as it were, at level (ii) of de Tocqueville's analysis, without ever achieving the transition that he models as level (iii).

Following de Tocqueville, we can take it that political institutions (i.e. the branches and levels of government, the collective actors of territorial and functional representation, various autonomous or self-governing agencies such as central banks or social security funds, the mass media, the electoral system, the bill of rights) together make up the opportunity structure, or framework of action and orientation, of individual citizens as well as political elites. These institutional patterns define the 'possibility space' of citizenship and political action. They provide a learning environ-ment which frames the citizens' points of access to the political process, shapes perceptions, defines incentives, allocates responsibilities, con-ditions the understanding of what the system is about and what the rele-vant alternatives are. These patterns function as a suggestive hidden curriculum of what the citizens can expect and hope for, what they can do, which of the citizens' competencies are needed, invited, discouraged, how to ascertain credibility, and in which way individuals can play a role in the shaping of public policies.

Political institutions and the observation of their actual functioning 'make' citizens in that they engender in them, as well as in elites, a percep-tion of duties, opportunities, and meanings. The citizen is constituted and positioned as an agent in politics by the institutions in and through which politics takes place. We learn what 'we', the citizens, 'are' through the hidden curriculum of day-to-day politics and its formative impact.

The analytical perspective proposed and employed by de Tocqueville (as well as later by Max Weber) looks upon patterns of political behaviour and attitudes as constituted not so much by individual properties (such as education, income, wealth), nor by individuals' value and ideological ori-entation or 'political culture', and neither by structural background con-ditions (such as indicators of political and economic stability and the respective policy outcomes), but by institutional contexts in which citizens are embedded and which endows them with a 'possibility space' of famil-iar options, meanings, political resources, and responsibilities.

Needless to say, this 'institutionalist' top-down perspective makes sense only to the extent that we can come up with an account of what explains the variations of institutional settings across space and time. Two answers to this question have been given. One focuses upon historical background conditions (such as size of a country, position within international trade and security relations, composition of its population by class, ethnicity, settlers vs. aborigines, the experience of civil and international war, etc.) and path-dependent institutional traditions. The other focuses on the strategic action of political elites and the ways in which they either comply with the letter and spirit of the institutional rules which the regime is made up of, or whether they, to the contrary, succumb to the temptation (or alleged 'necessity') to exploit, bend, pervert, and relate strategically and opportunistically to the institutional rules of the regime, thereby continuously redesigning it. Here, the question is whether decisions are being made 'under' the institutional rules that govern them or whether they are being made 'above' the rules and 'about' their particular mode of operation. Institutions are double-faced. On the one hand, they are 'inherited' and often show a great deal of tenacity. On the other, they are malleable and altered in the process of their day-to-day enactment by elites (and perhaps also non-elites).

Elites can interpret, alter, and revise in the interest of gaining or maintaining political control the institutional frame within which they operate. That does not imply that they regularly break the rules according to which they are supposed to operate, although sometimes of course they do. Yet while they remain perfectly within the bounds of the script of formal institutions, they invent styles and strategies for the conduct of office according to the problems they need to solve and the support they want to generate or maintain. The opportunities and incentives built into representative and competitive party and media politics lead them, given the kind of challenges that policy-makers must respond to in contemporary democratic polities, to choose opportunistic practices of governing which in turn cannot but generate disaffection. (The term 'opportunistic' does not stand for negative character features of the members of political elites, but for the dilemmas and tensions in their roles that necessitate a peculiar style of adaptive behaviour.) In line with this general hypothesis, I suggest that we look at the various symptoms of the liberal democratic *malaise* and discontent (such as dissatisfaction, distrust, illegitimacy, apathy, voter volatility, etc.) through the prism of the impact upon political institutions that results from opportunistic elite strategies and styles of conducting their office. To the extent this hypothesis holds true, 'disaffection' is less of a deviant or pathological response of those who exhibit it than a perfectly rational and easily understandable response to a drama of politics in which ordinary citizens are at the same time players and spectators.

What are the dilemmas and tensions of contemporary political systems to which the elite responses can be held responsible for provoking and inculcating the negative type of responses just mentioned? I will outline three types of answers to this question. First, in a time when policy-making is constrained by market-liberal precepts leading to the fiscal starvation of the state, on the one hand, and issues of international exposure ('globalization'), on the other, democratically competing political elites face the difficulty of making constituencies believe that it actually makes a difference whether they are in government or not. They need to convince voters that they are at all 'in control' and able 'to make a difference' in questions that are even remotely related to a distinctive notion of the common good of the political community, however that good may be conceived. Pressing problems of economic change, labour market regulation, social security, fiscal deficits, international competitiveness, demographic imbalances, inadequacies of the education and health systems, and many others are typically at any given moment of 'normal politics' to be dealt with simultaneously and without any overarching set of normative principles being available that could create coherence or an order of priorities among these diverse challenges. Each of the issues is embedded in a dense policy network of representative actors among whom working agreements must be negotiated and coalitions formed. As a result, the overall process of governance becomes, from the point of view of the citizen, ideologically colourless and cognitively opaque. As 'good' policy-making always aims at complying with the dual imperative of (a) 'solving problems' and (b) winning support, policies must be advertised in terms of the *group-specific interests* and advantages it offers to specific constituencies. This explains why public communication about governance is cast in an entirely functionalist mould ('which interests are being served?') rather than a normative one ('what principles of social and political justice can provide reasons for or against policy *x*?'). Yet consequentialist arguments concerning specific benefits, even provided that they can be objectively assessed, find the attention and support of ever smaller segments of a highly differentiated social structure. In contrast, encompassing collective benefits serving 'all of us' (economic growth is the standard example, an even better one being the prevention of climate change) are typically beyond the power of public policy makers to achieve. Adding to these dilemmas the phenomena of political corruption, or the blurring of the divide between private and public interests (in its dual form of either buying public decisions with private funds or feeding public funds into private pockets), we can appreciate why a great and apparently growing number of citizens look upon the 'political class' with a sense of distrust and animosity.

To illustrate the distinction between normative vs. functionalist frames in which policies are cast, let me use the issue of migration in German domestic politics. Like in many other countries, the issue is who should be granted asylum, residence, social, and citizenship rights. Any proposal concerning these questions can be argued for in terms of normative principles and obligations of justice, such as the obligation to care for refugees, the claim that an ethnic connotation of citizenship must be overcome, or the egalitarian demand that all people who are permanent residents and work in the domestic labour market must also be allowed to enjoy voting and other political rights. In short, what does a reasonably just migration regime provide for? At the same time, such proposals can also be argued for or, for that matter, criticized in functionalist terms, i.e. in categories of costs, benefits, and interests affected. The basic distinction here is that between *duties* and *costs*, the difference being that the fulfilment of duties always involves some costs, the costs resulting from duties cannot (or rather, should not) be saved or economized in the same way as they can (and rationally ought to be, wherever feasible) in economic contexts. As to the German debate on migration policy, it has been framed in terms of the distinction between two categories of migrants: people 'whom we need' (i.e. as bearers of scarce human capital) vs. 'people who need us', the latter category referring to refugees and asylum-seekers. The policy implication has been framed to be this: the more we need to recruit of the former, the fewer we can afford to admit of the latter of these two categories. This calculus of costs and interests that has largely displaced the discourse of rights and obligations, in the field of migration policy as well as other fields, is also likely to have a depoliticizing implication: the calculus of how costly or beneficial the admission of certain categories of people will be transcends the competence of ordinary citizens and must thus be left to the decision of experts, whereas normative judgements on rights and obligations can be left to the ordinary citizen who is (by definition) capable of making and appreciating reasonable arguments. My speculation is that the underutilization of this capability is what leaves citizens disaffected.

My second and (equally sweeping) generalization is this. The 'political class' is typically aware of the widening affective and cognitive distance that exists between the citizenry and itself, as well as of the ensuing risk of further losing support. In response, it tries to bridge the gap by *populist appeals to cultural values* and the emotions attached to them, such as the emotions of indignation or enthusiastic approval. One familiar pattern is politicians acting as 'anti-politician politicians', i.e. as ordinary people with common-sensical views and lifestyles and a heartfelt disgust for bureaucracy, taxes, and other negative features of 'the state' and 'big government'. Another one is the incitement and exploitation of fears (e.g. of terrorist acts or other kinds of crime) and hopes (e.g. for new wonder drugs) for political gain. Another familiar pattern of political elites' rhetorical self-presentation is the expression of concerns for community values, family values, religion, national identity, and patriotism. Politicians thereby frame themselves as decent and respectable personalities who are deeply concerned and committed to values that everyone shares. No doubt that may even be true, and they certainly can succeed with large parts of the audiences which these messages are intended to reach. But it is nevertheless a strategy of building a kind of counterfeit charisma by which politicians overstep the bounds of their office and colonize the moral life of their constituencies. A local candidate showing up, without being invited, at a neighbourhood garden party (with a TV team happening to be nearby), or a spokesperson of the opposition party instrumentalizing the horror and sadness caused by the recent murder of a child for accusing the governing party for having been soft on crime, are instances of the purposive use of people's moral sentiments and emotions. For the mandate of elected politicians in a liberal democracy is not to provide moral guidance or emotional satisfaction to constituencies, but to conduct good legislation and public policies. While parts of these constituencies, and the media in particular, will be quite receptive to such manifestations of 'political kitsch', others will react with disgust and disaffection.

My third point is related to the key concept of any democratic theory, which is *accountability*. The necessary minimum of such accountability obviously consists in general elections. However, it is in the nature of elections that the electorate answers questions put before them by political elites; it cannot address questions to the elites or question the alternatives party elites have posed. One problem with elections as the basic democratic accountability mechanism is that they occur relatively rarely. Even more serious is the problem that they are extremely modest and undemanding in terms of the thoughtfulness they require of the voter casting his or her vote. The choice of the yes/no/abstention alternatives may well be based upon well-considered reasons and a fully 'adequate understanding' (Dahl 1992: 47–48) of the issues at hand, but it can as well be guided by momentary impulses or a misleading campaign trick of one of the competing candidates or parties. There is nothing in the solitude of the voting booth, as well as the anticipation of that solitude, that would activate the deliberative capacity of voters. Moreover, the yes/no/abstention code does not allow to ask questions, present arguments, substantiate objections, or transmit specific demands voters may want to bring to the attention of democratic rulers. To be sure, there are plenty of facts and arguments presented in the course of election campaigns, but these are always arguments being advanced not *for* a point of view, but *from* the strategic point of view, namely that of attracting votes. Nor can we rely on the print and electronic media performing the function of adequately educating and informing voters, as media organizations, and in particular the commercial ones, have their own agenda to pursue.

For all these reasons, it has been convincingly argued, for old and new democracies alike (see Rose-Ackerman 2005), that a merely 'electoral' democracy is deficient in terms of the extent to which it is actually able to hold governing elites accountable. Their institutionalized practices amount to a systematic underutilization of the intelligence and the moral resources of the citizenry and its capacity for making informed judgement (see Offe and Preuss 1991). As citizens have very limited autonomously organized opportunities to ask elites for arguments and information, to evaluate both in terms of its accuracy and reasonableness, and to learn from each other in the process of doing so (which includes reflection and learning about their 'interests rightly understood'), a number of additional institutional mechanisms have been proposed that would enhance democratic elite accountability. These are not the subject of the present discussion. However, as long as democratic practice is stuck at the level of the electoral mechanism of accountability (plus the bargaining between governments and collective actors behind closed doors), it is not entirely unreasonable if the realities and outcomes of such impoverished kind of accountability test is met with a sense of disaffection and disenchantment.

These endogenously generated attitudes amount arguably to a moral crisis of the practice of democracy and an apparently growing disaffection, or affective distance, to the political life of liberal democracy. Charles Maier (1994: 59) speaks of 'a flight from politics, or what the Germans call *Politikverdrossenheit*: a weariness with its debates, disbelief about its claims, skepticism about its results, cynicism about its practitioners'. The finding of a profound and pervasive distrust of political leaders in all parties is virtually ubiquitous and uncontested (see Nye *et al.* 1997). Not only for the US, the diagnosis is uncontroversial: 'Americans' direct engagement in politics and government has fallen steadily and sharply over the last generation ... Every year over the last decade or two, millions more have withdrawn from the affairs of their communities' (Putnam 1995a: 68). Indicators such as 'declines in voter turnout, trade union membership, prestige of politicians, citizen interest in public affairs, in the perceived role of legislatures, in the extent and intensity of party identification, and in the stability of electoral preferences' (Schmitter 1995: 18) all point in the same direction, as does the new popularity of the term 'the political class' with its dismissive and contemptuous undertones. As a consequence, political institutions do not encourage, absorb, and engage the interests, as well as the cognitive, moral, and emotional resources of citizens – who thereby somehow *cease* to be *citizens*, as opposed to subjects, spectators, semi-bored consumers of 'infotainment', voters obsessed by myths and resentment, or simply victims of disinformation campaigns. The phenomenon is so consistent and widespread that it appears dubious to trace it to external determinants of people's 'attitudes' and 'opinions', rather than to the institutional contexts which endogenously generate and reinforce these dispositions.

One important aspect of this institutionally induced political alienation is what might be called 'cognitive flooding'. Every new item that appears on the agenda of public policy, including items of great and universal political concern, seem to have an ever shorter initial phase when ordinary citizens can feel confident to know everything that is necessary to know in order to form competent judgement on preferred political responses. After this period (which, according to my subjective estimate, may last about two weeks) there is already 'too much' to know and to consider in order for average citizens to avail themselves of what they would rely on as their own 'reasoned opinion'. As the gap between what we need to know and what we feel we actually know is rapidly widening, mass constituencies are reduced to political analphabetism, while the circle of the 'competent' shrinks to the tiny minority of those who have the time, opportunity, or professional mandate to immerse themselves into all the relevant complexities. In the meantime, political elites and media busy themselves with the task of feeding mass constituencies with those prefabricated views and basic (if distorted) pieces of information on which we all depend.

Types of disenchantment with the practice of liberal democracy

I wish to conclude this exercise in conceptual clarification and hypothesis-building with a *tableau* of 'disenchanted' responses. In order to specify all the deficiencies that we try to address with the concepts of disaffection, dissatisfaction, frustration, apathy, etc., we need to contrast these conditions (just as 'illness' is understood as the deviation from 'health') to the notion of the 'good' or fully competent citizen. Here is a sketch of what (the civic-republican version of) such a citizen looks like:

> The good democratic citizen is a political agent who takes part regularly in politics locally and nationally, not just on primary and election day. Active citizens keep informed and speak out against public measures that they regard as unjust, unwise, or just too expensive. They also openly support politics that they regard as just and prudent. Although they do not refrain from pursuing their own and their reference group's interests, they try to weigh the claims of other people impartially and listen to their arguments. They are public meeting-goers and joiners of voluntary organizations who discuss and deliberate with others about the politics that will affect them all, and who serve their country not only as taxpayers and occasional soldiers, but by having a considered notion of the public good that they genuinely take to heart. The good citizen is a patriot.
>
> (Shklar 1991: 5)

This ideal type of a democratic citizen is, to reduce this rich description to a schematic construct, someone who combines two sets of characteristics. For one thing, he or she has some '*cause*' ('considered notion of the public good') that is believed to be capable of being promoted in political life. This is some value, interest, group, or concern that – ultimately in the name of some notion of justice – should be served by the makers of public policy. For the other, the democratic citizen is reasonably confident that the institutional resources and mechanisms ('public meetings, voluntary organizations, elections, paying taxes') that the political community has at its collective disposal are capable of *actually processing* and promoting those 'causes', and that the citizens wishing to promote some cause can confidently and effectively rely on these institutional mechanisms to do so. These two variables – let us call them 'political engagement' and 'sense of political efficacy' – relate to the substantive *content* and institutional *forms* of political life, or to its *ends* and *means,* or the *specific* and the *general.* Either of theses variables can be dichotomized and combined to yield four groups of cases. To complicate things, I propose to add the elite/mass distinction to some of the cells of the resulting two-by-two matrix.

As in all such routines of conceptual exploration, the plus/minus combinations are of greatest interest. The plus/plus combination represents the *ideal democratic citizen* at the mass level and, at the elite level, the committed politician who 'stands for' some programmatic cause and, following Max Weber, lives 'for', rather than 'off', politics and a distinctive vision of the public good. In extreme contrast, the minus/minus combination ('*privatism*') represents the apathetic, perhaps cynical, and at any rate disenchanted citizen who does not perceive any meaningful place or role being provided to him or her by political institutions. At the same time, not much is seen to be missed by this fact, as the person in question sees *private* (family, occupational, religious, associational, consumption) and not *political* life as the scene or appropriate context where his or her important concerns and interests can be pursued. Politics is not held to be 'worth the effort', because what counts is seen to be outside of politics anyway, and political institutions (including the notion of 'the country') are at best dubious as to their worthiness of the citizens' confidence; this is the essence of post-modernist and neo-liberal dispositions towards political life. The 'privatism' type shies away from the complexity of politics and policies and the cognitive opaqueness of decision processes, which have made reasonably competent political participation more demanding in cognitive terms, while fiscal and other constraints imposed upon an essentially post-interventionist (as well as post-Cold War and, in Europe, post-national) political life have diminished both the interest-based and passion-based modes of involvement of citizens. As a consequence, politics itself has changed in ways which makes it both more difficult to understand and follow and less consequential (or more boring) in terms of the material benefits and emotional appeals it has to offer. Moreover, the remaining emotional appeals (on which both competitive strategies of media reporting and populist elite politics relies) are often of a negative, scandalizing, and implicitly 'anti-political' nature. They are designed to stir up audiences' sense of indignation (with politics as a 'dirty business') and thus to undermine the reputation and respectability of the 'political class', its authority and activities. Both the perceived realities of political life and the strategies of media converge on suggesting to the citizenry that politics is rarely 'worth the effort'. While rational and well-focused distrust is arguably healthy for the viability of democratic political life, the opposite may be said for the framing of politics in terms of a generalized anti-political suspicion and a detachment from issues of justice.

Perhaps more interesting than privatism is the combination of strong loyalty with political institutions and low intensity of political causes. Citizens belonging in this category, call them *conventionalist*, do follow the political process with attention and without a sense of being left out, but they do so without providing any input or even substantively adequate and relevant judgement of their own. They relate to politics in terms of spectator sports or personality show, without being able to (or finding it worth the effort to) evaluate, take sides, or pass independent judgement on issues and programmes. If mobilization of this kind of citizen occurs at all, it follows the 'populist' logic: both the issues over which the mobilization occurs and the standards and values applied to them are unreflective evaluative intuitions invoked by political leaders. There is also an elite-level equivalent to this 'a-political' conduct of politics: the all-purpose politician specializing in the brokerage of power without a sense of purpose and values, prudence, and justice of his own. The absence of authentic causes and programmatic visions can take the form of careerism, opportunism, or the ritualistic defence of agencies, parties, and budgets. This is the syndrome that Richard von Weizsäcker (1992), the former German president, had in mind when he criticized leaders of political parties for their routines of maximizing and monopolizing power without having any idea, or sense of purpose, for which causes and objectives to deploy that power.

The inverse combination is that of strong causes with low confidence as to the capacity of established political institutional procedures to respond to and process the issues making up these causes. This disposition may result in a number of behavioural and attitudinal outcomes. One of them is involvement in '*non-conventional*' *politics*, such as the politics of new social movements. The pattern of movement politics is to develop and practise new (and mostly perfectly legal) channels of political representation and communication in addition to existing routines and mechanisms of association and representation. A more radical outcome of the combination of strong causes with weak confidence is the turn to *violent militancy*, terrorism, and other illegal forms of political action, including the separatist denial of the validity of some established political authority and political community. The type of disaffection we encounter here amounts to the negation, typically fuelled by passionate emotions of resentment, fear, and hatred, not just of the institutional order of political life, but of the underlying political community to which actors no longer wish to belong (secessionist movements and separatism) or from which they want to exclude others (xenophobic violence).

This disposition can manifest itself in overt and active forms, but it can also take the latent and passive form of rejection of authority, non-identification, and the virtual dissociation from the political community over which this authority is established. In this passive version, we may speak of *political cynicism*, or a sense of futility of politics and the pervasive incompetence of political elites. For instance, almost half of all those asked in a German survey a question on 'Which party is best capable of solving the problems of Germany?' answered by choosing the answer 'none of them' (*Die Woche*, July 21, 2000). Withdrawal from political life that is the result of accumulated frustrations (which may be also due to a lack of trust in the cooperation of a significant number of others) is, at the surface of it and in behavioural terms, hard to distinguish from the syndrome of 'privatism'.

Conclusions

In conclusion, let me briefly reflect on the impact the various phenomena of disaffection, alienation, and dissatisfaction might have upon the viability and stability of the democratic regime form. Why is disaffection 'bad' – be it in itself or in terms of its consequences? To be sure, it is bad in terms of the normative ideals derived from the republican tradition, such as those evoked in the above quote from Judith Shklar. Assessments of the causal impact of disaffection, however, range from mildly benign to strongly alarmist. Distrust and even some measure of cynicism concerning the 'political class', its members, and its procedural routines may be considered a syndrome that positively *strengthens* democracy, as it helps to reduce participation and attention in 'normal politics' to tolerable levels, maintains a repertoire of capacity for mobilization for 'extraordinary' causes and critical conditions, and activates the search for additional and alternative modes of mobilization and representation, such as new social movements.

A less favourable assessment claims that the spread of disaffection creates space and opportunities that might be exploited by anti-liberal and/or anti-democratic political entrepreneurs and their populist projects. The danger of backlash into hyper-mobilization has been cited, as underutilized political 'slack resources' are available for the populist support of charismatic ideas and leaders who promise to relieve people from their widely shared sense of frustration and powerlessness. Similarly, the fear has been voiced that disaffection breeds non-compliance and defection, with the law in general (and tax laws in particular) meeting with more or less passive obstruction and becoming ever more difficult to enforce, thus generating a *post-modernist* spiral of state impotence and mass cynicism. Third and finally, the gloomiest of visions concerning the consequences of political disaffection is the fear that the institutional order of liberal democracy and its principles might itself be challenged as a consequence, thereby giving rise to anti-democratic and authoritarian mobilization. It is hard to see what the intellectual resources could possibly be on which such radical and 'principled' challenge of liberal democracy could be based – except, arguably, a fundamentalist revival of *theocratic* theories of the political order and 'good' politics.

But, at least as far as the OECD world is concerned, liberal democracy as a regime form does not show any signs of being in danger because any non-democratic ideas or models have a chance to win mass support. To the idea it is in danger at all, it is so because the democratic political process itself, as it is perceived and experienced by the citizen, has the potential of undermining the loyalty, commitment, and confidence of citizens. While there is very little that speaks 'against' liberal democracy in theory, there is also very little that speaks 'for' its practice. This practice, instead, instils doubts concerning all three items: the *rules* and operative procedures of the conduct of public affairs; the *objectives* and actual accomplishments of governance; and the *reference unit* in terms of which the (whose?) 'common' good is conceptualized.

The practices of political elites to which the deformation of citizenship must be attributed are, as I said, by no means arbitrarily chosen. They are rather necessitated and imposed upon elites by the nature and dynamics of a globalized political economy, the media, and the institutional logic of competitive party democracy itself. These contexts define strategies, constraints, and opportunities that elites have no choice but utilizing and exploiting. By doing so, they teach a hidden curriculum to ordinary citizens about the nature of democratic politics and the role of citizens in it. It is the corrosive impact of this curriculum and its suggestive lessons of disenchantment, cynicism, and withdrawal that even rational and committed citizens find it ever more difficult to withstand in our 'disaffected' democracies.

Notes

1 The term figures prominently in the title of a recent book edited by Pharr and Putnam (2000).
2 Recently the concept of 'disaffected groups' has been employed by the Secretary General of the United Nations, Kofi Anan, when he addressed the International Summit on Democracy, Terrorism, and Security on 11 March 2005. Outlining a UN strategy to combat terrorism, he stated as the first element of that strategy the need to 'dissuade disaffected groups from choosing terrorism as a tactic to achieve their goals'.
3 This conceptualization of legitimacy is quite commonplace in today's political analysis. 'Legitimacy is ... here understood as a widely shared belief that it is my moral duty to comply with requirements imposed by state authorities even if these requirements violate my own preferences or interests, and even if I could evade them at low cost. . . . Democratic legitimacy is about good reasons that should persuade me to comply with policies that do not conform to my own wishes' (Scharpf 2000: 4, 13).
4 To this, it might rightly be objected that theocratic fundamentalist revivals advocating the 'will of God' as rightfully governing and taking precedence over the 'will of the people' are the only remaining instance of a principled anti-democratic political theory.
5 Note the stark contrast to the situation after the 'first wave' of democratization after the First World War and during the entire inter-War period. At that time,

not only large segments of the middle class, but also numerous members of the intellectual and literary elite felt attracted by and actually significantly supported the 'totalitarian' ideologies of fascism and Stalinism and their political ambitions. At least in consolidated democracies, no analogue for such potential for ideological defection from liberal democracy is evident (or indeed conceivable) today.

6 This is in stark contrast to the situation of the inter-War period in Europe and elsewhere, when theorists of both the far Right and far Left could in fact make influential, as well as most consequential, anti-democratic arguments.

7 Page numbers in brackets refer to the respective volume of de Tocqueville (1961).

8 For an account of these, see Maletz (2005).

9 See Elster (1993: 107 and 112 ff).

10 In modern political theory, the classical source from which de Tocqueville probably adopted his analytical model is Montesquieu's *L'Esprit des Lois* (and more particularly from book 11, ch. 6, 'On the Constitution of England'), where the author undertakes a 'proto-Tocquevillean' analysis of the British system of government. It is still not widely understood and appreciated to which considerable extent the political sociology of Max Weber, who wrote two generations after de Tocqueville, is a continuation and elaboration of the work of the latter. What Weber is concerned with is how certain institutional settings shape and cultivate the particular kind of 'modal personality' ('*Menschentum*', as he puts it), the moral and political qualities of which reflect the qualities of the institutions in question. For instance, he vehemently criticized the fact that the semi-authoritarian protectionism that characterized the political system of Imperial Germany would breed a kind of 'timid' and 'politically uneducated' bourgeoisie incapable of assuming a political role of responsible participation and leadership.

11 In fact, the rich contemporary literature on 'deliberative' democracy attempts to remedy this deficiency (which it thereby highlights) through normative models and institutional designs. For a recent and highly suggestive example, see Ackerman and Fishkin (2004).

12 In German political theory debates, one of the symptomatically most often-quoted theorems is condensed in a sentence from the constitutional lawyer Ernst-Wolfgang Böckenförde. It reads: 'Der freiheitliche, säkularisierte Staat lebt von Voraussetzungen, die er selbst nicht garantieren kann'. ('The liberal secular state depends upon premises that itself cannot guarantee by its own means.') This is the precise opposite of de Tocqueville's account of American democracy, which, in his view, induces the learning processes on the results of which it thrives.

3 The multidimensionality of political support for new democracies

Conceptual redefinition and empirical refinement

Richard P. Gunther and José Ramón Montero[1]

This chapter explores some attitudes of political support which are relevant to the performance, quality, and survival of newly established democratic systems. We intend to explore the existing relationships among these attitudes and their distinctive effects on one basic element that define the nature of the relationship between citizens and the state: the political intermediation processes. Relevant attitudes towards democracy are of several different kinds, and may have differing but significant impacts on democratic performance. This is especially so for newly established democracies. Mass-level attitudes supporting democracy are often regarded as the bedrock of democratic stability and an important ingredient for the functioning of a healthy democracy, and much of the literature on democratic consolidation therefore places considerable emphasis on the establishment and dissemination of democratic attitudes and values (e.g. Linz and Stepan 1996: 6; and Przeworski *et al.* 1995: 59). In the following pages we present a detailed analysis of various attitudes towards democracy and some of its consequences in seven democratic systems that have emerged from the 'Third Wave' of democratization since the mid-1970s – in Bulgaria, Chile, Greece, Hungary, Portugal, Spain, and Uruguay.

In contrast with much of the earlier literature on these democratic attitudes, we argue that it is extremely important to differentiate clearly among different types of attitudinal orientations. In our previous work,[2] we found that such attitudes must be clearly separated into three different clusters, which we called *democratic support, political discontent,* and *political disaffection.* In the first part of this chapter we present a summary of findings demonstrating that these are three entirely separable and conceptually distinct attitudinal domains.

We then turn our attention to patterns of political behaviour that are associated with these attitudes. As we have also demonstrated somewhere else (Gunther, Montero, and Torcal forthcoming), these three sets of attitudes have quite different behavioural correlates or consequences: a lack of fundamental support for democracy is strongly associated with votes for anti-system parties; political discontent is clearly linked with votes against the incumbent party or governing coalition; and political disaffection is part of a broader syndrome of alienation and disengagement from active involvement in the political process. These attitudes of political disaffection, which is at the centre of the present volume, interact in varying ways with information flows through primary and secondary personal contacts, and from the communications media, but in some respects the direction of causality linking these attitudes to political intermediation is uncertain or reciprocal. As we demonstrate in the second part of this chapter, the politically disaffected tend strongly to be uninvolved with important intermediation channels; but it is unclear whether behavioural disengagement fosters disaffection, or disaffection simply leads to marginalization from most facets of organized politics.

Three concepts and seven countries

Most published studies of attitudes toward democracy share two characteristics. First, they tend to assume that attitudes towards the political system constitute one single attitudinal domain, or at most, two. In his seminal work on this subject, David Easton (1965) argued that such orientations could be broken down into two categories, which he called *diffuse support* and *specific support* for democracy. Other studies did not even go this far and indiscriminately mixed a wide variety of attitudinal orientations into their analyses assuming that they occupied a common conceptual domain. This is, they argue, because Easton's original conceptualization was so vague as to lead invariably to research that is 'ambiguous, confusing and noncumulative' (Kaase 1988: 117), because the relevant measurement problems are insuperable (Loewenberg 1971), because this distinction is tautological and derived exclusively from the employment of an inferior methodology (Craig 1993), or because citizens are simply not capable of distinguishing between them (Muller and Jukam 1977).[3] Unfortunately, in our view, by including such seemingly distinct orientations as basic support for democracy and satisfaction with the current performance of governmental institutions within a single attitudinal domain, this literature has produced a plethora of inconsistent findings and a great deal of confusion about the impact of democratic attitudes on individual-level political behaviour and the overall performance and legitimacy of democratic systems. For that reason, we will demonstrate why it is important to differentiate more clearly among these different types of attitudinal orientations.

A second claim often found in this literature posits a close (if not deterministic) relationship between citizens' levels of satisfaction with the performance of political institutions or the economy, and support for the democratic regime *per se*. Weatherford (1987: 13), for example, states that 'Over the long run, of course, legitimacy is wholly determined by policy performance'. Fuchs, Guidorossi, and Svenson (1995: 342) add that 'the stability of representative democracy depends (. . .) on the level of satisfaction'. And Adam Przeworski (1991: 95) flatly asserted, 'As everyone agrees, the eventual survival of the new democracies [in post-Soviet Eastern Europe] will depend to a large extent on their economic performance. And since many among them emerged in the midst of an unprecedented economic crisis, economic factors work against their survival'. Some scholars have even suggested that the legitimacy of established Western democracies is increasingly dependent on their performance (see Fuchs and Klingemann 1995: 440).

In earlier publications (Gunther and Montero 2000; Montero, Gunther, and Torcal 1997b) we tested some of these propositions and found no support for them. We found that the most commonly used indicators constituted three attitudinal domains that were both conceptually and empirically distinct from one another. And we found that fundamental support for democracy was not contingent upon satisfaction with the performance of the economy, the incumbent government, or of democracy in general.

Two of the three clusters of attitudes toward democracy that emerged from our earlier analysis are roughly similar to Easton's distinction between diffuse and specific support. *Democratic support* pertains to citizens' beliefs that democratic politics and representative democratic institutions are the most appropriate (indeed, the only acceptable) framework for government. This is the key attitudinal component of regime legitimacy. Such beliefs focus on the political regime in the aggregate, and should be expected to be stable over time and immune from the influence of such factors as the popularity of the government and partisanship – specifically, the correspondence between the citizens' partisan preferences and the party of the incumbent government – and evaluations of concrete institutions and their performance (Hibbing and Theiss-Morse 1995). Democratic support or legitimacy is a relative concept; no system should be expected to be fully legitimate in the eyes of each and every citizen, and the intensity of positive support for these institutions varies from one person to another. Accordingly, legitimacy may be considered to be 'the belief that, in spite of shortcomings and failures, the political institutions are better than any others that might be established' (Linz 1988: 65). This definition is also relative insofar as it refers to the belief that a democratic political system is the 'least bad' of all forms of government. As Linz (1978: 18) has written, 'ultimately, democratic legitimacy is based on the belief that for that particular country at that particular juncture, no other type of regime could assure a more successful pursuit of collective goals'.[4]

In contrast, *political discontent* is based on 'peoples' judgements about the day-to-day actions of political leaders and the operation of governmental institutions and processes' (Kornberg and Clarke 1992: 20).[5] In other words, political dissatisfaction arises from citizens' evaluations of the performance of the regime or authorities, as well as of their political outcomes (Farah, Barnes, and Heunks 1979). It should thus be expected to fluctuate over time in accord with the government's performance, the condition of the society and economy, or the performance of key political institutions.[6] And since it focuses on partisan political leaders and the governments they lead, it would not be surprising to find that, other things being equal, citizens supporting the same party as that of the incumbent government would be more positive in their assessments than those who voted for the opposition.[7] Its more commonly used antonyms, political dissatisfaction or discontent, can be regarded as expressions of displeasure resulting from the belief that the performance of the government or political system is falling short of the citizens' wishes or expectations (di Palma 1970: 30). More generally, dissatisfaction is a reflection of frustration derived from comparing what one has with what one hopes or expects to have (Gamson 1968). In political terms, it results from perceptions on the government's inability to deal effectively with problems regarded by citizens as important (Dahl 1971: 144; Morlino 1998: 127–131).

The third cluster of attitudes that we shall explore, *political disaffection*, is conceptually distinct from both of those described above, although it is often indiscriminately lumped together with measures of citizen support for and satisfaction with democracy. Following di Palma (1970: 30; also see Torcal 2002a: ch. 3, 2002b, and 2002c), we regard political disaffection as a certain estrangement of members of the polity from both its core political institutions and, more generally, from politics. Its indicators include disinterest in politics, a sense of personal inefficacy, cynicism and distrust, the belief that political elites do not care about the welfare of their citizens, low levels of political confidence, and a general sense of detachment from the political system and/or its most relevant institutions (Montero, Gunther, and Torcal 1997b). Political discontent may be regarded as the result of a negative evaluation of the performance of incumbent authorities and political parties, although it might be accompanied by a positive orientation toward the democratic system as a whole. In contrast, political disaffection is a reflection of a fundamentally distrusting and suspicious vision of political life and the institutions and mechanisms of democratic representation. And unlike discontent (which our earlier analysis found to ebb and flow in accord with current assessments of the performance of incumbents or democratic institutions), attitudes of disaffection are remarkably stable. In addition, while discontent is closely associated with partisanship (with supporters of opposition parties generally more critical of the performance of the government and dissatisfied with its policy outputs than those who identify with the incumbent party), disaffection is more far-reaching and indiscriminate in its objects of negativity, although it does not entail a denial of the regime's legitimacy.[8] In short, the disaffected hold political attitudes that are distinctly different from those who have been referred to as 'dissatisfied democrats' (Klingemann 1999: 54; Dalton 2004: 45 ss.).

Let us begin this exploration of attitudes towards democracy by examining the extent to which these attitudes fall into separable dimensions in six of the new democracies included within the Comparative National Elections Project, as well as in Portugal. Post-election surveys undertaken in Spain (1993), Greece (1996), Uruguay (1994), Bulgaria (1996), Portugal (2002), Hungary (1998), and Chile (1993) included identical or very similar items measuring the three core concepts of democratic support, political discontent, and political disaffection.[9] The geographical, institutional, and social diversity of the cases analysed in this study facilitates our efforts to test the generalizability of our initial findings concerning the separability of these three attitudinal domains (based heavily on our multi-method analyses of Spain). In addition, their greatly different historical experiences and democratization trajectories enable us to speculate about the origins of these democratic attitudes in widely varying contexts, as well as to explore their behavioural consequences and implications for regime stability.

As can be seen in Table 3.1, these countries spanned the full range of democracies arrayed in accord with our core measures of democratic legitimacy, with Greece near the very top in terms of the extent of support for democracy, while support for democracy in Bulgaria is much lower.[10] The Portuguese data (derived, as noted, from a 2002 survey that was not part of the CNEP project) utilized a response format that precludes a direct comparison of frequency distributions with these others, but the overwhelming level of support for democracy in Portugal would have placed it near the top of this rank-ordering of countries.[11]

The surveys conducted in Spain, Uruguay, and Chile included as a measure of support for democracy the respondent's agreement or disagreement with the proposition that 'Democracy is the best political system for a country like ours'. The other surveys also included a second measure of democratic support, which asks respondents to choose among the following three sentences: 'Democracy is preferable to any other form of government'; 'Under some circumstances, an authoritarian regime, a dictatorship, is preferable to a democratic system'; and 'For people like me, one regime is the same as another' (with the latter recoded to fall between the other two as an intermediate category). Both in the remaining text and in the following tables, these two indicators will be labelled as *Democratic support* and *Democratic vs. authoritarian [regimes]*, respectively. Most of the CNEP surveys also included three different measures of what we hypothesize will fall into a separate 'discontent' cluster. These are the respondent's degree of dissatisfaction with 'the way democracy is functioning in his or her country' (*Satisfaction with democracy*); the level of discontent over 'the political situation of the country' (*Political situation*); and the

Table 3.1 Two indicators of support for democracy in CNEP democracies in comparative perspective, 1993–2000[a] (in percentages)

Country	Democratic support		
	Agree	Don't know/It depends	Disagree
Uruguay (1994)	88	7	4
Greece (1996)	87	9	4
Spain (1993)	79	14	7
Chile (1993)	79	11	10
Hungary (1998)	72	18	10
Bulgaria (1996)	57	24	19
Hong Kong (1998)	62	14	24

Country	Democratic vs. authoritarian regimes			
	Democracy always preferable	They're all the same	Sometimes authoritarian regime best	Don't know, No answer
Denmark	93	2	5	1
Norway	88	2	5	5
Greece	**85**	**3**	**11**	**1**
Portugal	83	4	10	4
West Germany	84	5	8	3
The Netherlands	82	5	9	5
Spain	**81**	**7**	**8**	**4**
Italy	81	10	7	2
Uruguay	**80**	**8**	**6**	**8**
France	77	11	7	6
Great Britain	76	11	7	6
Argentina	71	11	15	3
Belgium	70	10	10	10
Bolivia	64	15	17	4
Chile (2000)	**64**	**16**	**17**	**3**
Ireland	63	21	11	6
Peru	63	14	13	10
Venezuela	62	13	19	6
Colombia	60	18	20	2
Bulgaria	**59**	**14**	**25**	**2**
Hungary	**58**	**25**	**7**	**10**
Chile	**54**	**23**	**19**	**4**
Mexico	53	17	23	7
Ecuador	52	23	18	7
Brazil	50	21	24	5

Sources: For the first indicator in Bulgaria, Chile, Greece, Hong Kong, Hungary, Italy, Spain, and Uruguay, as well as the second indicator in Bulgaria, Greece, and Hungary, CNEP surveys; and for the second indicator in Latin American and European countries, Lagos (1997) and *Eurobarometer 37*, 1995.

Note

a *Democratic support* includes answers to the question on whether 'Democracy is the best form of government for a country like ours'; *Democratic* vs. *authoritarian regimes* includes preferences towards the items of each column. Countries are ordered in descending order in each indicator.

extent of dissatisfaction with 'the economic situation of the country' (*Economic situation*). Three variables that we regard as indicators of disaffection were also included in the questionnaires administered in each of these countries. *Politics complicated* reflects agreement or disagreement with the statement, 'Generally, politics seems so complicated that people like me cannot understand what is happening'; *Politicians don't care* is the respondent's agreement or disagreement with the proposition that 'Politicians do not worry much about what people like me think'; and *No influence* taps into the respondent's belief in or rejection of the idea that 'People like me do not have any influence over what the government does'.[12]

Preliminary examination of the other sets of attitudes that we analyse in this chapter presents a very different picture. With regard to levels of dissatisfaction with the economy, the political situation of the country and the functioning of democracy vary considerably from one country to another, and these cross-national patterns do not correspond with the levels of support for democracy presented in Table 3.1. Respondents in Portugal and, especially, Bulgaria are by far the most negative in their assessments of the state of the economy (with 64 and 96 per cent, respectively, describing it as 'bad'; this compares with 60 per cent in Greece, 58 per cent in Spain, 50 per cent in Uruguay, and just 14 per cent in Chile). These assessments of the economy closely parallel those of the political situation of the country, with Bulgarians once again by far the most negative (81 per cent describing conditions as 'bad') and Chileans most positive (only 26 per cent), with respondents in the other countries in-between (with between 52 and 60 per cent evaluating political conditions negatively). When asked to describe the functioning of democracy in their countries, respondents were substantially more satisfied, but again Bulgarians anchored the negative end of the continuum (46 per cent 'bad'): this stood in sharp contrast with Chile (11 per cent), Uruguay (12 per cent), Spain (13 per cent), Portugal (15 per cent), and Greece (19 per cent). There were far fewer cross-national differences with regard to the attitudes associated with disaffection. The range of respondents agreeing with the 'politics is complicated' item was from 43 per cent in Bulgaria to 56 per cent in Greece, while national scores on the 'politicians don't care' item ranged from a low of 60 per cent to a high of 75 per cent. Only with regard to the 'no influence' item is the range of national-level responses more substantial (from a low of 56 per cent in Uruguay to a high of 80 per cent in Hungary).

Dimensional analyses of democratic attitudes

Tables 3.2, 3.3, and 3.4 present the results of two different approaches to analysing the dimensional structures underpinning the clustering of these attitudes and behaviours in our sample of countries. Measures of bivariate association (Tau-b) among all of these items appear in the matrices composed of the first five, six, or seven columns of these tables. The final two or three columns display the loadings that emerged from an exploratory factor analysis of all of these items following a Varimax rotation of the principal component solution. For all countries except Chile, a similar latent structuring emerges that strongly reflects three distinct attitudinal dimensions: democratic support, political discontent, and political disaffection.

It is clear from the data for Spain, Uruguay, and Greece in Table 3.2 that Factor 1 is made up of items involving political discontent. As we hypothesized, all three measures of dissatisfaction belong to this cluster; the magnitude of the factor loadings, the percentage of variance explained by this factor (ranging between 24.1 and 29.4 per cent),[13] and the bivariate measures of inter-item association are all strong and statistically significant (at the 0.001 level or better). It is also noteworthy that the degree of satisfaction with the functioning of democracy in all three countries was strongly linked to assessments of the economic and political conditions of the country. In sharp contrast, basic support for democracy is, at best, weakly related to dissatisfaction with the economic or political situation of the country. In Uruguay, there is no statistically significant relationship between support for democracy and either of these two measures of discontent, while in Spain and Greece the relationships are quite weak (ranging between Tau-b scores of -0.06 and -0.11). Dissatisfaction with the performance of democracy is moderately associated with our measures of democratic support (with Tau-b scores ranging from -0.14 to -0.22), but the factor analyses indicate that support for democracy and the three discontent measures are *not* part of the same attitudinal domain. In Spain, support for democracy simply fails to fit with the other items in the discontent cluster, while in both Uruguay and Greece the two measures of democratic support constitute their own separate attitudinal dimension. It is also clear that, as hypothesized above, the disaffection items cluster together to make up a third distinct attitudinal dimension, although the small percentages of variance explained by this factor (just barely above what would have been produced by random chance) indicates that the variables in this cluster are rather loosely associated with one another. Overall, however, the most noteworthy finding regarding the disaffection measures is that they are not at all statistically linked to democratic support items, and that in Spain and Uruguay are very weakly associated with indicators of political discontent, as well.[14]

In order to subject these hypotheses to more rigorous empirical tests, a 'confirmatory factor analysis' was performed using these same variables clustered in accord with the three latent factors described above.[15] The results confirmed the same dimensional structure for all three countries. All of the individual variables were found to be linked to one another as in the initial clusters that emerged from the exploratory factor analysis whose results are presented in Table 3.2.[16] Moreover, the correlations

Table 3.2 The dimensionality of attitudes towards democracy: factor analysis and Tau-b correlations in Spain (1993), Uruguay (1994), and Greece (1996)[a]

Spain	Economic situation	Political situation	Satisfaction with democracy	Democratic support	Politics complicated	No influence	Loadings	
							Factor 1	Factor 2
Economic situation	–						**0.762**	−0.035
Political situation	0.43**	–					**0.802**	−0.016
Satisfaction with democracy	0.28**	0.31**	–				**0.687**	−0.125
Democratic support	−0.06*	−0.10**	−0.14**	–			0.306	0.348
Politics complicated	0.00	0.01	0.05	0.00	–		0.021	**0.639**
No influence	0.06*	0.06	0.08*	0.04	0.17**	–	−0.056	**0.651**
Politicians don't care	0.14**	0.13**	0.21**	0.08*	0.25**	0.28**	−0.247	**0.728**
Variance explained (%)							28.1	19.9

Uruguay	Economic situation	Political situation	Satisfaction with democracy	Democratic support	Politics complicated	No influence	Loadings		
							Factor 1	Factor 2	Factor 3
Economic situation	–						**0.811**	0.076	−0.126
Political situation	0.36**	–					**0.767**	−0.108	0.014
Satisfaction with democracy	0.25**	0.21**	–				**0.609**	−0.018	0.359
Democratic support	0.00	−0.07	−0.14**	–			0.028	0.050	**0.934**
Politics complicated	0.08*	−0.01	0.00	0.03	–		0.106	**0.752**	−0.092
No influence	0.01	0.06	0.00	0.04	0.19**	–	−0.052	**0.615**	0.186
Politicians don't care	0.04	0.11**	0.03	0.00	0.32**	0.22**	−0.100	**0.760**	−0.028
Variance explained (%)							24.1	21.9	14.6

Greece	Economic situation	Political situation	Satisfaction with democracy	Democratic support	Democratic vs. authoritarian	Politics complicated	No influence	Loadings		
								Factor 1	Factor 2	Factor 3
Economic situation	–							**0.823**	−0.094	0.009
Political situation	0.47**	–						**0.849**	−0.072	0.021
Satisfaction with democracy	0.29**	0.34**	–					**0.612**	−0.217	0.314
Democratic support	−0.08	−0.11***	−0.22**	–				0.130	0.032	**0.788**
Democratic vs. authoritarian	−0.08	−0.09*	−0.19**	0.29*	–			0.025	−0.090	**0.802**
Politics complicated	0.13**	0.08*	0.16**	−0.01	−0.08	–		−0.040	**0.730**	−0.052
No influence	0.12**	0.12**	0.15**	−0.02	−0.08	0.22	–	−0.090	**0.677**	−0.011
Politicians don't care	0.19**	0.17**	0.21**	−0.05	−0.08	0.32**	0.28**	−0.173	**0.729**	−0.027
Variance explained (%)								29.4	16.0	14.3

Note

a Levels of statistical significance (2-tailed) are *** $p<0.001$; ** $p<0.01$; * $p<0.05$.

among latent factors further revealed that these clusters are independent of one another: these inter-factor correlations ranged between 0.00 and 0.19. Given our particular interest in the relationship between discontent and fundamental support for democracy, it is most noteworthy that these correlations were negligible in all three cases: 0.07 for Spain, 0.04 for Uruguay, and 0.07 for Greece. Overall, the root mean square error of approximation (RMSEA) 'goodness-of-fit' statistic reveals that these three-factor models adequately capture the nature of the relationships among these variables: the RMSEA statistic for Spain is 0.055, for Uruguay is 0.067, and for Greece is 0.054.[17]

Similar patterns emerge from analyses of the underlying structure among these political attitudes in Portugal, Bulgaria, and Hungary, despite the fact that these three countries have suffered worse economic and/or political crises than the first three countries we have examined. In contrast with the relatively tranquil transitions to democracy in Spain, Uruguay, and Greece, the downfall of the Oliveira Salazar and Marcelo Caetano dictatorship in Portugal was followed by over a year of revolutionary chaos and tumult. Indeed, it was not until a year and a half later that a counter-coup by more moderate military officers set Portugal on the path towards democracy and ultimate regime consolidation. Nonetheless, as can be seen in Table 3.3, the pattern of relationships among these individual variables and dimensional factors is precisely the same as we found above. There is no statistically significant relationship between dissatisfaction with the condition of the economy or the performance of the incumbent government, on the one hand, and a measure of support for democracy (which is quite similar to our Democratic support),[18] on the other. And the degree of association between basic support for democracy and dissatisfaction with the performance of democracy (-0.09) is significantly weaker than we saw in Spain, Uruguay, and Greece. Similarly, the two disaffection measures included in this survey were not substantially associated with either the democratic support or political discontent measures. A confirmatory factor analysis is supportive of these findings. The absence of some key variables and slight differences in item wording lead to weaker goodness-of-fit with the three-factor model than we have observed above (the RMSEA statistic is 0.090), and the factor loadings among items within each cluster are lower than we observed in analyses of Spain, Greece, and Uruguay.[19] But the correlations among the discontent, disaffection, and democratic support factors are extraordinarily low, ranging between -0.01 and $+0.01$. Among these findings, the latter data relating to the separability of the three dimensions are the most significant theoretically (see also Magalhães 2005).

In light of the severe economic crisis and the collapse of law and order that accompanied the transition to democracy in Bulgaria, it is not surprising to find that the aggregate level of support for democracy in that country is lower than is to be found in most other democratic systems and at the same time that it has the highest levels of political discontent and disaffection (as we summarized in the presentation of frequency distributions above). The data presented in Table 3.3, however, indicate that, despite some coincidence at the aggregate level, at the individual level the relationships between dissatisfaction with the economic and the political situation of Bulgaria, on the one hand, and two measures of support for democracy, on the other, are not only statistically insignificant, but they are of the wrong sign! And the correlation between the latent factors of discontent and democratic support that were generated by the confirmatory factor analysis was just 0.02 – a figure that was lower than comparable statistics for Spain, Uruguay, and Greece. As we saw in these countries and in Portugal, dissatisfaction with the performance of democracy in Bulgaria has somewhat stronger bivariate linkages with each of our two measures of democratic legitimacy, but these relationships (Tau-b scores of −0.21 and −0.24) are still only of moderate strength. Perhaps most importantly, the factor loadings reveal that support for democracy and satisfaction with the political and economic situation of the country constitute two distinctly different attitudinal domains, with dissatisfaction with the performance of democracy straddling the two dimensions. Given the logical overlap between the face content of that item (satisfaction with the performance of democracy) and our measures of democratic legitimacy (the belief that democracy is the best form of government for the country), this empirical overlap is not surprising. Accordingly, the RMSEA statistic for the three-factor model in Bulgaria (0.081) reveals that the model fits these patterns of relationships among variables somewhat less well than we saw above in the Spanish, Uruguayan, Greek, and Portuguese analyses, but that this model still provides a reasonable mapping of these relationships. It is important to note, however, that the correlations among the three latent factors that resulted from the confirmatory factor analysis (ranging between −0.03 and 0.02) are even lower than we found in those three other countries, reflecting an even higher level of independence among those dimensions, and that the factor loadings among the variables within each cluster are acceptably strong.[20] The overall conclusion to be drawn from these data is that the link between support for democracy in Bulgaria and assessments of the economic situation is surprisingly weak.[21] The Bulgarian data also reveal that those attitudes that we hypothesized would fall within a distinct political disaffection cluster do, indeed, inhabit a separate attitudinal domain, and are only weakly (or not at all) associated with those making up the political discontent and democratic support. This can be seen in the results of the exploratory factor analysis presented in Table 3.3, and also in the extremely low correlations between disaffection and the two other latent factors in the confirmatory factor analysis: −0.01 with discontent, and −0.03 with the democratic support cluster.

The case of Hungary provides another opportunity to explore the dimensionality of democratic attitudes in a post-communist country that

Table 3.3 The dimensionality of attitudes towards democracy: factor analysis and Tau-b correlations in Portugal (2002), Bulgaria (1996), and Hungary (1998)[a]

Portugal

	Economic situation	Political situation	Governmental performance	Satisfaction with democracy	Democratic support	Politics complicated	Factor 1	Factor 2	Factor 3
							Loadings		
Economic situation	–						**0.767**	0.037	0.117
Political situation	0.30***	–					**0.741**	0.005	0.012
Satisfaction with democracy	0.17***	0.19***	–				**0.588**	0.015	-0.342
Democratic support	0.01	-0.02	-0.02	-0.09*	–		0.002	-0.004	**0.947**
Politics complicated	0.00	-0.03	-0.03	0.00	-0.02	–	-0.101	**0.812**	-0.081
No influence	0.08***	0.07***	0.07***	0.03	-0.01	0.27**	0.148	**0.791**	0.075
Variance explained (%)							25.8	21.1	17.1

Bulgaria

	Economic situation	Political situation	Satisfaction with democracy	Support for democracy	Democratic vs. authoritarianism	Politics complicated	No influence	Factor 1	Factor 2	Factor 3
								Loadings		
Economic situation	–							-0.035	**0.799**	-0.071
Political situation	0.39***	–						-0.019	**0.790**	-0.005
Satisfaction with democracy	0.20***	0.18***	–					0.526	0.480	0.001
Democratic support	0.05	0.03	-0.21***	–				**0.822**	-0.087	-0.073
Democratic vs. authoritarian	0.01	0.01	-0.24***	0.47*	–			**0.822**	-0.008	-0.022
Politics complicated	-0.05	-0.02	0.03	-0.17***	-0.10***	–		-0.199	0.187	**0.578**
No influence	0.10***	0.08**	0.02	0.01	-0.05	0.14	–	0.036	-0.105	**0.731**
Politicians don't care	0.11***	0.04	0.04	-0.01	0.01	0.13**	0.34*	0.031	-0.125	**0.737**
Variance explained (%)								22.5	19.0	16.7

Hungary	Economic situation	Political situation	Support for democracy	Democratic vs. authoritarian	Politics complicated	No influence	Loadings		
							Factor 1	Factor 2	Factor 3
Economic situation	–						**0.889**	0.024	-0.062
Political situation	0.60***						**0.884**	0.071	-0.041
Satisfaction with democracy	-0.05	-0.07	–				-0.047	-0.004	**0.769**
Democratic support	-0.08**	-0.09	0.21***	–			-0.043	-0.100	**0.752**
Democratic vs. authoritarian	-0.02	0.02	-0.05	-0.20***	–		0.100	**0.738**	-0.139
Politics complicated	0.07**	0.10***	-0.05	-0.05**	0.27***	–	0.103	**0.699**	0.130
No influence	0.09**	0.10**	-0.09**	-0.15**	0.30***	0.24***	0.101	**0.690**	-0.131
Variance explained (%)							25.9	20.2	16.0

Note

a Levels of statistical significance (2-tailed) are *** $p < 0.001$; ** $p < 0.01$.

also had to confront serious economic difficulties (although by no means as severe as in Bulgaria) simultaneous with democratization. In this case, however, the key elites of the non-democratic predecessor regime initiated and willingly collaborated in far-reaching processes of economic and political liberalization, as well as with the early stages of the democratization process itself. Accordingly, we can take advantage of this fundamental difference in the transition process to manipulate effectively one of our central explanatory variables – the formative role of political elites. As can be seen in Table 3.3, the results of the exploratory factor analysis and the bivariate measures of association clearly indicate that the two items in this satisfaction/optimism cluster[22] are dimensionally distinct from those dealing with democratic support. The independence of these two clusters of attitudes is further reflected in the extremely low correlation between these two latent factors that was generated by the confirmatory factor analysis (0.02). The clustering of attitudes constituting the disaffection dimension is also clear-cut and quite consistent with our earlier findings. The latent factor of disaffection items correlates with those of democratic support and discontent at extremely low levels, 0.04 and 0.02, respectively. And neither the discontent nor disaffection item cluster is strongly related to the two measures of democratic legitimacy, which clearly constitute a third attitudinal dimension in the factor analysis. Thus, the three-dimensional structure of these attitudes found in Spain, Uruguay, Greece, Portugal, and Bulgaria also emerges from our analysis of Hungary. Indeed, the RMSEA statistic for Hungary (0.044) indicates a closer fit with the three-factor model than in the first three countries we analysed.[23]

These findings are highly significant for theories of democratic consolidation. Despite frequently bold predictions to the contrary,[24] in none of these countries is dissatisfaction with the political or economic situation of the country strongly associated with fundamental support for democracy. Even the bivariate link between democratic legitimacy and the broader measure of dissatisfaction with the 'performance of democracy' is only of moderate strength, and is not located in any of these factor analyses within the same attitudinal domain as support for democracy.

It is only in the case of Chile in 1993 that we encounter evidence suggesting that support for democracy is significantly linked with the items in the discontent cluster. As can be seen in Table 3.4, the bivariate measures of association (Tau-b) linking the belief that democracy is the best form of government for Chile and dissatisfaction with the economy with the political situation of the country and with the performance of democracy range between -0.12 and -0.24, and the exploratory factor analysis placed support for democracy in the same cluster as those satisfaction measures.

A confirmatory factor analysis testing our three-dimensional model, however, produced strikingly different results. While the correlation

Table 3.4 The dimensionality of attitudes towards democracy: factor analyses and Tau-b correlations in Chile, 1993[a]

Indicator	Economic situation	Political situation	Satisfaction with democracy	Democratic support	Politics complicated	No influence	Loadings	
							Factor 1	*Factor 2*
Economic situation	–						**0.642**	−0.250
Political situation	0.39***	–					**0.718**	−0.220
Satisfaction with democracy	0.27***	0.34***	–				**0.736**	−0.024
Democratic support	−0.12**	−0.19***	−0.24***	–			**0.604**	0.190
Politics complicated	0.16***	0.15***	0.10**	−0.02	–		0.119	**0.696**
No influence	0.10***	0.11***	0.04	0.01	0.20***	–	0.005	**0.629**
Politicians don't care	0.17***	0.16***	0.09***	0.01	0.33***	0.26***	−0.071	**0.759**
Variance explained (%)							30.1	19.3

Note

a Levels of statistical significance (2-tailed) are *** $p < 0.001$; ** $p < 0.01$.

Table 3.5 Correlations among latent factors and RMSEA statistics from confirmatory factor analysis[a]

Country	Discontent/ Democratic support	Democratic support/ Disaffection	Discontent/ Disaffection	RMSEA statistics
Spain	0.07	0.02	−0.12	0.055
Uruguay	0.04	0.19	0.00	0.067
Greece	0.07	−0.02	−0.11	0.054
Portugal	0.01	−0.01	0.00	0.090
Bulgaria	0.02	−0.03	−0.01	0.081
Hungary	0.02	0.04	−0.02	0.044
Chile	0.10	0.04	−0.08	0.031

Note

a The Root Mean Square Error of Approximation (RMSAE) is a goodness-of-fit statistic that is sensitive to the complexity (i.e. the number of estimated parameters) in the model. Values less than 0.05 indicate very good fit, values as high as 0.08 reflect reasonable errors of approximation, and values above 0.10 indicate poor fit.

between the latent factors of democratic support and discontent is slightly higher (0.10) than we found with the other cases, the overall pattern of correlations among latent factors (summarized in Table 3.5) definitely reveals the same clustering of items as in the other countries. Most striking in this regard, the RMSEA statistic produced by the Chilean confirmatory factor analysis (0.031) indicates *better* fit with the three-factor model than in those other countries!

Why are the findings of the exploratory and confirmatory factor analyses for Chile inconsistent? One potential explanation lies in the combination of certain unusual characteristics of Chile's transition to democracy and the particular alignment of political forces at the time of the Chilean election survey (Hunneus and Maldonado 2003). These attitudinal patterns are to some extent the product of a deep cleavage in the Chilean polity separating those on the centre and left with strongly pro-democratic attitudes, who tended overwhelmingly to vote for parties belonging to the Concertación coalition, from those on the right, who harboured reservations about the merits of democracy, favourably evaluated the economic accomplishments achieved under the military dictatorship, and gave their electoral support to candidates and parties that are generally sympathetic towards the Pinochet regime (Tironi and Agüero 1999; Torcal and Mainwaring 2003). Political discontent, as noted earlier in this chapter, is strongly associated with one's partisan preferences: supporters of the incumbent party (in any democratic system) tend to be much more satisfied with the political and economic conditions of the country than are those who support the opposition party. Accordingly, we contend that the link in Chile between low levels of support for democracy *and* dissatisfaction with various performance indicators is an artefact of the particular alignment of political forces at the time of this survey. More broadly, these findings suggest that the roles played by competing sets of political elites can have a substantial and lasting impact on fundamental support for democracy among their respective sets of followers.

Political disaffection and political intermediation

To what extent are these attitudes toward democracy related to social or political processes involving political intermediation? By political inter-mediation we refer to the set of interaction processes through which cit-izens receive information and mobilization stimuli about parties, candidates, policies, and politics in general (see Gunther, Montero, and Puhle forthcoming). In this section of the chapter, we will systematically explore the relationships linking political disaffection to the three sets of intermediation channels: membership in secondary associations, direct face-to-face contacts with individuals in different types of social networks, and exposure to the media. We will also examine disaffection vis-à-vis some patterns of political involvement that are central to the functioning of democratic systems. In doing so, we will test a variety of hypotheses in which attitudes toward democracy and patterns of political behaviour are treated variously as causes or as consequences of flows of political informa-tion through intermediation channels.

Having determined the dimensional clustering of these various atti-tudes, we can simplify the following steps in this analysis by constructing scales measuring political discontent and disaffection. The *Discontent* scale was constructed out of dissatisfaction with the economic situation, with the political situation, and with the functioning of democracy.[25] A second scale was created by adding together responses to the three *Disaffection* measures: 'Politics is too complicated', 'People like me do not have any influence', and 'Politicians don't care'. And *Democratic support* is oper-ationalized as positive responses to the statement that 'Democracy is the best form of government for a country like ours'.

Disaffection and social capital

It has been frequently argued that the development of attitudes related to a strong 'civil society' and the development of 'social capital' are essential for the health of democratic politics. Central to both of these sets of hypotheses is a high level of affiliation with secondary organizations. As is well known, the most prominent defender of this view is Robert Putnam (2000 and 2002a), who argues that social capital (which is developed through embeddedness in social networks and involvement in voluntary associations) is the cement of civil society, is the source of formal and informal organizations, and is conducive to an efficient democratic performance. Active membership in organizations instils 'in their members habits of cooperation and public-spiritedness, as well as the practical skills necessary to partake in public life'. Moreover, 'voluntary associations are places where social and civic skills are learned: [they are] "schools for democracy" ... [and] serve as forums for thoughtful deliberation over vital public issues ... [as well] as occasions for learning civic virtues, such as active participation in public life' (Putnam 2000: 338–339). In short, associational involvement is taken *per se* as having positive consequences towards oneself through the learning or the reinforcement of basic skills for participation in the social and the public arenas, towards others through the strengthening of social trust, and towards the political system through the spill-over of democratic attitudes.

To what extent is organizational membership related to attitudes toward democracy? Putnam (1993 and 2000) has inconclusively explored some of these relationships. Norris (1999a and 1999b: 21–22) and Newton (1999a: 17), while not strong advocates of the social capital approach, have broadened the social capital argument to include not only citizens' trust in each other,[26] but also their confidence in political institutions. As Newton (1999b: 179) put it, political confidence and social trust are considered to be 'different sides of the same coin'. From this perspective, *political* confidence is at least to some extent a by-product of *social* trust, and is exogenous to the political system (see Mishler and Rose 2001: 31). Several scholars have recently demonstrated that social trust and political confidence are indeed associated, but that membership of voluntary associations has only a small impact on social trust and is irrelevant to democratic support or political involvement (Morales and Geurts forthcoming; Zmerli *et al.* forthcoming). Other scholars, however, have warned that not all secondary associations may produce the same beneficial effects (Stolle and Rochon 1998). Accordingly, and on the basis of preliminary analyses of these data, we found that it is important to separate membership in those organizations that are explicitly political (such as political parties and, in the European context, trade unions) from those that are at least ostensibly non-partisan (e.g. religious organizations and business or professional groups) or are almost certainly uninvolved in political matters (sports associations, youth groups, etc.).[27] Separate scales were therefore created to capture membership in one or more of each of these two types of organization.[28]

The bivariate relationships (Tau-b) between membership in each of these two types of organization, on the one hand, and each of our three clusters of attitudes towards democracy, on the other, are presented in Table 3.6. As can be seen, the statistical associations are weak or nonexistent with regard to both support for democracy and political discontent. In only two countries (Spain and Bulgaria) is the linkage between membership in political organizations and support for democracy statistically significant. But even in these cases the relationships were quite weak, and were further weakened in a subsequent round of analysis in which education was introduced as a control. And in no country is there a statis-

Table 3.6 Correlations (Tau-b) between organizational membership and attitudes toward democracy[a]

Membership	Democratic support	Political discontent	Political disaffection
Political organizations[b]			
Spain	0.06*	0.04	−0.08**
Greece	0.04	−0.03	−0.13**
Uruguay	0.04	−0.01	−0.09**
Chile	−0.05	−0.03	−0.04
Hungary	0.00	0.03	−0.06*
Bulgaria	0.10**	−0.06*	−0.10**
Portugal	−0.02	0.06*	−0.08**
Non-political organizations[c]			
Spain	0.03	−0.04	−0.03
Greece	−0.03	−0.05	−0.13**
Uruguay	0.00	0.05	−0.06*
Chile	−0.02	0.00	−0.04
Hungary	0.03	−0.05	−0.16
Bulgaria	0.05	−0.06*	−0.08**
Portugal	0.06	0.03	0.00

Notes
a Levels of statistical significance (2-tailed) are ** = 0.01; * = 0.05.
b Includes membership in political parties and trade unions (except in Portugal, where respondents were not asked about party membership).
c Includes membership in professional, religious, cultural, ecological, youth, sports, feminist, and neighbourhood associations, parent–teacher organizations, and others (except in Portugal, where it included only those belonging to business, farmer, and professional associations).

tically significant relationship between membership in non-political organizations and support for democracy. Similarly, the linkage between aggregate levels of membership in secondary organizations and political discontent is also weak or non-existent in the great majority of these countries.

This is not to say, however, that membership in specific organizations has no impact on political discontent. As we noted in our earlier analysis, political discontent is highly contaminated by partisanship, such that individuals supporting opposition parties or groups are predisposed to be more dissatisfied with the performance of government and democracy in general, or vice versa, than are supporters of the governing party or parties. While measures of organizational membership in the aggregate are not linked to political discontent, membership in organizations that are highly politicized, if not closely linked to political parties, is associated with political discontent in a statistically significant manner. In the cases of Spain and Portugal, for example, affiliation with trade unions (which are dominated by communist and/or socialist parties) correlates significantly with measures of political discontent.[29]

Not surprisingly, there is a stronger (and negative) association between political disaffection and organizational membership, particularly with regard to membership in political organizations. But this statistical association begs the important question of direction of causality. Since disaffection involves a general estrangement from both politics and society, one could argue that individuals with disaffected attitudinal predispositions simply choose not to join organizations, particularly of the political variety. The reverse direction of causality could also be posited in which organizational membership fosters attitudes that are the opposite of those associated with political disaffection and societal estrangement. Clearly, these cross-sectional data cannot resolve that question of direction of causality.

Overall, there is little evidence to ground an assertion that fundamental support for democracy is rooted in widespread membership in secondary associations. Even when an elaborate multiple regression analysis was performed, with democratic support as the dependent variable, only in the case of Bulgaria did a statistically significant relationship emerge.[30] Organizational membership may play a crucial role in efforts to mobilize the electorate during election campaigns, but it does not have the decisive importance that advocates of civil society or social capital sometimes assert with regard to core attitudes relevant to the legitimacy of democratic regimes.

Disaffection and face-to-face interaction

The frequency of face-to-face discussion of politics with family, friends, neighbours, or fellow workers, however, is more substantially associated with each of these three sets of democratic attitudes, at least in some countries, as can be seen in Table 3.7. Support for democracy is positively associated with frequency of political discussion in Spain and Bulgaria: those who are more supportive of democracy in these countries tend to discuss politics more frequently. Again, it is not clear if the supportive attitude towards democracy encourages political discussion, or if talk about politics is conducive to positive attitudes towards democracy. In Chile, however, the direction of this relationship is reversed, although the relationship is rather weak. A mixed pattern of findings is also revealed with regard to the relationship between frequency of political discussion and political discontent. This relationship is significant only in Greece and Chile, where dissatisfaction with the performance of government, economy, and/or democracy itself is negatively associated with the frequency of political discussion.

Much stronger and more consistent findings are found with regard to the link between frequency of political discussion and disaffection. In all of the countries examined, political disaffection is moderately or strongly associated with the avoidance of political discussion. Once again, interpretation of this relationship is greatly complicated by questions regarding

Table 3.7 Correlations (Tau-b) between frequency of discussion of politics (with family, friends, neighbours, or fellow workers) and attitudes toward democracy[a]

Country	Democratic support	Political discontent	Political disaffection
Spain	0.10**	−0.04	−0.14**
Greece	0.01	−0.10**	−0.14**
Uruguay	0.05	0.06	−0.24**
Chile	−0.11**	−0.17**	−0.16**
Hungary	0.03	0.01	−0.25**
Bulgaria	0.18**	−0.03	−0.11**

Note
a Levels of statistical significance (2-tailed) are ** $p < 0.01$.

the direction of causality. It is quite likely that those who are politically disaffected choose to avoid discussion of politics with family, friends, neighbours, or fellow workers; it is less plausible to argue that infrequent discussion of politics 'causes' political disaffection. Moreover, the introduction of other 'control' variables, such as education, somewhat weakens this relationship.

Disaffection and involvement in politics

To what extent does political disaffection have an impact on individuals' predispositions towards active involvement in politics? The extensive research literature on political participation has repeatedly demonstrated that political involvement is a function of a number of other social attributes and experiences as well. In particular, in most countries better educated citizens tend to participate more actively in politics than the uneducated or poorly educated; the young are typically much less involved in democratic politics than those in middle age; and women in many countries are less politically active than men. Thus, an analysis of the causal impact of disaffection, *per se*, on political involvement (conceptualized here as interest in and knowledge about politics as well as frequent discussion of politics) must introduce simultaneous controls for the impact on political behaviour of these other potentially causal variables as well. Accordingly, it is necessary to begin our exploration of the impact of disaffection and various forms of intermediation on political involvement by including those other relevant factors as independent variables in multiple regression equations analysing, as the dependent variable, the level of an individual's involvement in politics. But before that multivariate analysis can be undertaken, the zero-order correlations (Tau-b) between political involvement and each of these potentially causal variables should be examined. These bivariate relationships can be seen in Table 3.8.

Table 3.8 Correlations (Tau-b) between some sociodemographic factors, political disaffection, and organizational membership with involvement in politics[a]

Country	Age	Gender	Education	Political disaffection	Non-political organization membership	Political organization membership
Spain	−0.06**	−0.21**	0.28**	−0.25**	0.10**	0.14**
Greece	−0.10**	−0.04	0.01	0.05	−0.08*	0.13**
Uruguay	0.03	−0.11	0.26**	−0.27**	0.08**	0.13**
Chile	0.08*	−0.13**	0.07**	0.02	0.00	0.02
Hungary	0.13**	−0.12**	0.24**	−0.17**	0.12**	0.07**
Bulgaria	−0.01	−0.16**	0.42**	−0.13**	0.07**	0.28**
Portugal	−0.02	−0.12**	0.15**	−0.24**	0.09**	0.11**

Note

a Levels of statistical significance (2-tailed) are are ** $p<0.01$; * $p<0.5$.

Consistent with the findings of a multitude of studies of political participation, education is positively and strongly associated with involvement in
politics in most countries (see, for instance, Nie and Stehlik-Barry 1996).
Only in Greece is there no statistically significant relationship between
education and involvement, while in Chile the relationship is weak, and in
Portugal is only of moderate strength. Gender is also quite consistent as a
predictor of political interest, information, and discussion: in all of these
countries, women are less involved in politics than men, although, as we
will see in the following round of multivariate analysis, the introduction
into the equation of other independent variables – especially education –
weakens this relationship; in Hungary and Bulgaria, those controls actually reverse it. Finally, with regard to the last of the sociodemographic
control variables included in our analysis, age exerts a decidedly mixed
influence on involvement in politics, and nowhere do we find the moderately strong positive relationship existing in most established democracies.
Contrary to the United States, for example, where the young exhibit very
low levels of involvement in conventional forms of political involvement,
in Greece and Spain young people are significantly more engaged in politics. And, unlike in many established democracies, socialization experiences of the older age cohorts (such as the trauma of the civil war in
Spain, the political repression of the early stages of the authoritarian
regime, and the depoliticization and anti-democratic propaganda of its
later phases) have apparently discouraged active involvement in politics
and encouraged much higher levels of political disaffection among older
citizens (see Montero, Gunther, and Torcal 1997b; and Torcal, Gunther,
and Montero 2002).

Disaffection is strongly and negatively associated with political involvement in all of these countries except Greece and Chile. These same two
countries stand out as puzzling exceptions when we examine the relationship between organizational membership and involvement: in Chile, there
is no statistically significant relationship with membership in either political or non-political organizations, while in Greece, belonging to both
types of secondary associations actually leads to *lower* levels of involvement
in politics. In all other countries, however, there are statistically significant
relationships in the predicted direction. It is also noteworthy that in all of
those countries except Hungary there is a stronger positive impact of
membership in political organizations (parties and trade unions) than in
non-political organizations, with which these correlations are relatively
weak or of moderate strength. The difference between membership in
these organizations is particularly strong in Bulgaria. From one perspective, the relationship between affiliation with political organizations and
involvement in politics is obvious, verging on the tautological. From
another perspective, however, these findings have significant implications
for commonly stated claims growing out of the social capital literature.
It appears that the *type* of organization to which one belongs has an

important bearing on whether group membership leads to higher levels of involvement in politics. When a member is surrounded by other individuals who are politically interested and motivated, and when the nature of the organization tends to channel consistent messages reinforcing one particular political view, then the mobilizational impact of group membership can be quite substantial (see also Morales 2004: 212 ss.). However, when the recruitment of group members is more random with regard to political viewpoint, and/or the basic purpose of the organization is irrelevant to politics (e.g. bowling leagues), then the positive relationship between group membership and political involvement is much weaker.

How do these bivariate relationships hold up when simultaneous controls for the impact of other variables are introduced? Table 3.9 presents the results of multiple regression analyses of political involvement (with the involvement scale serving as the dependent variable) and all of the aforementioned variables introduced as independent variables. The ability of these equations to predict respondents' levels of involvement in politics in Chile and Greece is very weak, explaining just 4 and 5 per cent, respectively, of variance in political involvement. This may help to account for some puzzling sign reversals regarding the Beta scores for some key independent variables. We shall therefore focus our attention on the results for the other countries, whose R scores are much more robust, ranging from 0.342 to 0.554.

In Spain, Uruguay, Hungary, Bulgaria, and Portugal, political disaffection is consistently associated with low levels of political involvement, and in three of those countries the relationships are quite strong. In Spain, Uruguay and, especially, Bulgaria, membership in a politically relevant organization is substantially more strongly associated with political involvement, while in Portugal membership in political and non-political organizations is roughly of equal strength. It is only in Hungary where the positive impact of both types of organizational membership largely vanishes when controls are imposed capturing the causal impact of other variables. Overall, however, it can be said that both political disaffection and organizational membership remain as statistically significant determinants of involvement in politics even after other variables (including the extremely powerful impact of education) are taken into account.[31]

Disaffection, involvement, and media exposure

To this point, we have dealt with the impact of political disaffection in very general terms, using as the hypothetical dependent variable an aggregate scale of involvement with politics. Let us conclude this analysis of the consequences of disaffection by breaking down political involvement into several specific manifestations. As we shall see, this more detailed investigation leads to an intriguing and somewhat surprising conclusion regarding the *quality* of political participation of disaffected citizens.

Table 3.9 Regression analysis of involvement in politics: standardized beta coefficients (and T scores)

Variable	Spain	Greece	Uruguay	Chile	Hungary	Bulgaria	Portugal
Age	0.13 (4.7)	−0.13 (−3.7)	0.11 (3.3)	0.10 (3.1)	−0.09 (−3.6)	0.15 (4.7)	0.12 (3.5)
Gender	−0.14 (−5.7)	−0.10 (−2.9)	0.05 (1.5)	−0.14 (−4.0)	0.28 (10.6)	0.14 (4.5)	−0.08 (−2.8)
Education	33 (11.7)	−0.03 (0.8)	0.25 (7.4)	0.13 (3.5)	0.28 (9.9)	0.47 (14.3)	0.16 (4.6)
Political disaffection	−0.21 (−8.8)	0.05 (1.5)	−0.21 (−6.5)	0.06 (1.8)	−0.10 (−3.7)	−0.08 (−2.5)	0.24 (−8.4)
Non-political organization membership	0.07 (3.0)	−0.08 (−2.2)	0.02 (0.6)	−0.06 (−1.7)	0.04 (1.4)	0.00 (0.1)	0.06 (1.9)
Political organization membership	0.09 (3.8)	−0.13 (−3.7)	0.09 (2.8)	0.00 (0.3)	0.00 (0.1)	0.16 (5.2)	0.06 (2.0)
R	0.462	0.213	0.392	0.201	0.394	0.554	0.342
R^2	0.213	0.045	0.153	0.040	0.155	0.307	0.117

Table 3.10 Correlations (Tau-b) between the political disaffection scale and interest in politics, political information, and exposure to media[a]

Country	Interest in politics	Newspaper reading	Listen to radio news	Watch news on television	Political information
Spain	−0.27***	−0.18***	−0.13***	−0.09***	−0.18***
Uruguay	−0.28***	−0.15***	−0.05	0.00	−0.20***
Greece	−0.19***	−0.19***	−0.08**	−0.01	−0.17***
Portugal	−0.28***	−0.20***	−0.18***	MD	−0.10***
Hungary	−0.28***	−0.17***	−0.11***	−0.17***	−0.19***
Bulgaria	−0.10***	−0.17***	−0.03	−0.03	−0.10***
Chile	−0.24***	−0.18***	−0.06**	−0.11***	−0.22***

Note
a Levels of statistical significance are: *** $p < 0.001$ or better; ** $p < 0.01$; MD = missing data.

The first column of figures presented in Table 3.10 clearly reveals that
political disaffection is strongly correlated with low levels of interest in
politics, as measured by the respondent's self-report; the only partial
exception is Bulgaria. This lack of interest is reflected in a strong propensity of the disaffected in all of these countries to read about politics in the
newspapers less frequently (second column). The same tendency is also
reflected in exposure to news about politics through radio broadcasts
(third column), although the relationship is significantly stronger in some
countries than in others. A much weaker and more variable association
between disaffection and exposure to political news can be seen in the
fourth column: with the single exception of Hungary, the association
between disaffection and the frequency with which respondents follow
political news on television is much weaker than is the case with regard to
newspaper reading (Spain and Chile), or is not even statistically significant (Uruguay, Greece, and Bulgaria). In short, disaffected citizens are
much less likely to follow politics regularly through newspaper reading
than are other citizens, but in most countries are not so averse to television coverage of politics.

Given their lack of interest in politics and less frequent exposure to it
through the newspapers, the disaffected are substantially less informed
about politics than are other citizens. In all of the countries analysed in
this study, the disaffected were less likely to identify prominent political
figures correctly in a four-item 'information test' that was embedded in
the CNEP questionnaires (see the data in the fifth column of Table 3.10).
This finding, in conjunction with those concerning exposure to specific
sources of political information, is consistent with an argument frequently
set forth in the literature on the media and politics. As Ranney (1983),
Sartori (1998), and Gunther and Mughan (2000) have argued, television
does a much poorer job than newspapers in conveying a large volume of
policy-relevant information to citizens (with few exceptions, such as Great

Britain). Thus, even though the disaffected are not much less likely to watch the news on television than other citizens, this exposure is insufficient to offset the 'information deficit' that results from their markedly less frequent newspaper readership.

Political disaffection is also consistently associated with a propensity to avoid involvement in discussions of politics, and the disaffected are less likely to try to convince others to agree with their political views and support their preferred candidates (see the first two columns of Table 3.10). Thus, exposure to political stimuli through primary, face-to-face interpersonal networks is significantly lower among the disaffected. So, too, is the propensity to belong to one or more secondary associations (political or not). The Tau-b statistics presented in the third column of Table 3.10 indicate that this relationship holds up in all of these countries, although it is weaker in Chile, Portugal, and Spain. Not surprisingly, the disaffected are less likely in all countries to have attended a political rally during the election campaign and to have engaged in volunteer work on behalf of a party or candidate.

At the same time, it is noteworthy that disaffected citizens (except in Hungary and Portugal) are no less likely to participate in elections than are other citizens, and in Uruguay they actually vote with *greater* regularity. The consistent finding, across all countries, that the disaffected are less interested, less exposed to and informed about political news, less engaged in face-to-face discussions of politics, and less likely to belong to a secondary association of any kind, while at the same time (except in Hungary and to a lesser extent in Portugal) they vote regularly in elections, raises interesting questions about the quality of democratic citizenship in those countries where political disaffection is high. As Torcal and Lago have demonstrated (in this volume), disaffected citizens in new democracies cannot extract information about politics from their environment so as to compensate their low levels of political interest and exposure to political news. They also experience a combination of reinforcing stimuli for their lack of both political involvement and conventional or unconventional political participation. Disaffected citizens have of course less difficulties for casting their votes, since voting is an activity not particularly costly and one in which problems related to knowledge of politics can be easily solved through a number of informational shortcuts and political heuristics. But their much lower levels of participatory activities strengthen the inequality of governmental outcomes, enlarge the distance between citizens and representatives, and weaken the accountability and responsiveness of democratic governments.

Conclusions

The findings of this comparative analysis provide powerful and consistent evidence that in new democracies fundamental support for democracy, satisfaction with the performance of the system, and orientations and behavioural patterns reflecting disaffection from politics make up attitudinal domains that are both conceptually and empirically distinct from one another. Only in the case of Chile did we encounter evidence of a substantial overlap between items otherwise falling into the separate democratic support and discontent dimensions. But this statistical association, we argued, was an artefact of the particular alignment of partisan forces in Chile throughout all of the elections examined in this study, with the anti-system party serving as the principal party of opposition.[32] With regard to all other countries, the relationships between measures of satisfaction with the political and the economic situations of the country, on the one hand, and support for democracy, on the other, were very weak. The link between dissatisfaction with 'how democracy works' in the respondent's country and measures of democratic legitimacy is somewhat stronger, but the strength of these bivariate relationships is surprisingly modest given the logical overlap between the 'face content' of the two items. It is clear that support for democracy is not strongly linked to discontent in anything remotely approaching a deterministic relationship.

Without exception, the principal behavioural correlate of the three items making up the disaffection scale was a low level of involvement in politics and a low exposure to media in following political news. These strong and consistent empirical findings reinforce the construct validity of our concept of political disaffection, and they provide additional evidence of the autonomy of that attitudinal dimension from other types of democratic orientations. In no country did either the exploratory or the confirmatory factor analyses place disaffection in the same attitudinal domain as support for democracy or political discontent. And bivariate measures of association between disaffection and attitudes belonging to the other two attitudinal domains were generally weak or, at best, moderate in strength.

Notes

1 The authors would like to express their deep gratitude to Lorenzo Brusattin and particularly to Mariano Torcal for their collaboration and assistance in conducting the various rounds of confirmatory factor analysis that play such a significant role in this empirical study.

2 E.g. Montero, Gunther, and Torcal (1997b); and Gunther and Montero (2000). Also see Hibbing and Theiss-Morse (1995) and Klingemann (1999).

3 In our view, this latter claim is patently incorrect. Citizens who have recently experienced a transition from a dictatorship are able to both distinguish between authoritarian and democratic rule, and to separate their evaluations of system performance (satisfaction) from their support for the current democratic regime (legitimacy). See Morlino and Montero (1995) and Rose, Mishler, and Haerpfer (1998: ch. 5).

4 For a related but different concept of support of democracy based in the so-called 'Churchill notion' as a lesser evil, see Rose and Mishler (1996) and Shin and Wells (2001). See also Morlino (1998: ch. 3) and Diamond (1999: ch. 5).

For the case of advanced industrial democracies, Dalton (2004) has defended an excessively comprehensive concept of political support which combines both five levels or aspects (political community, regime [principle, norms and procedures, and institutions], and authorities) and two types of orientations (affective and evaluative).

5 For enlightening discussions of political discontent, or satisfaction with the performance of democracy and/or democratic institutions, see Schmitt (1983); Fuchs, Guidorossi, and Svensson (1995); Remmer (1996); Anderson and Guillory (1997); Nye (1997); Anderson (1998a and 1998b); Norris (1999b); Newton and Norris (2000); Foweraker and Krznaric (2000); and Linde and Ekman (2003). For a critique of alleged analytical deficiencies in this indicator, see Canache, Mondak, and Seligson (2001). The October 2001 edition (vol. 22, no. 4) of the *International Political Science Review*, edited by Richard I. Hofferbert and Christopher J. Anderson, was devoted to the theme of 'The Dynamics of Democratic Satisfaction'.

6 In an earlier empirical study of Spain (Montero, Gunther, and Torcal 1997), we have analysed this contrast between the stability over time of attitudes pertaining to democratic support or legitimacy (a similar characteristic to political disaffection, as we shall see), on the one hand, and the considerable fluctuation of satisfaction with performance of democracy, or the incumbent government, or the condition of the economy, on the other. This pattern of stability vs. fluctuation has also been found in other countries; see, for instance, Klingemann (1999); Finkel, Muller, and Seligson (1989); and Gibson (2000). For an analysis of the internal dimensionality of these orientations, see Cusack (1999).

7 The current state of the economy is not the only subject on which these assessments are based. While the economy of course generally shows a strong relationship with satisfaction with the performance of democracy (see, for instance, Anderson and Guillory 1997; Franz 1986; and Tóka 1995), other studies have demonstrated the limited effects of the political economy of attitudes linking satisfaction with democratic performance (see Clarke, Dutt, and Kornberg 1993; Linz and Stepan 1996: ch. 5; and McAllister 1999). Among the many other factors that affect the evaluation of the performance of new democracies are those related to a rejection of the former regime (Morlino and Montero 1995; Mishler and Rose 1999); respect for fundamental liberties (Diamond 1999: 192; and Hofferbert and Klingemann 1999); a public awareness of the limited capacity of government to resolve problems or, more generally, to 'deliver' (Kaase and Newton 1995: 75); the patience of citizens who realize that solving some problems may take several years (Rose and Mishler 1996; Bruszt 1998); high levels of corruption (Seligson 2002; and Anderson and Tverdova 2003); and the timing of elections (Nadeau *et al.* 2000).

8 This point is also stressed in Klingemann (1999) and Hofferbert and Klingemann (2001); also see Hibbing and Theiss-Morse (1995). For different conceptions of disaffection, see Morlino and Tarchi (1996), and Pharr and Putnam (2000), although the latter never presents an explicit definition of disaffection.

9 In addition, the inclusion of some of these items in the 1985 Four Nation Study (Greece, Italy, Portugal, and Spain) and the 1996 Italian and 2000 Chilean CNEP surveys makes it possible for us to test one crucial hypothesis, although so many of the other items were not included in those surveys as to preclude broader comparisons with the other countries in this initial dimensional analysis.

10 Although there are more recent data (see Lagos 2003, who reports a similar ordering of countries with data from *Eurobarometer* 2000 and *Latinobarómetro* 2002), we have kept the 1995 data in Table 3.1 for being closest in time with the 1993 CNEP data.

11 The Portuguese item asked respondents about the following statement: 'Democracy may have problems, but it's better than any other form of government'. Thirty-three per cent of respondents strongly agreed with this statement, and another 48 per cent agreed; only 4 per cent and 1 per cent, respectively, disagreed or strongly disagreed, while 14 per cent said they did not know how to respond. In 1985, a different question, which had an identical item format to what is in the text later labelled as *Democratic* vs. *Authoritarian*, was included in the Four Nation Study of Portugal, Spain, Greece, and Italy. The percentages of those survey respondents who selected the democratic alternative ranged between 61 per cent in Portugal (with 23 per cent not answering this question) and 87 per cent in Greece, with Italy and Spain falling between these two extremes with 70 per cent of those interviewed supporting democracy; see Morlino and Montero (1995: 236).

12 Those items with agree/disagree response categories were recoded as follows: agreement was coded as 1, disagreement as 3, and 'it depends', 'neither' or 'both' as 2, with a non-response coded as missing data.

13 It should be noted that there were no significant differences between the results obtained from this Varimax rotation and an Oblimin rotation (whose results are not presented in the table). Not only were the factor loadings resulting from these two approaches very similar, but the percentage of variance explained was identical, with respect to each of the factors for all three countries.

14 These findings have been remarkably consistent over time; similar results were obtained from analysis of data collected in 1979 and 1982 post-election surveys, which contained many of the items that were subsequently included in the CNEP surveys; see Maravall (1997: ch. 5) and Torcal (2001 and 2002a: ch. 3), who reach the same conclusions using different data sets, variables, and statistical analyses.

15 In a confirmatory factor analysis, a specific structure of clustering among variables is hypothesized and empirically tested. This approach not only generates 'goodness-of-fit' statistics, but also allows for the calculation of correlations among the variables within each cluster and between these 'implicit factors'.

16 Factor loadings for the three items in the discontent cluster (except for the one item set initially at 1.00) ranged between 0.61 and 0.87 for Spain, 0.55 and 0.94 in Uruguay, and 0.51 and 0.80 in Greece. Factor loadings among items in the disaffection clusters ranged between 0.48 and 0.50 in Spain, 0.95 and 0.98 in Uruguay, and 0.98 and 1.14 in Greece.

17 The RMSEA is a goodness-of-fit statistic that is sensitive to the number of estimated parameters in the model, which is to say, its complexity. Values less than 0.05 indicate very good fit, and values as high as 0.08 reflect reasonable errors of approximation, while values above 0.10 indicate poor fit.

18 It should be reiterated that, unlike the indicator on Democratic support in the CNEP surveys, which provided only three possible responses (agree, disagree, and 'it depends') with regard to the statement that 'Democracy is the best political system for a country like ours', the Portuguese 2002 election study allowed respondents to strongly agree, agree, disagree, or strongly disagree with the proposition that 'Democracy may have problems, but it's better than any other form of government'.

19 Within the discontent cluster, the factor loadings for the *Satisfaction with democracy* and *Governmental performance* variables are just 0.15 and 0.10, respectively (with *Economic situation* = 1.0); and within the disaffection cluster, *Politicians don't care* has a factor loading of just 0.14 (with *Politics complicated* = 1.0).

20 Among the discontent items (with political situation set at 1.0), *Economic situation's* factor loading was 0.74, and that of *Satisfaction with democracy* was 0.50;

among the disaffection items (with *Politics complicated* equal to 1.0), the factor loading for *No influence* was 0.88, and that of *Politicians don't care* was 0.80.

21 This finding is consistent with those of Mishler and Rose (2001), and Evans and Whitefield (1995). While the former study found that in seven Central and East European democracies the impact of political performance is greater than that of economic performance (and its impact is increasing), the latter study revealed that the combined impact of five different variables measuring current, prospective, and retrospective assessments of the performance of the economy in eight post-Soviet Eastern European democracies explained less than five per cent of the variance in support for democracy. See also Vassilev (2004).

22 Unfortunately, none of our standard 'satisfaction' items was included in this survey. The closest to our item tapping satisfaction with the economic situation of the country is a question measuring the respondent's confidence that the economy will improve in the coming year (included as *Economic situation* in Table 3.3). The Hungarian questionnaire also lacked an item dealing with the respondent's level of satisfaction with the performance of democracy. As a means of fleshing out the satisfaction dimension, a measure of the respondent's confidence that his/her financial situation will improve over the coming year was included in the analysis. Despite these differences in the wording of the satisfaction items, the data presented in Table 3.3 are perfectly compatible with our earlier findings: the two economic optimism measures are highly intercorrelated.

23 The correlations among the three latent factors in the confirmatory factor analysis range from 0.02 to 0.04.

24 Among many others, see, for instance, Fuchs and Roller (1998).

25 In the case of Hungary, the two indicators used instead were lack of confidence in both the economy and that the respondent's financial situation will improve in the coming year.

26 It should be noted that Newton departs significantly from Putnam's argument. Putnam (1995a: 666) claims that 'causation flows mainly from joining to trusting', while Newton (1999a: 16–17) has argued that the direction of causality may flow in the opposite direction.

27 To undertake this analysis, a scale was created measuring the number of organizations to which respondents belonged. This is based upon an extensive battery of questions in which respondents were asked whether or not they belonged to over a dozen different types of organizations. Two of these were organizations directly involved in politics: these are membership in political parties and membership in trade unions. The others were organizations that ordinarily are not so directly involved in politics: these included professional associations, fraternal organizations, youth organizations of various types, sports organizations, etc. Two different scales were constructed by adding together positive responses to questions about each type of organizational membership (with membership scored as one and non-membership coded as zero). The range of the scales was from zero to as much as five (with the latter capturing those respondents belonging to five different organizations). Most respondents in our sample of countries either did not belong to any organization or belonged to only one. Since few individuals in countries belonged to more than one or two organizations, several of these categories were very sparsely populated. And since these skewed distributions would have depressed various measures of association, these categories were recoded to reflect (depending on the distribution of respondents in each country) membership in one or more, or two or more organizations.

28 The actual distribution of respondents among these categories with regard to

political organizations (parties and trade unions) is as follows: in Spain, Greece, and Chile, 92 per cent belonged to no organizations, and 8 per cent to one or more; in Uruguay, 95 per cent did not belong to a political organization and 5 per cent to one or more; in Hungary, 13 per cent belonged to one or more political organization, while 87 per cent did not; in Bulgaria, 23 per cent of respondents belonged to one or more political organizations, while 77 per cent did not; and in Portugal, 12 per cent belonged to trade unions (and the questionnaire did not include an item tapping membership in political parties). With regard to *non-political organizations* distributions of respondents were the following: in Spain, 14 per cent belonged to one organization, 6 per cent to two or more, while 80 per cent did not belong to any organization; in Greece 12 per cent belonged to one organization, 3 per cent to two or more, and 85 per cent to no organization; in Uruguay, 8 per cent belonged to one or more organizations while 92 per cent belonged to none; in Chile, 23 per cent belonged to one organization, 10 per cent to two or more organizations, and 67 per cent belonged to none; in Hungary, 91 per cent did not belong to any organization, while 9 per cent belonged to one or more; in Bulgaria, 6 per cent belonged to one or more organizations, while 94 per cent belonged to none; and in Portugal, 1 per cent belonged to two or more organizations, 7 per cent belonged to one, and 92 per cent belonged to none.

29 Data regarding these statements are not shown.

30 Independent variables in this multivariate analysis included age, gender, education, subjective social class identification, income, party identification, left–right self-placement, frequency of discussion of politics, membership in political organizations, and membership in non-political organizations. With our standard measure of Democratic support as the dependent variable, the R^2 statistic measuring the percentage of variance explained was just 0.07 in Greece, 0.04 in Chile, and 0.01 in Hungary and Portugal. Only in Bulgaria did it reach 0.17, and the Beta score for the variable measuring membership in non-political organizations amounted to just 0.10 (significant at the 0.01 level). Membership in political organizations in Bulgaria was not statistically significant in this OLS analysis.

31 See also Thomassen and van Deth (1998), who nonetheless use different indicators and analyse only some Central and Eastern European countries.

32 Indeed, we predict that if electoral turnover were to occur in Chile, bringing the post-pro-Pinochet party to power, there would be a 'sign reversal' with regard to the relationship between support for democracy and the discontent items.

Part III

Causes I: institutional disaffection and social capital

4 Institutional confidence and social trust

Aggregate and individual relations

Kenneth Newton

According to Robert Putnam's 'bowling alone' thesis, the increased levels of political disaffection to be found in some Western democracies have their origins in the decline of social trust and social networks of modern society. As the opening chapter of this volume points out, social trust is the most important component of a broad syndrome of values, attitudes, and behavioural patterns that are indispensable antecedents of political confidence and other civic attitudes. It quotes Putnam (2000: 137) as saying, '...people who trust others are all-round good citizens'. This chapter, therefore, is about the relationship between social trust and political confidence. It deals with social trust because it is a key component of social capital, and perhaps the best single indicator and measure of it. It deals with confidence in parliament because this is a good indicator of political disaffection, defined as a set of critical attitudes towards the institutions of government. Indeed, parliament (or whatever the legislative assembly is called) is the main representative body in a democracy, and so declining confidence is a serious matter. Confidence in parliament is about something deeper and more fundamental than the more volatile measure of trust in particular governments or politicians, and so it is a good measure of political disaffection.

The idea that trust is vital for democracy is not a new one. The crucial importance of trust in society was recognized in the social contract theories of Thomas Hobbes and John Locke, and from a completely different perspective by Adam Smith, who pointed out that it was essential for free-market commercial transactions. Their concern with trust was carried forward into the nineteenth and twentieth centuries by an equally diverse range of writers from Claude Henry de Saint Simon, Alexis de Tocqueville, and Herbert Spencer to Ferdinand Tönnies, Georg Simmel, and Max Weber.[1] In recent years the social sciences have seen a new wave of interest in trust on the part of sociologists, psychologists, economists, philosophers, and political scientists.[2] Many, if not all of these writers agree with Simmel (1950: 326) that 'trust is one of the most important synthetic forces in society'.

An explicit link between social trust and political life was picked out by de Tocqueville, who argued that involvement in the local community and its voluntary organizations teaches 'the habits of the heart' of trust, reciprocity, solidarity, and co-operation, which are the necessary foundations of democracy (see also Bellah *et al.* 1985). Trust, de Tocqueville argued, is created in the dense network of voluntary organizations and clubs (especially political associations) that brings people together and teaches them how to co-operate and compromise in order to achieve common goals. Similarly, John Stuart Mill argued that participation in civic life was an end in itself and a great teacher of the skills and attitudes necessary for democracy. In the last decade or so, the subject of trust has been picked up and driven on by (contested) evidence of its progressive decline in some Western societies, and by the enormous interest in social capital theory of Putnam (see 1993, 2000), which seeks to explain both the origins and the political effects of these trends. Social trust is crucial to social capital theory, either as the core of the concept or as the best single indicator of it.

In this chapter, I will argue that there are serious empirical difficulties with the de Tocqueville/social capital theory of trust and with the claim that it is rooted and nurtured in membership of voluntary organizations. It seems that there is no direct, necessary, or simple link between social trust, on the one hand, and levels of political disaffection, on the other. This is because survey research shows that the individuals who express *social* trust are not necessarily those who express *political* trust. On the contrary, there is some evidence that they are found in different groups in the population and, apparently, for different reasons. Moreover, membership of voluntary organizations seems to have a rather weak association with social trust, and barely any relationship with political trust.

Nevertheless, while the de Tocqueville/social capital theory of trust and civic engagement does not work when individuals are the units of analysis, there is some truth in it when it is tested, as it should be, at the aggregate cross-national level of analysis. However, even at the aggregate cross-national level, the association between social trust and political disaffection is not particularly strong, because it is not at all simple or direct. The final part of this chapter tries to disentangle the relationship in a way that makes sense of aggregate cross-national data and some appropriate case studies.

Individual comparisons: social trust

Trust is not easily defined.[3] It may even be classified as an essentially contested concept. It also has many synonyms – mutuality, empathy, reciprocity, civility, respect, solidarity, toleration, and fraternity – and it may be that one of these terms captures the significance of the basic idea of trust more satisfactorily. Yet we should not be lured into the belief that other terms are necessarily better. They simply have not been subject to the same scrutiny, and were they to be examined closely they would almost certainly be found wanting in clarity of meaning and precision of application. Trust is likely to be as good or bad a concept as any, and, in any case, it is not the purpose of this chapter to dispute the meaning of words. For present purposes, trust is defined here as the belief that others will not knowingly or willingly do you harm, and, at best, that they will act in your interests, given the opportunity. This is close to Hardin's (1998: 12–15) definition of trust as 'encapsulated interest'.

A more important problem for empirical research is the way in which the standard survey question has usually been interpreted. The question ('Generally speaking would you say that most people can be trusted, or that you can't be too careful in dealing with people?') is often assumed to tap the inner or psychic traits of individuals who reveal their psychological identity as trusters or misanthropes in their responses. An individualistic theory of the social-psychologists about trusting personalities, on the one hand, and misanthropic personalities, on the other, lies at the heart of this assumption (see Erikson 1950; Allport 1961; Rosenberg 1956 and 1957; Cattell 1965; and Uslaner 2002). One implication of the theory that trust is a core personality trait is that there are trusting and distrusting personalities, and it follows that trusting is a general orientation towards society as a whole; trusters and distrusters do not distinguish between different things requiring different degrees of trust and distrust – they tend either to trust or to distrust across the board.

However, trust is less an expression of an inner psychic state than an evaluation of the external world; it is a product of the society people live in. People who say they trust others are telling us less about themselves and about their core personality characteristics, than about the trustworthiness of the society in which they find themselves. In other words, answers to the standard trust question are an indicator of how individuals evaluate their social world, as much as they are an indicator of individual personality types.

We can see this in the enormous cross-national variations in social trust, which range from Norway (65 per cent) to Brazil (3 per cent). Not only are there huge national differences, but countries of the same type generally have similar trust scores. The Scandinavian and northern European nations (Norway, Sweden, Denmark, the Netherlands, Finland) are invariably grouped right at the top of the international league table with trust scores of 50 per cent or more. Other West European nations (Ireland, Iceland, Germany, Switzerland, Italy, Belgium, and Austria) are grouped below them in the 50 to 33 per cent range. Many ex-Soviet bloc countries are grouped in the middle of the table (Ukraine, Serbia, Bulgaria, Czech Republic, Bosnia, Albania, Slovakia, Latvia, Croatia, Belarus, Russia, Estonia, and Lithuania), with 30 to 20 per cent, and the poorer nations of the developing world fall out at the bottom (Brazil, Turkey, Peru, Puerto Rico, Colombia) with scores of 10 per cent or less. This suggests that trust is not only affected by individual considerations such as socialization experiences and family life, but also strongly influenced by social factors common to the populations of countries and world regions.

Nor is trust all of a piece. People distinguish between different things according to the degree of trust they feel they merit. They can trust their family but not their neighbours, their own social group but not their government, their fellow citizens but not foreigners, and they can trust a political party or political leader at that particular point in time, but not the same party or leader ten years later.

There are three reasons for opting for this approach to trust. First, different forms of trust do not form a single syndrome. As the correlations in Table 4.1 show, there is a fairly strong positive relationship between trust in the family and trust in fellow countrymen ($r = 0.30$***), but the correlations between other aspects or types of trust are low, and some of them are even negative. For example the association between trust in people and trust in fellow countrymen is -0.16***. One can predict very little or virtually nothing about trust in government from trust in family members, or trust in fellow countrymen, or trust in people in general. This strongly suggests that there are different forms of trust, and that people usually distinguish between different social and political objects according to their trustworthiness.

The figures in Table 4.1 are calculated from pooling responses to the trust question in 12 countries, but much the same results are produced when the correlations for separate countries are computed (Table 4.2). The figures are statistically insignificant in 13 countries, but, even when they are statistically significant, they rarely reach substantively interesting levels. The figures clearly confirm Kaase's (1999: 14) conclusion that 'the

Table 4.1 Individual level simple correlations between World Values measures of trust in 12 nations, 1990[a]

Variable	People	Government	Family
Government	−0.03***		
Family	−0.06***	0.05***	
Countrymen	−0.16***	0.14***	0.30***

Source: Newton (1996b: 180).

Notes
a *** Significant at 0.001; $N = 13,802$. The three questions asked were:
  'Generally speaking would you say that most people can be trusted [scored 2], or that you can't be too careful in dealing with people [1]?'
  'How much do you trust the government to do what is right? Do you trust it almost always [scored 4], most of the time [3], only some of the time [2], or almost never [1]?'
  'I now want to ask you how much you trust various groups of people. Using the responses on this card, could you tell me how much you trust your family/the British (substitute your nationality for "British"): completely [scored 5], a little [scored 4], neither trust nor distrust them [3], do not trust them very much [2], do not trust them at all [1]?'

Table 4.2 Individual level simple correlations between interpersonal trust and confidence in parliament[a]

Country	Correlation	(N)	Country	Correlation	(N)
Austria	0.05	(600)	Japan	−0.02	(541)
Belgium	0.06	(839)	Netherlands	0.09	(411)
Canada	0.01	(916)	Norway	0.04	(785)
Denmark	0.11**	(586)	Portugal	0.03	(579)
Finland	0.10	(357)	Spain	0.06	(585)
France	0.04	(380)	Sweden	0.09**	(832)
Iceland	0.02	(542)	Turkey	0.07	(355)
Ireland	0.10**	(485)	United Kingdom	0.09**	(661)
Italy	0.08**	(9,791)	United States	−0.01	(1,015)
			West Germany	0.12***	(944)

Source: World Values Survey (WVS), 1990.

Note

a ***Significant at 0.001; **significant at 0.05. For social trust, the questions asked are included in Table 4.1. For confidence, it was the following: 'Please look at this card and tell me for each item listed, how much confidence you have in them, is it a great deal [scored 4] quite a lot [3], not very much [2], or none at all [1]'? This question is asked about parliament (or the equivalent representative institution), and repeated for the police, the courts, the armed forces, and the civil service.

statistical relationship between interpersonal trust and political trust is small indeed'.[4]

The second reason for doubting the social-psychological interpretation of the standard trust question is that levels of trust in society can rise and fall quite quickly, apparently in response to changing social and political circumstances. As Hardin (1993) observes, trust involves the continual accumulation and updating of experience. Consequently, while social trust does not normally fluctuate very much in a given country over time, it can do so. For example, social trust in West Germany increased steadily after the war as the nation moved from Nazi fear and paranoia into the post-war period of peace, prosperity, and democracy. It rose from 9 per cent in 1948 to 19 per cent in 1957, to 27 per cent in 1973, 37 per cent in 1983, and 45 per cent in 1993 (Cusack 1997). A 36 per cent change in a 45-year period cannot be explained in terms of population replacement by different personality types alone. Response to changing social, political, and economic change seems to play a role.

The third reason for questioning the idea that there is a single dimension underlying different forms of trust, and that this forms a core personality trait, is that levels of social and political trust can change quite rapidly and independently of each other within the same country. For example, social trust in Finland was at a very high level compared with most other nations in 1980, and by 1990 it was even higher. In the same period confidence in the Finnish parliament dropped from 65 to 34 per cent – from one of the highest to one of the lowest in West Europe within a decade (Newton 2001). The evidence suggests that social and political trust are not necessarily associated with each other, do not necessary vary together, and do not seem to be basic and enduring personality traits.

If trust is not entirely or only a core personality characteristic, what are its other origins? This may be judged from the results of the regression analysis of social trust in 20 Western nations presented in Table 4.3. Social trust, according to these figures, is most closely associated with a set of variables measuring success and satisfaction with life – social class, income, education, happiness, life satisfaction, job satisfaction, and national pride. One or a combination of these is associated with social trust in 15 of the 20 countries. Happy, successful, proud, and satisfied people, it seems, are likely to be comparatively trusting (see also Delhey and Newton 2003).

The conclusion that social trust is not at all closely associated with confidence in parliament is confirmed in the regressions. Only 6 of the 20 coefficients are statistically significant, and even these fail to reach the highest level of statistical significance. By and large political factors are not generally associated with social trust. It is social factors, including class, income, education, job satisfaction, and national pride that do most of the work in the regressions. But it must also be said that the regression results on social trust are poor. At best 30 per cent of the variance is explained, at worst 1 per cent, and usually 10 per cent or less. According to these figures, the origins of social trust remains a puzzle; it seems to have little systematic or strong associations with the individual characteristics of citizens, either within or across nations. The firmest conclusions that we can draw at this stage, therefore, are negative ones: social trust is not closely associated with the measure of political trust (confidence in parliament), and it is not closely or consistently associated with variables describing the individual characteristics of populations.

Individual comparisons: political confidence

Political trust has much the same theoretical relationship to politics as social trust has to social life, which is to say that citizens trust their political leaders when they believe that they will not knowingly or willingly do them harm, and will, so far as possible, look after their interests. Citizens have confidence in political institutions when they believe they operate effectively according to democratic principles of justice and impartiality. Just as there are many terms that are similar to social trust or closely associated with it, so there are many similar or closely associated with political trust – civic mindedness and participation, citizenship, political interest and involvement, a concern with the public interest/public good, political tolerance, an ability to compromise and co-operate in political life, and confidence in political institutions. The last is chosen as the indicator here because it is a good measure of political disaffection, as spelled out in Chapter 1.

Table 4.3 Individual level regressions of social, economic, and political variables on social trust in 20 OECD nations, 1990[a]

Variable	United States	France	United Kingdom	West Germany	Italy	Belgium	Spain	Eire	Japan	Sweden
Voluntary organization	0.09** (3.01)		0.14*** (3.31)		0.13*** (3.43)	0.11** (2.94)			0.11* (2.53)	0.12*** (2.10)
Age	0.10*** (3.42)		0.13* (2.54)							
Success/satisfaction										
Education	0.10** (3.04)		0.12* (2.45)	0.10** (2.68)		0.09* (2.14)			0.15** (2.82)	
Occupational class/ income	0.12*** (3.67)			0.07* (2.22)				0.12* (2.12)	0.10* (2.14)	0.09* (2.14)
Life satisfaction	0.09** (3.09)			0.16*** (3.43)	0.08* (2.06)					0.11* (2.38)
happiness				0.08* (2.04)						
Job satisfaction										
National pride				0.05* (2.32)		0.08* (2.04)				
Political interest/liberalism										
Right wing	-0.09** (2.97)	-0.13* (2.38)								
Confidence in parliament			0.09* (2.04)	0.12** (3.13)	0.08* (2.34)			0.10* (2.02)		0.09* (2.46)
Interest in/discuss politics					0.14** (2.98)					
Maintaining order										-0.12** (3.50)
Open government										
Religious						0.11* (2.14)				
Adjusted R^2	0.08***	0.05***	0.05***	0.08***	0.08***	0.04***	0.02	0.06***	0.07***	0.09***
F ratio	11.62	1.95	2.42	4.10	4.25	2.54	1.38	2.35	2.99	4.67
(N)	(1,114)	(380)	(661)	(944)	(791)	(839)	(585)	(485)	(541)	(822)

Table 4.3 cont.

Variable	Finland	Switzerland	Austria	Turkey	Canada	Netherlands	Denmark	Iceland	Norway	Portugal
Voluntary organization		0.15** (3.24)	0.15*** (3.63)			0.10* (2.01)	0.09* (2.94)	0.09* (2.10)		
Age					0.14*** (3.77)			0.10* (2.12)	0.09* (2.01)	
Success/satisfaction										
Education					0.18*** (4.62)					0.11* (2.21)
Occupational class/income					0.09* (2.29)			0.09* (2.08)		
Life satisfaction happiness	0.18* (2.39)								0.11** (2.98)	0.10* (2.01)
Job satisfaction										
National pride	0.12* (2.22)	0.13** (2.77)			0.07* (2.20)	0.15** (2.88)				
Political interest/liberalism										
Right wing							-0.11* (2.57)	-0.09* (2.11)		
Confidence in parliament							0.11** (2.80)			
Interest in/discuss politics	0.12* (1.98)		0.13* (2.48)		0.09* (2.31)					
Maintaining order								-0.09* (2.08)	-0.08* (2.25)	
Open government						0.10* (2.03)				0.09* (2.13)
Religious					0.08* (2.05)			0.10* (2.28)		
Adjusted R^2	0.05*	0.07***	0.05***	0.02	0.10***	0.11***	0.08***	0.08***	0.09***	0.01
F ratio	1.84	3.05	2.40	0.75	5.47	3.43	3.59	3.26	4.65	1.24
(N)	(357)	(530)	(600)	(355)	(906)	(411)	(586)	(542)	(785)	(579)

Source: World Values Survey, 1990.

Note

a Levels of statistical significance are *** 0.001; ** 0.05; * 0.1; t statistics in brackets.

Like social trust, political trust seems to be a reflection of the external or objective state of political life. It is not so much an expression of an internal personality trait, as an evaluation of the external political world. Low political trust and confidence (that is, high or rising political disaffection) suggest that something in the political system is thought to be functioning poorly. It may be that the performance of politicians or institutions, or both, is poor, or that the expectations of the population are too high, but either way low trust and confidence tells us that something is wrong.

This brings us to the question, who expresses high political trust and confidence and why, and whether there is a connection between social trust and political confidence? To try to answer this question Table 4.4 presents the results of regression analysis of political confidence in 19 nations. The figures show that confidence in parliament is most closely associated with a range of political variables, including, in rough order of importance:

1 interest in politics and an inclination to discuss it (positive);
2 pride in the nation and in its political system (positive);
3 a belief in open government, a low priority given to national order (positive), and a belief that the country is run for the benefit of a few big interests (negative); and
4 the left–right variable (positive and negative). The sign changes in different countries because those on the political right are more likely to express confidence in parliament when they have a right-wing government, and those on the left more likely to express confidence when the left is in power (Anderson and LoTempio 2002).

As in Table 4.3, the figures in Table 4.4 show a weak and patchy association between social trust and political confidence. The coefficients are statistically significant in seven of the 19 nations, but they usually fail to reach the highest levels of significance and are often substantively quite small. Once again we find little evidence of a connection between social trust and political confidence. A comparison of both tables shows that social trust and political confidence are usually associated with a different range of variables. Whereas social trust is most closely associated with a set of social variables, especially success and satisfaction measures, political confidence is more usually associated with political variables. Perhaps unsurprisingly, in retrospect, social trust appears to be a social phenomenon connected with social conditions, while political trust seems to be a political phenomenon most closely associated with political variables.

Individual comparisons: voluntary organizations

We are born into families, we cannot avoid the state, and most of us have to work; in contrast, voluntary organizations, clubs, intermediary associations,

Table 4.4 Individual level regressions of social, economic, and political variables on confidence in parliament in 19 OECD nations, 1990[a]

	United States	France	United Kingdom	West Germany	Italy	Netherlands	Denmark	Belgium	Spain	Eire
Political variables										
Right wing	0.09** (2.98)	−0.19** (2.93)	0.10* (2.41)	0.12*** (3.49)			0.13** (2.97)			0.13** (2.79)
Open government		0.13* (2.46)	0.16*** (4.30)	0.17*** (5.39)	0.14*** (4.09)	0.18*** (3.61)		0.11** (3.14)		0.11** (2.62)
Need for national order										
Interest in/discuss politics				0.09* (2.18)	0.13** (2.85)	0.18** (2.91)		0.15*** (3.56)		0.16*** (3.18)
Pride in nation/political system				0.13*** (3.73)	0.12** (3.28)	0.10* (2.03)		0.14*** (3.94)	0.18*** (5.79)	
Country run for few big interests									−0.08** (2.76)	
Other variables										
Social trust			0.07* (2.04)	0.11*** (3.43)	0.09* (2.38)				0.12*** (3.41)	
Education		0.16* (2.35)	0.10* (2.20)				0.12** (2.80)			0.09* (2.02)
Age	−0.09** (3.03)			0.09** (2.62)						
Occupational class/income	−0.07* (2.05)								0.09* (2.47)	
Job satisfaction										0.16** (2.89)
Voluntary organizations										
Happiness			0.08* (2.02)							
Satisfaction with household finances			0.10* (2.39)							
Adjusted R^2	0.02***	0.05*	0.17***	0.15***	0.05**	0.09***	0.02*	0.06***	0.17***	0.12**
F ratio	3.39	1.87	7.33	8.82	3.09	2.84	1.60	3.40	5.04	4.52
(N)	(1,114)	(380)	(661)	(944)	(791)	(411)	(586)	(839)	(585)	(485)

Table 4.4 cont.

	Iceland	Japan	Sweden	Finland	Austria	Turkey	Canada	Norway	Portugal
Political variables									
Right wing	0.17*** (3.84)	-0.08* (2.20)							
Open government		0.15*** (3.62)	0.21*** (6.36)	0.27*** (5.44)	0.12** (2.98)			0.15*** (4.17)	
Need for national order	-0.10* (2.22)	-0.11** (2.67)							
Interest in/discuss politics	0.18*** (3.60)	0.13** (2.64)	0.19*** (4.77)	0.19** (3.19)	0.17*** (3.40)			0.10* (2.31)	0.11* (2.07)
Pride in nation/political system	0.10* (2.19)	0.14** (3.24)	0.16*** (4.73)	0.14** (2.79)	0.18*** (4.43)	0.41*** (8.85) / 0.10* (2.12)	0.44*** (14.65)	0.10** (2.73)	
Country run for few big interests						-0.19*** (4.31)	-0.18*** (6.03)		
Other variables									
Social trust			0.08* (2.46)						
Education			0.08* (2.16)						
Age									
Occupational class/income								0.09* (2.26)	
Job satisfaction			0.11** (3.13)						
Voluntary organizations				0.11* (2.18)					
Happiness									
Satisfaction with household finances									
Adjusted R^2	0.05***	0.13***	0.14***	0.17***	0.06***	0.43***	0.30***	0.05***	0.04
F ratio	2.31	4.98	7.01	4.44	2.65	12.58	18.18	3.00	1.98
(N)	(542)	(541)	(832)	(357)	(600)	(355)	(935)	(785)	(579)

Source: World Values Survey, 1990.

Note

a Levels of statistical significance are *** 0.001; ** 0.05; * 0.1; t statistics in brackets.

secondary associations, and community groups are wholly voluntary. Unlike any other area of life, membership is entirely up to individuals who engage in a set of co-operative activities for mutual benefit and satisfaction. For this reason voluntary associations have played a special role in sociological, anthropological, and political theory from de Tocqueville, Émile Durkheim, Simmel, Tönnies, and J. S. Mill to William Kornhauser, Gabriel Almond and Sidney Verba, Clifford Geertz, and Putnam. At the individual level, voluntary associations are said to teach trust and social understanding because they bring together a variety of people, sometimes with disparate backgrounds and different values, to work together. They teach empathy for others, the ability to compromise and co-operation, the ability to rub along with different social types – they encourage the 'habits of the heart' of civilized social relations. They breed and enforce reciprocity – it is difficult to cheat in business if you know you will meet your victim at the golf club on Saturday.

On the societal level voluntary associations are said to create the cross-cutting ties and social networks that bind society together by its own internal conflicts. They create social bonds between like-minded people and can build bridges between different social groups. The cross-pressures they produce help to create moderate social and political opinions, and, at the same time, they give citizens a sense of security that comes from community and belonging. They form the organizational basis of a democratic, participatory culture and the basis of a well-founded civil society. They enable governments to function more effectively by providing channels of communication between elites and masses, and by creating the private organizations and institutions necessary for public policy-making and implementation.

Although many theorists stress the political benefits of private associational life, the empirical evidence to support their various claims is rather thin and weak. First, the argument that social and political trust are close cousins that build and reinforce each other is not supported by the evidence in Tables 4.3 and 4.4. Second, at the individual level voluntary organizations are not particularly strongly associated with social trust, and barely related to political trust at all. There *is* an association between voluntary activity and social trust in some countries, but it is not found in all, and not strong in any. It is difficult to find hard, robust, or convincing evidence in Tables 4.3 and 4.4 to support the theory that social trust, political confidence, and membership of voluntary associations form a close and mutually supportive nexus.

On reflection, it is difficult to see why voluntary associations should be so important for social trust and political confidence, whatever their impact on society may be in other respects. Most people do not spend a lot of time on voluntary activities, compared with the time they spend in school, work, the family, or the neighbourhood. These are likely to be more important arenas for the generation of trust than voluntary organizations (Newton 1999a: 16; Levi 1996: 48). For example, education shows a very strong association with trust, and the last few years of further education appear to be particularly important (Verba, Scholzman, and Brady 1995: 514; Putnam 1995b: 667). Second, those who spend a great deal of time in voluntary organizations, the activists, do not seem to differ greatly from the ordinary members who spend comparatively little time with them (Newton 1999b: 173).

The third reason for questioning the argument that activity in voluntary associations (either bridging or bonding) generates trust, is the problem of cause and effect (van Deth 1996). Do voluntary organizations generate trust, or do the trusting join voluntary associations? This involves trying to untangle the complex relationships between trust, activity in associations, and related variables, including objective social characteristics (class, income, education) and subjective social attitudes (life satisfaction and happiness). The most likely story seems to be that while voluntary activity may strengthen and reinforce trust, it is more likely that those with high class, income, and education, who are also likely to find society trust-worthy and to express life satisfaction and happiness, are more likely to be active in voluntary groups (for a different view see Putnam 1993: 171–176, and 1995b: 666). In other words, the main causal path goes from trust to membership, rather than the other way round.

In sum, the first sections of this chapter have shown (i) that social trust and political confidence are not closely associated; (ii) that they, in turn, are associated with different configurations of social, economic, and polit-ical variables, although the associations in both cases are weak and patchy, and that (iii) while members of voluntary organizations show a slight tend-ency to be socially trusting in *some* societies, there seems to be no strong or general association between voluntary associations and social trust, and a weaker association of voluntary activity and confidence in parliament. At this point, the classic theory claiming a close connection between social and political trust, and a close connection between both of them and membership of voluntary organizations, seems questionable.

Cross-national comparisons

It would be odd, indeed, if the classic theory originated by de Tocqueville had barely more than a grain of truth in it. Apart from its *prima facie* plausibility, it is an old and venerable theory, and a great many of the most distinguished names of social and political theory have subscribed to it in the nineteenth and twentieth centuries. However, there is another approach to the theory. If the standard measures of social and political trust are to be interpreted as judgements about the external world in which people find themselves, then the analysis of trust should focus not on individuals but rather on the trustworthiness of society at large. Rather than seeing trust as a socio-psychological characteristic of individuals, perhaps we should compare whole societies and their collective levels of trust? (Pharr, Putnam, and Dalton 2000a: 26). If social capital is a property of societies, not individuals, it should be studied as a social or collective phenomenon, not as an individual one. In this sense, citizens do not so much 'have' social capital or carry it around with them, as access it and benefit from it as part of their social environment. They can also contribute to it by their behaviour in everyday life. According to this view social capital is a public good. Individuals do not own it, as they own a house or a car, but social systems generate it as a context in which individuals operate.[5] Therefore, research on trust and social capital should not compare individuals, but social systems – networks, groups, communities, societies, or nation states.

Political confidence is also best approached at the aggregate level. If confidence in political institutions is based upon evaluations of how the political system is working, then it is likely to be affected by such things as inflation, unemployment, political corruption or incompetence, victory or defeat in war, economic growth, a rising or falling crime rate, and governments whose records inspire confidence, or the lack of it. These are indicators of government performance that affect everybody.[6] They may not affect all citizens to the same extent, but they are likely to affect most of them to a greater or lesser extent. Therefore, attitudes of political trust or distrust are distributed fairly randomly across society and expressed by a wide variety of people. Hence, political trust does not generally correlate strongly with the usual set of individual variables – age, income, education, gender, religion, or class – and, therefore, the analysis of political trust should focus attention not on individuals, but on political systems as a whole. If this is correct, then the absence of an association between social and political trust at the individual level is not of great importance for social capital theory. What matters is the relationship at the aggregate level of community, society, or nation. And because the measure involves government and politics, we must compare units of the political system, either local municipalities, political regions, states, or nation states.

The association between social trust and political confidence, using nation states rather than individuals as the units of analysis, is shown in Figure 4.1. This plots average social trust against confidence in parliament scores for 65 nations in the early 1990s.[7] The results show a group of countries in the bottom left-hand quandrant of the scattergram, where both trust and confidence in parliament are comparatively low. The group includes Brazil, Peru, Colombia, Macedonia, Argentina, Romania, Slovenia, Portugal, the Dominican Republic, Belarus, South Korea, Latvia, Russia, Poland, Nigeria, Mexico, Bulgaria, Croatia, East Germany, Turkey, Montenegro, and Armenia. On average about 15 per cent of the citizens in this group of countries expresses a willingness to trust others, and on a 4-point scale their confidence in parliament score averages about 1.9. In the extreme cases of Brazil, Peru, Colombia, and Macedonia, society is more

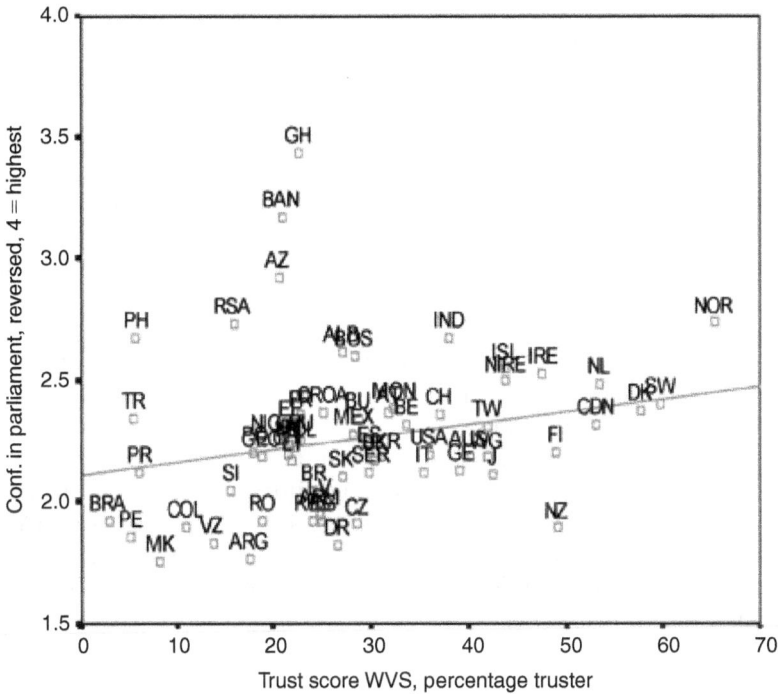

Figure 4.1 Social trust and confidence in parliament (sources: WVS Wave II and Wave III, *N* = 65 countries).

accurately described as 'no trust' than 'low trust', and the parliamentary confidence scores are the lowest of any of the 65 nations. In contrast, there is another, smaller, group of countries where both social trust and confidence in parliament are relatively high, including Norway, Sweden, Denmark, Canada, the Netherlands, Northern Ireland, the Republic of Ireland, Australia, West Germany, Japan, and the United States. Social trust averages around 50 per cent and confidence around 2.4. In the extreme case of Norway, social trust is over 65 per cent and confidence 2.8, compared with Brazil's 3 per cent and 1.9, or Peru's 5 per cent and 1.8.

These two clusters of countries fit the classic Tocquevillean theory. On the one hand, there are low trust countries where civil society is weak, social institutions rather poorly developed, and confidence in parliament is low because the system of government does not work well. The result is a vicious circle of low trust, inadequate social institutions, and poorly functioning government that is difficult to break. Creating democracy in such countries is a slow and difficult task that involves pulling up the system by its own boot straps. If social trust were higher and co-operation easier, social institutions could operate more effectively, and government policies in the public interest could be implemented more effectively and with greater justice. Equally, the causal chain also works in the opposite direction. If government and its policies inspired more confidence, it could help to create a framework in which social institutions could work more effectively, with the result that the conditions nurturing social trust and co-operation would be improved. But where social trust is low it is difficult in the extreme to create an effective and efficient government that can implement policies in the public interest, and inspire the confidence of its citizens.

On the other hand, there is a group of stable democracies, mainly the wealthy OECD nations, which are characterized by both comparatively high social trust and comparatively high confidence in parliament (Norway, Denmark, Sweden, the Netherlands, Canada, Finland, and Ireland). Their high levels of social trust and co-operation mean that they have well established and effective social institutions, which makes it easier for government to work effectively and in the public interest. The quality of their government helps to create a structure in which social institutions can operate effectively, which, in turn, enables a climate of social trust and co-operation to flourish. The result is a virtuous circle of high trust, well established social institutions, and good government that tends to sustain itself.

While the distribution of countries in Figure 4.1 suggests that this is the general case, it must also be said that the correlation between the social trust and confidence in parliament for all 65 nations is only 0.23, which, though significant at 0.05, is not a high figure, especially for aggregate data. It seems that while there is something in the argument that cross-national comparisons reveal a connection between social trust and political confidence, the relationship is not clear or strong. Another look at Figure 4.1 suggests three reasons for this. First, some of the data may not be of the highest reliability. The position of the most obvious outliers – Ghana, Bangladesh, Azerbaijan, the Philippines, and India – may be explained in this way. Second, it is possible that the question about confidence in parliament may be interpreted in a different way in some of the newest democracies. Countries such as South Africa, Albania, Bulgaria, Estonia, Croatia, and Bosnia express much higher levels of confidence in parliament than their social trust scores suggest, which may be because respondents in these countries do not always disentangle confidence in parliament from a belief in democracy. Placing a great deal of hope and faith in the principles of their new democracies, they may answer the question about parliament as if it were about parliamentary systems rather than about the operation of their parliament at the time. In established democracies such as Canada, Sweden, Switzerland, and Denmark, which lie much closer to the regression line, respondents may find it easier to express an opinion about the way their parliaments are working, while assuming a belief in democracy as a system of government.[8]

Third, and more important from the point of view of classic trust theory, there is another small group of countries where confidence in parliament is lower than one might expect given their social trust levels. In a previous article (Newton 2001), the special nature of Japan and Finland were discussed, but there is another case, Sweden, which shows a large and consistent increase in political disaffection over the past 20 to 30 years.[9] The reasons for this tell us something of importance about the association between social trust and political disaffection.

The case of Sweden

Between the 1960s and 1990s political support in Sweden fell more sharply than in almost any other Western democracy. In 1986, confidence in the Riksdag and the cabinet was 51 and 47 per cent respectively; by 1996 these figures had fallen to 19 and 18 per cent. In 1968, the 'year of revolutions', half the Swedish population believed that the Riksdag paid attention to what ordinary people thought, and 60 per cent believed that the parties were interested in people's opinions; by 1994 the figures were 28 and 25 per cent, respectively (Holmberg 1996: 107 and 112; see also Listhaug and Wiberg 1995: 320).

At the same time, there is no evidence of a decline of social trust or social capital in Sweden over the same period. On the contrary, participation in voluntary organizations, unusually high by world standards in the 1950s, remained high or climbed to even higher levels by the 1990s. In the post-war period the size of the voluntary sector grew in terms of membership size, number of organizations, level of activity, and financial resources. Informal social activity has also increased, especially in informal study circles, which, according to one observer, 'maintain a civic network right across social borders' (quoted in Rothstein 2002: 301). Nor is there any clear evidence of a decline in generalized social trust. It increased from 57 per cent in 1981 to 67 per cent in 1997, remaining at a constant 66 to 67 per cent over three surveys in 1990, 1996, and 1997.

If a decline in social capital and social trust does not account for a decline in political trust and confidence in Sweden in the late twentieth century, what does? Rothstein (2002) offers the following tentative explanation. 'It could be argued', he writes (p. 293), 'that the increased mistrust has resulted from a series of political scandals or from an increasing distance between the electorate and politicians'. In particular, what Rothstein calls 'organized social capital' in Sweden has broken down, that is, the special institutions that managed the incremental and consensual relations between the unions, the employers, and the (Social Democratic) government. The resulting failure of the incremental wage bargaining system produced a spiral of inflation, a series of currency devaluations, and a sharp decline in economic performance which took Sweden from fourth in the OECD wealth table in 1970 to eighteenth in 1997. In short, it was not the erosion of trust or social capital, but a disruption of the elite level institutions of economic co-operation, that caused Sweden's political disaffection.

Conclusions

The associations between social trust and social capital, on the one hand, and political trust and political capital, on the other, are not simple or straightforward. A relationship exists, as social capital theory predicts, but not at the individual level, where little can be predicted about an individual's political trust or confidence in public institutions on the basis of his or her social trust. Since social capital is essentially a social and collective property, not an individual or personal one, the relationship is found at the aggregate level of society as a whole, but even then it is a complicated and asymmetric one. While it is difficult to build the sort of democratic system that produces high levels of satisfaction with the political system without a solid foundation of social trust and the institutions that go with it, high levels of social trust and effective social institutions do not necessarily mean that satisfaction with the political system will be high.

Social and political trust are different things. Social trust is rooted in social conditions of everyday life, while political confidence is mainly a function of how well the political system is performing. Across the globe the highest levels of social trust are usually associated with the lowest levels of political disaffection. Norway, Finland, Sweden, Denmark, and the Netherlands are examples. At the other extreme, the lowest social trust levels are usually found in countries with the highest levels of political disaffection. Figure 4.1 shows Brazil, Peru, Puerto Rico, Macedonia, Colombia, and Venezuela to be examples. This is because it is difficult to build democracy in poor countries that do not have the social institutions and attitudes of social trust and co-operation that are necessary for government to work effectively and efficiently. Therefore, low social trust is not normally associated with the sort of democracy that generates high levels of political satisfaction.

Conversely, countries with high levels of social trust are likely to have the social institutions and infrastructure that makes it possible to sustain an advanced democracy. They are well founded civil societies, with a high level of social trust and reciprocity, an ability to compromise and co-operate, and an array of private and public institutions that are the necessary foundations for good government. In these cases, high social trust and political confidence tend to go hand in hand. Norway, Sweden, Denmark, Canada, and the Netherlands are examples.

But high social trust does not necessarily or automatically go with high levels of political confidence. Because the two are based on different considerations – social trust on social factors, and political confidence on political factors – the link between them can be broken. Finland, Japan, and New Zealand are examples. All three maintained relatively high levels of social trust and voluntary activity in the 1990s, or even improved on their stock of social capital, but political confidence declined and political disaffection rose sharply because of economic and political difficulties. In this sense, social trust and social capital may well be a necessary condition of political trust and political capital, but not a sufficient one. One cannot have the kind of effective democratic government that breeds political confidence without a solid foundation of social trust, but one can have a solid foundation of social trust without high levels of political confidence. In many cases, there is a direct relationship between social trust and political confidence, but this is not always true.

It is exceedingly difficult to build the kind of democratic government that breeds confidence in parliament if levels of social trust are not high to start with. The two are causally connected, though in an indirect way, because social trust is a foundation for effective social institutions, and effective social institutions are a foundation for good government, which inspires confidence in its citizens. Therefore, low social trust most usually means low political confidence. In this sense, the classical theory of social trust and the modern theory of social capital are both right.

But the reverse is not necessarily true. High social trust countries do not always retain their normal high level of political confidence. On the contrary, political disaffection can increase strongly, while social trust and other measures of social capital remain unaffected. While high social trust is generally associated with high confidence, this is not always the case. Political confidence is most closely associated with political factors, and a reversal of political fortunes in the best established of democracies can lead to a rapid fall of political confidence, as it did in Finland, Japan, and Sweden. In this sense, the classical theory of social trust and the modern theory of social capital are wrong. But the difference between low trust/high political disaffection countries (Brazil, Peru, Venezuela), and the high trust/high political disaffection countries (Finland, New Zealand, Japan), is that political disaffection can be rapidly reduced in countries with a good foundation of social trust, community life, and strong social institutions.

Notes

1 For a brief history of the interest in trust see Misztal (1996).
2 See Arrow (1972: 357); Baier (1986); Gambetta (1988); Coleman (1988 and 1990: 306); Ostrom (1990); Fukuyama (1995); Seligman (1997); Hardin (1996 and 1998); Braithwaite and Levi (1998); Warren (1999a); Inglehart (1999b); and Uslaner (2002).
3 See Barber (1983); Baier (1986); Gambetta (1988); Hardin (1991, 1993, and 1996); Misztal (1996); Seligman (1997); Braithwaite and Levi (1998); and Warren (1999a).
4 Some recent evidence suggests rather convincingly that good measures of social

trust, confidence in parliament, and satisfaction with democracy (using a battery of questions with an 11-point rating scale for each) reveal strongly significant correlations between social and political trust at the individual level (Zmerli *et al.* forthcoming; Jagodzinski and Manabe 2004). However, these results are so different from many other research findings that their reliability must be independently confirmed.

5 I do not wish to imply that social capital cannot be an individual property at all, but that it is *also* a collective property. The person who lives in Manhattan, who would not dream of leaving their apartment without locking and bolting it several times, may not think twice about leaving their place in the country unlocked when they go off shopping. Trust is context specific. As we have already seen, it is much higher in some countries and even regions of the world than in others, not because of individual variations in personality but because of social environments and cultures.

6 A simple example may help here. Assume that we are interested in satisfaction with rail services. It would make very little sense to interview people travelling on the same train and compare the opinions of social groups (according to class, education, gender, age, ethnic origin, religion) about the price, comfort, safety, reliability, and punctuality of the service because, travelling on the same train, they would all give pretty much the same answers. There would be some variation in individual responses, but these would probably be according to rather random and personal occurrences. But it would be sensible to compare the responses of people using the railway services in different countries.

7 The countries are: Albania (Alb), Argentina (Arg), Armenia (Arm), Australia (Aus), Austria (At), Azerbaijan (Az), Bangladesh (Ban), Belarus (Be), Bosnia (Bos), Brazil (Bra), Britain (Br), Bulgaria (Bu), Canada (Cdn), China (Chi), Colombia (Col), Croatia (Croa), Czech Republic (Cz), Denmark (DK), Dominican Republic (DR), East Germany (EE), Estonia (Es), Finland (Fi), France (Fr), Georgia (Ge), Germany (De), Ghana (Gh), Hungary (Hu), Iceland (Isl), India (Ind), Ireland (Ire), Italy (It), Japan (J), Latvia (Lv), Lithuania (Lt), Mexico (Mek), Moldova (Mol), Montenegro (Mon), Northern Ireland (NIre), the Netherlands (NL), New Zealand (NZ), Nigeria (Nig), Norway (Nor), Pakistan (Pak), Peru (Pe), the Philippines (Ph), Poland (Po), Portugal (Pr), Puerto Rico (PR), Romania (Rom), Russia (Russ), South Africa (RSA), South Korea (SK), Serbia (Ser), Slovakia (Sl), Slovenia (Slo), Spain (Esp), Sweden (Sw), Switzerland (Ch), Taiwan (Tw), Turkey (Tr), Ukraine (Ukr), Uruguay (UY), United States (USA), Venezuela (Vz), West Germany (W.Ger), and Yugoslavia (Yu).

8 In 24 OECD countries, where data reliability is comparatively good, and where the confidence in parliament question is likely to have a similar meaning, the simple correlation between social trust and confidence in parliament rises from 0.23 for all 65 countries to 0.34, which is significant at 0.05. Though higher than the figure for the larger number of countries, the OECD figure is not a strongly significant figure either, but then there are rather few cases and not a great deal of variance to explain.

9 Note that while Sweden is shown to have a high level of social trust and confidence in parliament in the 1990s, the latter fell substantially in the previous period, and it is the change rather than the absolute level that is of interest here.

5 Democracy and involvement

The benevolent aspects of social participation

Jan W. van Deth

Democracy and democratic attitudes

Democracies cannot function without some minimal level of loyalty or affection. Loyalty and affection are necessary if systems are to be able to cope with the fact that many political decisions are, almost by definition, characterized as zero-sum games; this is a stylish way of saying that citizens cannot expect to get what they want unless somebody picks up the bill. Without a minimum attachment to the way political decisions are taken, unfulfilled demands and the obligation to meet the costs of social arrangements will gradually result in discontent, frustration, protest, or withdrawal. This notion has been a platitude among scholars and observers of political systems at least since Lane (1959b) and Almond and Verba (1963) presented their seminal work on the fragile balance between legitimacy and effectiveness, on the one hand, and the features of civic culture on the other hand. According to this line of argument, a democracy can only withstand the centripetal forces of sustained rivalry, the preponderance of group interests, and the rising frustrations of minorities if it enjoys a minimum level of loyalty and affection from citizens.

Instead of stressing the requirement of a minimum level of loyalty for the survival of democratic processes, we could reformulate this problem in terms of political disaffection, understood as 'a spirit of disloyalty to the government or existing authority'.[1] To turn the question round in this way is neither a frivolous exercise nor a mere word game, for where such negative orientations are absent or successfully suppressed, democracies are likely to survive. The advantage of this approach, therefore, is that it enables us to abandon the assumption that an engaged citizenry is a necessary condition for the survival of democratic decision-making processes. While conventional interpretations stress the need for positive political attitudes as a kind of antidote to dissatisfaction and frustration, focusing on the possible implications of negative attitudes signifies starting out from the much more restricted assumption that feelings of political indifference or apathy do not, *per se*, constitute a serious threat to democratic politics. We cannot even rule out the possibility that citizens show signs of political indifference precisely because they have faith in the way the system operates (van Deth 2000). The complexity of the relationship between political disaffection and the survival of democratic regimes is already clear from the discussion of the concepts in the editors' Introduction to this volume. In line with di Palma (1970), they define political disaffection as the subjective feeling of powerlessness, cynicism, and lack of confidence in the political process, politicians, and democratic institutions, but with no questioning of the political regime. Furthermore, they distinguish between two sub-dimensions of disaffection: political disengagement (that is, a lack of political engagement) and institutional disaffection (that is, a lack of confidence in political institutions). In the case of existing democracies, therefore, the decisive question is, what factors and mechanisms could prevent the spread or intensification of feelings of political disengagement and institutional disaffection among citizens? The development of positive democratic attitudes, especially political engagement, is the issue at the heart of many studies examining civil society and the potential that social capital has to generate certain benefits. Putnam's (1993, 1995a, and 1995b) famous use of the concept of social capital, in particular, has stimulated the debate on the prerequisites for the survival and performance of democratic political systems. According to Putnam (1993: 167), social capital refers to 'features of social organization, such as trust, norms, and networks'. In other words, social capital comprises both structural dimensions (that is, institutions and networks) as well as cultural dimensions (that is, social norms and values, and particularly trust).[2] Clearly working in the Tocquevillean tradition, Putnam presumes that membership of voluntary associations is of vital importance for a minimum level of civic virtue, going on to argue that the strength of American democracy is due to the existence of a wide variety of those associations. Consequently, the decline of civil society is partly a result of a decline in the membership of many types of associations, clubs, groups, and organizations.[3] More particularly, the decline in citizens' 'engagement with their communities' is seen as lying behind a series of major social problems, as well as of the political system's incapacity to resolve these problems. Social norms and values, but in particular trust among citizens, constitute the cultural dimensions of social capital (Putnam 1993; Fukuyama 1995; Inglehart 1997b). Indeed, a 'reciprocal relationship' exists between social capital and democracy (Sides 1999; Rosenblum 1998: 36–41).

Notwithstanding the appeal and apparent plausibility of this line of reasoning, it has always been obvious that civil societies do not constitute the remedy for all the ills of advanced democracies. Even more significantly, however, we cannot ignore those who suggest that civil society may also give rise to anti- and non-democratic attitudes. These would constitute, in the words of Fiorina (1999), 'a dark side of civic engagement', while Putnam himself (2000: 352) has written more generally about 'the dark side of social capital', at the same time as one of his early critics refers to 'social and unsocial capital' (Levi 1996). These negative dimensions should not be treated as an aberration but rather as an intrinsic feature of civil society: '. . . *all known forms of civil society are plagued by endogenous sources of incivility*' (Keane 1998: 135; emphasis in the original).[4] Rising levels of political disaffection may be one of the unavoidable, negative consequences of the development of existing civil societies, outweighing or at least diminishing the expected beneficial results that figure so prominently in Tocquevillean speculations.[5]

This chapter examines the relationship between the structural aspects of social capital (membership of voluntary associations) and political attitudes. Does social participation indeed promote positive feelings towards democracy or, to be more precise, does it lead to a decrease in political disengagement? Moreover, if the latter were found to be true, does social participation inevitably result in the over-representation of active citizens and hence to biased representation of interests? Since the available cross-national empirical evidence is rather limited, and was not collected specifically to permit analysis of political disaffection, these questions would appear to be difficult to answer. However, rather than retreating into the comfortable area of speculation and 'theorizing', here I will attempt to assess the empirical plausibility of the arguments made about the possible benevolent consequences of social participation in a number of European democracies.

The negative implications of social participation

Given the huge debate and literature on the positive consequences of increased social capital, it would be easy to overlook its potentially more negative features. That such negative aspects do exist is indicated by the fact that both Fiorina (1999) and Putnam (2000) explicitly discuss the 'dark side', and various other authors briefly mention possible damaging, harmful, or unpleasant aspects of civil society and social capital. From these authors it is possible to identify a number of different interpretations of the impact that civil society and social capital has for political orientations. What is probably the most widespread interpretation of the potentially negative political consequences of civil society goes to the very heart of the argumentation used by proponents of civil society; this is what Beem (1999: 182) has labelled 'counterproductive forms of civil society'. Precisely because social involvement enhances social capital (social skills, contacts, personal trust), this mechanism can be exploited to the benefit of *any* organization, regardless of its criminal or non-democratic character. The examples most frequently cited in this context include the Mafia, the Red Army Faction (RAF) in Germany, skinheads, the Ku Klux Klan, the Nation of Islam, or the Irish Republican Army (IRA) (van Deth 1997: 7; Fiorina 1999: 396; Beem 1999: 180–182; della Porta 2000).[6] Yet, unless we can distinguish between 'bad' and 'good' organizations, it will be impossible to draw any conclusions about the potential political consequences of counterproductive forms of civil society. 'Bad' and 'good' character of organizations exist in the eyes of the beholder; what one observer judges negatively might be much less controversial for someone else. That is not to say, of course, that we should ignore the sinister consequences of social capital, but simply that the evaluation of the political impact of social involvement as positive or negative depends entirely on some a priori evaluation of the specific organizations.[7]

A second and rather trivial type of interpretation follows directly from the fact that norms and values constitute inherent (cultural) dimensions of social capital. If these norms and values are negative towards the political system, or even towards the political regime itself, then the level of negative political orientations increases by definition as these norms and values obtain a more significant place in society due to the activities of voluntary associations. From this perspective, the content of norms and values is simply treated as exogenous. A rather more sophisticated subvariant of this interpretation is based not on the existence of explicitly non-democratic attitudes, but rather on a general aversion towards organized decision-making processes in complex societies. For many advocates of the benign effects of social capital and civil society, '...the local, the face-to-face, and the many sites in which conversation can take place ... are inherently good, while the professionalized, staffed, nationalized, computerized operation of the thousands of associations that get typed as special interests are always bad' (Schudson 1998: 280). Because political decision-making processes are the arenas for special interests par excellence, the spread of romantic support for small-scale organizations would stimulate negative political feelings since politics is considered to be part of the large-scale, professionalized, and institutionalized parts of society.[8] Instead of treating values and norms simply as given and exogenous, emphasis on the impact of participation in small-scale organizations leads to the conclusion that these generate negative political attitudes or at least feelings of indifference.[9] This interpretation contradicts conventional approaches, which emphasize the development of civic skills and interpersonal trust within small-scale organizations as the basis for the development of social trust and, consequently, for positive political feelings.

A third interpretation of the political consequences of social capital focuses on the biased representation of interests due to the assumption that social participation is unequally distributed in line with the unequal distribution of social capital (Schlozman *et al.* 1999). In his extensive overview of the normative uses of the concepts 'good governance' and civil society, Warren (1999b: 21) highlights the 'public sphere effects' and the positive consequences of social participation: 'when associations "go public" they can leverage their influence in ways that can compensate for a lack of other kinds of power. Silence serves the wealthy and powerful well, and public argument is a primary means through which poorer and weaker members of society can have influence'.[10] Why, however, should organizations be used especially by the 'poorer and weaker' rather than by the 'wealthy and powerful'? Is it not much more likely that the latter dominate decision-making processes precisely because they are wealthy and powerful? Faith in the potentially benign consequences of social participation seems to rest on a significant underestimation of the 'unbalanced representation of interests', as well as an extremely limited understanding of the roles and functions of organizations. Fiorina (1999), in particular, has drawn attention to the fact that public debate in the United States is heavily dominated by special interest groups which manage to control decision-making processes. The successful mobilization of special interests in voluntary organizations, therefore, is more likely to reflect existing 'imbalances' in the distribution of social capital than to compensate for these inequalities. Even in those cases when the signal and warning functions performed by arising organizations of the poorer and weaker parts of society are considerable, the actual outcomes of struggles probably reflect the interests of more resourceful or more involved groups. Rather than extending the opportunities for democratic decision-making, the very success of mobilizing specific interests based on social capital tends to reproduce and strengthen existing inequalities.

These three visions of the negative consequences of social capital for political attitudes and decisions in democratic political systems serve here as the starting point for the empirical analysis and interpretation of social participation and disaffection. Since the first interpretation (the counterproductive forms of civil society) depends entirely on exogenous information and specific presumptions, this analysis focuses on the last two arguments. According to the first, a general aversion to complex and formalized decision-making procedures would be expected to foster negative political feelings, especially among participants in groups that provide opportunities for direct, face-to-face contacts and co-operation (sports clubs, clubs devoted to certain hobbies, youth organizations, and the like). Such feelings can be broken down into political discontent, on the one hand, and political disaffection (especially political disengagement), on the other. Second, successful social mobilization is expected to lead to biased representation of specific political interests. When these two very different interpretations are combined, the assumption would be that higher levels of social participation in specific voluntary associations correlates with political discontent and political disaffection, and this despite the fact that the interests of the groups concerned are relatively well represented. The empirical analyses focus on three main concepts and the relations between them: social participation, political disengagement, and political discontent. Although certainly not unimportant, for the sake of the clarity of the argument in the limited space available, the second sub-dimension of political disaffection, that is, institutional disaffection, is not analysed here.

Satisfaction, interest, and saliency

Disaffection is an ambiguous term. Even in a volume devoted exclusively to the study of *Disaffected Democracies* (Pharr and Putnam 2000), one looks in vain for a clear-cut conceptualization of the term. After the stating that they '...find no evidence of declining commitment to the principles of democratic government or to the democratic regimes' (2000: 7), the editors simply go on to provide a list of 'specific indicators' of affection and disaffection: 'attachment to and judgements of political parties, approval of parliaments and other political institutions, assessment of the "political class", and assorted evaluations of political trust' (2000: 8). A large number of empirical studies have conclusively demonstrated the existence of a generalized commitment to the principles of democracy among the citizens of Western democracies, as well as the fact that this does not imply uncritical acceptance of government policies or devotion to the political authorities.[11] In fact, the opposite is true. Although most citizens support democratic decision-making processes, there is evidence of considerable discontent and indifference towards actual decisions and decision-makers.

As the volume edited by Pharr and Putnam, as well as the Introduction to the present volume by Torcal and Montero highlights, empirical research has employed very different measures or indicators of political disaffection. Moreover, existing studies based on survey data about the orientations of citizens in different countries only offer a very limited number of possible instruments. Since the main objective here is not to analyse extreme feelings of political disloyalty or aversion, but rather feelings of indifference and estrangement, straightforward indicators of political discontent and political disengagement are required. Both a relatively low level of satisfaction and a lack of interest in politics could be the consequence of a purely instrumental attitude towards political decision-making processes, and need not be accompanied by negative political feelings. However, a high level of discontent and an evident lack of political engagement could hardly exist in the absence of negative feelings about the political process. Rather than examining attitudes in terms of trust or support, negative political feelings are measured here, first, by relatively low levels of satisfaction with democracy and, second, by restricting the concept of political disaffection to political disengagement. For this last concept, two indicators will be used here: one for subjective political interest and another one for political saliency, that is, the relative importance citizens attach to politics.

The concept of *political discontent* is measured here through a direct question about citizens' level of satisfaction with democracy. Respondents are invited to indicate their degree of overall satisfaction with the way democracy functions in their country ('very satisfied', 'fairly satisfied', 'not very satisfied', 'not at all satisfied').

Our first indicator of *political disengagement*, in turn, is constructed from the answers given to a direct question about the respondent's level of subjective political interest: 'generally speaking, are you interested in politics' ('a great deal', 'to some extent', 'not much', 'not at all'). Subjective political interest reflects 'the degree to which politics arouses a citizen's curiosity' (van Deth 1990: 278), or, in other words, citizens' 'attentiveness to politics' (Zaller 1992: 18) and their potential readiness to participate. A minimum level of subjective political interest is a self-evident requirement for any democratic political system: without such a minimum level, citizens would not even be aware of the political process, or of the opportunities this affords them to defend their interests or to take part in collective action.

However, the conventional indicator of subjective political interest, in particular, may be too limited to capture the relevant aspects of respondents' relation to politics and political life. Therefore, a second conception of political disengagement can be defined in terms of *political saliency*, that is, the relative importance of political as opposed to other matters or affairs. Citizens may be interested in politics, but this does not necessarily mean that they will actually consider politics important or even relevant to their lives. People might be much more strongly inclined or obliged to use their scarce resources for other more important, more relevant, more pleasant, less threatening, or less demanding areas of life, than following political decision-making processes (van Deth 2000). Moreover, a low level of political saliency surely does not constitute a threat to democracy as long as people do not lose interest out of frustration with governmental politics or political processes.[12] Compared with other matters, politics might be interesting but just not considered important by many people.

The measure of political saliency used here reflects this idea of the relative importance of politics and has been constructed from the response given to a survey question about the significance of various areas of individual citizens' lives. For each of six different items (work, family, friends and acquaintances, leisure, politics, and religion) respondents are invited to indicate 'how important it is in your life' on a 4-point scale ranging from 'very important' (1) to 'not at all important' (4). The saliency of politics is then operationalized as the ranking of the relevant item among this set of six. For example, if politics is the only item to receive the highest score (usually, but not necessarily, score [1]), then the saliency of politics is at a maximum; if 'politics' is the only item to receive the lowest score (usually, but not necessarily, score [4]), then the saliency is at its minimum level. Since, with six items and four response categories, ties are unavoidable, the precise ranking is also based on the mean number of items receiving the same score as politics. For instance, a respondent marking both 'politics' and 'work' as 'quite important' (score [2]), 'family' as 'very important' (score [1]), and the remaining items as 'not at all important' (score [4]), scores 2.5 on the political saliency scale. In this way, the scale for subjective interest is complemented by a scale for political saliency ranging from 'very high' (1) to 'very low' (6) (van Deth 2000).

Finally, we need information about *social participation*. In several surveys, respondents have been presented with a list of organizations and invited to say to which, if any, they belong. A typical variant of this question would read as follows:[13]

From the following list, could you tell me which organizations you are a member of or whose activities you participate in?

- Social welfare and charitable organizations;
- Religious or parish organizations;
- Cultural or artistic associations;
- Political parties;
- Trade unions, professional organizations, employer organizations;
- Human rights movements or organizations;
- Organizations for the protection of animals, nature, the environment;
- Youth organizations (scouts, youth clubs, etc.);
- Consumer organizations;
- Sports clubs associations;
- Hobby or special interest clubs/associations (collectors, 'fan-clubs', computer clubs, etc.); and
- Other clubs or organizations.

Although the exact wording and format of the questions vary in different surveys, and the coding schemes used are not identical, research has tended to confirm the general conclusions about cross-national similarities and differences in the levels and modes of social participation presented by Curtis, Grabb, and Baer (1992). Various researchers have analysed the response to this type of question in an effort to construct more general and equivalent measures (Wessels 1997; van Deth and Kreuter 1998; Morales 2001). However, given the very serious problems encountered in this respect, the 12 kinds of organizations listed above will be analysed separately here.

In order to verify empirically the existence or otherwise of possible less positive consequences of social participation for the political orientations of citizens, we require evidence about distinct aspects of engagement and political interest. Empirical information on the saliency of political matters is particularly hard to find. Since this concept is crucial for the arguments presented, only data sets including information on this dimension of political involvement can be used to this end. In accordance with this criterion, *Eurobarometer 49.0* study (data collected in Spring 1998) was selected for analysis,[14] and the data for Belgium, Denmark, Germany, Greece, Spain, France, Ireland, Italy, the Netherlands, Portugal, Great Britain, Austria, Sweden, and Finland pooled in order to carry out the empirical analysis.[15] The data for Northern Ireland and Luxembourg were not included in the analysis due to the very limited numbers of cases.

The political antecedents of social engagement

Does social participation correlate with more positive feelings towards the political system and, as a result, lead to the unbalanced representation of interests? Although it would certainly be desirable to count on much less ambiguous indicators of negative political feelings, with the available data it is nevertheless possible to make a preliminary evaluation of the empirical worth of the arguments about the impact of social participation discussed above. Let us begin by considering the political antecedents of social participation, and then go on to analyse its consequences for interest representation.

Social and political engagement

In order to trace the possible political antecedents of social participation, we first compare the characteristics of members and non-members of voluntary associations. If associational membership, for whatever reasons, correlates with greater satisfaction with democracy, interest in politics, and saliency, we would expect to find higher levels of these political attitudes among members than among non-members of associations. Furthermore, this general finding should hold regardless of the kind of voluntary association in question. For instance, sports clubs and employers' organizations all provide opportunities for developing skills and interpersonal trust which, according to conventional Tocquevillean reasoning, lead to positive political orientations. However, if we follow the more controversial interpretation that participation in local, face-to-face organizations implies a rejection of professional and institutionalized special interests organizations, then members of sports clubs should have less positive political feelings than members of employers' organizations. A comparison of political feelings of members and non-members of different types of organization should provide the empirical evidence needed to evaluate these rival interpretations.

Figures 5.1a, 5.1b, and 5.1c show the levels of satisfaction with democracy, political interest, and political saliency of members and non-members of 12 kinds of voluntary associations in 14 European countries.[16] The format of these graphs is rather unusual. First, two points indicate the average levels for members and non-members of each type of association; and then, in order to facilitate interpretation, straight lines connect the two points for each category of organization. For each type of organization, therefore, two points are shown in each graph: one corresponds to the average results of members and the other of non-members. For instance, Figure 5.1a shows that about 59 per cent of the members of political parties are satisfied with democracy and 85 per cent interested in politics. The corresponding figures for non-members of political parties are 53 per cent and 40 per cent, respectively, the straight line indicating the difference between members and non-members. The graphs can be used to examine the differences between members and non-members of each organization in four different ways:

1   Members and non-members may differ in terms of their average levels on the first indicator (*x*-axis) of political orientations. For instance, the average level of satisfaction with democracy is clearly higher among members of sports clubs than among non-members (63 per cent as opposed to 53 per cent), and this effect is rather less pronounced for members and non-members of political parties (59 per cent as compared with 53 per cent).

2   Members and non-members may differ in terms of their average levels on the second indicator (*y*-axis) of political orientations. For instance, the average level of political interest is clearly higher among members of sports clubs than among non-members (51 per cent as opposed to 40 per cent), and this effect is much stronger for members and non-members of political parties (85 per cent as opposed to 40 per cent).

3   Members and non-members may differ in terms of the relative impact of the two indicators of political orientations, that is, the gradient of the line connecting the points for these two groups may vary. For instance, members and non-members of sports clubs differ in terms of their satisfaction with democracy but hardly at all with respect to their level of political interest (gentle slope), while members and

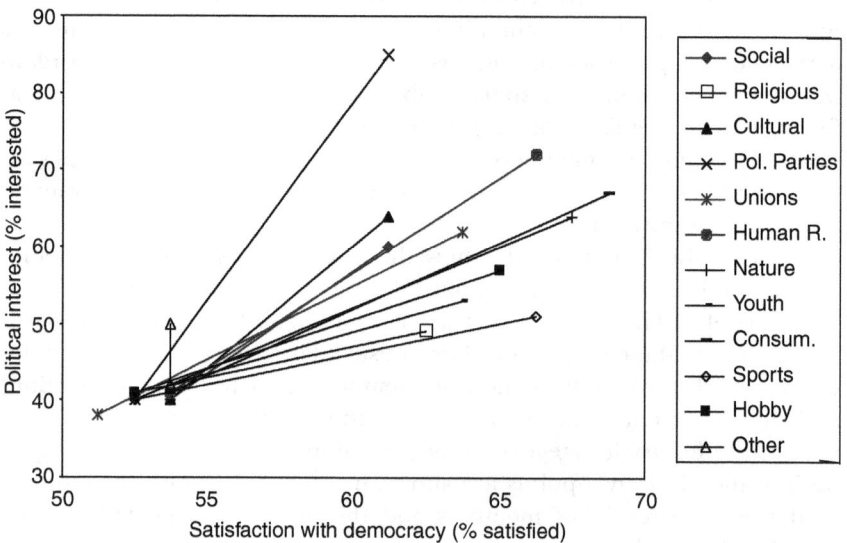

Figure 5.1a Satisfaction with democracy and subjective political interest among non-members (left points) and members (right points) of voluntary associations, 1998.

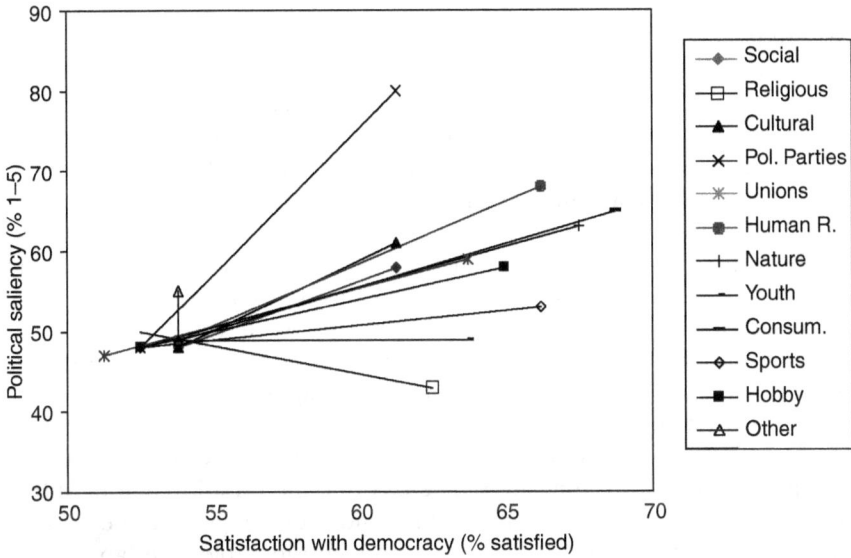

Figure 5.1b Satisfaction with democracy and political saliency among non-members (left points) and members (right points) of voluntary associations, 1998.

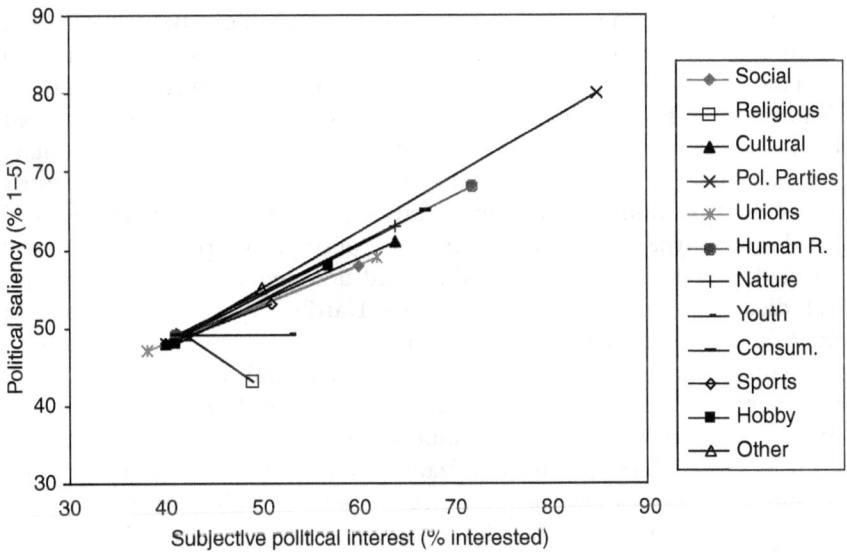

Figure 5.1c Subjective political interest and political saliency among non-members (left points) and members (right points) of voluntary associations, 1998 (source: *Eurobarometer 49.0,* 1998).

non-members of political parties show pronounced differences in both indicators (steep slope).

4   In general, the intensity of the combined effects of the two indicators is summarized in the distance between the points for members and non-members (that is, the length of the line connecting the points for these two groups). For instance, members and non-members of cultural organizations are more similar (short line) than members and non-members of youth organizations are (longer line).

Even a superficial glance at Figures 5.1a, 5.1b, and 5.1c is suffice to reveal that members and non-members of associations differ in terms of their satisfaction with democracy, political interest, and the importance or saliency of politics in their lives. The results for non-members all converge in the lower left-hand corners of the three graphs, indicating that about 52 per cent of non-members are satisfied with democracy, about 40 per cent are interested in politics, and about 50 per cent consider politics to be quite important in their lives. The fact that the variation among different non-member groups for these three indicators appears to be remarkably low is hardly surprising given the considerable overlap among non-members of different associations.[17] For instance, the non-members of hobby clubs are also non-members of unions, and therefore the two points for these non-member groups are virtually identical.

Figure 5.1a provides initial confirmation of the positive implications of social engagement for political orientations. In this diagram, political discontent (satisfaction with democracy) and the first of our two indicators of political disengagement (political interest) are shown for members and non-members of different organizations. For all the organizations in question, the points for their respective members are located to the northeast of the points for non-members. In other words, members of voluntary associations are in fact more satisfied with democracy and more interested in politics than non-members are.[18] Although this conclusion applies to all the different types of association, the level of subjective political interest in particular does vary among members and non-members of these groups, as indicated by the variation of the *y*-axis. Hardly surprisingly, members of political parties, human rights movements, and consumer associations, in particular, show much higher levels of political interest than non-members do.[19] In contrast, there are virtually no differences in the levels of political interest among members and non-members of religious groups, sports clubs, youth organizations, and 'other' associations. Membership of a social organization correlates with a higher level of satisfaction with democracy, but the differences in terms of political interest are clearly tied to the type of association in question. In other words, negative political feelings (discontent and disengagement) are higher among non-members of voluntary associations irrespective of the type of organization considered. Differentiation between different kinds of voluntary associations is specially relevant for distinctions between the levels of political interest among members and non-members: whereas the level of satisfaction with democracy varies between 60 and 65 per cent among all members only, the corresponding figures for political interest range from about 45 to 85 per cent. These findings show that discontent and disengagement have quite different consequences, as reflected in the slopes of the vectors in Figure 5.1a. This first finding clearly highlights the need to distinguish between political discontent, on the one hand, and political disaffection, on the other. We will return to the distances between the various points below.

The second indicator of political disengagement (political saliency) and the average level of political discontent among members and non-members of different associations are shown in Figure 5.1b. The general conclusions drawn in the previous paragraph are confirmed here, albeit with two clear exceptions. As in Figure 5.1a, virtually all points for non-members cluster neatly in the lower left-hand corner of the graph, while the corresponding points for members are located to the northeast of these points for non-members. Yet, in the case of religious organizations, and to a lesser extent youth groups, these points fall in the southeast, indicating that members of these voluntary associations attach less importance to politics than non-members do.[20] Besides, members and non-members of sports clubs and 'other' organizations do not differ much in terms of the relevance they attach to political phenomena as compared with other aspects of life. In other words, social participation in certain types of organizations is clearly related to political disengagement. Here, too, the conclusion is that distinct levels of political saliency among members and non-members are evidently related to the type of association in question, and that differences are again apparent for members of political parties, human rights movements, and consumer associations.

The similarities between the results presented in Figures 5.1a and 5.1b are reflected in Figure 5.1c, which shows, for a number of organizations, the relationships between the two indicators of political disaffection used here. From Figure 5.1c it is apparent that much higher levels of both political interest and political saliency are found particularly among members of political parties, human rights movements, and consumer associations. In contrast, only very slight differences exist between members and non-members of sports clubs, youth organizations, and 'other' associations. At the same time, it is clear that religious organizations constitute a rather exceptional case: the relevance of politics among members of religious organizations is lower than among non-members (although the levels of subjective political interest actually do show the expected distinction, with higher levels of subjective political interest among members of religious organizations than among non-members).

From the results presented in Figures 5.1a, 5.1b, and 5.1c, it is apparent that membership of almost any type of voluntary association correlates with more positive attitudes towards democracy and politics, while less positive feelings are found above all among non-members of voluntary associations. This broad conclusion, however, requires further refinement, because the differences between members and non-members are closely tied to the actual type of association in question. Since the average levels of political discontent and of the two indicators of political disengagement are more or less the same for all non-members, irrespective of the kind of organization in question (see the clustering of points in the lower left-hand corners of Figures 5.1a, 5.1b, and 5.1c), any conclusions about the correlation between social participation and political orientations must necessarily be rather cautious: we can speak in terms of relatively lower levels of negative feelings among members of specific groups (that is, the points to the right in Figure 5.1 are more or less distant from the cluster of non-members to the left). Differences between distinct voluntary associations, therefore, can easily be seen if we compute the distances or vector lengths between members and non-members in the three-dimensional space defined by political discontent and the two indicators of political disengagement. Although this does not take the slope of the various vectors into account, the information obtained neatly summarizes the overall difference between members and non-members of voluntary associations. If we order the types of organizations according to their distances, we obtain the following result:[21]

Shortest distance   1 'Other' clubs or organizations (10.0);
　　　　　　　　　　2 Religious or parish organizations (13.3);
　　　　　　　　　　3 Youth organizations (scouts, youth clubs, etc.) (13.6);
　　　　　　　　　　4 Sports clubs associations (16.3);
　　　　　　　　　　5 Hobby or special interest clubs/associations (21.4);
　　　　　　　　　　6 Social welfare and charitable organizations (23.2);
　　　　　　　　　　7 Cultural or artistic associations (28.0);
　　　　　　　　　　8 Trade unions, professional, and employer organizations (28.6);
　　　　　　　　　　9 Protection of animals, nature, the environment (30.7);
　　　　　　　　　10 Consumer organizations (32.8);
　　　　　　　　　11 Human rights movements or organizations (37.7);
Longest distance   12 Political parties (55.7).

The relative lengths of these vectors confirm the existence of politically relevant differences between members and non-members in the cases of political parties and consumer and human rights organizations, while the difference between members and non-members of religious organizations, youth clubs, and sports clubs are much less significant. All this can be seen from the precise figures for the distances listed above.

Before we accept these inferences about the need to distinguish between the various kinds of organizations insofar as political orientations are concerned, it is necessary to carry out one further empirical test. Both political discontent and political disengagement depend, at least in part, on socio-demographic characteristics such as the respondents' level of education, gender, and age (van Deth 1990). If particular socio-demographic categories of citizens' tend to be over-represented in certain voluntary associations, then the identified differences in the political attitudes of members and non-members could simply be a reflection of the different profiles of the two groups. In order to confirm this possibility, two tests have been carried out: one to examine the average differences between members and non-members after statistically controlling for various individual characteristics, and another analysing the specific impact of social participation when these individual characteristics are included in (logistic) regression models in which the degree of political discontent (satisfaction with democracy) and of political disengagement (political interest and political saliency) are the dependent variables.

The results of the first test are shown in Table 5.1. In a preliminary step, the average scores for satisfaction with democracy, political interest, and political saliency have been corrected for respondents' level of education, their gender, and age.[22] Then, the respective residual scores have been computed and used to test the null-hypothesis that there is no difference between the two groups (that is, members and non-members of a given type of voluntary association). A parametric F-test has been carried out (one-way analysis of variance) to test the match between the mean levels of satisfaction, interest, and saliency among members and non-members of the type of organization in question. To avoid biased estimates due to the heavily skewed distributions of a number of the variables analysed, a non-parametric Kolmogorov–Smirnov test was added to see whether the two groups come from the same population (or from populations with the same distributions) (Siegel 1956: 127).

The results presented in Table 5.1 unequivocally confirm the conclusions noted above: members and non-members of voluntary associations clearly differ in terms of their levels of both political discontent and political disengagement. Members of 'other' organizations seem to constitute a heterogeneous category that does not show a substantially higher level of satisfaction with democracy than non-members.[23] Levels of subjective political interest among members and non-members differ for each kind of voluntary association: only in the cases of youth organizations and sports clubs do members and non-members show more or less identical levels of political saliency.[24] This first complementary test reinforces, therefore, the general conclusion that social participation is associated with clear differences in political discontent, as well as political disengagement. Even after controlling for the effects of education, gender, and age, members and non-members of voluntary associations show notable differences in terms of political discontent and political disengagement. At the

Table 5.1 Political discontent and political disengagement among members and non-members of voluntary associations, 1998 (F-Test and Kolmogorov–Smirnov Test of Residual Scores[a]; $N=14{,}624$)

Groups[b]	Political discontent				Political disengagement							
	Satisfaction with democracy[c]				Subjective political interest[d]				Political saliency[e]			
	F-Test		K-S Test		F-Test		K-S Test		F-Test		K-S Test	
	F	Sig.	Z	Sig.	F	Sig.	Z	Sig.	F	Sig.	Z	Sig.
Social	23	0.000	2.6	0.000	223	0.000	6.9	0.000	30	0.000	3.4	0.000
Religious	46	0.000	3.6	0.000	81	0.000	4.1	0.000	31	0.000	4.9	0.000
Cultural	8	0.004	2.5	0.000	213	0.000	6.8	0.000	93	0.000	4.3	0.000
Political parties	10	0.002	1.8	0.002	708	0.000	11.1	0.000	523	0.000	9.1	0.000
Unions	82	0.000	5.0	0.000	342	0.000	9.4	0.000	40	0.000	3.4	0.000
Human rights	8	0.004	2.1	0.000	155	0.000	5.9	0.000	110	0.000	4.3	0.000
Nature, environment	58	0.000	4.3	0.000	229	0.000	6.9	0.000	77	0.000	4.7	0.000
Youth	7	0.008	2.0	0.001	60	0.000	3.9	0.000	6	0.015	1.3	0.081
Consumer	31	0.000	3.2	0.000	111	0.000	5.2	0.000	59	0.000	3.4	0.000
Sports clubs	103	0.000	6.6	0.000	97	0.000	5.4	0.000	3	0.075	3.1	0.000
Hobby clubs	40	0.000	3.5	0.000	118	0.000	5.2	0.000	23	0.000	3.3	0.000
Other	0	0.834	0.6	0.903	24	0.000	2.4	0.000	15	0.000	1.8	0.003

Source: *Eurobarometer 49.0*, 1998.

Notes

a Scores corrected for the level of education, gender, age, and age-square of each respondent.
b For all organizations, members (1) and non-members (2).
c Four categories ranging from very satisfied (1) to not at all satisfied (4).
d Four categories ranging from very interested (1) to not at all interested (4).
e Six categories ranging from high saliency (1) to low saliency (6).

same time, we find further confirmation of the exceptional character of religious organizations (and to some extent youth and sports clubs) in this respect.

A second test of these conclusions about the correlation between social participation and political discontent and disengagement is based on the presumption that membership of voluntary associations has consequences for the degree of satisfaction with democracy, political interest, and political saliency. In order to isolate the impact of membership from other factors (logistic) regressions have been carried out in which the three indicators of discontent and disengagement and saliency are the dependent variables, and the conventional socio-demographic characteristics (education, gender, age) again form the first block set of independent variables. Only after these background variables were included in the models were the variables for membership of different kinds of voluntary associations incorporated into the calculations. The principal results of the analyses are presented in Table 5.2. It is immediately apparent that the model hardly explains political discontent as measured by the level of satisfaction with democracy, and that in fewer than half of the voluntary associations listed does membership have any statistically significant explanatory impact on this attitude.[25] These associations in question include organizations as varied as religious groups, unions, and environmental groups, as well as hobby and sports clubs. As for political disengagement, let us first consider the explanation of the level of subjective political interest. Here, the coefficients indicate that membership of every type of voluntary association does have a significant impact on political interest, with the sole exception of religious organizations. The exceptional position of religious organizations is also confirmed by the results of the model in which political saliency is the dependent variable. In this case, significant coefficients are obtained for religious organizations, the positive sign indicating that being a member of this kind of association increases the likelihood that politics is considered irrelevant. At the same time, membership of social organizations, youth clubs, and sports clubs does not have a significant impact on the level of importance which respondents attribute to politics. Apparently, participation in any type of association except religious organizations has clear positive consequences in terms of political disengagement as measured by the level of subjective political interest. For satisfaction with democracy and political saliency, the picture is more ambiguous, as only certain kinds of voluntary associations have a modest impact on the explained variance.

At first sight, the results summarized in Tables 5.1 and 5.2 might appear contradictory. Although the levels of both political discontent and disengagement differ significantly between the members and non-members of virtually every type of voluntary association (Table 5.1), the impact of membership on political orientations is modest, and varies depending on the orientation and type of organization in question (Table

Table 5.2 Predictors of political discontent and political disengagement, 1998 (logistic regression; N= 15,248)

Predictor	Political discontent			Political disengagement					
	Satis. democracy[a]			Subj. political interest[b]			Political saliency[c]		
	B	Pred. B	Sig.	B	Pred. B	Sig.	B	Pred. B	Sig.
Education[d]	−0.049	0.952	0.000	−0.161	0.851	0.000	−0.087	0.916	0.000
Gender	−0.009	0.991	0.785	−0.637	0.529	0.000	−0.473	0.623	0.000
Age	0.026	1.027	0.000	−0.032	0.969	0.000	0.005	1.005	0.321
Age squared	0.000	1.000	0.000	0.000	1.000	0.002	0.000	1.000	0.000
Social[e]	−0.024	0.976	0.674	−0.259	0.772	0.000	−0.089	0.915	0.132
Religious	−0.259	0.771	0.000	−0.041	0.960	0.470	0.537	1.711	0.000
Cultural	0.040	1.041	0.521	−0.413	0.662	0.000	−0.247	0.781	0.000
Political parties	−0.058	0.944	0.441	−1.690	0.185	0.000	−1.201	0.301	0.000
Unions	−0.251	0.778	0.000	−0.494	0.610	0.000	−0.173	0.841	0.000
Human rights	−0.047	0.954	0.632	−0.522	0.594	0.000	−0.377	0.686	0.000
Nature, environment	−0.241	0.786	0.000	−0.396	0.673	0.000	−0.350	0.705	0.000
Youth	−0.034	0.966	0.671	−0.319	0.727	0.000	0.027	1.027	0.741
Consumer	−0.212	0.809	0.018	−0.293	0.746	0.002	−0.291	0.748	0.002
Sports clubs	−0.386	0.680	0.000	−0.190	0.827	0.000	−0.049	0.952	0.240
Hobby clubs	−0.200	0.819	0.000	−0.322	0.724	0.000	−0.229	0.796	0.000
Other	−0.022	0.978	0.750	−0.334	0.716	0.000	−0.167	0.847	0.019
Constant	−0.231	0.793	0.048	2.820	16.780	0.000	1.050	2.858	0.000
Nagelkerke's R^2	0.039			0.214			0.101		

Source: *Eurobarometer 49.0*, 1998.

Notes

a Categories dichotomized in satisfied (1 + 2) and dissatisfied (3 + 4).
b Categories dichotomized in interested (1 + 2) and not interested (3 + 4).
c Categories dichotomized in high saliency (1–5) and low saliency (5.5–6).
d Level of education measured by age when finishing education ('still studying' recoded in actual age).
e For all organizations, members (1) and non-members (2).

5.2). This result is paradoxical only if we presume that social participation leads to particular political orientations. However, unless we distinguish between the various kinds of voluntary association, this interpretation holds neither for the level of political discontent nor for political disengagement as measured by political saliency. The fact that members and non-members of virtually every type of voluntary association differ significantly in their political orientations does not mean that these orientations are a consequence of social participation.[26] Only in the case of political disengagement, as measured by subjective political interest, does membership of every organization except religious groups appear to have a clear and positive impact on engagement. The beneficial consequences of social participation, therefore, are rather limited and specific, and the apparent distinction between members and non-members should not lead us to succumb to the temptation to conclude that increased social participation *per se* promotes more healthy political attitudes.

Interest representation

Politics is organization, and organization implies change in balances of power and opportunities. Since members of voluntary associations clearly differ from non-members in terms of their political orientations (as documented in Figure 5.1 and Table 5.1), it is very likely that some political interests are better represented than others. This potential bias is not related to the question of whether social participation leads to specific attitudes (as shown in Table 5.2). Irrespective of tangible causal connections in this respect, the very existence of significant variation implies differences in the articulation of demands and expectations. This bias is an unavoidable side-effect of social participation (Schlozman *et al.* 1999). The important question would not seem to be whether such a bias exists, but which organizations display the greatest differences between members and non-members in this respect.

One widely used indicator of overall political ideological orientations is citizens' self-placement on the left–right scale. This indicator basically reflects the amount of social change desired, with positions on the left suggesting a preference for greater equality and social solidarity, and a position on the right indicating a stronger attachment to the status quo and existing inequalities (Klingemann and Fuchs 1990; Inglehart 1977). Respondents are usually invited to indicate their favoured position on a straight line running from 'left' (1) to 'right' (10), without being given any further information as to the meaning of these terms. Since there is no obvious reason why members of, say, sports or hobby clubs should have different opinions about social change to those of non-members of these organizations, we will first consider the null-hypothesis that no such differences exist. However, various types of organization such as unions or environmental groups are generally set up exclusively to bring about societal change, making it very likely that their members will have a more leftist orientation. Consequently, the hypothesis to be tested is, first, that on average members and non-members of 'ordinary' voluntary associations do not differ in terms of their ideological orientations, and second, that members of pure interest groups will generally locate themselves further to the left than other citizens do.

The empirical evidence necessary to test this interpretation is shown in Figure 5.2. It presents the information about members and non-members in a similar format to that used in Figure 5.1, straight lines linking the points for the two groups. The horizontal axis in Figure 5.2 represents the mean left–right placement. From the projections of the points for members and non-members on this axis, it is clear that members of human rights organizations tend to place themselves on the left, and members of religious groups and hobby clubs on the right of the ideological spectrum. In the case of all the other types of organizations, neither members nor non-members differ significantly from the mean position of the population as a whole. Most surprisingly, even in the case of political parties, we find virtually identical left–right placements among members and non-members. Apparently, membership of voluntary associations has very little impact on citizens' ideological orientations, with the clear exceptions of human rights groups and religious organizations.

Even relatively modest deviations in left–right placements could have significant consequences for the representation of certain interests, especially if members of associations try to influence the political opinions of their friends and relatives more frequently than non-members do. In order to explore this hypothesis, the ideological self-placement of the respondents in Figure 5.2 has been combined with an indicator of their willingness to engage in political discussions and attempt to persuade other people to adhere to their own political positions. The indicator used here is 'opinion leadership'. It comes as no surprise to find that members of political parties have most interactions of this type. We find more modest levels among members of human rights groups, consumer organizations, cultural organizations, and environmental groups, while members of all other associations show more or less the same level of engagement as non-members.[27] These results suggest that membership of voluntary associations hardly leads to the over-representation of specific interests. With the exception of human rights groups (for which an extreme left-position is complemented by moderate levels of opinion leadership among its members), membership of every other kind of voluntary association is insignificant, either because the mean ideological placements of members and non-members are identical, or because attempts to convince other people are so rare. The fact that a large majority of the members of political parties try to convince other citizens is of little consequence, since there are virtually no differences in the left–right self-placements of members and non-members. Likewise, it would seem

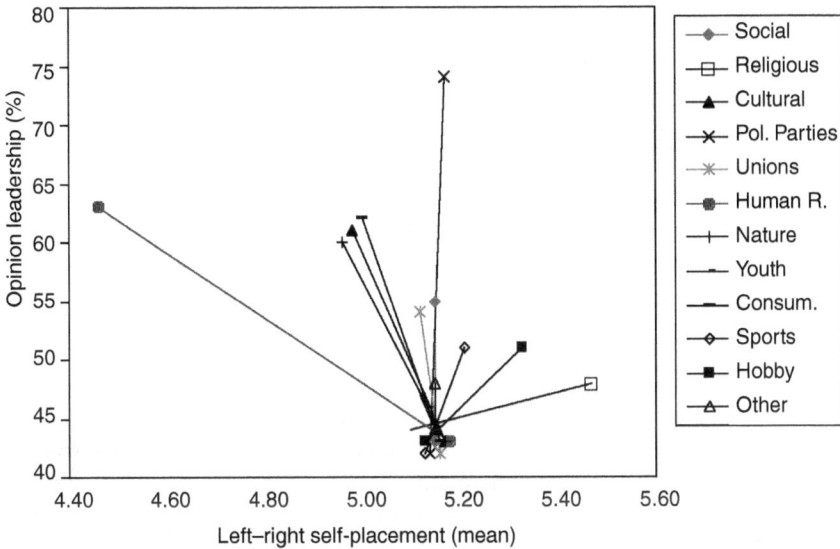

Figure 5.2 Left–right self-placement and opinion leadership among non-members (lower points) and members (higher points) of voluntary associations, 1998 (source: *Eurobarometer 49.0*, 1998).

unlikely that the deviant ideological orientations of members of religious organizations implies the over-representation of these ideas: here the degree of opinion leadership between members and non-members is practically indistinguishable.

Before we draw the reassuring and encouraging conclusion that social participation does not imply biased representation, we would be well advised to consider respondents' average ideological orientations. It is possible that within broad categories of voluntary associations, different clubs in the same category may have very different left–right orientations. For instance, we may find a liberal or left-wing consumer organization alongside consumer organizations with more conservative or right-wing leanings. In the case of political parties, unions, or professional organ- izations, such neutralizing effects might skew the averages shown in Figure 5.2. In order to uncover these effects, the degree of ideological extremism has been measured and operationalized as the distance between respon- dents' self-placement on the left–right scale and the centre of the spec- trum.[28] The mean scores on this scale of extremism have then been combined with the levels of opinion leadership of members and non- members (see Figure 5.3). Even a cursory glance at this graph reveals the fallacies resulting from only considering average left–right positions. Quite clearly, the average position of political parties in Figure 5.2 is highly misleading; members of political parties are characterized by very distinctive left–right orientations, which only disappear because all parties are placed in a single category. Since party members frequently engage in political discussions, members of different parties will articulate their different ideological positions. This situation can hardly be considered to constitute evidence of the misrepresentation or biased representation of specific interests. Citizens are aware of the ideological orientations of the different political parties and, almost by definition, party members are expected to try to convince other people of the virtues of such positions. The only anomalous case is that of human rights organizations, but their fairly left-wing position is already apparent in Figure 5.2. For all other organizations, average ideological positions appear to be unproblematic when distinguishing members and non-members since these positions do not show large variations. Moreover, the figures for the degree of extremism again show that the issue of the representation of political orientations is irrelevant for almost all voluntary associations: the lower corner of Figure 5.3 is heavily populated by non-members as well as members, and only members of political parties and human rights groups declare positions at any distance from this cluster.

The picture of the differences between members and non-members of different kinds of voluntary associations painted in Figures 5.2 and 5.3 can be examined more closely by testing the null-hypotheses that mean that ideological self-placements and scores of extremism are identical for

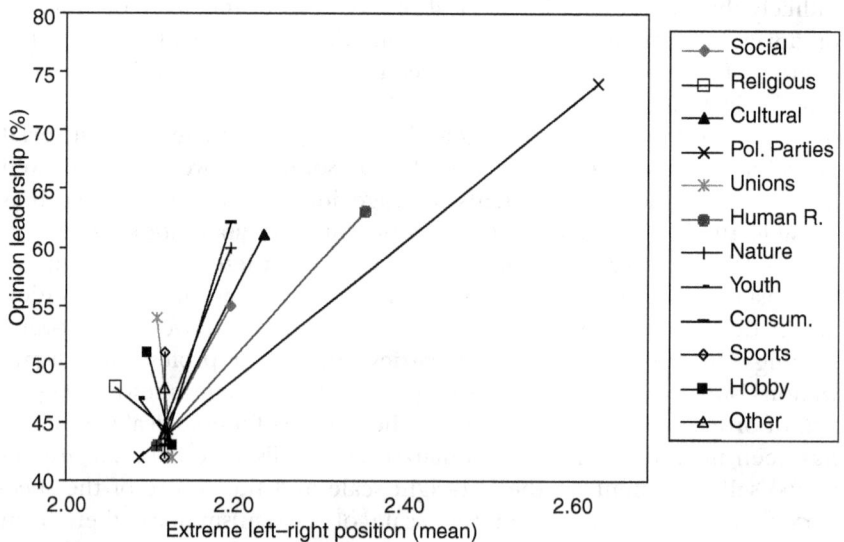

Figure 5.3 Extreme left–right position and opinion leadership among non-members (lower points) and members (higher points) of voluntary associations, 1998 (source: *Eurobarometer 49.0*, 1998).

members and non-members, and that both groups are drawn from the same population. As in the previous section, the scores for these two indicators have been corrected for the impact of respondents' education, gender, and age. Accordingly, the null-hypotheses have been tested directly through individual parametric and non-parametric tests for each kind of voluntary association. The results of these analyses are summarized in Table 5.3. In contrast to the findings for political discontent and political disengagement (included in Table 5.1), the two types of test produce very different results: the levels of significance of the F-tests indicate far smaller differences between members and non-members than the corresponding levels for the K-S-tests. Apparently, political parties are not the only kind of organizations to show almost identical scores for members and non-members, although the distributions of the scores between these two groups differ considerably.

The results in Table 5.3 unambiguously support the conclusion that the average ideological position of party members is identical to the position of non-members, whereas party members are distinguished from other citizens in terms of their political extremism. At the same time, members of human rights groups and cultural associations clearly differ from

Table 5.3 Left–right ideological placement and ideological extremism, 1998 (F-Test and Kolmogorov–Smirnov Test of Residual Scores[a]; $N= 12,815$)

Groups[b]	Left–right placement[c]				Extremism[d]			
	F-Test		K-S-Test		F-Test		K-S-Test	
	F	Sig.	Z	Sig.	F	Sig.	Z	Sig.
Social	2	0.235	1.7	0.005	6	0.018	2.1	0.000
Religious	36	0.000	3.2	0.000	6	0.014	1.8	0.003
Cultural	17	0.000	3.2	0.000	9	0.003	2.5	0.000
Political parties	1	0.485	2.9	0.000	132	0.000	5.0	0.000
Unions	2	0.189	2.2	0.000	1	0.289	2.0	0.000
Human rights	68	0.000	4.2	0.000	17	0.000	2.4	0.000
Nature, environment	16	0.000	2.9	0.000	5	0.022	2.0	0.001
Youth	0	0.595	1.6	0.012	0	0.792	1.0	0.280
Consumer	6	0.014	2.4	0.000	2	0.167	2.7	0.001
Sports clubs	8	0.005	2.4	0.000	0	0.592	1.6	0.011
Hobby clubs	12	0.001	2.4	0.000	2	0.183	2.0	0.001
Other	0	0.628	0.8	0.599	0	0.746	0.9	0.332

Source: *Eurobarometer 49.0*, 1998.

Notes
a Scores corrected for the level of education, gender, age, and age-square of each respondent.
b For all organizations, members (1) and non-members (2).
c Ten categories self-placement scale ranging from left (1) to right (10).
d Five categories ranging from middle position (1) to extreme left or right (5).

non-members in terms of their left–right positions as well as their extremism. The opposite is true of youth organizations and 'other' groups, for which no significant distinctions are found between members and non-members for any of the indicators or with any of the tests. The pattern is less clear-cut in the case of the other types of association, with insignificant differences for the mean scores accompanied by significant differences in the actual distributions.

In order to consider the direct consequences of social participation for ideological orientations and extremism (logistic) regression analyses have been carried out with right-placement, left-placement, and degree of extremism as the respective dependent variables. The inclusion of education, gender, and age in the models in the very first step controls for possible variation in socio-economic characteristics.[29] Although the overall statistical fit of the models presented in Table 5.4 is rather poor, it is evident that (with just three exceptions) there are no significant differences between members and non-members. Religious groups constitute the first exception, as extreme positions (both on the right and left) are more frequent among non-members than among members. Political parties are the second exception. In this case, we see that non-members are more likely to declare right-wing leanings than members are, and that they are less likely to select left-wing positions. Finally, the results for human rights groups indicate that extreme positions (both to the right and to the left) are less likely among non-members than among members.

Probably the easiest way to summarize the various findings about the biased representation of different ideological positions among members and non-members of voluntary associations is to begin by highlighting the rather uncontroversial conclusion that, generally speaking, membership of different kinds of organizations *per se* scarcely implies any over-representation of particular interests. Only in the case of easily recognizable groups such as political parties and human rights organizations, do members and non-members' ideological positions and levels of involvement in political discussions differ substantially. Membership of religious organizations correlates with right-wing orientations, but this deviation seems hardly relevant: members of these organizations simply do not try to convince other people of their political opinions. Hence, it does not appear that the biased representation of specific interests as captured through left–right self-placement is an undesirable or harmful by-product of membership of voluntary associations. Except in the rather obvious case of organizations explicitly established for that purpose, voluntary associations do not function as alternative settings for political debate.

In conclusion

Morris Fiorina (1999: 415–416) is certainly right when he states that 'contrary to the suggestions of pundits and philosophers, there is nothing

Table 5.4 Predictors of right and left ideological placement, and ideological extremism, 1998 (logistic regression; N = 12,815)

Predictor	Right placement[a]			Left placement[b]			Extremism[c]		
	B	Pred. B	Sig.	B	Pred. B	Sig.	B	Pred. B	Sig.
Education[d]	0.045	1.046	0.000	0.019	1.020	0.020	0.010	1.010	0.173
Gender	0.167	1.182	0.002	-0.065	0.937	0.149	0.131	1.140	0.001
Age	-0.024	0.977	0.003	-0.001	0.999	0.859	-0.015	0.986	0.012
Age squared	0.000	1.000	0.000	0.000	1.000	0.296	0.000	1.000	0.003
Social[e]	0.067	1.069	0.432	-0.057	0.944	0.427	0.076	1.079	0.219
Religious	0.223	1.250	0.004	0.459	1.583	0.000	-0.189	0.828	0.001
Cultural	-0.148	0.863	0.126	-0.284	0.753	0.000	0.143	1.154	0.031
Political parties	0.635	1.886	0.000	-0.461	0.631	0.000	0.714	2.042	0.000
Unions	-0.141	0.868	0.043	0.052	1.053	0.364	-0.108	0.898	0.029
Human rights	-0.798	0.450	0.000	-0.617	0.540	0.000	0.206	1.229	0.042
Nature, environment	-0.116	0.890	0.225	-0.191	0.826	0.011	0.091	1.095	0.167
Youth	-0.027	0.974	0.834	0.074	1.077	0.472	-0.070	0.932	0.429
Consumer	0.011	1.011	0.935	-0.119	0.888	0.254	0.091	1.095	0.320
Sports clubs	0.136	1.146	0.031	0.104	1.109	0.052	-0.009	0.991	0.847
Hobby clubs	0.156	1.169	0.057	0.205	1.228	0.005	-0.064	0.938	0.295
Other	-0.037	0.963	0.732	0.101	1.106	0.280	-0.090	0.914	0.250
Constant	-2.085	0.124	0.000	1.169	3.217	0.000	-0.577	0.562	0.000
Nagelkerke's R^2	0.028			0.021			0.018		

Source: Eurobarmeter 49.0, 1998.

Notes

a Categories dichotomized in right (8–10) and non-right placement (1–7).
b Categories dichotomized in left (1–3) and non-left (4–10).
c Categories dichotomized in extreme (3–5) and non-extreme difference (1–2).
d Level of education measured by age when finishing education ('still studying' recoded in actual age).
e For all organizations, members (1) and non-members (2).

wrong with those who do not participate, rather, there is something unusual about those who do'. However, his statement refers to participation itself, and not to the desirable objective of having an 'attentive public' characterized by some degree of political interest. Political discontent in combination with political disengagement (as reflected both in subjective interest and political saliency) suggests the existence of negative political feelings among citizens. In turn, these feelings might be strengthened if specific interests were over-represented and dominated political discussions.

In the analyses displayed here, we started by presuming that membership of all kinds of voluntary association correlates with both relatively high levels of political satisfaction and political engagement. This Tocquevillean interpretation is convincingly supported by the empirical findings in the case of political disengagement as measured through the indicator for subjective political interest. However, the picture changes when we consider political saliency: members of religious groups in particular attach relatively less importance to politics than non-members do. These results confirm the need to distinguish conceptually between political discontent on the one hand, and the two indicators for political disengagement on the other. We have also considered the question of ideological differences between members and non-members of voluntary associations. In this respect, the rather trivial conclusion arrived at is that political parties and human rights groups opt for extreme positions in terms of left–right orientations, which they use in attempts to convince other people of their ideas. As for other voluntary associations, the average ideological positions of members and non-members are either virtually indistinguishable or irrelevant due to the lack of political debate. The general conclusion, therefore, is that membership of different kinds of voluntary associations has far fewer political implications than is generally presumed in many popular interpretations. The positive side-effect of this situation is that specific interests are not strongly over-represented in consequence of differences in social participation among active and less active sectors of the population. Putnam's (2000: 351; emphasis in the original) question, '*Is social capital at war with liberty and tolerance?*', would appear to attach too much significance to the consequences and relevance of membership of voluntary associations for political orientations. Once again, Eliasoph's (1998) observations should be recalled: face-to-face contacts in clubs and organizations promote the avoidance of political topics and the 'evaporation of politics' from public life.

Various limitations should be borne in mind when considering these conclusions. First, the empirical data used here refer exclusively to (West) European democracies, and it is quite possible that today Tocquevillean interpretations apply primarily to American society, just as they did in the 1830s.[30] The fact that we did not find strong effects of social participation in any type of voluntary association might reflect the existence of substantively different political cultures on either side of the Atlantic. Second, even though it is clear that profoundly negative political feelings are not widespread among citizens of European democracies, the indicators used here (level of satisfaction with democracy as an indicator of political discontent, and levels of political interest and political saliency as indicators of political disengagement) may be too far removed from concepts such as disloyalty and alienation to reveal the existence of potentially more dangerous attitudes for a democracy, such as alienation or frustration. And if no threats are found to begin with, no threats will be found in the subsequent analyses. However, it should be emphasized that the conclusions presented here are not based on the results obtained for a single indicator, but rather from all the different data contained in the distinct elements of Figure 5.1, and in Figures 5.2 and 5.3. When all this has been taken into account, it is clear that membership of voluntary associations is associated with clear differences in political orientations which, on closer inspection, do not appear to threaten either the democratic decision-making processes or the balanced representation of specific interests. Membership of religious organizations, political parties, or human rights groups imply different positions, the most remarkable finding being the evident irrelevance of politics for, and right-wing preferences of, members of religious organizations.

Beem (1999) judged faith in the benevolent consequences of civil society as 'romantic and unpersuasive'. In his view (1999: 180–181), 'the civil society movement is largely convinced that more civil society means more trust, more solidarity, and ultimately moral and civic unity'. However, if civil society is assumed to encompass lower levels of both political discontent and political disengagement, this statement is corroborated by the empirical analyses presented here, with the unequivocal exception of membership of religious organizations. At the same time, the expected 'dark side' of civil society or social capital hardly surfaces in our findings. Accordingly, the evident inequalities in social participation apparently do not have the expected negative consequences in terms of political representation. The other side of the coin is, of course, that social participation only has a modest positive impact on political attitudes. These conclusions might be unspectacular or disappointing in the eyes of a sceptical observer, but they are certainly neither romantic nor unpersuasive.

Notes

1 This definition is taken from the *Oxford English Dictionary* (2nd Edition, 1999) which defines 'disaffected' as 'Evilly affected; estranged in affection or allegiance, unfriendly, hostile; almost always *spec*. Unfriendly to the government or to constituted authority, disloyal'.
2 In one of the very first publications on the subject, Coleman (1990: 302) defined the common features of social capital by their functions: 'They all

consist of some aspect of social structure, and they facilitate certain actions of individuals who are within the structure'. See Haug (1997) or Schuller *et al.* (2000) for excellent reviews of the different definitions and applications of the concept 'social capital', and Jackman and Miller (1998) or Edwards and Foley (2001) for critical overviews of the use of the concept in political science. Early critiques of Putnam's work are presented by Levi (1993 and 1996).

3 The terms 'associations', 'organizations', 'clubs', and 'groups' will be used synonymously to refer to voluntary associations of the type listed below.

4 See Keane (1998: 114–156) for an extensive overview of the historical roots of the concept 'uncivil society'.

5 To quote Putnam (2000: 351; emphasis in the original) once again, the 'classic liberal objection to community ties' can be neatly summarized with the question, *'Is social capital at war with liberty and tolerance?'*

6 In probably one of the most remarkable and terrible examples of the observation that cultivated behaviour has no implications for the moral quality of the decisions or actions taken, Keane (1998: 128) draws attention to the very civilized German officers and executives meeting in Spring 1942, sipping champagne and smoking cigars while deciding how to proceed with the Final Solution.

7 For instance, Warren (1999b: 26; emphasis in the original) has attempted to clarify this point: 'Good governance, viewed through civil society, already suggests the liberal democratic good of *collective self-governance*'.

8 The point is summarized neatly by Beem (1999: 14): 'when civil society is operating as it should, it stands in healthy opposition to the state'.

9 The mechanisms by which politics are avoided in face-to-face groups have been very convincingly explored in Eliasoph (1998). In order to avoid political arguments, members of clubs and groups will restrain from starting political discussions, which, in turn, encourages the 'evaporation of politics'. Warren (1993: 227) expects similar consequences. However, he stresses the self-selection and homogeneity of groups when accounting for the absence of political debates, as well as the fact that for political groups 'goals are action-oriented'.

10 Schattschneider's (1960: 40) famous dictum ('...it is the weak, not the strong, who appeal to public authority for relief. It is the weak who want to socialize conflict, i.e. to involve more and more people in the conflict until the balance of forces is changed') is hard to ignore in this context. See Couto and Guthrie (1999: 59–69) for a concise discussion of participation in civic organizations.

11 See Kaase and Newton (1995) for an extensive overview of this literature and an assessment of the main interpretations.

12 For an early application of this interpretation in empirical research, see the distinction between 'quiescent' and 'disenchanted' citizens in studies on the nature and persistence of political saliency as discussed by Nie and Andersen (1974: 575–578); see also van Deth (1990: 298–301). A discussion and empirical application of the concept of political saliency is provided by van Deth (2000).

13 The text of this question comes from *Eurobarometer 49.0*, 1998.

14 *Eurobarometer 49.0* contains a special section on political interest designed by the author. The data were compiled for the project 'Political Interest, Involvement and Affection', funded by the German National Science Foundation DFG (Grant 630/2-1), whose generous support is gratefully acknowledged here. I would also like to thank Martin Elff and Sonja Zmerli for their help in preparing the data used here.

15 Since this chapter does not seek to make generalizations or estimates about Europe as a whole, the analyses are unweighted.

16 In these calculations, the responses 'very satisfied' (1) and 'fairly satisfied' (2) of the question on satisfaction with democracy have been combined in order to

get round the problem posed by the low numbers of cases. Similarly, the two highest categories for subjective political interest (1 and 2) have been combined, as have the highest scores (1 to 5) on the saliency index.

17 About 41 per cent of respondents do not belong to any kind of association, and only 16 per cent identify themselves as members of more than two different kinds of organizations. The average number of different kinds of memberships is 1.20 ($N = 15{,}248$).

18 On the basis of empirical findings for the relationships between membership of different associations and a variety of political orientations in Belgium, Hooghe (1999: 17) concludes that, in general, all kinds of associations, in one way or another are correlated with the attitudinal scales. This result is clearly in line with the outcomes summarized in Figure 5.1a.

19 This finding reflects the more general formulation presented by La Due Lake and Huckfeldt (1998: 581): 'the production of politically relevant social capital is a function of the political expertise within an individual's network of relations, the frequency of political interaction within the network, and the size or extensiveness of the network'.

20 The atypical position of religious organizations is emphasized in many studies, see for instance Rosenblum (1998: 73–111); Putnam (2000: 65–79); Verba *et al.* (1995), or Greeley (2001).

21 The Euclidean distances computed are presented in brackets in the ordering of the various associations listed below.

22 In order to deal with the well-known curvilinear relationship between age and political involvement, the square of the exact age of the respondents has been added as a fourth controlling variable (alongside education, gender, and age) in all the computations presented here.

23 Obviously, this observation was already evident from Figure 5.1a.

24 Notice that the significant difference identified in the political saliency of members and non-members of religious groups is that, as can be seen in Figure 5.1b, non-members attach more importance to politics than members do.

25 One noteworthy finding concerns the clearly insignificant impact of gender on levels of satisfaction with democracy. Apparently, this is one of the few instances where men and women do not show evident differences in terms of their political orientations.

26 Similarly, Stolle (1998: 521) convincingly showed that trust is not (only) a consequence of social participation, but that 'people who join associations are significantly more trusting than people who do not join'. Unfortunately, the longitudinal data required to test this kind of interpretation are not available.

27 This result is clearly in line with Eliasoph's (1998) observation that members of voluntary associations generally tend to avoid political debates.

28 In other words, respondents choosing '5' or '6' on the left–right dimension score '1' on the extremism scale, those selecting '4' or '7' obtain '2', and so on until '1' and '10' on the left–right scale get the highest code '5' on the extremism scale.

29 In order to avoid the fallacy of not distinguishing between left- and right-wing groups and to obtain dichotomized scores, the left–right self-placement is split into two variables: one for left placement (scores '1' to '3' versus '4' to '10'), and one for right placement ('8' to '10' versus '1' to '7').

30 On the United States see, for instance, the discussions about political trust by King (2000) or Rosenblum (1998), and Putnam (2000: 65–79) for the specific role of religious groups. As Putnam (2000: 65) remarks, 'churches and other religious organizations have a unique importance in American civil society'. Fukuyama (1999: 267) directly relates the spread of American civil society to 'religion, and in particular sectarian Protestantism'.

6 Understanding the relationship between social capital and political disaffection in the new post-communist democracies

Geoffrey Evans and Natalia Letki

Among the many important questions raised in the Introduction to this book figure two key issues. First, how is political disaffection related to the performance of democracies? And second, what is the relationship between political disaffection and various aspects of social capital? In this chapter we address both of these questions in a comparative analysis of the post-communist democracies of East Central Europe (ECE).

In the West, there is an extensive body of comparative research tracing the decline in public confidence in political institutions and government practices (Norris 1999a; Pharr and Putnam 2000). In East-Central Europe, however, this issue has made less of an impact on the research agenda. Here, levels of satisfaction with political institutions and their performance are not assumed to have followed any linear downward path. A number of studies, of course, examine the patterns and sources of satisfaction and dissatisfaction with democratic processes in Eastern Europe. Partly as a result of measurement issues, academic opinion as to whether public opinion towards the new democratic systems is positive is divided (Klingemann 1999; Mishler and Rose 1996 and 1999; and Tóka 1995). Debates over the explanation for levels of approval have focused on the relative impact of economic and political factors on support for democracy (Evans and Whitefield 1995; Przeworski *et al.* 1996) or on theories of modernization and cultural legacies which have tried to establish and account for longer-term tendencies (Lipset 1959, 1994). Political and economic factors have both been shown to be significant predictors of satisfaction with democracy, while debates about modernization and culture have, by their very nature, proved harder to test in any precise way (Whitefield and Evans 1999).[1] In this chapter, however, we examine one particularly influential approach to understanding the emergence and maintenance of effective democratic systems and, by extension, the nature and level of popular support for these systems: social capital theory. More precisely, we examine the putative role of social capital in providing a basis for satisfaction with democracy in the region and thus providing a bulwark against political disaffection.

As is well known, the concept of social capital has recently become one of the most popular and enthusiastically studied phenomena in the social sciences. Although many theorists have dealt with this phenomenon (see, for example, Coleman 1990 or Newton 1997), the most influential approach is undoubtedly that developed by Robert Putnam (1993: 173–176; and 2000). Putnam maintains that the crucial prerequisites for the appearance and growth of social capital are 'norms of generalized reciprocity' and trust, which are learned through participation, especially in various kinds of organizations.[2] In *Making Democracy Work* (1993), he also demonstrated a strong correlation between the functioning of government and levels of civic participation in a given community.[3] The assumption that there is a connection between participation and the quality of government is, of course, hardly new; it was a central theme in de Tocqueville's *Democracy in America*, and has been an important premise of research on civic participation from the 1960s onwards. However, *Making Democracy Work* was the first exhaustive, systematic empirical analysis of the relationship between these two phenomena. Since publication of Putnam's seminal work, the explanatory potential of social capital, defined as 'features of social organization such as networks, norms and social trust that facilitate coordination and cooperation for mutual benefit' (Putnam 1995a: 67), has provided a powerful attraction for political scientists (see Jackman and Miller 1996a, 1996b, 1998, and Letki and Evans 2005, however, for a dissenting view). Consequently, the last few years have brought numerous empirical studies focusing on the role social trust plays in modern democracy (see, for example, Putnam 1995a, 1995b, 2000; Hall 1999; Foley and Edwards 1996; Paxton 1999; van Deth *et al.* 1999). Research in Italy, the United States, Great Britain, and other Western European countries seems to justify the enthusiasm of those who point to social trust as constituting the (still) 'missing link' of the chain between civic participation and institutional success.

A key assumption in this approach is that effective political institutions and interest representation are likely to produce positive perceptions of the workings of democracy among the electorate. In his study of Italy, for example, Putnam (1993: 78) concludes that 'in the regions that are relatively successful by our "objective" measures, people from all walks of life are relatively satisfied, while in the low-performance regions most people are dissatisfied'. From this perspective, the main factor underlying popular satisfaction with democracy is the performance of new political institutions and electors' ability to make themselves heard through the party and electoral systems; the sources of effective government are supposedly themselves partly a result of stocks of social capital. In short, social trust leads to *better political performance*, and thus provides a basis for satisfaction with democracy (Putnam 1993, 2000).

Despite evident differences in recent historical experiences and the current social situation, a similar pattern of association between democracy and communal life has been assumed to exist in ECE (see, for example, Rose 1998, 1999; Rose *et al.* 1997; Inglehart 1999b). Inglehart (1999b: 103, emphasis added), for instance, concludes that 'the World Values Survey data reveal a strong positive correlation between interpersonal trust and the functioning of democratic institutions *throughout the world*'. Our first aim in this chapter, therefore, is to test empirically the applicability of 'social capital theory' to the countries of ECE using far more detailed measures of experiences and perceptions than have hitherto been employed.[4]

We will also develop an argument concerning the relations between social trust and political disaffection that reverses the usual direction of causation between the two phenomena. In line with Jackman and Miller (1998), we argue that social trust should itself be endogenized (Letki and Evans 2005). Thus, according to earlier theories of social capital (the best example is probably James Coleman's [1990] *Foundations of Social Theory*), trust would be a result of an institutional setting, not its source. Trust is more important as a resource in the absence of formal rules and accountable rule-makers, as was the situation under communist rule, than in highly predictable and regulated liberal democratic systems. Therefore, trust can plausibly be understood as resulting from the process of individuals' adaptation to the institutional setting rather than determining their capacity to adapt or their strategies of adjustment. The idea that social trust is a product rather than a cause of democracy has also been considered by Muller and Seligson (1994). Their study of cross-national patterns across 27 societies found that established democracies such as Belgium, France, and Italy showed significantly lower levels of trust than Guatemala or Panama (1994: 646).[5] They concluded that social trust is an outcome not a determinant of the effectiveness of a political system. In the rest of this chapter we present our evidence and argument that ECE shows patterns of social trust that are consistent with the idea that trust is endogenous rather than exogenous in its relation to political disaffection; that trust results from political disaffection rather than vice versa.

The first part of the analysis assesses the empirical coherence of attitudinal and behavioural measures of social capital in post-communist countries by examining the connections between an index measuring social trust (including general trust, norms of reciprocity, and beliefs about cooperativeness) and different types of non-political participation: we take associational membership, membership of trade unions, and religious communities to indicate 'civic engagement'. We then examine the relationships between these indicators and an index of political disaffection (including evaluations of the implementation of democracy, the responsiveness of political representatives, and perceptions of political efficacy). The relations between social trust, civic engagement, and political disaffection are analysed at both the aggregate and individual levels. At the individual level we also control for the impact of other predictors of political disaffection, such as socio-economic status. In the Conclusions we consider whether social capital, thought by many to be the 'engine' of modern Western democracy, helps to explain reactions to democratization and the consolidation of democracy in post-communist countries.

Measuring stocks of social capital

Although social capital has become a popular and extensively studied phenomenon, it is still rather vaguely defined. The most popular definition (Putnam 1993, 1995a, 1995b, 2000; Coleman 1990) mixes two types of components: attitudes (trust, faith in cooperation, or reciprocity) and behaviour (membership of voluntary associations or other forms of participation). According to Putnam (1995a: 73), 'social trust and civic engagement are strongly correlated; the greater the density of associational membership in a society, the more trusting its citizens. Trust and engagement are two facets of the same underlying factor – social capital'. Accordingly, stocks of social capital are often 'measured' through indicators such as membership of associations, charitable behaviour, and political engagement (Putnam 1993, 1995a, 1995b, 2000; Hall 1999). Although a strong correlation between trust and participation is assumed in post-communist countries (see, for example, Rose 1998, 1999; Rose *et al.* 1997; Inglehart 1999b), it is not in fact clear that such a relation actually exists. Our first task in this chapter, therefore, is to present our measures of the attitudinal and behavioural components of social capital and to discover whether these are indeed empirically two facets of the same phenomenon.

Social trust

Social trust is defined here as 'a set of institutionalised expectations that other social actors will reciprocate co-operative overtures' (Boix and Posner 1998: 686). We selected five items as indicators of individuals' beliefs about trust that (because they imply trust and faith in cooperation, and reflect a general vision of the norms and rules of social interactions) collectively make up a relatively broad and comprehensive measure of social trust:

(B3a)   'It is human nature to cooperate with other people';
(B3b)   'Most people can be trusted';
(B3c)   'If someone is in serious trouble, no one else cares about it';
(B3d)   'If you are not always on your guard other people will take advantage of you'; and
(B3e)   'A person cooperates with other people only when he or she sees it is in his or her own interest to do so'.

All of these items have an 'agree–disagree' format with 5-point response scales. For B3a and B3b 'strongly disagree' is 1 and 'strongly agree' 5, while for B3c, B3d, and B3e the coding is reversed. 'Don't know' responses have been recoded to the mid-point of the scale. Factor analysis detected two main dimensions (B3a and B3b form one positively worded dimension, and the remaining three a second, negatively worded dimension), and the reliability test for the five items indicated that Cronbach's alpha is a rather low 0.54. Nevertheless, to balance the scale and avoid acquiescence bias, all five items were used to construct an index of social trust (see Heath, Evans, and Martin 1994, and Evans and Heath 1995 for discussion of this approach to scale construction). Figure 6.1 displays the distribution of responses to each of the five statements.

Respondents almost unanimously agree with the statement about human nature being cooperative. Moreover, while it might appear 'alarming' that only some 50 per cent of respondents show trust in other people, this resembles the reported results for the most 'civic' nations – Great Britain and the United States (Hall 1999; Putnam 1995a; Inglehart 1999b). In the case of the remaining three items, however, respondents giving 'negative' answers (i.e. 'strongly agree' and 'agree') outnumber those expressing trust and faith in cooperation. Although 42 per cent of respondents would expect help and support from other people (B3c), almost 80 per cent are afraid that others may take advantage of them, and over 70 per cent do not believe in unselfish cooperation. In general, these results cannot be considered to be either unambiguously 'negative' or

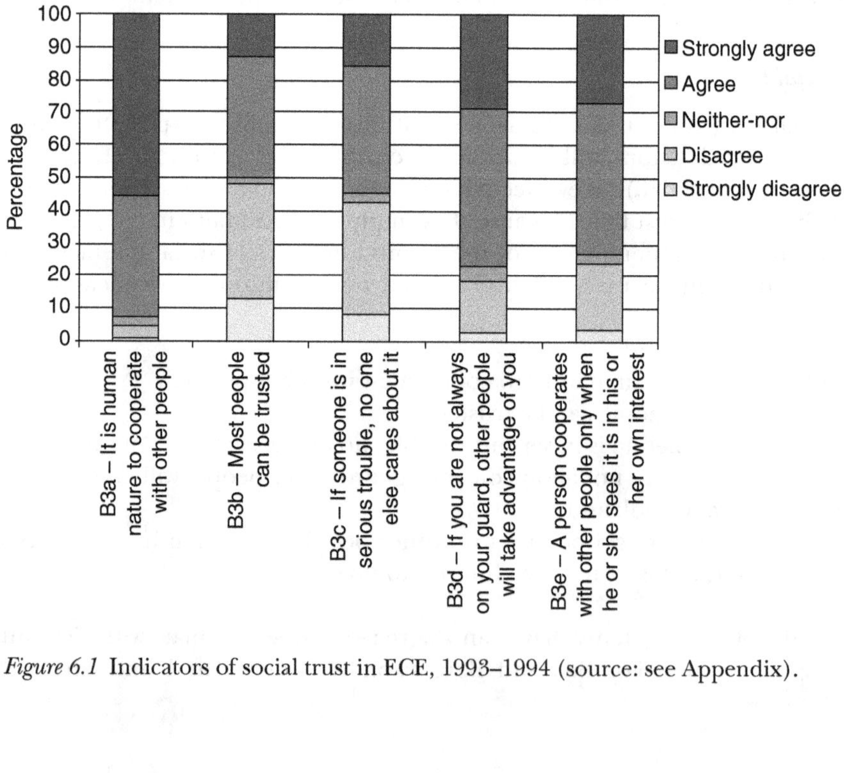

Figure 6.1 Indicators of social trust in ECE, 1993–1994 (source: see Appendix).

'positive' in tone. They may well reflect the hardships of transformation as well as a communist legacy of distrust. And their most important feature is that they provide us with a range of responses across items that differ in terms of their general levels of agreement and disagreement, and thus allow the construction of a normally distributed multiple-indicator measure of the concept of social trust (see Martin *et al.* 1993).

Figure 6.2 displays the average scores on the social trust index for each country. The index score is the average of scores on all five items. As the chart shows, 'stocks' of social trust differ significantly between countries. Three clusters of countries can be identified. Hungary and the Czech and Slovak Republics have average scores in social trust, ranging from 2.76 to 2.78; Bulgaria, Lithuania, and Poland score between 2.89 and 2.91; and a third, looser cluster of Ukraine, Russia, Belarus, and Estonia score between 3.07 and 3.18. While the first cluster seems intuitively predictable based on the various countries' geographical location and economic characteristics, the second cluster would appear much more unexpected given the presence of Poland. Even more 'counterintuitive' is the fact that Ukraine, Russia, and Belarus boast higher levels of average social trust than countries that are further advanced in the transition towards market democracy. It is also interesting that Romania, despite showing high levels of support for democracy and the free market at the time of the survey (Evans and Whitefield 1995), has by far the lowest score on the index of social trust. In general, with the exception of Romania and Estonia, the countries whose institutions perform better systematically register lower levels of social trust.[6]

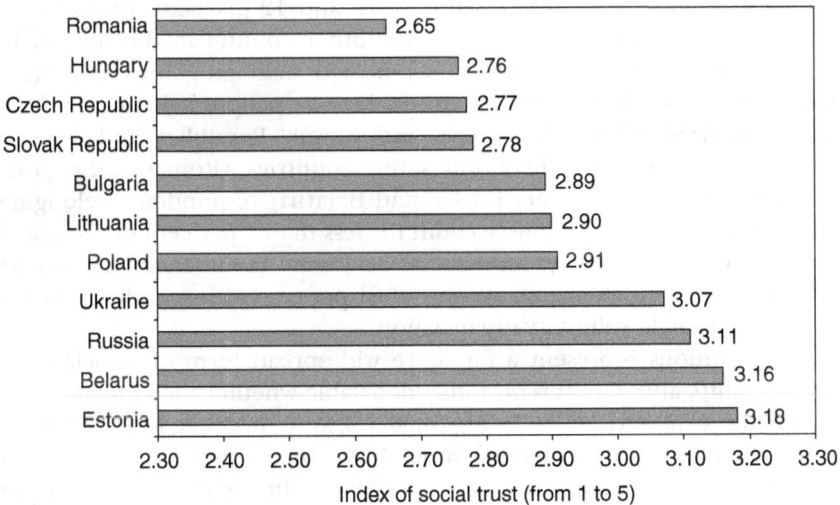

Figure 6.2 Social trust in ECE, 1993–1994 (source: see Appendix).

As noted above, social trust is believed to be 'closely related to . . . civic engagement' (Putnam 1995b: 665), that is, to acts of participation focused not on politics, but on local community organizations. To examine this assumption we first present our measures of the main types of civic association membership in ECE and then see how this relates to social trust.

The behavioural dimension of social capital: civic associations, trade unions, and religious community membership

One of the 'definitional' elements of social capital is membership of voluntary organizations (Putnam 1993, 1995a, 1995b, 2000; Hall 1999). We asked our respondents about membership of a wide range of voluntary organizations. These included business and professional associations, farmers' organizations, church groups, local and community groups, sports or social clubs, armed forces associations, ethnic organizations, and workplace committees. Sports or social clubs were the most popular type of organization, but even in this case only 6 per cent of respondents reported belonging to one. The least popular categories of organization are ethnic and armed forces associations, to which only 1 per cent of the respondents belong. The levels of membership of particular types of associations are similar across the countries of ECE, albeit with a few exceptions: farmer associations are extremely popular in Romania, where 9 per cent of respondents report belonging to one. Church groups attract very few members in Belarus, Russia, and Bulgaria (1 per cent or under), but are more than nine times more popular in Hungary. The popularity of local/community groups in the Czech and Slovak Republics is above average (7 and 5 per cent, respectively). Sports groups are also significantly more popular in both countries (16 and 12 per cent, respectively) and Estonia (10 per cent) than in any other country in the region. In Poland, absolutely no respondents reported belonging to a workplace committee. The three countries in which most people belong to at least one organization are the Czech and Slovak Republics and Estonia (around 30 per cent). In a full seven countries (Romania, Bulgaria, Lithuania, Poland, Ukraine, Russia, and Belarus) respondents belonging to three or more associations account for less than 1 per cent of the population. Overall, therefore, levels of associational membership are rather low. Figure 6.3 shows that an average of 81 per cent of respondents do not belong to a single voluntary organization.

Trade unions represent a far more widespread form of associational membership, although it is obviously debatable whether such membership is actually voluntary in ECE. Figure 6.3 also shows that levels of trade union membership are indeed quite high: on average 29 per cent of respondents were union members (in Belarus this figure reached 64 per cent).[7] Although in many cases trade unions are the direct heirs of communism in terms of their organizational structure, human capital,

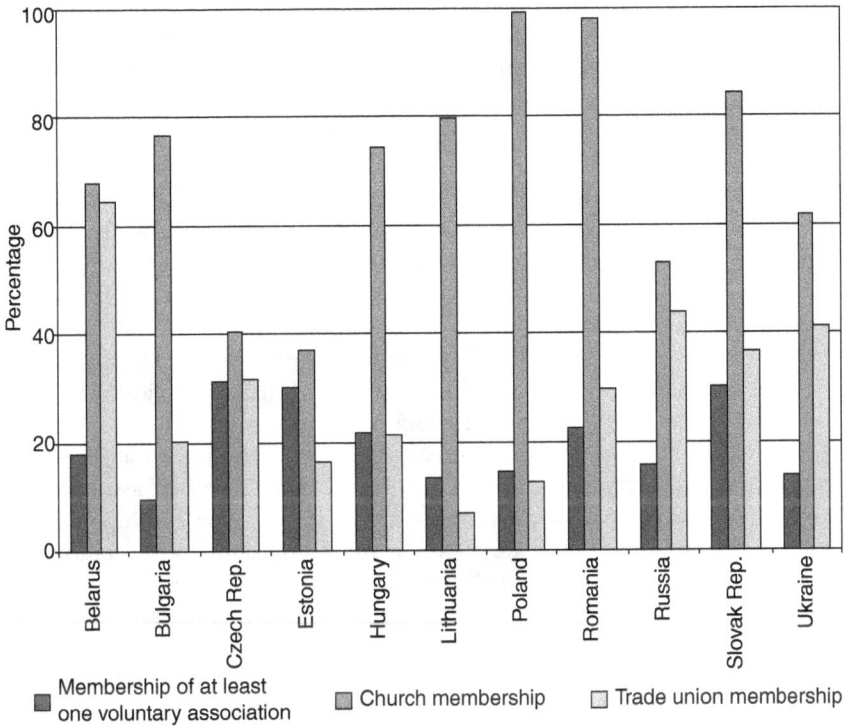

Figure 6.3 Behavioural dimensions of social capital: membership in voluntary associations, church groups, and trade unions in ECE, 1993–1994 (source: see Appendix).

and material resources, they still constitute the most popular type of 'association'.[8]

The final indicator of the behavioural dimension of social capital we use here is church membership, measured through self-declared religiosity. According to Putnam (1993: 107), 'organized religion, at least in Catholic Italy, is an alternative to the civic community, not a part of it', while in his most recent work (2000: 67) he concludes that 'religiosity rivals education as a powerful correlate of most forms of civic engagement ... [The] studies cannot show conclusively that churchgoing itself "produces" social connectivity – probably the causal arrow between the two points in both directions – but it is clear that religious people are unusually active social capitalists'. Similarly, in mainstream 'civic culture' research, religiosity, and church service attendance are recognized as constituting significant, positive, civic forms of behaviour (see, for example, Brady *et al.* 1995).

As can be seen from Figure 6.3, we find striking national differences in church membership: in Poland and Romania just 2 per cent of respondents declare themselves to be atheists, while in Estonia and Czech Republic this figure rises to some 60 per cent (63 and 60 per cent, respectively). In this respect, the major disparity between the two parts of the former Czechoslovakia is particularly interesting: in the Slovak Republic only 16 per cent of respondents are non-believers, 44 percentage points less than in the Czech Republic. This probably reflects historical opposition to the Catholic Church in Bohemia and Moravia dating back to Jan Huss's rebellion and which intensified during subsequent periods of conflict with the country's Catholic Hapsburg rulers. In the other countries, atheists make up between 20 and 38 per cent of the population.[9]

The social capital thesis implies that in countries with higher levels of trust we should also find more citizens engaged in the activities of voluntary associations, trade unions, or religious communities. However, Figure 6.3 indicates that there is no positive correlation between these three elements of 'civic community': countries with higher levels of associational membership are more secular, while trade union membership is unrelated to the other two indicators. Nor is there any significant relationship between associational membership and social trust ($r = -0.228$). Estonia, and the Slovak and Czech Republics display very different levels of trust, but very similar (and relatively high) figures for membership of voluntary associations. Belarus, Russia, and the Ukraine have considerably higher levels of social trust than Lithuania and Poland, but similar proportions of association members. Again, we also find that more unionized societies are not more trusting ($r = 0.346$, but statistically insignificant): despite relatively high union membership, Romania, has the lowest level of social trust in the region, while Lithuania, Poland, Bulgaria, and Estonia have much higher 'stocks' of trust accompanied by very low levels of unionization.[10]

Finally, Figure 6.4 shows the proportion of respondents in a country who reported belonging to a church by levels of social trust. It seems that a pattern is visible in this respect (although it is weakened by the low position of the Czech Republic on the dimension of religiosity for the reasons suggested above). This pattern, however, is the opposite to the one we would expect on the basis of the arguments identifying church membership as a powerful generator of social trust: in ECE the more religious societies appear to be, if anything, less trusting ($r = -0.541$, significant at $p < 0.1$).

Our findings, therefore, generally challenge Putnam's (1993: 171) claim that 'trust lubricates cooperation. The greater the level of social trust within a community, the greater the likelihood of cooperation. And cooperation itself breeds trust'. In post-communist Europe, social trust is not connected to the civic character of a country (measured through associational membership) or to labour organization (measured through

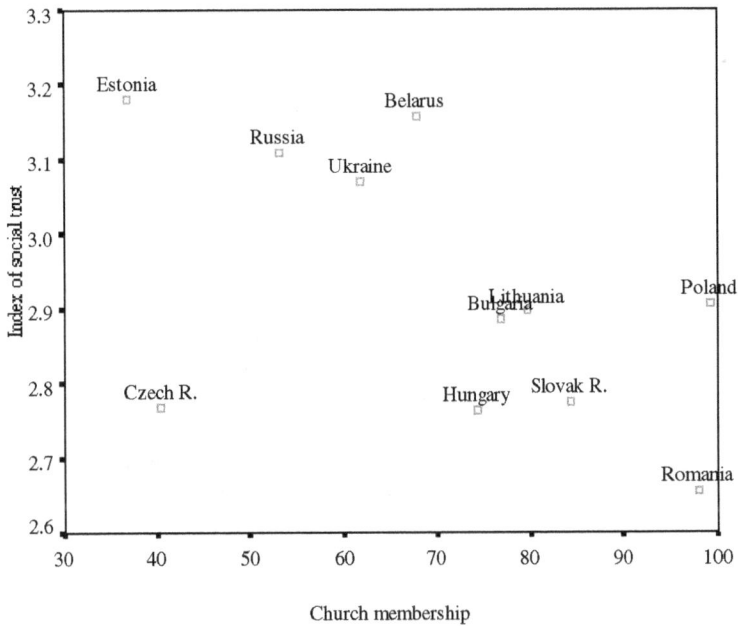

Figure 6.4 Social trust and church membership in ECE, 1993–1994 (source: see Appendix).

unionization); and it is negatively associated with church membership (measured through levels of religiosity). Hence our evidence does not support the most popular definition of social capital, which emphasizes the strong positive correlation between levels of social trust and levels of civic participation.

Social trust and civic participation: individual level relationship

So far, we have focused on the association between civic engagement and social trust at the national or aggregate level. However, it is also important to see if differences in individuals' level of social trust can be explained by participation. This analysis includes the three types of participatory activities described above, as well as six variables capturing respondents' socio-economic status: gender, age, education level, job situation, whether the respondent has children or not, and income (coefficients not shown here).

Table 6.1 shows the *b* coefficients for the participatory activities obtained by applying linear regression models to the data from each country. These models suggest that there is almost no relationship between participation and social trust: associational membership is insignificant in all 11 countries; trade union membership is significant in three (Czech Republic, Russia, and Ukraine); and church membership in only two (Belarus and Hungary). Interestingly, the individual level relationship between trust and church membership mirrors the aggregate-level findings: it is negative, that is to say, members of religious communities are less trusting than atheists. Again, these findings contradict claims concerning the positive role of civic participation in generating social trust (Brehm and Rahn 1997; Putnam 1993, 1995b, 2000; Inglehart 1997b): in ECE the individual-level link between attitudinal and behavioural aspects of social capital is in most cases non-existent, and in some countries it is negative.

The highest R^2s (in Hungary and Poland) are below 0.09, and most of the explanatory power of the models is contributed by background characteristics rather than civil or political involvement. In most countries, education is the most important and significant predictor (the exception is Belarus); it is sometimes accompanied by income (positively correlated with trust) or job status (the unemployed are less trusting). In general, in ECE socio-economic status is a much better predictor of trust level than civic involvement is.

Social capital and political disaffection

Now let us consider the main question in our study: the relationship between social capital and political disaffection. Social capital is believed to be important for the growth and success of Western democracies (Putnam 1993; Inglehart 1990; Fukuyama 1995). But does it play the same role in protecting the young post-communist democracies from corrosive levels of political disaffection? If so, its presence is likely to be important for the future of countries undergoing transformation from non-democratic regimes to democracy. As Jackman and Miller (1996a: 633) point out, 'it is often asserted that democratization will continue to face severe handicaps in the southern European cone, much of Latin America, and most strikingly in Eastern Europe and Russia, given the strong legacy of authoritarianism in the recent past'. Moreover, according to many accounts, social capital has a significant impact on the functioning of the political and economic systems, and its level is therefore likely to be particularly important for the future of countries undergoing the 'dual transition' from non-democratic, non-market regimes to market democracy in ECE.

This section first examines respondents' opinions about the functioning of the new democratic political systems of Eastern Europe.[11] We operationalize political disaffection as a set of beliefs comprising lack of trust in politicians, lack of confidence in political institutions, and lack of a sense of internal and external efficacy (Pharr and Putnam 2000). Seven items were chosen to measure respondents' opinions about these aspects

Table 6.1 Social trust regressed onto civic participation and background indicators in ECE, 1993–1994[a]

Countries	Associational membership		Trade union membership		Church membership		Total R²	% of total R² explained by presented variables
	b	s.e.	b	s.e.	b	s.e.		
Belarus	-0.042	(0.052)	0.041	(0.043)	-0.001**	(0.017)	0.035	14.3
Bulgaria	-0.041	(0.056)	-0.022	(0.045)	0.000	(0.012)	0.023	4.3
Czech Republic	0.011	(0.035)	0.082***	(0.035)	0.050*	(0.014)	0.039	25.6
Estonia	0.055	(0.036)	0.012	(0.044)	-0.018	(0.018)	0.024	8.3
Hungary	0.023	(0.049)	0.080	(0.048)	0.031***	(0.014)	0.092	17.4
Lithuania	0.039	(0.047)	0.049	(0.062)	0.008	(0.014)	0.022	9.1
Poland	0.073	(0.052)	0.042	(0.056)	0.023	(0.014)	0.086	16.3
Romania	0.012	(0.042)	0.032	(0.041)	0.002	(0.013)	0.044	4.5
Russia	0.002	(0.048)	0.128*	(0.035)	0.038**	(0.014)	0.034	23.5
Slovak Republic	-0.033	(0.037)	0.024	(0.038)	0.002	(0.010)	0.033	12.1
Ukraine	0.010	(0.040)	0.099*	(0.031)	0.015	(0.011)	0.020	30

Source: See Appendix.

Note

a Figures are b coefficients from OLS, with standard errors (s.e.) in parenthesis. Levels of significance are ***$p \leq 0.001$; **$p \leq 0.01$; and *$p \leq 0.05$.

of the working of the political system in their country.[12] These items refer to the evaluation of the practice of democracy (A1b), confidence in the government (B1e, F1g), and respondents' sense of political efficacy (B1h, F1b, F1e, and F1i):[13]

(A1b) 'How would you evaluate the actual practice of democracy here in [country] so far?';

(B1e) 'The government acts for the benefit of the majority of the society';

(B1h) 'Everyone has an influence on the election of the government';

(F1b) 'People like me have no say in what the government does';

(F1e) 'Elected officials don't care much what people like me think';

(F1g) 'On the whole, what governments do in this country reflects the wishes of ordinary people'; and

(F1i) 'There is no point in voting because the government can't make any difference'.

Although factor analysis detected two dimensions (F1b and F1e form a separate factor reflecting the different direction of the wording of the questioning in both cases, rather than any difference in substantive focus), Cronbach's alpha for the seven items is an acceptable 0.61. All seven items are positively correlated with each other and strongly correlated with the composite scale. Removing any item from the scale would reduce the reliability of the scale as measured by Cronbach's alpha. Again, as in the case of the index of social trust (and other studies of political ideology [for example Heath, Evans, and Martin 1994; Evans and Heath 1995], to balance the scale all seven items were used, including those that load onto the second dimension, thus increasing the validity of the scale. Figure 6.5 presents the distribution of responses to each question.[14]

Only just over 20 per cent of respondents express a positive opinion of the way democracy is being implemented in their countries, while 46 per cent judge this negatively (A1b). Two of the three items referring to the government give rise to a more optimistic picture: 34 per cent think that the majority of the society benefits from the government's actions (B1e) and 46 per cent believe in the efficacy of government (F1i). However, as many as 56 per cent of respondents disagree with the statement that the government's actions reflect 'the popular will' (F1g). Moreover, the three items referring to respondents' political efficacy indicate a sense of 'political powerlessness'. A full 65 per cent of respondents do not believe in the most basic feature of democratic systems (that citizens can influence the election of the government [B1h]), while 72 per cent think they cannot influence the government's actions (F1b), and 73 per cent agree that officials are not interested in the opinions of 'ordinary' people (F1e). In general, these figures indicate that citizens in the new Eastern and Central European democracies held a negative opinion of their political systems

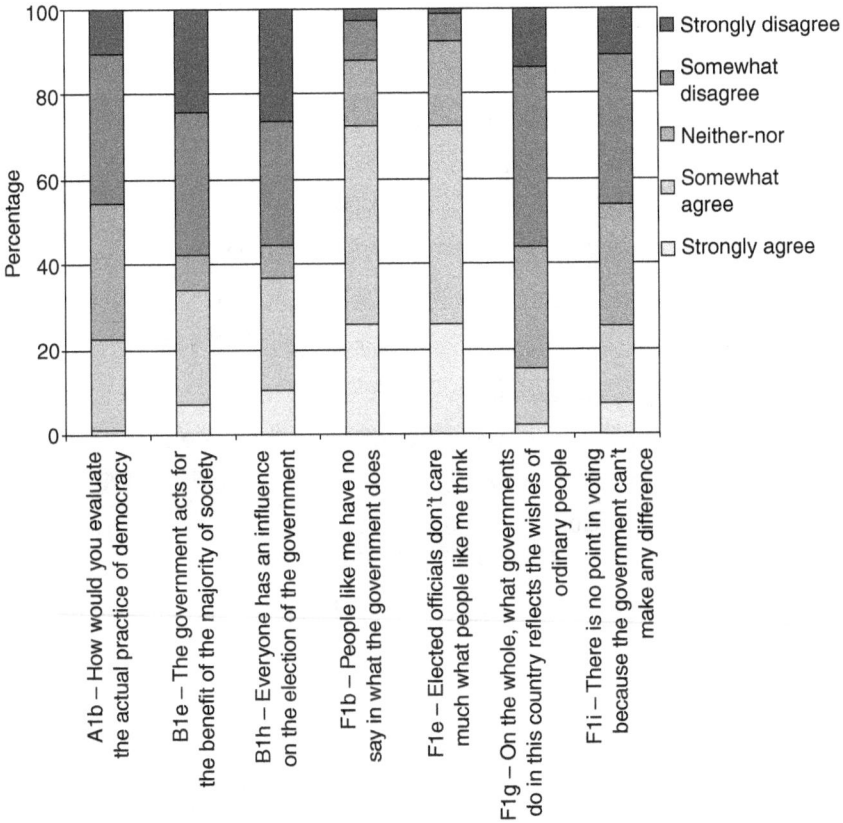

Figure 6.5 Indicators of political disaffection in ECE, 1993–1994 (source: see Appendix).

in the mid-1990s. And this applies not only to perceptions of the democratic functioning of their political systems, but also to their feelings of political inefficacy.

Figure 6.6 shows that, as would be expected given the distributions in Figure 6.5, political disaffection scores are high (that is, significantly above 3.0) in all countries. Country scores do not vary greatly: there are substantial and statistically significant differences between the lowest (the Czech Republic and Romania) and the highest scoring countries (Ukraine and Russia). More importantly, however, Figure 6.7 also shows that the cross-national distribution of political disaffection is very similar to that of social trust. In fact, the aggregate correlation between social trust and political disaffection is 0.83. Once more, one of the general claims of social capital theory finds no support here; although there is a strong (and significant at

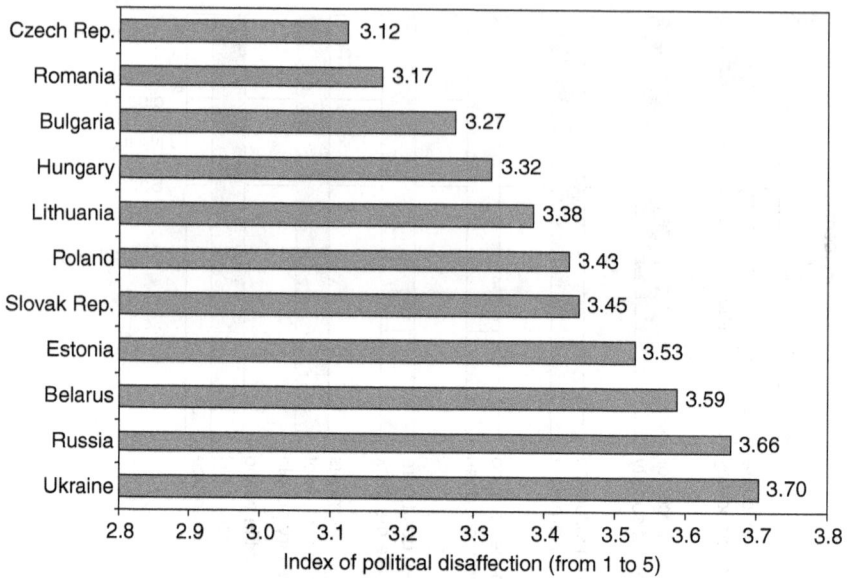

Figure 6.6 Political disaffection in ECE, 1993–1994 (source: see Appendix).

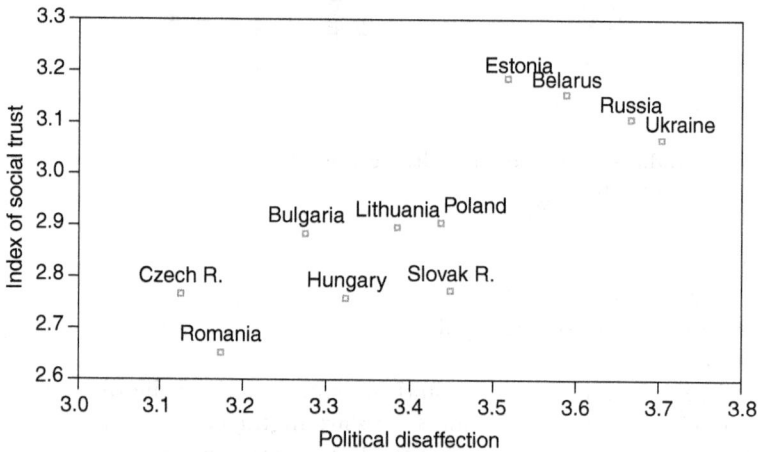

Figure 6.7 Social trust and political disaffection in ECE, 1993–1994 (source: see Appendix).

$p < 0.01$) country-level association between social trust and political disaffection, this association is positive.

However, while trust and disaffection are strongly correlated, the association between political disaffection and civic participation is not significant. None of the types of civic involvement (membership of associations, trade unions, and churches) show any clear or statistically significant pattern when plotted against levels of disaffection.[15]

Predicting political disaffection at the individual level

Finally, we have examined the relations between social capital and political disaffection at the individual level. As will be seen, the individual-level analysis produces a very different picture of the relationship between trust and political disaffection to that found at the national, aggregate level.

Table 6.2 presents the result of a series of linear regressions predicting political disaffection. The *b* coefficients are those estimated for models including, in addition to indicators of social capital, socio-economic characteristics (gender, age, education, income, job situation, and whether a respondent has children or not).[16] As can be seen, the explanatory power of the models varies significantly from country to country, as the R^2s range from 0.024 in Belarus to 0.131 in the Czech Republic, with the average value of 0.146.[17] The strongest predictor in all countries (with the exception of Bulgaria) is social trust, but on average this only explains 1.3 per cent of the variance. Background characteristics in most countries are insignificant for explaining levels of disaffection; even in the countries where socio-economic status variables are significant (Estonia and Russia), their net share of the explanation of variance is minimal. Among the participatory activities, associational membership and church membership are the most common predictors: they are significant in, respectively, four and five countries. Interestingly, only in Poland are all four indicators of social capital statistically significant predictors of political disaffection.

The most important finding obtained from this analysis, however, is that while the correlation between trust and satisfaction does vary (from -0.099 in Belarus to -0.254 in the Czech Republic), in every case the effect of social trust on political disaffection is negative. Citizens who are more trusting are also less disaffected with politics in their country. When the controls are added, we see a moderate decline in the size of these coefficients, but they all remain statistically significant.

Conclusions

Social capital theory maintains that social trust is positively correlated with networks of civic engagement, on the one hand, and negatively correlated with disaffection from politics, on the other. As a result, social trust

Table 6.2 Political disaffection regressed onto social trust, civic participation, and background indicators in ECE, 1993–1994[a]

Countries	Social trust		Associational membership		Trade union membership		Church membership		Total R^2	% of total R^2 explained by presented variables
	b	s.e.	b	s.e.	b	s.e.	b	s.e.		
Belarus	−0.079*	(0.024)	−0.040	(0.042)	0.040	(0.035)	−0.009	(0.014)	0.027	51.9
Bulgaria	−0.132*	(0.017)	−0.161*	(0.040)	0.033	(0.032)	0.018***	(0.009)	0.067	68.7
Czech Republic	−0.288*	(0.030)	0.007	(0.040)	0.069	(0.039)	−0.048**	(0.016)	0.141	61.0
Estonia	−0.121*	(0.019)	−0.060*	(0.029)	0.034	(0.035)	−0.049*	(0.015)	0.112	28.6
Hungary	−0.195*	(0.026)	−0.027	(0.044)	0.067	(0.044)	−0.039**	(0.013)	0.100	69.0
Lithuania	−0.137*	(0.018)	−0.051	(0.037)	−0.133*	(0.049)	0.014	(0.011)	0.059	64.4
Poland	−0.144*	(0.021)	−0.186*	(0.041)	−0.058	(0.045)	−0.064*	(0.011)	0.111	64.9
Romania	−0.213*	(0.026)	−0.092	(0.040)	0.006	(0.039)	0.006	(0.012)	0.089	70.8
Russia	−0.157*	(0.021)	−0.009	(0.040)	0.046	(0.030)	−0.005	(0.012)	0.118	33.1
Slovak Republic	−0.197*	(0.025)	−0.011	(0.035)	−0.037	(0.036)	−0.008	(0.009)	0.078	73.1
Ukraine	−0.152*	(0.016)	−0.012	(0.032)	0.011	(0.025)	−0.018***	(0.009)	0.049	79.6

Source: See Appendix.

Note

a Figures are b coefficients from OLS, with standard errors (s.e.) in parenthesis. Levels of significance are ***$p \le 0.001$; **$p \le 0.01$; and *$p \le 0.05$.

contributes to the quality of democratic government. The existence of such a relationship has been demonstrated in empirical studies of Western countries. However, our analysis of post-communist countries shows that the social capital theory is not 'universal'; social trust is not always positively influenced by civic participation and is not always negatively associated with disaffection with institutional performance. Levels of social trust in East Central Europe are not particularly low, yet citizens in this region seem relatively disillusioned with the ongoing political and economic transformation. Country-level analysis reveals no significant pattern of association between social trust and civic participation, and a positive association between trust and political disaffection. Thus social trust is not significantly related to the 'civicness' of the community; and the more trusting the citizens the lower the level of approval of the workings of the political system and the higher the level of political disaffection. This would seem to suggest that if democracy succeeds in East Central Europe, it is not interpersonal trust and faith in cooperation or norms of reciprocity – all key elements of social capital theory – that help make it work. Furthermore, civic participation itself does not predict levels of political disaffection.

Similarly, at the individual level, our analysis indicates that in the Eastern and Central European countries social trust is not predicted by either of the main sets of 'conventional' determinants, that is, patterns of civic engagement and socio-economic characteristics. Educational attainment is the only consistent predictor. Social trust and civic participation are certainly not closely linked elements of a coherent concept, and membership of civic associations is only a very weak predictor of political disaffection.

So far, then, these findings all point to the limited applicability of social capital theory for understanding levels of political disaffection in East Central Europe. Nonetheless, at the individual level, social trust is associated with lower levels of disaffection. This is what would be expected on the basis of conventional formulations of social capital theory. Why is this so? Why should this one prediction of social capital theory hold when others do not? To account for this apparent anomaly, we need to reconsider how stocks of social trust might develop in non-democratic societies and to distinguish this process from one that accounts for how individual differences in trust might arise.

First, consider how stocks of trust develop. Social capital theory assumes that in democratic systems social trust emerges through communitarian experience of participation in democracy itself. This does not explain, however, how it develops in systems where such 'positive' participation is lacking. Presumably, in non-democratic societies there must be mechanisms other than participation in a democratic system that generate social trust. Otherwise, social trust would only be the property of established, developed democracies. What might these mechanisms be? Our suggestion is that in an environment where a government fails to provide adequately for its population, where cynicism with respect to the political system is prevalent, where the national economy is in disarray,[18] people develop networks of social trust that compensate for these very inadequacies. In other words, the causal relation is exactly the opposite of that assumed in Putnam's theory of social capital and its effects on political systems. As a result, in the case of post-communist regimes we would indeed expect a correlation between high levels of social trust and high levels of political *dis*trust; the observed aggregate-level correlation between trust and political disaffection is consistent with this hypothesis. Moreover, we have demonstrated elsewhere, using objective indicators of political performance, that the improvement in the quality of democracy in East Central Europe is linked to a decline in levels of interpersonal trust (Letki and Evans 2005).

In contrast, at the individual level, differences in trust in 'generalized others' are likely to depend on individuals' psychological characteristics and their life-course experiences. In other words, the factors responsible for overall stocks of social trust and for individual variations in social trust are quite different: aggregate variations in stocks of social trust are likely to be conditioned by long-term contextual factors, such as the functioning of the political system, while individual differences are likely to reflect more immediate processes involving variations in individual experience. These same processes might be expected to generalize individual differences in confidence in politicians, a key element of notions of political disaffection. This may then explain the positive relationship between distrust and political disaffection at the individual level.

Explanations of differences in stocks of social trust at the country level thus derive from macro-level features of social and political systems, while the sources of individual differences within these systems are more contemporary in nature and probably relate to experiences of the new political systems in East Central Europe. This interpretation also makes sense of our finding that, contrary to claims that social trust can only be generated in a democratic context, there are reasonably high levels of interpersonal trust in post-communist countries. There is no basis for assuming that trust was absent under the previous communist regime in the region: distrust of state structures should not be mistaken for distrust of fellow citizens. Quite the contrary, cooperation, reciprocity, and trust in others were resources necessary for survival in situations of economic scarcity and political arbitrariness. As Gibson (2001: 51) puts it, 'perhaps in response to the totalitarianism of the past, Russians have developed extensive social networks with high levels of political capacity'. While much research focuses on the role of *blat* networks and informal exchange in the political and economic system in Russia (see, for example, Ledeneva 1998), the Russian experience can be extended to other post-communist countries as well. Dependence on the spoken word and informal connections are particularly strong and important in the context of institutional uncertainty and unpredictability. As Knack and Keefer (1997: 1.253) emphasize, 'interpersonal trust can . . . provide an imperfect substitute for government-backed property rights or contract enforcement where governments are unable or unwilling to provide them'. Situations of this sort are therefore likely to result in the emergence of strong norms of interactions and reciprocity (Coleman 1990). The negative correlation between national levels of political or economic satisfaction and social trust are quite consistent with these arguments; in countries where citizens evaluate the workings of democracy and the market positively and see themselves as influential, they have less need to rely on networks of informal relations with others than do citizens who live in countries where the state and market institutions are largely inefficient. When the political and economic systems respond to citizens' needs, generalized trust is less necessary.[19]

Consequently, we would agree with Kenneth Newton (1999b: 185–186; and this volume) when he concludes on the basis of results from analysis of the World Values Surveys (WVS) and *Eurobarometer* data 'that there is not a close or consistent association between social and political trust. . . . In other words, social capital is not necessarily translated into political capital and political capital seems not to be dependent on social capital'.[20] But we would propose instead that a more conditional model of the relations between trust and politics is required. As our analysis shows, in East Central Europe there are relationships (albeit operating in different directions at different levels) between social trust and political disaffection; we assume that political (dis)trust is a component of the latter. We therefore need to understand at some more abstract level the conditions under which these ostensibly contradictory outcomes might occur. There are systematic differences between East Central Europe and Italy or the United States that can provide a further set of hypotheses to be tested in order to explain this apparent difference in contextual effects between Eastern and Western Europe. This is especially likely to be the case given that we have seen that some relationships identified in research on the West do seem to hold: that is, individuals' social trust scores are negatively related to their sense of political disaffection.

To conclude, it would appear that in East Central Europe politically dysfunctional and disaffected societies tend to have more trusting citizens. But high levels of social trust do not appear to cause political disaffection. Rather, levels of trust can plausibly be seen as a product of citizens' strategies of 'getting by' in societies in which the political system and the economy do not function effectively. In other words, in societies where government and the economy are dysfunctional, people develop networks of trust in order to cope. The causal direction of the relationship between trust and politics is thus reversed: trust does not influence politics, politics influences trust. This does not undermine the explanatory edifice that is currently being constructed around the concept of social capital, but it does signal the need to specify more precisely the conditions under which different processes occur. Far from social trust being necessary for political and economic success in East Central Europe, a declining level of trust may well be a result – or symptom – of the stabilization and consolidation of the political and economic situation in the region. The findings presented in this chapter do not refute the relevance of social capital and trust for understanding popular support for a political and economic system, but they do suggest that it is necessary to specify the mechanisms at work more clearly. They also indicate that to do so it is necessary to go beyond the assumptions developed in models of the relations between social capital, trust, and political disaffection in Western liberal democratic contexts.

Appendix 6.1 The surveys

Country	Sampling frame	Sampling	Response rate	Date
Belarus	Adult population Housing offices' residence List of individuals	1. 7 regions 2. 26 settlements 3. Local councils 4. Individuals from residence lists randomly	Names issued: 1,300 + 650 Achieved sample: 1,200	Summer 1993
Bulgaria	Adult population (18+) 1992 census of households	Two-step cluster 1. 211 census districts (from 42,000) 2. Random: 12 households from each	Names issued: 2,532 Achieved sample: 1,932	Summer 1993
Czech Republic	Adult population (18+) List of voters from 1992 in sampled localities	1. 8 regions 2. 182 sampling points (localities) from 13,410 3. 2,104 addresses, of which: 1,681 random list sampling (electoral register) + 423 random route + 111 quota	Names issued: 2,104 Achieved sample: 1,409 + 111	Spring 1994
Estonia	Adult population (18+) 1989 census of households	1. 5 regions 2. 15 counties 3. 321 sampling points 4. Random-route/household 5. Kish matrix/respondent	Names issued: 2,285 Achieved sample: 2,029	Summer 1993
Hungary	Adult population (20+) Central register of population (1992)	1. 12 counties representing regions 2. 78 sampling points 3. Random selection of individuals	Names issued: 1,703 Achieved sample: 1,314	Spring 1994

continued

Appendix 6.1 Continued

Country	Sampling frame	Sampling	Response rate	Date
Lithuania	Adult population (18+) Random route (rural) Register office address lists (urban)	1. 5 regions 2. 180 sampling points 3. Rural – random route urban – address list	Names/addresses 2,982 issued: Achieved sample: 2,000	Summer 1993
Poland	Adult population (18+) Central register of individuals	1. 8 regions 2. 4 types of settlements	Names issued: 2,040 Achieved sample: 1,729	Summer 1993
Romania	Adult population (18+) Electoral records	1. 4 provinces 2. 4 types of settlements 3. Electoral constituencies (126 from 51 settlements)	Names issued: 2,000 Achieved sample: 1,621	Summer 1993
Russia	Adult population (18+) Lists of 'privatization vouchers'	1. 10 regions 2. 56 settlements 3. Individuals from list of vouchers	Names issued: 2,420 Achieved sample: 2,030	Summer 1993
Slovakia	Adult population (18+) List of voters from 1992 in sampled localities	1. 4 regions 2. 215 sampling points (localities) from 4,191 3. 2,014 addresses of which: 1,100 first wave; 914 second wave. Random list sampling (electoral register) + 68 quota	Names issued: 2,014 Achieved sample: 1,443 + 68	Spring 2004

Notes

1 Przeworski (1991: 184), for example, has modelled the political dynamics of transition societies as a learning process in which citizens start out with relatively little knowledge of market economies and often exaggerated views of its possibilities. Citizens' political response to the transition, in his view, is a function of the degree to which economic experience departs from their expectations. Rose (1992) and Whitefield and Evans (1994) propose political learning models.

2 As Putnam (2000: 134–135, 137) writes, 'The touchstone of social capital is the principle of generalized reciprocity.... The norm of generalized reciprocity is so fundamental to civilized life that all prominent moral codes contain some equivalent of the Golden Rule ... In short, people who trust others are all-round good citizens, and those more engaged in community life are both more trusting and more trustworthy'.

3 To explain the influence of civic participation on governmental performance, Putnam (1993) makes reference to rational choice theory and stresses positive effects of social capital such as the reduction of transaction costs and increased predictability of cooperation, as well as the widespread belief that cooperation is more advantageous than individualism. In a similar vein, Boix and Posner (1998: 686–693) have attempted to systematize 'the mechanisms that link social capital with good performance in government' and point to five dimensions of the relationship: the relation between the articulation of citizens' interests and expectations and the political elite's responsiveness (verified later through elections); the reduction of costs of policy and rules implementation; the transformation of citizens' preferences from particularist to collectivist; the increased effectiveness of bureaucracy (trust and reciprocity within the agencies); and leaders' ability 'to make necessary compromises without losing the support of their group members'.

4 See the Appendix to this chapter for a description of the surveys undertaken in 1993 and 1994 in 11 Eastern and Central European countries.

5 Their sample contained several so-called 'European-oriented' countries and six Central American countries, but no Eastern European countries (Muller and Seligson 1994: 648).

6 'Institutional performance' refers to political as well as economic performance; these can be estimated on the basis of the World Values Survey (WVS) and Organization for Economic Cooperation and Development (OECD) and European Bank for Reconstruction and Development (EBRD) reports (Hellman 1998).

7 The level of unionization in ECE is generally high: 42 per cent of respondents in paid employment were members of trade unions.

8 For evidence showing the positive impact of membership in a communist organization on participation in democratic politics in post-communist status, see Letki (2005).

9 Need and Evans (2001) provide more detailed information on religious participation in ECE.

10 Plots of these non-significant associations are available on request.

11 Although political and economic performance can be measured by means of 'objective' indicators, such as Freedom House rankings and Gross National Product (GNP) per capita, we use measures taken from our surveys that more directly tap citizens' experience of transition. For a critical evaluation of the validity of Freedom House rankings as a measure of the quality of democracy, see Bollen (1993). Evans and Whitefield (1995) provide a critique of official measures of economic experience in Eastern Europe.

12 Some of these items are derived from the established tradition of survey
research into the concept of political efficacy originating in Campbell, Gurin,
and Miller's (1954) study. The concept and its related indicators have usually
been employed as part of the political culture approach to comparative analysis, as in Almond and Verba (1963) and Barnes *et al.* (1979), but they can
clearly also be interpreted within a rational choice framework concerned with
the perceived pay-offs of democratic systems (Evans and Whitefield 1995).
Here, we do not have to make a choice about the 'cultural' or 'rational' status
of answers to the questions.

13 All variables were recoded into 5-point items, with answers 'don't know' and
'neither-nor' aggregated into the middle point of the scale. In the cases of A1b,
B1e, B1h, and F1g, answers were coded as 'very negatively/strongly
disagree' = 1, 'negatively/disagree' = 2, etc., while in the cases of F1b, F1e, and
F1i the direction was reversed, i.e. 'strongly agree' = 1, 'agree' = 2, etc.

14 In the case of item A1b, the labels 'strongly agree', 'agree', 'disagree', and
'strongly disagree' refer to 'very positively', 'positively', 'negatively', and 'very
negatively', respectively.

15 The correlation coefficients are, respectively, -0.290, 0.429, and -0.242. Plots
of the relations between political disaffection and membership of associations,
trade unions, and churches are available on request.

16 Although, according to Putnam (1995a: 78), socio-demographic factors should
not affect political disaffection ('across our six national surveys, approval of the
activities of the regional government is uncorrelated with *any* of the standard
sociological categories'), the literature on political culture and civic participation suggests that they can be expected to have significant explanatory value
(Parry *et al.* 1992; Verba *et al.* 1971; Brady *et al.* 1995). We have therefore
included them in our models.

17 For the pooled sample, controlled for country effects.

18 Elsewhere we have shown the close relationship between political and economic satisfaction, and by implication political and economic performance, in
the Eastern and Central European countries (Evans and Whitefield 1995).

19 Some authors go as far as to suggest that democratization can undermine trust:
as a result of 'the overwhelming failures of the planned economies ... cooperation between family and friends [emerged] as a means of coping with a dysfunctional system. This sense of community has been broken up by the move to
the market and to democracy leading to a loss of trust and to an increase in
opportunism' (Rose-Ackerman 2001: 415).

20 Similarly, Paxton (1999) examined the decline of social capital in the United
States and concluded that trust in individuals and confidence in institutions
are relatively independent; there has been a significant decline in the former,
whereas when public scandals associated with, for example, legislative and
executive institutions are taken into account, the trend in the latter is rather
different.

Part IV

Causes II: politics and institutions

7 Political disaffection and democratization history in new democracies*

Mariano Torcal

Representative democratic regimes have spread out all over the countries of Southern Europe and the vast majority of countries in Asia, Latin America, and the former Eastern Europe. These 'new democracies' have very defined symptoms of political disaffection: lack of interest in politics; cynicism towards everything related to politics, institutions of representation and politicians; and a sense of alienation from all things political. Since the 1960s, an increasing 'confidence gap', or increasing 'symptoms of disaffection', have also been observed among citizens of advanced Western industrial countries (Barnes *et al.* 1979; Lipset and Schneider 1983; Dalton 1988, 1999; Nye, jr. 1997; Pharr and Putnam 2000).[1] Is there any difference in the levels of political disaffection among old and new democracies?[2]

I will discuss in this chapter different levels of political disaffection in a series of Western and Latin American democracies. Following the definition of political disaffection presented in the Introduction of this volume, I will compare cross-national levels of the two dimensions of political disaffection: institutional disaffection and political engagement. To measure political engagement, I will use indicators of interest in politics and salience of politics. To measure institutional disaffection, I will use confidence in institutions and responsiveness of the system (external political efficacy). The discussion will not be limited to the comparative analysis of those aggregate levels. I will also discuss the different nature of political disaffection in new democracies, since the factors explaining disaffection at the individual level are somewhat different in new democracies. Most studies of political disaffection focus on established democracies, attempting to explain the origin and existence of attitudes about politics in countries which have had representative democracies for 50 years or more. In other words, democracies whose citizens have accumulated considerable 'democratic experience' and have been exposed to inclusive-gradual political mobilization. However, citizens in new democracies do not have the 'recent and prolonged' experience that would enable them to evaluate the functioning, achievements, and performance of their newly established democratic institutions. More importantly, their only references for evaluating the institutions and practices of political representation are often linked to pseudo- or non-democratic experiences of their past. In older democracies, on the other hand, these negative references are not so salient and their socializing impact is much smaller. This enables citizens in older democracies to evaluate the present with a future perspective, using the democratic ideal as the dominant reference point. As a recent study has argued, 'differences in the historical origin of political confidence and the generational argument offer plausible explanations for some broad, cross-national patterns in political confidence' (Katzenstein 2000: 130).

Comparative levels of political disaffection

This section contains a preliminary analysis of cross-national comparative data on political disaffection. Although some of the data presented portrays an inconclusive picture of the comparative levels of political disaffection, it shows that overall political disaffection is slightly higher in new democracies. However, a higher level of political disaffection is not one of the distinctive features of new democracies: many old democracies also present high levels, while a few new democracies display relatively low levels.

Starting with the comparative levels of institutional disaffection, we can observe that, despite a marked decline in institutional trust in the United States[3] and Western Europe[4] over recent decades, the institutional confidence gap is a little wider among new democracies.[5] In any case, it is almost impossible to distinguish new and old democracies based only on the comparative levels of institutional confidence. Comparative data from the 1990 World Values Survey (Table 7.1) show that citizens in Spain and Portugal have the lowest levels of institutional trust in Western Europe,[6] particularly with respect to parliament, public administration, and the legal system.[7] But this group of citizens critical of representative institutions also includes more traditional democracies such as Italy. In general, citizens in Southern European democracies give more negative evaluations of basic institutions such as parliament, public administration, and the legal system. They have more positive views of big business, the Church, and the Armed Forces, although their assessments of these institutions are also below the European average. Although data from Greece on institutional confidence are not available in this comparative survey, other scholars have shown that Greek citizens displayed positive evaluations of representative institutions following the transition to democracy; this also appears to be undergoing a shift towards institutional mistrust (Dimitras 1987: 64–84; Mendrinou and Nicolacopoulos 1997: 22–29). These findings reveal a general syndrome of lack of political institutional confidence among citizens in Southern European democracies, including second-wave democracies such as Italy.

The comparative data for institutional confidence in some new Latin American democracies paint a similarly fuzzy picture. Table 7.2, which gives the percentage of citizens who are very or quite confident in a series of institutions, shows that only the Church and the Armed Forces receive majority approval. The only exceptions are Argentina and Paraguay, where citizens have less confidence in the Armed Forces, even though support for the military is still higher than that for all other institutions in Argentina and the majority of other institutions in Paraguay. This is significant when we bear in mind that the Armed Forces in these countries have often been discredited by recent authoritarian experiences. Overall, with the significant exceptions of Chile and Uruguay, two third-wave democracies, confidence in political parties, trade unions, courts, the national Congress, and the public administration is relatively low in almost all Latin American countries.[8] Chile and Uruguay contrast with Venezuela, where institutional confidence is very low despite the fact that this country has been until recently under democratic rule since 1958. Therefore, although new democracies tend to have lower levels of institutional confidence, there are some significant exceptions such as Chile and Uruguay, and even Greece during the 1980s. Moreover, as exemplified by the cases of Venezuela and Italy, this lack of confidence is not exclusive to recently established regimes.

The lack of institutional confidence in many democracies is especially important for political parties. Although it is higher among new democracies, it also affects some old democracies. Unfortunately, there are few comparative data on confidence in political parties. The best available data come from the 1997 wave of the World Values Survey, but few Western European countries were included in this wave of the survey. Despite this shortcoming, the analysis of these data is very enlightening. Of all the countries for which data are available, Venezuela, a second-wave democracy, is the one with the highest level of distrust in political parties: some 60 per cent of Venezuelans say they have absolutely no trust in political parties. Close behind Venezuela come Argentina, with 49 per cent of 'nontrusters', Brazil with 47 per cent, Peru with 44 per cent, Chile with 37 per cent, Spain with 29 per cent, Uruguay with 26 per cent, and at a considerable distance Germany with 17 per cent, the United States with 16 per cent, Sweden with 11 per cent and Norway with 7 per cent. Although more comparative data are needed, recent studies in Southern Europe and Latin America have shown that anti-party sentiments are widespread throughout both regions, with the notable exceptions of Uruguay and Chile and, to a lesser extent, Greece (Torcal, Gunther, and Montero 2002: 265–268; Meseguer 1998: 99–111). These data reveal the scale of the clear disparities among the citizens of new and old democracies in terms of their level of confidence in political parties.

These findings on confidence in a set of institutions can be seen somewhat more clearly when we compare average indexes of overall institutional

Table 7.1 Confidence in institutions in 14 democracies, 1990–1991[a]

Country	Church	Armed forces	Education system	Legal system	Press	Unions	Parliament	Administration	Big business	Social security
Austria	50	29	65	58	18	35	41	42	42	68
Belgium	51	34	72	46	43	37	42	42	50	66
Denmark	47	46	81	79	31	46	42	51	38	69
France	50	56	66	57	38	32	48	49	67	70
Germany	39	39	53	65	34	36	50	38	38	70
Iceland	68	24	80	67	20	51	53	46	40	69
Ireland	72	61	73	47	36	43	50	59	52	59
Italy	60	46	47	32	39	33	31	25	62	37
Netherlands	32	31	65	63	36	53	53	46	48	69
Norway	45	65	–	75	43	59	59	44	53	–
Portugal	63	65	–	44	37	33	38	36	47	53
Spain	47	39	63	46	48	39	37	34	46	43
Sweden	37	49	–	56	33	40	47	44	53	–
United Kingdom	45	81	49	52	15	27	44	46	47	33
United States	67	47	55	57	56	33	45	60	50	53

Sources: World Values Surveys (WVS), 1990–1991.

Note

a Percentage of respondents stating that they have great or some confidence in institutions.

Table 7.2 Institutional confidence in seven Latin American countries, 1995 and 1996[a]

Institutions	Argentina '95	Argentina '96	Brazil '95	Brazil '96	Chile '95	Chile '96	Paraguay '95	Paraguay '96	Peru '95	Peru '96	Uruguay '95	Uruguay '96	Venezuela '95	Venezuela '96
Church	65	63	74	69	81	78	89	85	78	80	56	57	77	76
Armed forces	39	33	61	63	56	51	34	48	64	52	45	39	56	59
Unions	20	11	38	32	46	44	40	49	33	28	41	35	19	19
Courts	35	24	41	42	37	38	37	45	27	27	58	56	29	28
Big business	36	27	42	39	41	46	37	46	45	40	37	31	38	37
Public administration	28	20	29	28	44	39	20	34	32	28	43	38	22	18
Parliament	37	26	27	20	49	43	46	43	46	35	50	40	22	19
Political parties	27	17	17	17	33	28	23	38	21	20	41	33	16	12
Business associations	33	24	28	26	46	43	35	43	36	36	38	32	26	26
Government	39	20	32	25	60	52	37	40	71	50	47	37	27	16

Sources: *Latinobarometer* 1995 and 1996.

Note

a Percentage of respondents stating that they have great or some confidence in institutions.

confidence. These indexes are designed to show the two dimensions captured by a number of scholars when measuring European citizens' evaluations of a series of institutions, distinguishing between specifically political institutions, and other institutions in society.[9] Both indexes have therefore been designed with these two dimensions in mind. The first index only includes evaluations of those institutions that belong to the political system *per se* (parliament, public administration, and the legal system).[10] The second includes these three institutions as well as three other important social institutions (trade unions, the Church, and big business).

Although the inclusion of some of these institutions in the index is debatable, they have been used in comparative studies to show the declining levels of institutional trust in many Western democracies.[11] Table 7.3, which provides data for these indexes (the scale ranges from 4, great trust, to 1, none; hence 2.50 is a neutral position, in that it is neither negative nor positive), confirms that the citizens of Argentina, Belgium, Brazil, Italy, Peru, Portugal, Spain, and Venezuela have the lowest levels of institutional confidence.[12] This dimension further confirms the sense of estrangement existing between citizens and government in these countries.[13] However, differences among citizens of new and old democracies, although statistically significant for political institutions, are small, as we can observe from the averages presented at the bottom of Table 7.3. Furthermore, low levels of confidence in political institutions are neither an exclusive nor a defining characteristic of new democracies; the Chilean and Uruguayan cases represent new democracies with high confidence, while Italy and Venezuela are more traditional democracies with very low levels of confidence.

A very similar situation can be observed with the comparative analysis of citizens' perception of democratic openness or responsiveness (external political efficacy), another way of measuring institutional disaffection. Despite a marked decrease in the feeling of political efficacy in old Western democracies (Dalton 1999; Putnam, Pharr, and Dalton 2000: 13–20), Table 7.4 documents that, in general, citizens in the new democracies tend to declare to a higher degree that their political system and their representatives are the most unresponsive (see averages of old and new democracies in the last two rows). These differences in the average might be over-inflated because of the use of differently worded questions in Latin American countries. Both items are intended to tap the citizens' perception of the system and representatives' responsiveness, and, although the data are not fully comparable, they display reliable and valid differences across countries. Even with the exact same item included in the *Eurobarometer*, new democracies such as Greece and Portugal present the lowest levels of political efficacy among Western democracies. The data for Portugal confirm the high levels of cynicism and lack of political efficacy which, according to some authors, have characterized Portuguese citizens since the beginning of their political transition (Bruneau and

Table 7.3 Confidence in political institutions in 21 democracies, 1981 and 1990[a]

Country[b]	1981		1990	
	Political	Socio-political	Political	Socio-political
Argentina	–	–	1.80	1.90
Peru[c]	–	–	1.87	2.14
Venezuela[c]	–	–	2.03	2.29
Italy	2.17	2.21	2.09	2.30
Brazil	–	–	2.19	2.44
Portugal	–	–	2.24	2.32
Spain	2.44	2.40	2.30	2.35
Belgium	2.39	2.36	2.34	2.35
Uruguay	–	–	2.39	2.38
France	2.50	2.42	2.43	2.40
Austria	–	–	2.48	2.43
Sweden	2.56	2.46	2.48	2.42
United Kingdom	2.57	2.48	2.50	2.41
Germany	2.56	2.45	2.52	2.41
Netherlands	2.52	2.38	2.52	2.43
Ireland	2.55	2.59	2.55	2.61
United States	2.63	2.65	2.58	2.61
Iceland	2.20	–	2.58	2.56
Denmark	2.57	2.47	2.64	2.51
Norway	2.89	2.70	2.64	2.58
Chile	–	–	2.65	2.73
Average first- and second-wave democracies	2.51	2.47	2.46	2.45
Average third-wave democracies	–[d]	–[d]	2.21	2.32

Sources: WVS, 1980–1981 and 1990–1991.

Notes
a Figures are indices of average confidence in the institutions of the political system and in other social institutions.
b The countries are listed in order of their 1990 index of confidence in political institutions.
c The data for Peru, Venezuela, and Uruguay come from the 1995–1997 wave.
d In 1981 Spain was the only third-wave democracy included in the WVS.

Bacalhau 1978; Bruneau 1984a: 72–83; Bruneau and Macleod 1986: 152–155).

The results for Greece also reinforce the fact that, despite initial differences with respect to other Southern European countries (Dimitras 1987: 64–84), Greek citizens have already joined the Spanish and Portuguese in their negative opinions concerning the responsiveness of their democratic systems.[14] Nevertheless, these data also show that old democracies such as Belgium, Germany, or the United Kingdom have similarly low levels of

Table 7.4 External efficacy in seven Latin American countries, 1995–1997, and in 15 Western Europe Countries, 1997

Country[a]	% who agree that 'Public officials care about what people like me think' (1995)	% who considered that 'Politicians are concerned about the issues that interest you' (1996)
Brazil	16	8
Venezuela	16	10
Argentina	19	7
Chile	24	13
Paraguay	28	12
Peru	29	6
Uruguay	38	13
	% who disagree that 'Public services look less after the interests of people like me'[b]	% who disagree that 'The people who run the country are more concerned with themselves than with the good of the country'[b]
Belgium	19	6
Greece	20	13
Germany	20	16
Italy	26	11
Portugal	26	19
United Kingdom	26	22
Ireland	32	19
Spain	32	22 (17)[c]
Austria	34	32
Sweden	35	32
France	37	19
Finland	43	28
Denmark	50	57
Netherlands	50	59
Luxembourg	56	46
Average first- and second-wave democracies	34.1	27.5
Average third-wave democracies	25.7	12

Sources: For Latin America, *Latinobarometer*, 1995 and 1996; for Western Europe, *Eurobarometer 47.1*, 1997.

Notes
a The countries are listed in ascending order of the first item (first column).
b Percentage of those who disagree greatly or somewhat.
c The data in brackets for Spain represent the percentage obtained with the exact same question included in the *Latinobarometer*, 1996.

political efficacy. In the Latin American context, the new Uruguayan democracy presents higher levels of efficacy, whereas Venezuela is among the lowest in the rank.

The lack of correspondence between low levels of institutional disaffection and the third-wave democracies is just a demonstration that attitudes have nothing to do with the timing of democratization (after the 1970s). As some scholars have argued in a recent comparative study, it is not possible to identify a general trend or a particular group of new democracies suffering from special problems in this respect (Klingemann 1999: 47–48; Norris 1999b: 227). This suggests that the different trends observed in each country may be due to internal political factors that go beyond their recent authoritarian experiences and the third-wave phenomenon (Klingemann 1999: 52).

Are the preceding comparative levels of institutional-responsiveness disaffection in different countries also found in the case of the other dimension of political disaffection, political disengagement? Again, the differences between older democracies and new democracies do to some extent persist, although they are not consistent in many cases.

Tables 7.5 and 7.6 show the comparative levels of political interest found among the same set of democracies, displaying quite a similar pattern. While the citizens of new democracies generally tend to display lower levels of interest in politics, this pattern is not uniform. Spain and Portugal, together with Argentina, Chile, and Venezuela, show the lowest levels of engagement in politics and public affairs; but countries such as Uruguay, Peru, Brazil, and even Colombia display higher levels of political interest.

According to data from the World Values Surveys of 1981–1983, 1990–1991 and 1995–1997 (see Table 7.5), the levels of political interest are on average substantially lower in new democracies than in old ones (29 and 44 per cent, respectively). For instance, among Western democracies, Spain has the lowest and most rapidly decreasing levels of interest in politics of all the European countries analysed, making the Spaniards the most politically disinterested citizens in all the Western democracies.[15] Portugal, only included in the 1990 study, is also among the group of countries whose citizens are the most politically disinterested in Europe. The lack of interest in politics among the citizens of these two countries is also confirmed by data from the 1983–1990 *Eurobarometers*.[16] On average, over this period just 34 per cent of Spaniards declared that they were very or quite interested in politics. Lower figures are also found in Portugal and Italy (12 per cent).[17] Moreover, between 1983 and 1990, interest in politics rose more in most other European countries than in Spain, where it decreased until 1988 and remained virtually unchanged thereafter.[18]

However, Spanish and Portuguese levels are close to and even higher than those observed among very important and significant first- and

Table 7.5 Political engagement in Western and Latin American democracies, 1981–1997[a]

Country[b]	Interest in politics				Salience of politics 1990[c]	Salience of religion 1990[c]	Difference politics religion
	1981	1990	1997	Mean '81–'97			
United States	51	60	63	58	50	79	−29
Norway	50	72	69	64	50	40	10
Iceland	48	47	–	47.5	26	56	−25
West Germany	50	69	78	66	42	37	5
Sweden	44	47	51	47	45	27	18
France	64	38	–	51	33	43	−10
Denmark	38	54	–	46	43	31	12
Austria	–	54	–	54	35	59	−24
Netherlands	41	58	–	49.5	52	42	10
United Kingdom	42	49	–	45.5	43	45	−2
Uruguay	–	–	37	37	36	50	−14
Peru	–	–	32	32	38	84	−46
Brazil	–	–	31	31	51	90	−39
Colombia	–	–	29	29	26	84	−58
Italy	29	29	–	29	31	68	−37
Ireland	24	37	–	30.5	28	83	−55
Portugal	–	31	–	31	21	56	−35
Belgium	25	30	–	27.5	26	45	−19
Spain	29	25	26	27	21	53	−32
Argentina	–	–	26	26	31	67	−36
Chile	–	–	21	21	20	75	−55
Venezuela	–	–	19	19	27	85	−58
Average first- and second-wave democracies	–	–	–	44.2	37.1	53.1	−17.5
Average third-wave democracies	–	–	–	29.3	31.1	67.9	−36.7

Source: WVS, 1981, 1990–1991, and 1995–1997.

Notes

a The data in the first three columns are percentages of respondents stating that they are very or somewhat interested in politics (excluding the DK/DA). The last two columns are percentages of those who state that politics and religion are very or quite important in their lives (excluding the DK/DA).

b The countries are listed in order of their 1981–1997 averages.

c The data for the Latin American countries is from 1997.

Table 7.6 Political engagement in seven Latin American countries, 1995 and 1996[a]

Country[b]	Year	A lot or some	Little	None
Argentina	1995	19	34	28
Argentina	1996	26	29	44
Brazil	1995	10	42	38
Brazil	1996	23	42	35
Chile	1995	12	30	46
Chile	1996	19	34	47
Paraguay	1995	15	39	32
Paraguay	1996	34	50	17
Peru	1995	17	41	27
Peru	1996	22	39	38
Uruguay	1995	20	33	27
Uruguay	1996	36	32	32
Venezuela	1995	10	30	50
Venezuela	1996	16	28	56

Sources: *Latinobarometer* 1995 and 1996.

Notes
a In horizontal percentages.
b Countries are ranked in ascending order of political interest.

second-wave democracies such as Italy, Ireland, and, once again, Belgium. Furthermore, some of the new democracies in Latin America display lower levels of interest in politics than most European countries, but the gap is smaller (as in Uruguay and, to a lesser extent, Peru and Brazil). They even display higher levels of political interest than some traditional Western European democracies. This conclusion is confirmed by *Latinobarometer* data (see Table 7.6). Higher levels of political interest can also be observed among the Greeks, who display a relatively higher level of interest in politics (52 per cent) than Spain, Portugal, and some other new democracies, remaining stable over time according to the data from 1989 and 1993 (53 and 52 per cent, respectively). Only in 1996 was some decrease observed, as the proportion of Greeks who are very or somewhat interested in politics dropped to 41 per cent; even then, however, Greece still remained well ahead of Portugal and Spain in this respect.

Similar patterns can be observed when analysing political saliency and comparing this with the importance citizens attach to religion. Table 7.5 also gives the percentage of citizens who regard politics and religion as very or quite important in their lives. On average, the level of political saliency is slightly higher among old democracies (37 per cent), whereas the importance of religion is higher among the new ones. The data show that Spanish and Portuguese citizens give the least importance to politics in Europe, in stark contrast to their attitude to religion. Despite the intense secularization processes in both Spain (Montero 1994; Díaz-Salazar 1993) and Portugal (Bacalhau 1995: 65–67), in these two countries twice as many citizens attach importance to religion as attach importance to politics. This does not mean that citizens in Spain and Portugal give particular importance to religion, but rather that the number considering politics to be important is so low.[19] In Europe, Belgium, Iceland, Ireland, and Italy follow the same pattern. They are also politically disaffected societies in which religion is still relatively important (especially in the cases of Ireland and Italy). On the other hand, the importance of religion is consistently higher in Latin America. Only Uruguay is close to the European pattern. This is because, despite the varying levels of political affection in these countries, religion is considered important throughout the continent. But the importance given to politics matches and in some cases even outstrips European levels (as in Brazil, Peru, and to a lesser extent, Argentina).

Finally, despite the lack of comparable indicators of internal political efficacy, Table 7.7 summarizes the data on questions that, although not fully comparable, were designed to measure this attitude by portraying an adequate picture of the comparable levels of this attitude among some of the countries under study. On average, internal political efficacy is higher among old democracies. In fact, among the European citizens of the nine Western democracies included in this ISSP study, Spanish citizens display the lowest percentage of respondents stating that they do not understand important political issues (39 per cent).[20] Similar data on the other new democracies in Southern Europe show low levels of internal political efficacy in Greece and Portugal.[21] The lack of consistency in low levels of internal political efficacy among new democracies is even more remarkable in the light of Latin American data. It can also be seen in Table 7.7 that in Argentina and Uruguay 61 and 60 per cent of respondents, respectively, declare that 'politics is not complicated and can be understood'. Furthermore, the figure for the other countries is around 50 per cent, except in Brazil and Paraguay. Hence, in some Latin American countries we find a picture combining a high level of citizen confidence in their political abilities (internal political efficacy) and low levels of confidence in the responsiveness of the system (external political efficacy).

Summing up the comparative evidence on political disaffection, it can be seen that while slightly higher among the new democracies, it is not a defining or exclusive feature of these new democratic regimes. Equally, the levels of political disaffection found among new democracies vary depending on the dimension considered. The differences between cases are even greater with respect to political disengagement and do not seem to follow any identifiable pattern. It is, therefore, impossible to conclude the link between the third-wave democratization phenomenon and political disaffection, although the latter does tend to occur to a slight but significantly greater extent in new democracies. It is also difficult to find a pattern related to the type of transition to democracy that these countries experienced. For instance, Chile, Brazil, and Spain took similar paths to

Table 7.7 Internal political efficacy in Latin America, 1995, and in Western Europe, 1999

Country[a]	'I feel that I have a pretty good understanding of the important political issues...'[b]
Spain	39
West Germany	41
Sweden	41
United Kingdom	45
Norway	51
Italy	52
United States	56
France	57
Ireland	62
	'Politics is not so complicated and can be understood'[c]
Brazil	34
Paraguay	38
Venezuela	45
Chile	46
Peru	53
Uruguay	60
Argentina	61
Average first- and second-wave democracies	50
Average third-wave democracies	47.3

Sources: For Western Europe, ISSP 96, Role of Government III, 1999; for Latin America, *Latinobarometer*, 1995.

Notes
a The countries are listed in ascending order.
b Percentage of those who agree somewhat or a lot.
c Percentage of those who agree.

democracy, but they show important disparities in the level of political disaffection. A classification of democracies according to *current institutional settings* (pluralistic vs. majoritarian models) does not seem to correspond with the differing levels of political disaffection. Political disaffection is high in countries like Spain and Greece with parliamentary-pluralistic systems as well as in countries with presidential settings, such as Argentina and Venezuela, or semi-presidential ones, such as Portugal, whereas political disaffection is lower in countries with presidential systems such as Uruguay and Chile and traditional pluralistic, parliamentary systems like Norway, the Netherlands, and Sweden. Finally, as I have shown elsewhere (Torcal 2002a), there is no relationship between the levels of democratic support and political disaffection at the individual or aggregate levels.

Why, therefore, is this attitudinal phenomenon higher in new democracies? What factors account for the differences observed among the new democracies?

Democratic disaffection and the politics of the past

The comparative analysis of the levels of disaffection in the previous section seems to point to the importance of the democratic past in explaining the differences observed among countries. As McAllister (1999: 201) states, 'confidence [in institutions] is formed cumulatively within the mass electorates', for, as the same author notes, 'institutional confidence is strongly related to the period of time that democratic institutions have been in existence [and] is predicated on the frequency of free, competitive, national elections'. This is not a classical institutional argument about the origin of a lack of institutional confidence (Norris, 1999c); neither, I argue in this chapter, is the consolidation of pro-democratic attitudes just a matter of time under democratic rule as Converse (1969) has defended, or merely a question of citizens' experiencing repeated calls to elections.

Rather, the nature and evolution of these attitudes depend to a large extent on how a given democratic regime has been incorporating citizens into the political game and the degree of mobilization generated under it (democratic inclusiveness).[22] So, for example, a democracy with a well-established record of adopting exclusive rather than inclusive institutions and deliberative processes, together with the presence of exclusionary practices such as political manipulation, electoral fraud, or non-accountable political corruption, will inevitably suffer the consequences in terms of visible signs of disaffection. Hence, countries such as Venezuela and Italy show much higher levels of disaffection than Uruguay and Chile, regardless of the fact that the latter belong to the so called new or third-wave democracies. As will be argued here, what matters is the time spent living in a representative democracy which is not dominated by exclusionary institutions or practices which systematically challenge or call into question the basic institutions of political representation and produce systematic political demobilization. The nature of the democratic past manifests itself through its direct influence on the political disaffection found in the various countries. This influence is explored in this section, which presents a macro-analysis of data on disaffection and a series of contextual indicators. The starting point for this analysis is the hypothesis that the nature of a country's 'democratization history' will explain the levels of political disaffection in the present. In order to test this hypothesis, I have compiled a number of aggregate indices for various countries. These indices incorporate a series of social, economic, and political indicators that, according to the literature, could influence the levels of these attitudes found in a given society. I go on to examine the relationship between these indices and four attitudinal aggregate indicators, one for the support for democracy[23] and three for political disaffection: the proportion of citizens who generally feel that the authorities and the system as a whole are not responsive to their demands;[24] the percentage of citizens who declare that politics is very or somewhat important in their lives;[25] and the index of confidence in the institutions of political representation which has been discussed above and which includes confidence in parliament, the public administration, and the legal system.[26] The countries included in the analysis vary slightly depending on the data available, but the analysis still centres on the advanced capitalist societies of Western Europe and the United States, the Southern European countries, and the Latin American Southern Cone democracies.[27]

To test the three major hypotheses, four sets of variables with aggregate data were created: the influence of democratization history; the influence of current contextual political and institutional features; the influence of major economic and social achievements; and the level of modernization. The variables were as follows:

(A)   Three variables to measure past democratization history:[28]

1   Years of liberal and representative democracy from 1930 to 1997. I count only those years in which the country had a functioning democracy according to procedural criteria.[29]

2   The number of changes of political regime, either to or from a non-democracy (authoritarian or totalitarian), semi-democracy, or democracy, from 1930 to 1997.[30]

3   Duration in years of the longest period of uninterrupted democracy between 1930 and 1997.[31]

(B)   Five variables to measure some basic contextual political characteristics:

1   The type of constitutional design existing since 1995: (a) 'parliamentary democracy'; (b) 'mixed democracy'; and (c) 'presidential democracy' (see Mainwaring 1999).

2   Achievements in civil and political liberties, measured by the variations in the 'Political Liberties Index' and in the 'Civil Liberties Index' from the year before the introduction of the most recent democracy until 1997 or, in the case of democracies established before 1976, between 1976 and 1997.[32]

3   The party systems, measured by the average number of effective parties existing in each country from the beginning of democracy until 1990 or, in the case of democracies founded before 1976, between 1976 and 1997.[33]

4   The degree of social mobilization, measured by the average number of general strikes that took place from the foundation of democracy until 1990 or, if the democracy dates from before 1976, from then until 1990.[34]

5   The 'Corruption Index' produced by the Center for Corruption Research for the period 1980–1992.[35]

(C)   A further three variables to measure improvements in economic and social standards:

1   Social achievements and progress, measured by the variation in the country's 'Human Development Index' (HDI) from the last time that democracy was re-established until 1997 or, if a democracy was established before 1980, from 1980 to 1997.[36]
2   Economic achievements, measured by the average growth in GDP from 1975 to 1997.[37]
3   Growth in per capita income in constant US dollars from the creation of democracy to 1997 or, in the case of democracies established before 1976, between 1976 and 1997.[38]

(D)   And three modernization variables:

1   The level of GDP for 1997.
2   Cubic power of the GDP for 1997 in order to test the income threshold theory for modernization which maintains that there is an *N*-curve relationship between modernization and democratization.[39]
3   The Human Development Index (HDI) for 1997.

The results of a bivariate analysis of the relationship between these indicators and the aggregate levels of confidence in the political institutions and of external political efficacy are both consistent and revealing. As can be seen from the significant bivariate correlations given in Table 7.8, the variables most consistently related to the levels of institutional trust (first column) are essentially related to the democratization history and the modernization variables. There is also an important influence by some of the political context variables such as average number of general strikes and the corruption index, as well as the increase in per capita income. These results would certainly appear to confirm the importance of the relationship between institutional confidence and the democratic history of the societies under consideration, thereby opening a new venue for the significance of this variable. Only the group of the modernization variables seems to be of similar importance to the democratic history variables. The economic and social performance variables display a secondary or null importance with the exception of the rise in per capita income, which clearly contrasts with the absence of a significant relationship with the other main social and economic performance variables.[40] On the other hand, the increase in civil and political liberties does not seem, at first glance, to influence the degree of institutional confidence. It only has a low relation with one of the external efficacy items.

It is interesting to note the weak relationship found between institu-

Table 7.8 Bivariate relationships between some dimensions of political disaffection and democratic support with various aggregate economic, social, and political indicators[a]

Indicator	Trust in institutions	% Politically effective (item 1)	% Politically effective (item 2)	Salience of politics	Support for democracy
Democratization history					
Years of democracy since 1930	0.80***	0.45**	0.53*	0.34*	
Changes of political regime since 1930	-0.84***	-0.43*	-0.54**		
Duration of the longest period under democracy since 1930	0.77***	0.65***	0.73***	0.55***	
Modernization					
Income per capita 1997	0.78***	0.60***	0.68***	0.58***	0.60***
Cubic power of income per capita 1997	0.70***	0.69***	0.70***		0.46**
Human Development Index 1997	0.74***		0.50**		0.70***
Political context					
Institutions					
Average number of general strikes from introduction of democracy until 1990	-0.67***		-0.48**		
Effective number of parties from instauration of democracy to 1997					
Variation in Political Liberties Index from institution of democracy to 1997			-0.40*		
Variation in Civil Liberties Index from introduction of democracy to 1997		-0.64***	-0.70***		
Corruption Index 1980–1992	0.79***	0.44*	0.58***	0.45**	0.50**
Performance					
Variation in Human Development Index from institution of democracy to 1997				-0.46**	
GDP growth 1975–1997	0.58***				
Increase in per capita income from introduction of democracy to 1997	0.78***	0.65***	0.67***	0.45***	0.56***
(N)	(20)	(19)	(19)	(20)	(19)

Note
a Only statistically significant Pearson's correlations have been included. Levels of statistical significance are ***$p < 0.001$; **$p < 0.05$; *$p < 0.1$.

tional disaffection (confidence in institutions and external political efficacy) and some political contextual factors, including the constitutional
setting. Only the corruption index (which may reflect a cultural perception rather than a political reality)[41] and the number of general strikes
after the installation of democracy are significant. And, although the correlation is weaker than the variables mentioned above, this variable does
show a significant negative relation. In principle, this points towards the
existence of a relation between the lack of confidence in the institutions
of representation and the use of less conventional mechanisms of political
participation and expression.

On the other hand, the relationship between these same variables and
salience of politics is rather different, but also very revealing. There are
not such strong correlation coefficients, but the significant ones tend
again to confirm to some extent the relationship between political disengagement, the other dimension of political disaffection, and democratization history, as also the mobilization linked to it. The levels of the
importance of politics in citizens' lives are related to two of the democratic history variables, especially the one which measures the duration of
the longest period of democracy; the effect of political mobilization
during longer periods (under uninterrupted democratic rule) tends to be
a good predictor of citizens' levels of attention to political life. Furthermore, another good predictor of the different levels of this attitude in different countries is the cubic transformation of income. As Deutsch (1961:
493–514) argued in his classic work, social and political mobilization is a
function of modernity, and, regardless of the effect on democratization or
democratic stability,[42] the intensity of mobilization in South America has
had an N-curvilinear shape corresponding to the cubic transformation of
income per capita: strong during the 1950s and 1960s, and weak or non-
existent during the 1980s under repressive military rule. We can, therefore, tentatively speculate that, at the aggregate level, modernization,
together with the political mobilization linked to it, has an impact on the
levels of relevance of and interest in politics among citizens of different
countries. The impact of the institutional variables and economic
performance variables is either weaker or non-existent.

These findings on political disaffection at the aggregate level contrast
with the lack of relationship with support for democracy (see Table 7.8,
last column). Only the modernization variables, the increase in per capita
income from the introduction of democracy to 1997, and the corruption
index are of any statistical significance. These data confirm two important
points. First, they point to the distinct nature of disaffection and democratic legitimacy (highlighting one of the causes of the lack of relationship
between these variables) (see Gunther and Montero in this volume).[43]
Second, these data also show that the preceding hypotheses lack the
power to explain democratic support.

All these conclusions about the distinct levels of political disaffection among Western and Latin American democracies are, however, rather contingent, as they are based on simple bivariate relations. Therefore, in a bid to provide further confirmation for these conclusions, I developed three regression models: one in which the dependent variable is the percentage of citizens who generally feel that the authorities and the political system are not receptive to their demands; one with the percentage of salience of politics in life as the dependent variable; and the third in which the dependent variable is the index of institutional trust. I have not included, however, all the variables shown in Table 7.8 due to the existence of strong multicolinearity between some of them.[44] In general, I have only included one variable for each of the four groups of the major hypotheses discussed above (the one showing the strongest correlation in Table 7.8). In some cases, I have maintained two variables when they do not seem to create major problems for estimation.[45]

The models to be estimated are:

1 Institutional confidence $= \int$(democratization history variables, modernization, institutions in place, performance of the system).
2 External political efficacy $= \int$(democratization history variables, modernization, institutions in place, performance of the system).
3 Salience of politics $= \int$(democratization history variables, modernization, institutions in place, performance of the system).[46]

As can be seen in Table 7.9, the results of the estimation of these models provide definitive confirmation of the crucial role that democratization history plays in shaping these attitudes. In model 1, focusing on confidence in political institutions, the significant variables with a positive relationship (in order of importance) are years of democracy since 1930, number of general strikes, and increase in political and civil liberties since democracy was re-established. The last is the only variable related to performance (although it might be interpreted as a recent record of democratization history) that displays any relationship with institutional confidence, confirming the findings of Norris' (1999c: 232–234) recent comparative study. Nevertheless, I do not think that this is an indicator, as the author suggests, of current institutional political features, but rather of past democratic history (in fact, the correlation between the latter and the increase in political liberties is 0.44). Finally, I could not find any relation with the level of corruption at the aggregate level.

These findings, as well as the crucial importance of the individual country's democratization history, are confirmed once again in model 2 (also in Table 7.9), which estimates the relation with the degree of external political inefficacy. The relation with the number of years of democratic rule since 1930 and the variation in political and civil liberties are once again the strongest. The variables related to income differences (i.e. 1997 income levels and 1997 income levels to the cubic power) are not significant.

Table 7.9 Regression model with aggregate data of some indicators of political disaffection (Ordinary Least Square [OLS])

Variable[a]	Model 1 Dependent variable: Index of institutional confidence*100		Model 2 Dependent variable: External efficacy political		Model 3 Dependent variable: Salience of politics	
	Beta	Sig.	Beta	Sig.	Beta	Sig.
Years of democracy since 1930 or years under longest democratic rule	0.46	0.07	0.70	0.07	0.28	0.40
Average number of general strikes from introduction of democracy to 1990	0.42	0.06	0.57	0.04	n.i.	
Corruption index 1980–1992	−0.12	0.75	−0.71	0.11	0.28	0.51
Effective number of parties from introduction of democracy to 1995	−0.1	0.7	n.i		n.i	
Variation in Political and Civil Liberties Index from introduction of democracy to 1997	−0.42	0.06	−0.73	0.02	n.i.	
Increase in per capita income from introduction of democracy to 1997	−0.19	0.74	−0.19	0.73	−0.83	0.17
Income per capita 1997	−0.03	0.95	n.i		n.i.	
Income per capita 1997 to the cubic power	0.16	0.64	0.59	0.21	0.91	0.06
Constant	1.96		49		20.6	
R^2	0.85		0.64		0.44	
F	7.73		3.29		3.18	
(N)	(20)	0.00	(17)	0.04	(20)	0.04

Note
a Some variables discussed in the text have been taken away from this model given the lack of bivariate relationships observed in Table 7.8 and problems of multicolinearity; n.i. = not included.

Nevertheless, the variable measuring income levels in 1997 was not included due to high multicolinearity detected with the two preceding ones, and the tolerance levels (multicolinearity) produced by the other two income variables remain very high, generating very questionable statistical inference tests for the coefficients. It is clear, however, that the variables containing some information on income per capita have the same predictive capacity for the level of external political efficacy, although far from that detected by the years of democracy and variation of political and civil liberties. For instance, the different levels of modernization of Southern European societies do not correspond with the low levels of political efficacy observed in these countries and the differences among them. (Greece has the highest levels of political efficacy, for example.) This is also true of Argentina, Chile, and Brazil.

In model 3, the only significant predictor of the different levels of salience of politics is the '*N*-curve modernization' variable. Democratization history variables lose their predictive capacity as soon as this variable is included in the model (data not shown). Political mobilization does occur more under democratic rule than under authoritarian regimes. However, pseudo-democratic systems in Latin America during the 1950s and 1960s did implement populist-mobilizing strategies to legitimate their political regimes among demobilized populations, thereby changing their basic attitudes.[47] This is why, as suggested by the comparative levels in the previous section, engagement and attentiveness to politics are higher in those countries. A similar hypothesis, that is to say, one which emphasizes the effect of political mobilization on political engagement, has also been put forward to account for the higher levels of interest in politics in Eastern Europe.[48] Finally, we can conclude that these results challenge the significance, defended by other scholars,[49] of current economic performance, current institutional setting, and contextual political features.

The distinctive character of disaffection in old and new democracies

As we have seen in the analysis of the aggregate data presented in the previous section, the best predictor of the varying levels of political disaffection found in the countries under consideration is their democratic history or, to be more precise, their record of exclusionary and/or anti-democratic institutions, practices, and demobilizing political episodes. In this section, I argue that the effect of this democratization history not only explains differences in political disaffection at the aggregate level, but also explains political disaffection at the individual level. The main aim of the following pages is to show the distinct 'nature' of disaffection at the individual level in new democracies, as they are countries with long histories of democratic instability and protracted experiences of serious democratic disruption brought about by the aforementioned exclusionary institutions and practices in a context of social complexity. In short, I will show that the factors explaining political disaffection at the individual level are different in new democracies.

The basic argument concerning the different nature of political disaffection in new democracies is that the citizens of these countries do not have a valid point of reference from which to assess the performance and representative nature of the current political institutions or the achievements of the system. As a result, their opinions and attitudes with respect to the democratic institutions, politicians, and performance of the system will be much less dependent on direct experience of the existing institutions and their functioning, and will tend to reflect accumulated non-democratic or pseudo-democratic experiences in the past.

As we saw before, high disaffection is not a problem exclusive to new democracies. Some new democracies display low disaffection due to a successful, more distant democratic past, despite recent and sometimes traumatic non-democratic experiences. At the same time, there are democracies that, although not part of the recent 'third democratization wave', have high political disaffection due to their history of troubled democratic regimes. These exceptions reinforce the conclusion regarding the importance of the political past in shaping these attitudes. However, the problem of disaffection is different in these old, stable democracies precisely because of the effect of the past. Political disaffection in new democracies is the product of the 'democratization process of the past', whereas in old democracies it reflects the effect of the 'democratic past'. In old democracies, citizens have experienced democratic rule and have some experience on which to base their evaluation of the functioning and performance of the current institutions. Therefore, political disaffection derives from the negative evaluation of current socially excluding institutions, their representatives, their declining performance, and the long accumulation of frustrated expectations. In this respect, the causes of political disaffection in all non-third-wave democracies are the same – the result of accumulated democratic experience. The difference is that in those with high disaffection, the democratic history is full of episodes of failure, manipulation, instability, the use and abuse of exclusive institutional settings, and accumulated poor performance, whereas in countries with high affection the democratic history tends to be full of successes.

In contrast, political disaffection in new democracies – regardless of the levels observed – has a distinct origin and nature, also related with the political history, and is more closely linked to the socializing experiences of previous episodes of non-democratic or pseudo-democratic rule. In this respect, despite the almost similar presence of a certain degree of political disaffection in new and some old democracies, it does make sense to separate them when studying their nature at the individual level.

If this hypothesis is correct, the analysis of the variables that influence disaffection in the new and traditional democracies should produce very different results in each case. We should also expect the basic characteristics of the disaffected citizens to be quite distinct. I have already shown elsewhere that the characteristics of the disaffected citizens are quite distinctive in their educational, generational, and informational profiles: the disaffected in new democracies are younger than average, have less education, and are less informed (Torcal 2002a).

I will now present further evidence for the distinctive character of disaffection in new and old democracies. This is drawn from a comparative multivariate analysis of survey data: the WVS third wave (1995–1997), which includes a series of particularly interesting variables for this discussion. Using only the last wave of this comparative cross-national survey has two advantages: I can use more variables included in the questionnaire to test different hypotheses, and can include as well confidence in political parties in the institutional confidence index (only included in that third wave). On the other hand, it has one disadvantage: unfortunately, the survey did not cover all the countries under analysis here. I will, therefore, present the results obtained from survey data for 12 countries, comprising six first- and second-wave democracies and six of the so-called new democracies (16,367 cases).[50]

In order to verify the distinctive character of disaffection I have developed a general model to look at three different attitudes: institutional confidence, the importance of politics in life (salience of politics), and interest in politics (another indicator of political disaffection).[51] The independent variables chosen from the survey are the following:

(A)   Political and performance variables:

1   Ideological scale;[52] according to Newton and Norris (2000: 65) this is an essential variable in observing the effect of politics on individuals' institutional confidence.

2   Satisfaction with the way people in national office today are running the country.[53]

3   Perception of the level of corruption existing in the system.[54]

4   Evaluation of the extent of poverty in the country compared with the situation ten years earlier.[55]

5   Household's financial situation, used to test the effect of individual prosperity on political disaffection.[56]

(B)   Cultural variables:

1   Postmaterialist index,[57] since some literature has identified a relationship between this variable and internal political efficacy (Gabriel 1995: 357–389).

2   Social trust,[58] in order to test whether there is a relationship between the type of people who express trust in others and confidence in strong and effective institutions.

(C)   Sociological variables:

   1   Gender.[59]
   2   Age.[60]
   3   Education.[61]

(D)   I have also added a dummy variable in order to see whether the effect of being an established (0) or new (1) democracy has any effect on the levels of political disaffection.
     Thus, the general individual level model for political disaffection I propose to test is the following:

Model 1: $y = \beta + \beta_1 A + \beta_2 B + \beta_3 C + \beta_4 D + e_o$

To test my hypothesis on the specific nature of political disaffection in new democracies I will add two additional sets of variables in two steps:

(E)   Aggregate political variables:

   1   Number of years of democracy since 1930.
   2   Average number of general strikes since the introduction of democracy.

(F)   Interactions of some of the variables *A*, *B*, and *C* with the *D* dummy old/new democracy variable to test if the individual level variables do have a different impact in new democracies.
     Therefore, models 2 and 3 to be tested are as follows:

Model 2: $y = \beta + \beta_1 A + \beta_2 B + \beta_3 C + \beta_4 D + \beta_5 E + e_o$

Model 3: $y = \beta + \beta_1 A + \beta_2 B + \beta_3 C + \beta_4 D + \beta_5 E + \beta_6 F + e_o$

If my hypothesis about the distinct character of political disaffection in new democracies is correct, we should expect the following:

1   Coefficients of the interaction variables *E* should be other than zero ($\beta_6 \neq 0$), that is, statistically significant and negative for the satisfaction with the performing variables (since this should be less important in new democracies), positive for the social trust variables (since this variable partly represents the personal socializing experiences in new democracies), and, as I discussed in the preceding section, negative for age and education.
2   Coefficients of aggregate political variables *F* should be other than zero ($\beta_5 \neq 0$), that is, statistically significant. The strength and direction could change depending on the dependent variable: positive for

the years of democracy since 1990 and institutional confidence, and positive and stronger for the relationship between the average number of general strikes and interest in politics and relevance of politics in life.

Table 7.10 shows the results of the estimation of the three models for each of these three dependent variables. I have only shown the statistically significant beta coefficients with significance values of over 0.05.[62] The parameters estimated in these models confirm the hypothesis regarding the specific nature of political disaffection in new democracies. In model 3 under institutional confidence, the interaction for satisfaction with authorities is important, significant, and negative (beta −0.22), revealing that in new democracies confidence in institutions depends much less on the performance of the system, and more on social trust (significant and positive) and the perception of corruption. On the other hand, there is no consistent relationship in all democracies between education and institutional confidence, which also shows a reduced positive coefficient with age. In contrast, the effect of age and education is more negative and significant in new democracies, making it clear that in these democracies institutional disaffection is greater among the youngest and less educated citizens.

The interaction variables for political interest and relevance of politics are not significant except for age (higher among the younger) and education (higher among the better educated). Even though in some non-democratic countries political mobilization has often been focused on marginal sectors of society, it has a clearer effect on the more educated and younger citizens than on those who were directly exposed to attempts at mobilization or to greater political information during these periods in the past (e.g. Argentina, Peru, Brazil, and so on). In contrast, long-lasting political mobilization resulting from enfranchisement and political organization of all sectors of society has a more widespread effect on overall cultural levels with a slightly greater impact among older citizens. The particular relationship between age and education and these two attitudes in new democracies confirms the impact of past political history. However, much of the variance in these attitudes remains to be explained, as shown by the poor goodness of fit. Besides, the beta value of the old/new dummy variable in the models is very important, revealing that there are some additional factors to be included in the analysis in order to explain the lower level of political engagement in these countries. Additionally, the results reveal a number of very interesting findings, but perhaps most importantly:

(A)   With regard to institutional political disaffection:

1   The dummy variable for new/old democracies has a small but positive impact on institutional confidence, showing, as we saw in preceding sections, that some new democracies have greater levels

Table 7.10 Estimation of models explaining institutional trust and political engagement at the individual level 1995–1997 (Ordinary Least Square [OLS])[a]

Variables	Institutional confidence			Political interest			Salience of politics		
	Model 1	Model 2	Model 3	Model 1	Model 2	Model 3	Model 1	Model 2	Model 3
Years of democracy since 1930		0.13	0.13		0.18	0.18		0.11	0.11
Social trust in new democracies			0.07						
Social trust	0.14	0.13		0.11	0.10	0.09	0.11	0.10	0.10
Satisfaction with personal financial situation	0.08	0.07	0.07	0.06	0.03	0.03	v0.03		
Satisfaction with authorities in new democracies			-0.22						
Satisfaction with authorities	0.24	0.21	0.31	0.05	v0.03	0.03	0.05	0.03	
Poverty compared with ten years earlier	-0.04	-0.03	-0.03						
Postmaterialist Index				0.17	0.15	0.15	0.12	0.11	0.11
Perception of level of corruption in the system	0.20	0.17	0.13	0.09	0.06	0.08	0.04		
Perception of corruption in new democracies			0.10						
New democracies (0, 1)	0.06	0.07	0.13	-0.18	-0.30	-0.25	-0.09	-0.22	-0.31
Ideology in new democracies				-0.06	-0.05	-0.04			-0.06
Ideology			0.03	0.06	0.07	0.07			
Gender							0.03	0.04	0.03
Education in new democracies			-0.07			0.17			0.17
Education				0.09	0.11	0.06	0.11	0.12	0.07
Average number of general strikes from introduction of democracy to 1990			-0.13		0.22	0.24		0.19	0.21
Age in new democracies		-0.08	-0.09			-0.15			-0.08
Age	0.05	0.04	0.03	0.09	0.06	0.11	0.07	0.06	0.09
R^2	0.22	0.23	0.25	0.16	0.18	0.19	0.08	0.09	0.09
(N)	(10,043)	(10,042)	(10,043)	(10,452)	(10,452)	(10,452)	(10,404)	(10,404)	(10,404)

Sources: WVS, 1995–1997.

Note

a Only the statistically significant beta coefficients with a p value < 0.05 have been included.

of political affection (Chile and Uruguay) than their older counter-parts (such as Venezuela, Italy, or even France). The classification of countries according to the levels of political disaffection does not correspond with recent non-democratic and democratization experiences. However, when I added to model 2 the aggregate vari-able measuring the number of years of democracy since 1930, it also emerges as a powerful predictor at the individual level. Institutional political disaffection is a problem related to the political history of these countries that goes beyond the third-wave phenomenon.

2   The degree of satisfaction with the incumbent authorities is a powerful predictor of institutional confidence in the traditional democracies, confirming the importance of system performance in predicting this attitude, although, as we saw, this is much less significant in new democracies. The perception of corruption is the other performance variable with the greatest effect. This result con-firms the findings of recent studies which have argued that unful-filled expectations are important determinants of confidence in institutions, such expectations including the idea that the govern-ment should 'follow procedures that are unbiased' (Miller and Listhaug 1999: 189–201) and 'produce outcomes that neither advantage nor disadvantage particular groups unfairly. Addition-ally, citizens expect political leaders to operate in an honest ... manner' (della Porta 2000: 202–228). However, these expectations could be higher in different countries due to a lack of previous democratic experiences to compare with, explaining why the per-ception of corruption is much greater in the newer democracies than in the more-established ones; while 55 per cent of citizens in new democracies state that all or nearly all the authorities are involved in corruption, this figure drops to 44 per cent in the more traditional democracies (and to just 38 per cent when Venezuela is excluded). This also explains why this variable shows higher predic-tive capacity among new democracies.

3   However, institutional political disaffection is not a pure reflection of democratic system performance. Neither respondents' evalu-ations of the changing levels of poverty nor their personal eco-nomic situation have an impact. Institutional confidence depends to some extent on other cultural variables that reflect personal socializing experiences. In fact, and contrary to some recent find-ings, social trust has a greater impact on institutional confidence than some performing variables (Newton 1999b; Newton and Norris 2000; Mishler and Rose 2001). This is especially true for new democracies (see interactions in model 3).[63] The cultural change of postmaterialism does not have an impact.

4   Contrary to recent findings, ideology does not have any effect on institutional confidence (Newton and Norris 2000: 65).

(B)   With regard to political interest and political salience:

   1   The results of the estimation of both models are mirror images:
        both belong to the same dimension of political disaffection (polit-
        ical disengagement) and respond to the same processes and factors
        in their origin and evolution.
   2   The dummy new–old democracy variable is much stronger and
        consistent with this type of disaffection (lower among new demo-
        cracies), but the political aggregate variables are also good predic-
        tors, especially the average number of general strikes from the
        introduction of democracy to 1990. Even the mobilization pro-
        duced since the (re)establishment of democracy, shown in the
        average number of strikes, has a significant effect on the level of
        political disengagement.
   3   The cultural-socializing variables are the strongest attitudinal pre-
        dictors, confirming the importance of these dimensions on polit-
        ical engagement (Gabriel 1995: 357–387), whereas the performing
        variables have a very residual effect.
   4   Ideology has very little effect on political interest and none on
        salience of politics in life.

Conclusion

In this chapter I have compared different levels of political disaffection in
an important group of traditional and new democracies. The analysis displays the existence of substantive differences between these two groups of
democracies. Despite higher presence of political disaffection on average
among the new ones, political disaffection is not an exclusive phenomenon
of new democracies. Old established democracies might have citizens with
significant levels of political disaffection, whereas new democracies might
display a much better picture. Furthermore, cross-national differences on
political disaffection are not only a question of distinctive levels, but they
also point to the nature of this disaffection. Political disaffection among the
citizens of old democracies is positively related with education, information,
and participation experiences; in many new democracies, the relation with
these variables is negative. Critical citizens in new democracies are not
related so much with a rational assessment of the performance, openness,
and functioning of the current democratic institutions.

The third wave of democratization (the timing, the modern context
where it took place, and the existence of authoritarian rule during the
1970s) is not a clear factor for explaining the cross-national differences on
the levels and nature of political disaffection. The observed cross-national
differences are due to distinct democratization experiences. In new democracies, these democratization experiences are more frequently characterized by decades of convulsive processes of political exclusion for an

important part of the population and the presence of very erratic and distinctive mobilization episodes. These problematic democratization processes have left an enduring imprint in many citizens making them very critical of the democratic process, of politics, and of the mechanisms of democratic representation.

Notes

* I would like to thank Lorenzo Brusattin, Araceli Mateos, Irene Martín, José Ramón Montero, and Josep Pena, as well as two anonymous reviewers, for their interesting suggestions on an earlier draft of this chapter.

1 Some scholars have disputed the existence of this declining pattern, finding instead trendless fluctuations (Newton 1999b: 175). An argument against the internationalization of the decline of political confidence can be also found in Holmberg (1999).

2 By 'new democracies' we should understand the third-wave democracies established since the mid-1970s, whereas 'old democracies' are more traditional democracies established during the first and second democratization waves; see Huntington (1991).

3 It has also been argued that this decline in confidence taps confidence in incumbent authorities more than in institutions *per se*. See Lipset and Schneider (1983: 88–89); Merkl (1988: 32–33); and Dogan (1995: 57–71).

4 Some studies carried out during the 1980s and 1990s dispute the alleged decline in confidence in institutions. Some authors argue, for instance, that this has only affected government institutions, whereas confidence in national parliaments, for instance, has remained stable or even increased; see Listhaug and Wiberg (1995: 298–322). However, in more recent studies, scholars have demonstrated the presence of a clear decline in confidence in public institutions; see Dalton (1999: 62–69) and Newton and Norris (2000: 54–58).

5 For a similar comparative conclusion about the case of Spain, see Maravall (1984: 125–126). Despite a clear decrease in the United States and Great Britain, Maravall found significantly lower figures in Spain. The comparison includes references to the *output of the system*, i.e. approval and legitimacy given by citizens to the decisions made by incumbent authorities (30–33 per cent), bureaucratic authorities (81 per cent), and courts (47 per cent). For similar conclusions see Rose (1989: 14). The data come from Parisot (1988: Table 1).

6 For discussion and data showing the lower confidence in parliament among the Portuguese, see Bruneau and Macleod (1986: 152–155) and Bruneau (1984b: 38–39). In Spain, confidence in democratic institutions was higher in 1981 than in 1990, but still lower than among its Western European partners. See Merkl (1988: 31–33).

7 It is important to note that Spaniards only seem to trust the mass media (they come in third in the ranking of countries trusting the media) and trade unions (fourth). However, the former may not be very reliable and deserves further consideration, as this level of trust is not confirmed by other Spanish surveys, in which trade unions systematically appear as the institutions which enjoy the lowest levels of institutional trust among Spaniards. Moreover, membership and participation in trade unions in Spain is much lower than in the rest of Western Europe.

8 For similar conclusions, see Turner and Martz (1998: 66–70).

9 According to Listhaug and Wiberg (1995: 320), the distinction between political and private institutions can be observed in trends in confidence in a set of

European countries. Rose (1984) divides these institutions into those belonging to the government and other non-governmental institutions. And Döring (1992: 133–137) has distinguished between institutions of 'civil society' and institutions of 'established order'. Despite the different labels used, the relevant institutions are generally distributed very similarly between the two categories.

10 Political parties were only included in the 1997 WVS wave, which covers only a few Western European countries.

11 The classic study of this topic is by Lipset and Schneider (1983). These scholars demonstrated the decline in confidence in institutions by analysing trust in major industries (pp. 33–40), the educational system, big corporations, and the financial system (pp. 57 and 68); their data came from the Gallup, Harris, and NORC surveys.

12 This lack of institutional trust can also be concluded from the classic indicators of political trust. The 1994 CIRES survey, which includes these indicators, found that 77 per cent of Spaniards stated that rarely or never 'you can trust the government to do what is right'. The percentages in the United States for the 'rarely' or 'never' categories were only 45 per cent in 1972 and 68 per cent in 1978. Moreover, 70 per cent of Spaniards believed that 'the government is pretty much run by a few big interests looking out for themselves'. The percentages of Americans agreeing with this statement were only 53 per cent in 1972 and 67 per cent in 1978. For the United States data, see Miller *et al.* (1980: 257).

13 For similar conclusions, see Listhaug and Wiberg (1995: 302).

14 Already in 1989, 68 per cent of Greeks agreed with the statement 'politicians do not care about what people like me might think', and 77 per cent maintained that 'politicians only defend their own interests'. The percentage of people agreeing with both statements in 1993 increased to 72 and 82 per cent, respectively, and in 1996 only 29 per cent disagreed with the first statement. These data come from different Greek surveys: for 1989, the EKKE post-electoral study; for 1993, OPINION post-electoral study; and for 1996, the CNEP. This last survey includes a third neutral response category, 'it depends', selected by 14 per cent of the respondents. I want to thank Ilias Nikolapoulos, Nikiforos Diamandouros, and Takis Kafetzis for sharing these data, which were passed on to me by Irene Martín. Similar conclusions can be also observed in Mendrinou and Nicolacopoulos (1997: 22–29).

15 For similar conclusions, see Ester, Halman, and de Moor (1983: 79). These scholars also maintain that falling interest in politics among the Spaniards runs contrary to increasing interest observed in the rest of Europe, with the exception of France.

16 These data come from *Eurobarometer, Trends 1974–1993*, pp. 161–164. See also Montero and Torcal (1992: 261).

17 The averages in the other European Community (EC) countries are the following: Belgium, 34 per cent; Denmark, 67; Germany, 57; Greece, 52; France, 44; Ireland, 42; Luxembourg, 47; the Netherlands and United Kingdom, 55.

18 In Spain, interest in politics has increased 4 points since 1988, a smaller increase than that seen in the other EU countries with the exception of France and Holland, where it has decreased, and Luxembourg and the United Kingdom, with a 1 and 4 per cent increase, respectively. However, it is important to note that these countries display a much higher level of interest in politics than Spain. Moreover, in a recent comparative study, Gabriel and van Deth (1995: 410) have argued that, with very few exceptions, stability is the dominant tendency in the evolution of political interest in all Western European countries over the last two or three decades.

19 For similar conclusions, see Maravall (1984: 117–120); Montero and Torcal (1990: 131–134); Bacalhau (1995: 85–90); Morán and Benedicto (1995: 55–58).

20 These data come from the International Social Survey Program (ISSP), the Role of Government III survey, 1996–1999.

21 According to the Four Nation Study data, in Greece and Portugal 68 and 75 per cent of respondents, respectively, think that 'politics is too complicated for people like me'. Furthermore, contrary to what we have seen in the case of the other dimension of political disaffection, this situation in Greece has remained stable over time (55, 61, and 55 per cent of respondents agreed with this statement in 1989, 1993, and 1996, respectively).

22 According to Dahl (1971: 4–10), democratic inclusion (inclusiveness) is one of the major dimensions to classify political regimes and polyarchies. This dimension is measured by the right to participate in elections and hold offices. Therefore, institutions that foster democratic inclusion are those that recognize and encourage electoral and political participation in general. Although there is an explicit relationship between political contestation, the other dimension for measuring democratization, and inclusiveness, I do not consider political contestation as part of the phenomenon of democratic inclusion.

23 These data come from Torcal (2001, 2002c).

24 These data are given in Table 7.4.

25 These data are given in Table 7.5.

26 These data represent confidence in the three institutions. They were drawn from the 1990 World Values Survey and can be found in Table 7.5. Unfortunately, confidence in political parties was not included in the World Values Survey until 1997, and many of the other cases of interest to this research were not included in this latest round. Norris (1999c: 222) has developed a similar index of institutional confidence which also includes confidence in parties and in the government. I have excluded parties in order to consider a greater number of traditional democracies that were not part of the 1997 round of the World Values Survey. Moreover, excluding parties does not alter the conclusions of the present study. On the contrary, as will be seen below, the study of confidence in political parties serves to reinforce my conclusions. Including confidence in the government in the index is more problematic from my point of view since this indicator largely represents confidence in the incumbent authorities.

27 The countries included in the present analysis using the index of institutions and political saliency are the following: Germany, Argentina, Austria, Belgium, Brazil, Chile, Denmark, France, Ireland, Italy, the Netherlands, Norway, Peru, Portugal, Spain, Sweden, United Kingdom, United States, Uruguay, and Venezuela. For the analysis using the indicator of internal political efficacy, Greece and Paraguay could also be included, though Austria, the United States, Norway, and Sweden were excluded because data were not available.

28 As Altman and Pérez-Liñán (2002: 87) have asserted, there is a substantial difference between addressing the quality of democracy and the level of democratization of a political regime. By the same token, it is also important to distinguish the history of the quality of democracy and the history of democratization. Nevertheless, both are highly interconnected, and I will consider both past democratic history and democratization history as similar concepts. This is also why I consider years under democratic rule a good proxy for the history of democratization.

29 I have used Mainwaring's (1999: 14–20) classification of political regimes. He classifies governments as democratic, semidemocratic, or authoritarian (or totalitarian). I have only counted the democratic ones. To be classified as

democratic, a government must meet four criteria: (1) the president and legislature in presidentialist systems, or the legislature in parliamentary systems, are chosen in open and fair competitive elections; (2) these elected authorities have real governing power; (3) civil liberties are respected; and (4) the franchise includes a sizeable majority of the adult population. I have taken the data for the Latin American cases from Table 1 in Chapter 1 (Mainwaring 1999). I myself have computed the rest of the data for the other European and North American cases from other sources.

30 Computed from Mainwaring (1999: Table 1) and other sources.

31 These data for Latin America were collected from Mainwaring (1999: Table 2).

32 These data come from Freedom House (1985, 1992–1993, and 1996), and also from the web site www.freedomhouse.org/research.

33 The Latin American data come from 'Latin American Democracies Data set', collected by Scott Mainwaring, Aníbal Pérez-Liñán, and Daniel Brinks. The data for the other countries come from the ACLP Dataset. For the formula of the effective number of parties, see Laakso and Taagapera (1979: 3–27).

34 This includes any strike of 1,000 or more industrial or service workers that involves more than one employer and that is aimed at national government policies or authority; these data come from Banks and Muller (1995).

35 This index goes from 1, indicating considerable corruption, to 10, indicating no corruption. The data used here were taken from the web site www.gwdg.de/~uwvw, and are published by Transparency International Publishers.

36 These data were obtained from the *Human Development Report* 1999 and *Human Development Report* 2000.

37 These data come primarily from the OECD, *Historical Statistics*, various years; and OECD, *National Accounts* Vol. 1, various years.

38 These data come primarily from the OECD, *Historical Statistics*, various years; and OECD, *National Accounts* Vol. 1, various years.

39 O'Donnell (1973) challenges the classic modernization theories with respect to the relationship between modernization and democracy, arguing that rapid modernization created bottlenecks of development in most industrialized Latin American countries which triggered the emergence of military regimes in the 1960s and 1970s; see a similar argument Huntington (1968).

40 For a similar conclusion, see Miller and Listhaug (1999: 206–210); McAllister (1999: 201–203), and Pharr (2000: 179–180).

41 For a very interesting critique of this index reaching quite a similar conclusion about the validity of this item to measure corruption, see Heywood (2002).

42 For more sophisticated arguments critically revising the relationship between economic development and democracy, see Przeworski and Limongi (1997: 155–183) and Mainwaring and Pérez-Liñán (2000).

43 See also Gunther, Montero, and Torcal (2003).

44 Some variables presented coefficients with a tolerance of less than 0.1 and a very high Variance Inflation Factor (VIF).

45 Different tests have been carried out to ensure that these relations do not produce biased estimators or type II error in the test of significance.

46 To test the modernization hypothesis in models 1 and 2, I have included 1997 income and the cubic 1997 power of income, since both test different theories. However, 1997 income was not included for model 3 since there was no correlation (see Table 7.9). Finally, in models 1 and 2 I have included a new variable that combines the average increase in civil and political liberties (the indices of political and civil liberties), since the original two variables were found to be very closely related ($r = 0.8$). This variable was not included in model 3 due to the lack of relationship detected in the correlations.

47 As noted above, a perfect demonstration of this argument can be found in Stokes (1995).

48 For this argument and useful data on political interest, see Martín (2000).

49 Anderson and Guillory (1997: 66–81) argue in favour of the influence of constitutional design. Norris (1999b: 232–234), in addition to putting forward the same argument, also defends the importance of the electoral and party systems as well as the accumulated frustration of supporting losing opposition parties. Similar arguments can be found in Miller and Listhaug (1990: 357–386); Clarke, Dutt, and Kornberg (1993: 998–1021); Anderson (1995); Weisberg (1996); and Nye and Zelikow (1997: 268–276).

50 The countries included in the analysis are the following: Germany, the United States, Great Britain, Norway, Sweden, and Venezuela. Argentina, Brazil, Chile, Peru, Spain, and Uruguay are included as representative cases of new democracies.

51 The WVS does not include any of the traditional items to measure internal or external efficacy, so I have decided to use this indicator of political engagement.

52 Question V123 of the WVS questionnaire.

53 Question V165 of the WVS questionnaire: 'How satisfied are you with the way the people now in national office are handling the country's affairs? Would you say you are very satisfied, fairly satisfied, fairly dissatisfied, or very dissatisfied?'

54 Question V213 of the WVS questionnaire: 'How widespread do you think bribe taking and corruption is in this country? 1, Almost no public officials are engaged in it; 2, A few public officials are engaged in it; 3, Most public officials are engaged in it; 4, Almost all public officials are engaged in it'.

55 Question V171 of the WVS questionnaire: 'Would you say that today a larger share, about the same share, or a smaller share of the people in this country are living in poverty than they were ten years ago?'

56 Question V64 of the WVS questionnaire: 'How satisfied are you with the financial situation of your household? 1 means you are completely dissatisfied on this scale, and 10 means you are completely satisfied'.

57 Variable V100mpm of the WVS questionnaire containing the materialist-postmaterialist scale.

58 Variable V27 of the WVS questionnaire: 'Generally speaking, would you say that most people can be trusted or that you can't be too careful in dealing with people? 1, Most people can be trusted; 2, Can't be too careful'.

59 Question V214 of the WVS questionnaire.

60 Question V216 of the WVS questionnaire

61 Question V217 of the WVS questionnaire.

62 The variable was created with individual score loadings resulting from the following factor analysis: Legal system, 0.58; administration, 0.70, and national parliament, 0.77. Unlike Norris (1999a, 1999b), I did not include confidence in political parties for this part of the analysis only, in order to maintain consistency with the index analysed in previous sections.

63 For a different position in which social trust is considered to be part of the vicious circle see della Porta (2000: 202–228).

8 Confidence in parliaments

Performance, representation, and accountability*

Pedro C. Magalhães

Institutional confidence has become a major concern of both political scientists and policy-makers. An increasing number of studies have detected a decline in citizens' confidence in contemporary democracies which seems to encompass not only officeholders and parties but also, and perhaps more disturbingly, the political institutions themselves (Norris 1999c; Dalton 1999; Pharr, Putnam, and Dalton 2000b; Newton and Norris, 2000). As Torcal and Montero argue in the Introduction to this volume, lack of confidence in political institutions does not necessarily entail a lack of public support for democratic institutions or for the democratic regime as a whole. However, if, as they suggest, we treat lack of confidence as a symptom of *institutional disaffection* (a belief 'about the lack of responsiveness of the political authorities [representatives] and institutions') a low level of confidence in institutions would signal the presence of lived and perceived gaps between the interests of citizens and those of their representatives, which are in turn likely to be associated with low levels of political engagement, involvement, or efficacy. In other words, they suggest that we are in the presence of potential deficits in the quality of democratic rule that merit serious investigation.

From this perspective, confidence in parliaments is a topic deserving special attention. In an age of increasing party discipline and the 'governmentalization' of legislative policy-making in parliamentary democracies, one of the crucial functions of legislatures in the political system arguably remains that of 'mobilizing consent' between elections (Beer 1990: 46), producing 'among the relevant populace and elites a wider and deeper sense of the government's moral right to rule' and 'putting the legislative stamp of approval on initiatives taken elsewhere' (Packenham 1970: 527; see also Mishler and Rose 1994). However, parliaments would hardly appear able to perform these functions if they themselves have become the object of distrust on the part of citizens.[1] In the United States, for example, negative feelings towards Congress seem to have helped generate widespread lack of trust in politicians and governmental institutions in general (Hibbing and Theiss-Morse 1995). Therefore, the perception that confidence in parliaments has declined over the last decade points to the possibility that distrust may spill over to other institutions and actors in other industrialized democracies. Moreover, even if these provisional assessments of such a 'decline' were to turn out to be rather premature, national variations in citizens' levels of confidence in such a key democratic institution as parliament may provide vital insights into why political institutions in general are more trusted in some countries than in others.

Attempts at explaining institutional confidence have been plagued by two major dilemmas. The first involves the choice of culture- or performance-based interpretations of the sources of trust in or distrust of political institutions and actors. On the one hand, although some of the most persuasive arguments about the origins of institutional confidence employ cultural differences and socialization patterns as explanatory variables, the micro-foundations of such interpretations invariably suffer from a notable lack of empirical support. However, on the other hand, while governmental performance and popular satisfaction with policy outputs have indeed been shown to affect political confidence at both the individual and aggregate levels, they fail to account for the most evident phenomenon in industrialized democracies in this respect: the fact that citizens living in certain societies seem to display systematically lower levels of political confidence than citizens living in others, the sort of recurrent and structural phenomenon that seems impervious to circumstantial explanations.

One of the major goals of the various contributions to this volume is precisely to overcome the dichotomy between culturalist and rationalist approaches to political support. In this chapter, this is done by expanding the notion of institutional performance in order to encompass not only economic and policy outputs, but also the extent to which institutional rules – particularly those regulating elections and policy-making – facilitate citizens' input into policy-making. In other words, I suggest that, regardless of the impact that short-term governmental outputs may have on institutional confidence, the continuous operation of certain stable institutional arrangements is more likely to foster citizens' long-term confidence in political institutions than others.

However, when discussing which particular constitutional rules are likely to affect political responsiveness and the perception of this among citizens (and thus, are likely to affect institutional disaffection), we encounter a second dilemma, that revolving around the role of representation and accountability. On the one hand, the most persuasive arguments about the relationship between institutional rules and institutional confidence point to the positive effects of the type of political inclusiveness and congruence between citizens' interests and those of political authorities made possible by constitutional arrangements that foster power-sharing, i.e. those that typically prevail in so-called consensual democracies. On the other hand, however, these hypotheses tend to overlook the potential obstacle that such power-sharing may pose to the electoral *accountability* of governments, coalitions, and parties. In fact, this may be one of the reasons why the arguments about the relationship between consensual democracies and institutional confidence have yet to be empirically confirmed. I will attempt to overcome this second dilemma by suggesting that *both* representation and accountability should be taken into account when trying to identify links between institutional rules and citizens' beliefs about the trustworthiness of political institutions. Consensual election and policy-making rules (and the fair representation and negotiation between majorities and minorities they provide for) are indeed likely to foster voters' confidence in parliaments. However, electoral accountability should also matter: when the possibility of genuine alternation in power is neutralized and clarity of responsibility is undermined by the presence of strong institutional veto-players, citizens' confidence in legislative institutions is likely to diminish.

Institutional confidence, culture, and performance

The recent wave of research into confidence in political institutions has largely been driven by the desire to account for the purported decline in industrialized democracies of citizens' confidence in parties, governments, and parliaments above all. The best-known explanations for this tendency have been framed in what could be termed a cultural approach. This maintains that confidence in political institutions originates 'outside the political sphere in long-standing and deeply seeded beliefs about people that are rooted in cultural norms and communicated through early-life socialization' (Mishler and Rose 2001: 31). Two specific hypotheses have been generally advanced about the micro-foundations of this approach: the notions that interpersonal or social trust correlates strongly with confidence in institutions, and that citizens' basic value orientations affect their attitudes towards institutions and their performance.

From this point of view, 'trusters' – individuals who trust other people in general in face-to-face relations – should also have more confidence in political relations, objects, and institutions. Moreover, certain socialization experiences and social backgrounds – such as involvement in voluntary associations – are likely to be related to higher levels of interpersonal trust which, in turn, should spill over to political institutions. Thus, the decline in institutional confidence in Western societies would be explained by changes in patterns of socialization that have undermined social trust. In societies where citizens become increasingly disconnected from their extended families, friends, and neighbours, and where television has replaced civic-minded activities by 'privatized' and 'individualistic' forms of leisure, the 'networks, norms and social trust that facilitate coordination and cooperation for mutual benefit' have also decayed, a decay that, in turn, is strongly correlated with a general psychological disengagement from politics and government (Putnam 1995a, 1995b; Brehm and Rahn 1997; Campbell, Yonish, and Putnam 1999).

A rather different culturalist hypothesis about institutional confidence focuses on the role played by value orientations. Individuals oriented towards 'post-materialist' values (typically better educated and younger citizens) would also be more likely to reject traditional sources of authority and to criticize the established order, a set of attitudes that is alleged to undermine their confidence not only in hierarchical institutions but also in government in general. From this perspective, greater economic growth and well-being, as well as the expansion of schooling in industrialized democracies, have led to a 'post-modern' cultural shift, which has de-emphasized 'all kinds of authority, whether religious or secular, allowing much wider range for individual autonomy in the pursuit of individual subjective well-being', and leading, with respect to attitudes towards the political system, to a decline in institutional confidence (Inglehart 1999a: 238; see also Inglehart 1997a).

There are, however, two main problems with the cultural approach as applied to confidence in parliaments. The first is that it remains unclear whether the main phenomenon it accounts for – the decline in confidence in political institutions – in fact exists to be explained. Take the case of parliaments. While in the 1980s 'a key democratic institution like parliament experiences virtually no change in confidence' among European nations (Listhaug and Wiberg 1995: 308), the same was not true in the early to mid-1990s, when Klingemman (1999: 51) reported that 'lack of confidence in parliaments is particularly pronounced'. However, data from later periods suggest that this 'trend' has not continued, at least in Western Europe. Table 8.1 shows aggregate levels of confidence in parliament since the mid-1990s in all 15 European Union (EU) nations. It can be seen that confidence in parliaments actually seems to have increased in ten countries since the mid/late-1990s, sometimes quite significantly (as in the cases of Belgium, Sweden, Austria, or Italy), at the same time as the average for the 15 countries taken as a whole has risen from 44 to 49 per cent. This lends greater credence to the assertion that 'despite all the verbiage decrying the decline in trust, there is little actual evidence of a long-term secular decline, either in the United States or in Western Europe across the board' (Levi and Stoker 2000: 483).[2]

The second problem with the culturalist approach is that, at the individual level, interpersonal trust or value orientations (as well as the whole range of social background and/or socialization variables thought to be associated with them) have generally proved very poor predictors of institutional confidence, at least on the basis of existing measurements. Working with 1981 and 1990 pooled samples of survey respondents in 14 European countries (plus the United States and Canada), Listhaug and Wiberg (1995: 316–319), for example, found that of all the traditional socio-demographic variables only age has a consistent positive effect on institutional confidence, although this effect is very weak (particularly with respect to confidence in parliament and the legal system). Other studies

Table 8.1 Confidence in parliament in EU countries, 1997–2002[a]

Countries	1997	1999	2000	2001	2002	1997–2002 average	2002 in relation to 1997–2002 average
Luxembourg	57	61	64	64	65	62	+
Netherlands	64	62	58	62	58	61	−
Denmark	61	54	58	58	63	59	+
Finland	48	55	57	52	53	53	=
Sweden	48	42	49	50	59	50	+
Greece	51	51	44	49	51	49	+
Portugal	43	56	41	50	50	48	+
Spain	45	45	58	46	46	48	−
Austria	41	47	46	45	50	46	+
Germany	35	45	41	42	42	41	+
Ireland	38	36	38	41	45	40	+
United Kingdom	46	36	34	34	37	38	−
France	38	37	40	35	32	36	−
Belgium	20	26	42	41	43	34	+
Italy	29	28	35	32	38	32	+
Average	44	45	47	47	49		

Sources: *Eurobarometers 48, 51, 54.1, 55.1* and *57.1*.

Note

a Percentages of those who 'tend to trust' the lower chamber of their national parliaments.

have reached very similar conclusions,[3] lending credibility to McAllister's (1999: 200) assertion that, generally, 'the roots of democratic confidence in the social structure ... are weak'. Similar findings have been obtained about the direct impact of value orientations on individuals' confidence in governmental institutions. Although individuals sharing post-materialist values do seem to have less confidence in traditional institutions (such as the police, the armed forces, or the Church), the same does not hold for political institutions.[4] Finally, interpersonal trust also seems to be very weakly related to political confidence. As Kaase (1999: 14) puts it, after analysing eight Western European nations in three different years (1981, 1990, and 1996), 'the relationship in most cases is so small that interpersonal trust ... for all practical purposes cannot assume the role of an important antecedent to political trust'.[5]

This type of negative findings has shifted attention to an alternative approach to understanding political confidence. This is the performance-based approach, in which confidence is seen as 'politically endogenous', 'rationally based', and hinging on 'citizen evaluations of institutional performance' (Mishler and Rose 2001: 31). From this point of view, lack of confidence in political institutions would be a consequence of discontent with political and economic outputs. This approach has been successfully applied, for example, in studies revealing the impact on institutional confidence of macro-economic conditions such as unemployment or GDP levels (McAllister 1999: 197). Declining macro-economic performance and the rolling back of social welfare policies in industrialized democracies have also been identified as potential causes of the decline in public confidence in general (Alesina and Wacziarg 2000: 156–160; Katzenstein 2000: 143–148). Finally, others have focused on the extent to which the relationship between economic performance and trust is mediated by egocentric or sociotropic evaluations of the economy or levels of corruption (Listhaug and Wiberg 1995: 316–319; Miller and Listhaug 1999: 209; Mishler and Rose 2001: 50). The role of these sorts of policy outputs and their evaluations in fostering confidence is also one of the reasons why, more generally, a large number of studies has found institutional confidence to be 'contaminated' by a partisan component of support for incumbents: 'because the government is largely composed of institutions operated by incumbents, feelings about both should explain trust' (Hetherington 1998: 792). In other words, there is a 'home team' effect at work with respect to political confidence, whereby 'generalized trust goes up among people whose preferred party is in the Cabinet and goes down among people whose party is outside the ruling circle' (Holmberg 1999: 117–118).[6]

However, this emphasis on 'performance' as an explanation for confidence still leaves something to be explained. Table 8.1 serves, again, to illustrate this phenomenon. It is true that trends of decline in confidence in parliament seem to be rapidly followed by counter-trends of increased confidence. This, along with the significant fluctuations within some countries in the space of five years (amounting to over 10 percentage points in Sweden, Portugal, Belgium, Spain, and United Kingdom), suggest that lack of confidence in parliaments may indeed partly be an expression of the short-term inability of governmental institutions to deliver outputs that promote social and individual welfare. However, the most notable feature of confidence in parliament in Western Europe is not how it has risen or declined within countries, but rather the resilience of the differences between countries. In fact, since 1997, the differences between countries in terms of the percentage of individuals who 'tend to trust' parliament have often been quite high (reaching 44 percentage points in 1997), and most countries have consistently ranked either above or below the yearly average. While Luxembourg, the Netherlands, Denmark, and Finland consistently register the highest levels of confidence in parliament, Germany, France, Belgium, and Italy can be seen to be those where confidence has been systematically lowest, a phenomenon that is consistent with available data from previous periods.[7] Thus, a new problem emerges: although cultural explanations have generally fared worse than explanations focusing on performance when it comes to accounting for institutional confidence, performance-based explanations scarcely seem able to account for what seem to be structural and resilient differences between the industrialized democracies in this respect.

One way of overcoming this problem is to try to reconcile the cultural and the institutional performance approaches. McAllister (1999: 202), for example, points to the importance of the length of time democratic regimes have been in existence as a mediating variable between policy outputs and institutional confidence. Established democracies, which have had 'more time and opportunity to accumulate popular goodwill', may enjoy a 'reservoir of support' that leads citizens to blame incumbents rather than institutions for failures, causing 'the link between economic beliefs and democratic confidence to be weaker in the established democracies than in the newer democracies' (McAllister 1999: 202). In other words, 'culture' and 'performance' may interact, with the result that the impact of policy outputs in confidence is 'mediated via beliefs about the government' (McAllister 1999: 202). Others have suggested that, while performance is indeed crucial to explain confidence, the structural differences found between countries in this respect are explained by cultural factors. As Newton and Norris (2000: 61; see also Newton in this volume) have put it, 'if social trust helps build social capital and social capital, in turn, helps strengthen political institutions, then governmental performance may improve, inspiring citizens' confidence'. More generally, Torcal suggests in Chapter 7 of this volume that, both at the aggregate and individual levels, disaffection is a cultural disposition about politics which is formed over time as a result of the way different polities perform in terms of integrating citizens into the political game and averting exclusionary practices of corruption, fraud, and political manipulation.

The rest of this chapter focuses on another way of reconciling the cultural and institutional performance approaches. This is centred on the notions that the concept of 'institutional performance' needs to be expanded in order to include the way in which different electoral and policy-making rules boost or undermine the accountability of political institutions to citizens and their responsiveness to citizens' preferences; and that the impact of such rules is visible in terms of resilient attitudes of institutional disaffection, that resist the introduction of controls for short-term governmental performance and political preferences.

Confidence, representation, and accountability

Our ability to determine the potential impact of the performance of representative institutions on citizens' confidence in them is typically plagued by a serious problem: 'once economic measures are set aside, there is little agreement over which dimensions of performance are relevant across countries, time, and individual citizens' (Putnam, Pharr, and Dalton 2000: 24). However, it is nevertheless possible to extend the conceptualization of institutional performance beyond concrete policy outputs or outcomes. One way of doing this is by focusing on constitutional arrangements and their effects on two crucial aspects of democratic performance: the extent to which political actors and institutions are likely to be representative of, and accountable to, the citizenry.

As Manin, Przeworski, and Stokes (1999: 29) argue, the claim that free and fair elections facilitate an outcome in which 'governments will act on the best interest of the people' is based on two different views of democracy and representation. The first, the 'mandate' view, is one in which 'elections serve to select good policies or policy-bearing politicians'. The second, 'accountability', is one in which 'elections serve to hold governments responsible for the results of their past actions' (Manin, Przeworski, and Stokes 1999: 29), allowing citizens to maintain or oust incumbents from office in light of their performance.

Another way of thinking about this is to conceive representative democracy as 'a chain of delegation, in which those authorized to make political decisions conditionally designate others to make such decisions in their name and place' (Strøm 2000: 263). This type of delegation is potentially plagued by two problems. The first is the so-called 'adverse selection' problem, the tendency to select 'wrong' agents whose preferences are different to those of the principals (voters). However, a different 'moral hazard' problem emerges if conditions are such that agents, following elections, have the opportunity to act against the principal without suffering the full consequences of their actions.[8] Thus, insofar as political confidence stems from the belief 'that the political actor or institution will act in his interests (or at least not against his interests)' (Levi and Stoker 2000: 498), constitutional arrangements that minimize both adverse selection and moral hazard problems – and thus help satisfying both the 'mandate' and 'accountability' views of democracy – should foster greater institutional confidence.

What constitutional arrangements might those be? One thing we do know is that fulfilment of the 'mandate' view of democracy tends to be favoured by consensual institutional rules. Electoral systems that give rise to greater levels of proportionality in the conversion of votes into seats tend to minimize wasted votes, allow voters more meaningful choices among competing parties, and favour more accurate parliamentary representation of the different social interests and policy preferences in society. More generally, the combination of election rules that foster lower vote–seat disproportionality and policy-making rules that disperse power in legislatures has been shown to favour greater proximity between the preferences of the median voter and those of policy-makers (Huber and Powell 1996; Lijphart 1999: 288–298; and Powell 2000: 221–229).

As a result, theories linking constitutional rules and institutional confidence have tended to focus on the beneficial effects of consensual constitutional designs. In line with research by Anderson and Guillory (1997) (as well as Lijphart 1999: 275–300) on the relationship between consensual democracies and satisfaction with democracy, Norris (1999c: 221) hypothesizes that 'consensual institutions which maximize the number of "winners" produce higher levels of institutional confidence than winner-take-all majoritarian arrangements'. Banducci, Donovan, and Karp (1999: 538–539) similarly hypothesize that the shift from a majoritarian to a proportional representation system in New Zealand should engender more positive attitudes towards the political system – including trust in government – particularly among political minorities. More generally, Katzenstein (2000: 178) suggests that one of the reasons why the smaller European states do not seem to have experienced a decline in political confidence is their emphasis on a 'politics of institutional inclusion', in which 'electoral systems that are based on the principle of democratic representation and the need for governments to consist of politically encompassing coalitions ... tend to produce more winners and more political confidence'.

There is, however, one important problem with these hypotheses: they have failed to encounter empirical support. For example, the expected rise in trust in government following the adoption of proportional representations in New Zealand did not materialize, suggesting that 'the roots of distrust in government lie in something other than the rules used to translate votes into seats' (Banducci, Donovan, and Karp 1999: 552). Norris's (1999c: 224, 233) findings in this respect are even more striking: contrary to her expectations, institutional confidence in fact proved to be 'greater in countries with majoritarian rather than proportional systems', as well as lower in countries where both one-party government or extreme-multipartyism make it difficult for citizens to 'use elections as an opportunity to kick the rascals out'.

Thus, one possible explanation for these findings is that the effects that consensual democracies and institutions have for confidence have been estimated without controlling for the effects of the political and institutional features of democratic regimes that may place accountability under serious strain. At first sight, losses in accountability might seem a feature of all consensual democracies: 'majoritarian institutions generate governments that are farther from voters in policy space but more accountable' (Manin, Przeworski, and Stokes 1999: 47). However, three of the most crucial features ensuring that rulers remain accountable may actually cross-cut different types of political systems, defined by the extent to which their election rules engender disproportionality and their legislative policy-making rules disperse power.

One of these features is the majority status of the government, 'the first and most important element in determining clarity of responsibility' (Powell 2000: 52). Majority governments endow a party or a coalition of parties with control over enough votes to initiate and change policies in parliament, which in turn prevents such governments from assigning blame for performance failures to opposition parties and allows citizens to distinguish accurately who is responsible for legislative policy-making. It is true that majoritarian political systems are indeed more likely to engender single-party majorities, but several consensual democracies are also characterized by stable majority cabinets based on cohesive coalitions.[9] Thus, any positive effects that election and legislative policy-making rules may have on representation (and thus, confidence) can be assessed while controlling for the impact of government status on accountability.

Second, both majoritarian and consensual democracies may or may not be characterized by the presence of institutional veto-players beyond the lower chamber of parliament. These may include presidents with veto power over legislation, second chambers whose decisions cannot be overridden by simple or absolute majorities, or courts with the ability to veto bills or laws on grounds of their unconstitutionality (Tsebelis 2000, 2002). Such institutional veto-players are likely to have an effect on electoral accountability and, thus, on citizens' beliefs about the trustworthiness of parliaments. It is true that they may be conceived as mechanisms of 'horizontal accountability', checks on the power of otherwise unconstrained majorities that help lessen the loss of control experienced by citizens as they delegate power to representatives (Holmes 1995: 299–306; Persson, Roland, and Tabellini 1997; Strøm 2000: 277–278). However, they are also likely to operate as impediments to 'vertical' or 'electoral accountability': veto-players provide election-seeking incumbents with means to shift publicly the locus of decision-making, allowing them to claim credibly that forces external to the lower house and the majority that controls it have prevented them from keeping their electoral promises and forced them to renege on previous commitments (Arnold 1990; Twight 1991, 1994; Salzberger 1993; Elster 1994; Majone 1999).

Finally, some consensual democracies are often considered to thwart electoral accountability by fostering party-system fragmentation and the proliferation of parties as members of coalition cabinets, causing dilution of individual responsibility for policy outcomes and preventing citizens from gathering accurate information about agents' actions, assessing whether these actions were in their best interest or not, or assigning punishments or rewards. As Strøm (2002: 21) has put it, 'multiparty politics clouds and complicates the relationship between electoral contests and executive power', as 'the entire linkage between electoral results and control of the executive branch may become tenuous'. It is true that these problems of accountability may be mitigated by giving voters choices between identifiable alternative coalitions (Strøm 1990). However, voters are rendered powerless to assign damages and impose sanctions on meaningfully legislative majorities if – instead of alternation between blocs of parties in power – we find a larger party or a colluding group of parties that, while occasionally changing additional coalition partners, remain themselves indefinitely in power. In these cases, 'there is no wholesale alternation in power as a result of electoral contests', and 'the glue that keeps politicians in line and subjects them to popular control is particularly suspect' (Strøm 2002: 20). So, in order to estimate the effects of consensual constitutional arrangements on confidence in parliaments, we need to control for the potential negative effects of lack of alternation in power that result from the presence of a 'pivotal' (rather than 'alterna-tional') multiparty system.

In other words, accountability should matter for institutional confi-dence. How and to what extent is something that will be explored in the rest of this chapter through an empirical analysis of confidence in parlia-ment in Western European democracies. In general, two strategies will be followed. First, the effects of institutional rules on political confidence will be assessed, while measures of government performance and political pref-erences are used as control variables. As Mishler and Rose (2001: 31) argue, 'insofar as political institutions persist and perform relatively consis-tently over successive generations, political socialization and institutional performance should exert very similar and reinforcing effects on trust in institutions'. In other words, political institutions are relatively stable phe-nomena, and their continuous operation and distributional effects (particularly those that affect the fulfilment of the 'mandate' and 'account-ability' views of representation) can themselves be treated as socialization experiences, leading rational citizens to develop feelings of basic belief or disbelief about the responsiveness and trustworthiness of political institu-tions (Norris 1999c: 219–220; see also Torcel and Montero in this volume). And if this is the case, we should find that the impact of stable institutional rules on confidence in parliaments should resist the introduction of con-trols for measurements of performance and support for incumbent parties.

Second, the concepts of 'consensual' or 'majoritarian' democracies will not be used to explain institutional confidence here, as they seem to be excessively broad. As Norris (1999c: 221) notes, 'it is not clear what spe-cific institutions within majoritarian or consensual systems influence levels of public support', and 'in practice there is as much variation within, as between, these ideal-types'. Thus, in order to capture the long-term effects of institutional rules on institutional confidence, cross-sectional analyses of the institutional determinants of political confidence are probably well advised to focus on rules while controlling for the effects of some of their possible (but not inevitable, but rather historically and contextually con-tingent) political outcomes.

Before institutions: individual-level determinants of confidence in parliaments

A first step in the evaluation of the plausibility of cultural and institutional performance approaches to political confidence is to start by using indi-vidual-level independent variables. The data used here come from the *Eurobarometer* surveys, and more specifically *Eurobarometer 51.0*. This pre-sents the results of a series of surveys carried out in the EU countries between March and May 1999 (Melich 1999).[10] In these surveys, respondents in each country were asked the question, 'How much trust do you have' in 17 different political and civil institutions, ranging from the United Nations (UN) to the Church. In each case respondents were given two options: whether they 'tend to trust' or 'tend not to trust' the institution in question. One of the institutions asked about was the lower house of parliament.

Table 8.2 shows the results of logistic regressions of the dichotomous variable 'trust in parliament' (1 = 'tend to trust'; 0 = 'tend not to trust') on a series of variables measuring both socialization experiences and citizens' opinion of incumbents in a number of European countries. Cultural theories suggest that older individuals should display greater confidence in political institutions in general and parliament in particular, not only because of a life-cycle socialization effect on attachment to the political order but also because of a generational effect, whereby younger cohorts are more likely to hold post-materialist values of scepticism with respect to political institutions (Listhaug and Wiberg 1995: 318; Inglehart 1999a: 220). Education, in turn, should have a negative impact on trust in parliament, as greater education is associated both with a 'rational scepticism' hypothesis and a general post-materialist syndrome, and should therefore lead to lower levels of confidence (Listhaug and Wiberg 1995: 318).[11] Finally, in accordance with Putnam's argument about the decline of social capital and its relation to institutional trust, we can test the impact of two additional variables. One is a dummy variable simply measuring whether the respondent lives alone or not, which has been commonly used as a measure of social integration. Another is the level of exposure to television news, which should be negatively related to social and political confidence not only due to the alleged effects of television viewing as an individualistic form of leisure, but also by exposing citizens to increasingly negative portrayals of the political realm (frequency of political discussion – as a proxy for interest in politics – is introduced as a control variable).[12]

The institutional performance approach to political confidence will be, at this stage, assessed by estimating the impact of individual support for incumbent parties. 'Support for incumbent parties' is measured through a dichotomous variable that recodes, for each respondent in each country, the answers to a question about the intended vote in the next general election.[13] If the respondent declares her intention to vote for a party currently (at the time of fieldwork) supporting the governmental coalition, support for incumbent takes the value 1, otherwise the value is 0.[14] Ideological self-placement is introduced in order to be able to control for the effects of other factors that might affect vote choices regardless of evaluation of government performance. Finally, whether the respondent is unemployed (a personal experience that is likely to colour negatively the perception of overall system performance), gender, and income are also incorporated into the models as socio-demographic control variables.

Table 8.2 Effects of individual-level variables on confidence in parliament, 1999[a]

Variables	Belgium	Denmark	West Germany	East Germany	Greece	Italy	Spain	France
Gender (female)	−0.26	−0.69***	−0.16	0.16	−0.16	0.17	0.15	−0.07
Income	0.16	0.04	0.02	−0.10	0.13	0.12	−0.10	0.07
Age	−0.01	−0.01	0.01*	0.01	0.02**	0.01	0.02*	0.01
Education	0.05	0.03*	0.09**	0.01	−0.01	0.04	0.06*	0.05
Living alone	0.25	0.17	−0.31	−0.25	−0.05	−0.02	0.08	0.02
Exposure TV news	0.25	0.05	0.23	0.26	0.21	−0.09	0.21	0.19*
Political discussion	0.07	0.29*	−0.09	−0.02	0.13	0.37*	0.21	0.26
Unemployed	−0.62	−0.58	−0.55	−0.61*	0.47	−0.53	−0.34	−0.49
Ideological self-placement	−0.03	−0.05	−0.01	0.15**	−0.01	−0.07	0.25**	−0.01
Support for incumbents	1.18***	0.42*	0.34	0.45*	0.86***	0.13	0.41	0.34
Constant	−2.71	−0.18	−2.72	−1.79	−2.34	−1.60	−3.78	−2.39
Nagelkerke's R^2	0.11	0.08	0.07	0.05	0.09	0.06	0.15	0.05
(N)	(489)	(829)	(575)	(604)	(585)	(393)	(412)	(566)

Variables	Ireland	Netherlands	Portugal	Britain	Finland	Sweden	Austria
Gender (female)	−0.22	−0.16	−0.16	0.01	0.08	−0.12	0.19
Income	0.14	0.32**	0.12	0.06	−0.02	0.19**	0.01
Age	0.02*	−0.01	0.01	0.01	0.01	−0.01*	0.01
Education	0.14*	0.06*	−0.01	0.07*	0.01	0.02	0.08*
Living alone	0.23	0.34	0.78*	0.12	−0.09	−0.01	−0.24
Exposure TV news	0.30	−0.12	0.03	0.14	0.01	0.08	−0.03
Political discussion	−0.05	−0.04	−0.24	0.10	0.41**	0.42**	−0.13
Unemployed	−0.70	−0.62	0.37	0.11	−0.70*	−1.50**	−0.12
Ideological self-placement	−0.08	−0.07	−0.09	−0.02	0.16***	0.07	−0.05
Support for incumbents	0.65*	0.74***	0.44*	0.90***	0.26	0.64**	0.61**
Constant	−4.86	−0.11	0.57	−2.55	−0.08	−1.43	−0.98
Nagelkerke's R^2	0.12	0.11	0.05	0.10	0.06	0.08	0.06
(N)	(289)	(717)	(510)	(439)	(794)	(750)	(394)

Source: Melich (1999).

Note

a The figures represent logistic regression coefficients. Models were also run as linear regression models and the highest Variance Inflation Factor found was 1.84 for Education in the Portuguese model, suggesting that the precision of the estimates is not seriously affected by problems of multicollinearity. Levels of statistical significance are *** $p < 0.001$; ** $p < 0.01$; and * $p < 0.05$.

The results of the analysis tend to confirm the findings of a number of previous studies of institutional confidence. Variables measuring social practices and background have no consistent impact on Western Europeans' declared level of trust in their parliaments. The partial exception is education, but contrary to the expectations of the cultural approach, the coefficients' signs are positive for almost all cases and statistically significant in Denmark, West Germany, Spain, Ireland, the Netherlands, Britain, and Austria. In contrast, institutional performance variables fare rather better. This is especially true in the case of 'support for incumbents'; as predicted, the signs of the coefficients are always positive and emerge as statistically significant in all but five cases, even after controlling for individuals' ideological self-placement. Therefore, as Citrin (1974: 974) suggested many years ago when analysing the decline of trust in government in the United States and its implications, it seems that 'opinions about incumbents inevitably colour evaluations of political roles and institutions'.

Nevertheless, it would be premature to treat institutional confidence as a mere manifestation of political discontent with the powers that be. On the one hand, there is substantial variation between countries in terms of the actual scale of the effect of the 'support for incumbent' variable. In Belgium, for example, the probability of trusting parliament was 3.3 times higher for those who supported one of the incumbent parties in March–May 1999 (the Christian People's Party, the Social Christian Party, or the Walloon and Flemish Socialists parties) than for those who did not. In other countries, such as Britain, Greece, and the Netherlands, the odds of 'winners' trusting parliament are at least two times higher than those of 'losers'. However, in the remaining cases, the impact of support for the incumbent is much more modest.[15] Moreover, in every case, the explanatory power of the models is relatively low. As shown by the pseudo R^2 values – the highest of which is found in Spain (0.15) – while the introduction of political variables strengthens the explanatory power of the models in comparison with those that exclusively use social and cultural variables, the logistic regressions still leave considerable variance to be explained. This becomes clearer in Table 8.3, which shows the results of an estimation of the same model for a pooled sample, with model 2 including a set of dummy variables to estimate country-specific effects not captured by the remaining independent variables.

High levels of statistical significance and generally weak effects are to be expected when using a sample as large as that used to estimate the models in Table 8.3. While, therefore, these results cannot be interpreted as if a conventional size sample had been used, the substantive conclusions do not differ greatly from those obtained in the country analysis. Age has no significant impact on confidence in parliaments across Western Europe, while both education and exposure to TV news have positive effects on trust, thus running contrary to culturalist expectations.

Table 8.3 Effects of individual-level variables on confidence in parliament: pooled model estimates, 1999[a]

Variables	Model 1	Model 2 (including country dummies)
Gender (female)	−0.09*	−0.10*
Income	0.05*	0.07**
Age	0.01	0.01
Education	0.02***	0.02***
Living alone	0.07	0.06
Exposure TV news	0.10**	0.10**
Political discussion	0.10**	0.13**
Unemployed	−0.63***	−0.50***
Ideological self-placement	0.03**	0.02
Support for incumbents	0.63***	0.56***
Belgium		−1.42***
Denmark		−0.48***
West Germany		−0.68***
Greece		−0.78***
Italy		−1.32***
Spain		−0.42**
France		−0.92***
Ireland		−1.30***
Portugal		0.18
Britain		−0.89***
East Germany		−1.03***
Finland		−0.33**
Sweden		−0.74***
Austria		−0.28*
Constant	−1.27	−0.71
Nagelkerke's R^2	0.05	0.10
(N)	(8,346)	(8,346)

Source: Melich (1999).

Note

a The figures represent logistic regression coefficients. Model 2 uses $N-1$ country dummies, with the Netherlands as the reference category (the country with the highest percentage of individuals who trust their parliament). Levels of significance are ***$p<0.001$; **$p<0.01$; and *$p<0.05$.

Also predictably, whatever positive effect rightist ideology seems to have for confidence in the pooled model disappears when we control for country specificities, suggesting that its effects are unrelated to basic political value orientations and are instead caused by identification (or lack of it) with whoever happens to be in power in each country. Finally, the coefficient of support for the incumbent remains positive and significant. However, the model's R^2 doubles when we include countries as dummy variables, suggesting that, regardless of whatever citizens happen to think about incumbents, there are systemic variables that play an important role in explaining confidence in parliament. The following section addresses the role of some of these variables.

Institutional rules and institutional confidence

Above it was hypothesized that insofar as institutional rules affect the extent to which political systems foster representation and accountability, some types of rules should also have an impact on the extent to which citizens believe that parliaments act in their interests and are trustworthy. Three sets of rules will be addressed here: election rules, legislative decision-making rules, and institutional veto-players.

One common way of distinguishing between electoral systems in terms of their ability to make parliaments accurately reflect the political preferences of voters is the degree of disproportionality they engender. Hence, I have constructed a variable by simply measuring the disproportionality in the conversion of votes into seats in the lower chamber. The variable is based on the composition of the lower house of each country at the time of fieldwork (March–May 1999), using the Gallagher (1991) Least Squares Index.[16] For our cases, the values of the disproportionality index range from 0.3 per cent in Denmark to 19.4 in France.

It has also been hypothesized that the extent to which legislative policy-making rules disperse power, taking it away from governments and the parties that support them and increasing the influence of the opposition, should also have an impact on institutional confidence. In order to measure this legislative decentralization, I constructed an index based on the extent to which constitutional or internal parliamentary rules make legislative committees stronger and award rights to opposition parties in agenda-setting and legislative policy-making. This index, displayed in Table 8.4, takes into account six basic institutional characteristics of the legislative process: the existence of an institutionalized committee structure; committee rights to initiate and amend legislation; whether governments enjoy special prerogatives in agenda-setting; whether the allocation of committee chairs follows proportional or majoritarian rules; and whether opposition parties are able to voice their opinions in committee reports.

However, Western European nations pose a fundamental problem in terms of assessing the specific impact of election rules and legislative decentralization in institutional trust. As we can see in Table 8.5, all those countries whose electoral systems engender the lowest levels of disproportionality (below 4 per cent) also have medium or high levels of legislative decentralization. Conversely, those countries whose electoral systems engender the highest levels of disproportionality (above 8 per cent) are also those that display lower levels of legislative decentralization. In other words, although we are interested in focusing on institutional arrangements and their long-term effects on institutional confidence, those

Table 8.4 Index of legislative decentralization

Countries	Committee strength		Opposition rights				Index
	More than ten committees matching government departments	Committees with right to initiate legislation	Committees' unlimited amendment powers	Government lacks special prerogatives in agenda-setting	Proportional allocation of committee chairs	Right to make minority reports	
Austria	Yes	Yes	Yes	Yes	Yes	Yes	6
Sweden	Yes	Yes	Yes	Yes	Yes	Yes	6
Finland	Yes	No	Yes	Yes	Yes	Yes	5
Spain	Yes	No	Yes	Yes	Yes	Yes	5
Germany	Yes	No	Yes	Yes	Yes	Yes	5
Netherlands	Yes	No	No	Yes	Yes	Yes	4
Portugal	Yes	No	No	Yes	Yes	Yes	4
Italy	Yes	No	Yes	Yes	Yes	Yes	4
Belgium	Yes	No	Yes	Yes	No	Yes	4
Denmark	Yes	No	No	Yes	Yes	No	3
Greece	No	No	No	No	No	Yes	1
Britain	No	No	No	No	No	No	0
Ireland	No	No	No	No	No	No	0
France	No	No	No	No	No	No	0

Sources: Döring (1995) and Strøm (1998).

Table 8.5 Disproportionality and legislative decentralization

Disproportionality index	Index of legislative decentralization		
	Low 0–2	Medium 3–4	High 5–6
Low 0–4%		Netherlands	Sweden
		Denmark	Austria
		Belgium	Germany
Medium 4–8%	Ireland	Italy	Finland
		Portugal	Spain
High >8%	Greece		
	United Kingdom		
	France		

arrangements 'tend to fall into either proportional or majoritarian combinations of electoral and legislative rules' (Powell 2000: 38). Thus, legislative decentralization and disproportionality are predictably collinear in our pooled sample and cannot be employed simultaneously in any regression analysis.[17]

Nevertheless, the effects of either legislative decentralization and disprorportionality – both of which form part of the same cluster of 'consensual' rules – on confidence can be estimated while controlling for the effects of other political factors and institutional rules that may or may not be present: institutional veto-players, lack of political alternation, and whether cabinets are supported by majorities. Previously, we identified three types of institutional veto-players: presidents, second chambers, and courts with abstract powers of review. In the Western European countries included in the sample, there are no cases of presidents with veto power over legislation.[18] However, we do find cases where second chambers and courts do have veto powers over legislation. In Italy, Belgium, and Germany, upper chambers enjoy veto power over some or all types of bills. In the other countries considered here, upper chambers do not have the final say over legislation, as either their vote can be overturned by majorities in the lower house, or they simply do not exist (Patterson and Mughan 2001: 41–44). Similarly, in France, Germany, Spain, Portugal, Austria, Belgium, and Italy, special courts are entitled to review the constitutionality of legislation and veto or annul it through generally binding decisions. In the other countries, either judicial review does not exist at all or judicial decisions about the constitutionality of legislation apply only to concrete cases in trials and have no generally binding effects.

Tables 8.6 and 8.7 classify the countries in the sample according to the presence of such institutional veto-players. These tables reveal that there is only a relatively weak relation between the extent to which the policy-making process is encumbered by institutional veto-players and either disproportionality or legislative decentralization. Countries with election

Table 8.6 Disproportionality and institutional veto-players

Disproportionality index	Institutional veto-players		
	Neither bicameral veto nor constitutional review (0)	Either bicameral veto or constitutional review (1)	Both bicameral veto and constitutional review (2)
Low 0–4%	Denmark Sweden Netherlands	Austria	Belgium Germany
Medium 4–8%	Ireland Finland	Portugal Spain	Italy
High >8%	Greece United Kingdom	France	

Table 8.7 Institutional veto-players and legislative decentralization

Legislative decentralization	Institutional veto-players		
	Neither bicameral veto nor constitutional review (0)	Either bicameral veto or constitutional review (1)	Both bicameral veto and constitutional review (2)
Low 0–2%	Greece Ireland United Kingdom	France	
Medium 3–4%	Netherlands Denmark	Portugal	Belgium Italy
High 5–6%	Sweden Finland	Spain Austria	Germany

rules that engender low and medium levels of disproportionality present the whole range of variation in terms of the presence of institutional veto-players. Moreover, although no countries with highly disproportional election rules have both powerful upper chambers and constitutional courts, the existence of the *Conseil Constitutionnel* means that France cannot be considered a pure majoritarian model in terms of the combination of election rules and institutional veto-players.

Similarly, in countries with medium and high levels of legislative decentralization (policy-making rules in parliament which disperse power and boost the influence of the opposition) we also find the entire range of situations insofar as the presence or absence of institutional veto-players outside the lower chamber are concerned. Thus, our verifiable hypothesis is that although institutional veto-players may increase the horizontal accountability of power, they undermine citizens' ability to hold governments and legislatures directly accountable through elections. Hence, they should have a negative impact on confidence in parliament.

We can also test the effects of the extent to which elections actually result in alternation in government or mere partial replacement of minor coalition parties, i.e. whether a multiparty system is 'alternational' or 'pivotal' (Strøm 2002: 21). Most of the countries in our sample recurrently experienced meaningful alternations in power until 1999, whether they were majoritarian democracies (such as Britain, Greece, or France), prototypical consensual democracies (such as Finland, Denmark, or Sweden), or neither (Ireland).[19] Two countries, however, stand out due to the fundamental absence of alternation in the period running up to the survey. One of them is Austria, governed from 1987 to 2000 by a grand coalition between the Social Democratic Party (SPÖ) and the People's Party (ÖVP). Belgium is the other, as except for very brief periods, the Christian Democrats and the Socialists were the pivotal parties in almost all cabinet coalitions from 1945 until July 1999. Thus, in order to account for the potentially negative impact of lack of alternation on electoral accountability, a dummy variable for the Austrian and Belgian cases was created. Finally, although a more circumstantial phenomenon than the presence of institutional veto-players or the nature of the party system, the question of whether cabinets are supported by legislative majorities or not is also likely to play an important role in fostering clarity of responsibility, governmental accountability and, thus, institutional confidence. At the time of the survey, majority cabinets were found at almost all levels of electoral system disproportionality and legislative decentralization. Therefore, we can incorporate it as an independent variable.

Finally, two systemic variables were added in order to account for macro-economic factors known to have systematic effects on institutional confidence. These are levels of unemployment and Gross Domestic Product (GDP).[20] Both have already been shown to undermine institutional confidence: while the first directly denotes a failure of government performance, the latter's negative effect on confidence is thought to be related to the greater expectations of governmental performance which are expected to exist in more affluent societies (McAllister 1999: 197). Table 8.8 presents the results of logistic regressions of individual trust in parliament on a set of micro- and macro-level variables. Since disproportionality and legislative decentralization are collinear, two different models were used. Only one of the variables measuring the consensuality of political institutions was introduced into each model.

The results show, on the one hand, that variables associated with political and economic performance and evaluations of incumbents clearly have an impact on the extent to which Western Europeans trust the lower chambers of their national parliaments. Respondents' personal experience of unemployment and the overall unemployment rate in each country both have a significant negative impact. Support for an incumbent party has the greatest explanatory power of all variables included in the model, as individuals who express their intention to vote for any of the

Table 8.8 Effects of individual and macro-level variables on confidence in parliament: pooled model estimates, 1999

Variables	Model 3		Model 4	
	Coefficient	Wald	Coefficient	Wald
Cultural and social background explanations				
Gender (female)	−0.10*	4.93	−0.11*	5.31
Income	0.07**	7.34	0.07**	8.42
Age	0.01	2.03	0.01	2.12
Education	0.02***	13.89	0.02***	11.96
Living alone	0.08	1.89	0.07	1.22
Exposure TV news	0.09**	7.85	0.09**	8.90
Political discussion	0.09*	5.09	0.09*	5.43
Performance and partisanship (individual and macro variables)				
Unemployed	−0.56***	29.08	−0.55***	28.06
Ideological self-placement	0.02	2.02	0.02	2.21
Support for incumbents	0.63***	167.42	0.62***	161.36
Unemployment 1998	−0.04***	23.24	−0.05***	43.03
GDP per capita 1998	−0.01***	23.78	−0.01***	23.09
Institutional rules (macro variables)				
Disproportionality	−0.03***	31.46		
Legislative decentralization			0.10***	66.51
Majority government	0.04	0.50	0.03	0.27
Lack of alternation	−0.23**	7.54	−0.26**	9.55
Institutional veto-players	−0.16***	21.48	−0.19***	31.83
Constant	0.44		0.03	
Nagelkerke's R^2	0.07		0.08	
(*N*)	(8,346)		(8,346)	

Source: Melich (1999).

Note
a Levels of statistical significance are ***$p < 0.001$; **$p < 0.01$; *$p < 0.05$.

parties represented in the cabinet in their country are more likely to express confidence in their parliament than others, even after controlling for ideological self-placement and the overall macro-institutional context. All this lends support to the notion that political discontent and lack of confidence in institutions are not entirely unrelated phenomena, and that we should be wary of interpreting short-term shifts in institutional confidence as indications of long-term trends, whether positive or negative.

However, it is clear that institutional rules do also make a difference. In model 3, individuals living under lower house election rules that increase disproportionality in the conversion of votes into seats are clearly less likely to express confidence in their parliament. In model 4, legislative decentralization is shown to favour confidence in parliament, as could be predicted if we take into consideration that such decentralization is collinear with electoral proportionality and both are part of the same general construct of consensual democracy. Besides, in both models, individuals are shown to be less likely to trust their parliament the more the political system they live under allows for institutional veto-players outside the lower chamber and the less alternation is engendered by their party systems. This remains the case after we control for the impact of support for the incumbent and government status at the moment of the survey. The models' explanatory power increases in relation to the pooled model including only individual-level variables, almost matching the R^2 of the model with country-dummies.[21]

In this way, the extent to which constitutional arrangements allow for representation and accountability seem to produce relatively lasting effects on political confidence, which remain visible even when the impact of short-term economic and political factors is taken into account. Election and legislative policy-making rules that foster congruence between the median voter and policy-makers seem to foster citizens' confidence in their parliaments. However, any such confidence is undermined by factors that are not at all coterminous with consensual democracy and undermine electoral accountability. These factors are, on the one hand, 'pivotal' multiparty systems in which elections consistently produce no alternation, and are thus made inoperative as mechanisms of accountability; and, on the other, veto-players external to the lower house, allowing parliamentary majorities and coalitions to shift responsibility credibly for outcomes to forces and actors beyond their control.

Conclusions

We still have a long way to go in order to understand fully the nature and causes of institutional confidence in democratic regimes. This chapter provides only a snapshot of levels of EU citizens' trust in their parliaments in the late 1990s and of some of the factors that affect it. Moreover, as in the case of most previous studies, our ability to account for trust and distrust with respect to parliaments among Western publics remains limited in terms of the overall variance in individual attitudes explained.

However, we know now a little more than when we started. As other studies have argued, we saw that trust in or distrust of parliaments seem to be socially and culturally diffuse attitudes which are largely unrelated to social positions and long-term socialization experiences. Rather, support for incumbent parties plays a crucial role in accounting for confidence in parliaments, as do national and personal economic circumstances. This suggests that, as a dimension of political support, institutional confidence may experience rapid short-term changes within societies, and that any purported trends of secular 'decline' in confidence may be less evident than is suggested by cultural approaches.

Nevertheless, this does not mean that confidence is totally unrelated to values, beliefs, and norms, nor that it should be seen exclusively as a result of political discontent and short-term instrumental evaluations of system outputs. The analysis in this chapter provides some further clues as to what turns institutional confidence into an element of political culture that can be subsumed neither into the legitimacy afforded to the political regime as a whole nor into specific support for political actors and authorities (Listhaug and Wiberg 1995: 299; Torcal and Montero in this volume): confidence stems from citizens' expectations of whether or not institutions are likely to act in voters' interests, beliefs that are fostered by the long-term ongoing operation of institutional rules that facilitate (or otherwise) a match between the preferences of voters and rulers, as well as the latter's accountability to citizens.

From this perspective, the results do highlight the significant advantages of some aspects of consensual democracy in this respect. Electoral systems that reduce disproportionality when converting votes into seats, and legislative rules that foster power-sharing within legislatures seem to result in lower levels of institutional disaffection. Besides, one of the implications of the notion that voters seem to have more confidence in parliament when 'their party' is in government is the reinforcement of the trust-building nature of the very logic behind the model of consensual democracy: increasing the size and representativeness of majorities, instead of 'being satisfied with narrow decision-making majorities' (Lijphart 1999: 2). However, the positive impact on confidence of institutional rules that spread power and foster negotiation may be undermined if power-sharing between parties turns into fully fledged collusion that stops alternation in power from operating as a mechanism of electoral accountability. The same occurs in political systems where legislative policies may be vetoed by strong second chambers and constitutional courts with abstract powers of review. Accountability matters, regardless of whether democracies are generally majoritarian or consensual. In an age when, in response to the problems caused by the decreasing information available to voters about which interests parties actually represent, parliamentary systems have begun to rely increasingly on *ex post* mechanisms of accountability (such as empowering committees, independent agencies, central banks, and judicial institutions; Strøm 2000: 287), these results highlight the extent to which solutions may actually increase institutional disaffection among citizens.

Notes

* I am most grateful to Eva Anduiza Perea, Hanspeter Kriesi, Mark Warren, and especially José Ramón Montero and Mariano Torcal for their comments on earlier versions of this chapter.
1 In this chapter, the terms 'trust' and 'confidence' are used more or less interchangeably as applied to political objects. It should be noted, however, that,

sociologists and psychologists tend to use the two terms either to denote different concepts or to treat 'trust' as a particular type of 'confidence'. See for example Luhmann (1979) and Giddens (1990).

2 See also Katzenstein (2000: 128): 'scholarly assessments of changing levels of political confidence in Europe remain contested and (...) there is little prospect of convergent interpretations in the near future'.

3 Newton and Norris (2000: 65), with World Values Survey (WVS) data from the 1980s and 1990s for 17 countries, show that 'institutional confidence tends to be marginally higher among women, the middle classes, and older people', although 'the overall pattern by gender, class, and age displays a consistent but weak relationship across each model'. On the basis of their analysis of ten Eastern European democracies, Mishler and Rose (2001: 50) conclude that 'the effects of the socialization variables [education, age, gender, town size, and church attendance] on political trust are especially weak'.

4 Gabriel (1995: 370) notes that 'contrary to the assumption that the emergence of new value orientations leads to declining trust in government, only a small proportion of trust in government in all the countries under observation can be attributed to value orientations'. And Dalton (2000b: 259) specifically demonstrates that although postmaterialists are less likely to trust 'institutions that are identified with hierarchy, bureaucratic structures, and conservative political orientations..., the link between postmaterialism and other key institutions of democracy like parliament, the legal system, the civil service, and the press are quite weak'.

5 For similar conclusions, see also Newton (1999a: 180); Newton and Norris (2000: 63–64); and Newton in Chapter 4 of this volume. For a general evaluation of the literature on this point, see, for example, Katzenstein (2000: 128–129).

6 See also, among many others, Listhaug and Wiberg (1995: 316–319); Mishler and Rose (1997: 441); Norris (1999c: 231–233), and Anderson and LoTempio (2002).

7 Of the set of ten countries where WVS, European Value Survey (EVS), and *Eurobarometer* data have been consistently available since the 1980s, Belgium, Italy, and Britain have always been among the countries where confidence in parliament is lowest, while Sweden and the Netherlands stand at the opposite extreme. The most significant examples of major fluctuations since the 1980s and 1990s are Germany, France, and Finland (decline) and Denmark (increase), although, as we can see in Table 8.1, the downward trend in Germany and Finland has been reversed in recent years.

8 See, among many others, Kotowitz (1987: 550); Stiglitz (1987: 967); Kiewiet and McCubbins (1991), and Lupia (2001).

9 See the data in Powell (2000: 58–67).

10 The version used was second ICPSR version (Ann Arbor, MI: Interuniversity Consortium for Political and Social Research/Cologne, Germany: Zentralarchiv for Empirische Sozialforschung, 2001). Respondents from Northern Ireland and Luxembourg were excluded, the former due to the peculiar political context in the province and the latter on the grounds of the small sample size. Only individuals aged 18 or over were included in the sample.

11 Education was measured in response to the question, 'How old were you when you finished full-time education?' For respondents 'still studying' the variable was recoded with the answer to the question 'How old are you?'

12 Exposure to TV news was measured through respondents' answer to the question, 'About how often do you watch the news on television?' Values range from 4 ('everyday') to 0 ('never'). Political discussion was measured through the responses to the question, 'When you get together with friends, would you

say you discuss political matters frequently, occasionally, or never?' Values range from 2 ('frequently') to 0 ('never').

13 Another way of measuring institutional performance and its impact on confidence would be to use 'satisfaction with democracy' (SWD) as a predictor. I have done so with the following models and the impact of SWD on confidence in parliaments is considerable. However, as Linde and Ekman (2003: 405) show, although SWD 'taps the level of support for how the democratic regime works *in practice*. . ., it is suspiciously sensitive to the political-ideological orientations of the respondents'. Predictably, here, SWD is strongly correlated with support for incumbent, and thus the variable was abandoned.

14 Source for party composition of cabinets in March–May 1999 was Koole and Katz (2000).

15 In fact, mere correlational analysis already suggested as much: even without controlling for other variables, the highest values of Tau-b for the association between 'support for incumbent' and 'trust in parliament' are found in the Netherlands (0.17) and Belgium (0.16), although these are in any event not particularly high.

16 The source used for electoral data was Nordsiek (2003). Small parties classified as 'others' in election statistics were disregarded when calculating the index.

17 The correlation between the index of legislation decentralization and the index of disproportionality in the pooled sample is −0.80.

18 The French and Portuguese presidents do enjoy a final power of veto over governmental decrees, but their vetoes over parliamentary legislation can be overridden by majorities in parliament; see Shugart and Carey (1992: 148–166).

19 Confining ourselves to developments in the 1990s, in Finland, there was alternation between governments led by the conservative National Coalition Party (KOK), the Social Democratic Party (SDP), and the agrarian Finnish Center (KESK). Although the KOK was present in all cabinets until April 2003, the SDP was out of power between 1991 and 1995, while the KESK was in the opposition between 1995 and 2003. In Denmark, the Social Democratic Party (SD) has effectively alternated with the Conservative People's Party (KF) and, more recently, with the Liberal Party (V) at the head of coalition governments. In Sweden, the predominance of the Social Democratic Party in government did not prevent a centre-right government under Carl Bildt between 1991 and 1994. Finally, even Ireland experienced significant alternation in the 1990s, as the Fianna Fáil's control of power was interrupted between 1994 and 1997 by a coalition formed by Fine Gael, Labour, and the Democratic Left.

20 Source: Eurostat.

21 Models were also run using both country-dummies and macro-variables, but this predictably engendered intractable multicollinearity problems. Instead, in models 3 and 4 the highest Variance Inflation Factor (VIF) found was 1.62 for Institutional Veto-Players in model 4.

9 Political disaffection and political performance

Norway, 1957–2001*

Ola Listhaug

The theory of political disaffection promises a new approach to the analysis of the relationship between citizens and the polity. According to Montero, Gunther, and Torcal (1997b: 136), political disaffection is usually treated as a kind of syndrome, the most often cited symptoms of which are disinterest, inefficacy, unresponsiveness, cynicism, distrust, distance, separation, estrangement, powerlessness, frustration, rejection, hostility, alienation; more specifically, disaffection 'alludes to a more or less diffuse set of feelings as a result of which political affairs are seen as distant, unimportant, or meaningless'. These authors also contend that these attitudes may be independent of evaluations of political performance and overall support for democracy.[1] They suggest, moreover, that while disaffection is typical of new democracies, it may also be observed in established democracies. Norway is, by any standards, a mature democracy. Moreover, the country is very prosperous in per capita income terms and suffers from only very limited internal conflicts. Since the theory of political disaffection has been developed in the context of democracies which are potentially less stable and experience more pronounced internal conflicts than we have in Norway, examination of the Norwegian case may prove very enlightening if one wants to know how far the theory goes.

It is not always easy to decide what constitutes disaffection. It may fruitfully be explored only within a comparative frame (is a country's level of disaffection high or low compared with other countries?) or across time (is disaffection up or down?). In this chapter I will mainly pursue the second strategy. Comparisons over time may not only give us a better handle for assessing what is high or low, but will also be useful for establishing whether the phenomenon constitutes a syndrome or not. If trends over time are markedly different, one may conclude that a syndrome is observed; but if the patterns over time of the various indicators are quite similar, the cultural syndrome hypothesis would clearly begin to look weaker. The suggested indicators of disaffection bear a strong resemblance to some of the political support items in the American National Election Studies (Miller, Miller, and Schneider 1980; cf. Mason *et al.* 1985;

Weatherford 1992), which have partly been replicated in a number of countries outside the United States and more recently have become part of the main databases which are analysed in major comparative studies of political support (Kaase and Newton 1995; Klingemann and Fuchs 1995a; Norris 1999a). For better or for worse this constitutes a constraint on our study, since most of the survey questions that are asked in a time series format in Norway come from the Michigan studies.

The primary task of this chapter is thus to investigate if political disaffection is increasing or decreasing. To answer this question we will cast the net relatively wide and include attitudinal as well as behavioural dimensions that are crucial for understanding political affection. We analyse four problematic areas: internal political efficacy; trust in politicians; attachment to political parties; and confidence in political institutions. In addition, we present a short analysis of the level of democratic legitimacy in Norway as compared with other advanced countries. This comparison will allow us to examine the robustness of Norwegian democracy. Can political disaffection coexist with strong support for the democratic foundation of the polity, or will disaffection spill over into the principled attitudes? Before answering these questions, we first need to know if disaffection is a problem in Norway, and what the trends look like.

Dimensions, indicators, and context

We begin the analysis with a short discussion of the main dimensions of political disaffection as operationalized through time series data. It feels natural to start with the personal component of efficacy and move outwards from the individual toward political actors and institutions. Internal political efficacy is a measure of an individual's feeling of political competence to influence the political process (Campbell *et al.* 1954). How should we expect efficacy to develop over time? Two lines of arguments have been proposed. The first puts the emphasis on increasing cognitive skills and resources among citizens. The increase in political skills is driven by the growth of formal education and the expansion of mass media in society. The combined effects of these two processes should lead us to expect a slow, but persistent, upward movement in efficacy levels: when citizens are better educated and receive more information they should also feel more efficacious. The optimism of this scenario is soured somewhat by the argument that internal efficacy may also be affected by the structure of political alternatives. If political reality is becoming more complex (for instance, due to a weaker link between social structure and party choice, the emergence of new parties, the changing positions of old parties, or attitudinal cross-pressure, as exemplified in Norway by the two referendums on European Union [EU] membership), an individual may feel less able to cope with the more complex political environment and, in consequence, feel less efficacious.

Internal efficacy is closely linked to political participation. If efficacy is on the rise it would seem reasonable to suppose that citizen participation in politics will also increase. This increase is primarily expected to take place in forms of political action that go beyond voting at regular elections. It is possible to see such action as an indication of disaffection, but it could equally well be seen as a strengthening of the democratic link between citizens and the polity.

Indicators of trust in politicians enquire if political leaders or government are competent, honest, and trustworthy (Miller 1974; Miller and Listhaug 1998). Empirical research has demonstrated that levels of trust are affected by the evolution of political distance between government and the citizen in ideological as well as policy terms, by the parties' ability to integrate citizens into the political system, and by governments' economic performance (Norris 1999a; Holmberg 1999; Miller and Listhaug 1990, 1993, 1998; Listhaug 1995). A key issue in this line of research is to decide if trust follows a cyclical pattern or if there is ongoing linear decline.

The empirical analysis of disaffection will conclude with an analysis of regime institutions. According to the classification proposed by Norris (1999b), these categories can be seen as more general or diffuse than trust in politicians. A decline in confidence in political institutions and support for the principles of democracy would therefore be more problematic for the political system than disaffection with specific actors is. We compare public and private institutions in order to see if confidence in public institutions has declined more significantly than confidence in those in the private sector. Finally, since no time series data are available, we briefly compare the state of Norwegian democracy with that of seven advanced democracies.

Our data cover a period of more than 40 years. Norway has gone through enormous economic and political change in this period. Some of the changes will have a direct or an indirect impact on the levels of political support and affection in the Norwegian polity. At its most general, our study will ask how well the political system has adapted to long-term change as well as political events in the period. It is beyond the scope of this chapter to review Norway's development in this period in any depth, but a few comments should help contextualize the analysis below.

Economic growth has been strong and consistent throughout the period. With annual average growth of around 3 per cent for many decades, Norway is now one of the handful of richest countries in the world. This is not due to oil alone, the first thing that many outside observers think of, but can also be attributed to the overall development of traditional fisheries, the more recent explosive growth in fish farming, the modernization of the industrial base in metals and other raw materials, the emergence of an advanced service sector, and the promotion of a highly skilled and educated workforce.

Norway's affluence at the turn of the twenty-first century stands in marked contrast to the situation at the start of the period, when the effects of the Second World War were still deeply felt. In the decade after 1945 many of the country's resources were used to rebuild what had been destroyed during the German occupation. The postwar economy was controlled and regulated by government. Regulations were partly implemented in order to realize the goal of rebuilding the country, but were also driven by the Labour government's firm belief that state planning was the most efficient way of managing the economy in order to achieve the dual goal of economic growth and redistribution. The belief in government planning and control slowly gave way to deregulation and implementation of market principles in the economy. The move in this direction was strengthened by the Conservative-led government that was elected in 1981. The overall direction of policy was not reversed by Labour governments later in the decade and in the 1990s. Despite the market turn in some public policy areas, the Welfare State continued to expand, giving Norway one of the most comprehensive Welfare States in the world.

The early postwar period is often described as a period of political cooperation and consensus, in contrast with the 1920s and 1930s which had been characterized by the prevalence of class struggle and extreme ideologies. Though this is not entirely inaccurate, it should be remembered that Labour was by far the dominant party in the postwar decades, holding power through majority one-party governments between 1945 and 1961. This gave the other parties little influence on the main direction of public policy. Subsequently, Norwegian politics became more competitive. Labour continued to hold power most of the time, but the party was never again able to achieve a majority in the *Storting* (or Parliament). The bourgeois parties enjoyed significant periods of governmental power, notably in 1965–1971 and 1981–1986. Moreover, many of the governments in the 1980s and 1990s did not have majorities, and some only very weak parliamentary support. To survive, these governments relied on extensive bargaining and compromise with opposition parties.

Voting behaviour in the 1950s and early 1960s were still firmly entrenched in the structural cleavages outlined in Rokkan–Valen's famous model of electoral choice. Subsequently, cleavages have lost much of their power to explain the vote, class voting declining particularly sharply (Valen 1981; Listhaug 1997a; Ringdal and Hines 1995). While disputing the wisdom of much of the research into the decline of class voting in Western democracies, Evans (1999 and 2000) nevertheless concedes that the decline in Norway is real. The explanation for this weakening of the cleavages is partly socio-economic and partly political (Listhaug 1989, 1997a). Economic growth and affluence have weakened traditional class differences. Cultural secularization, the weakening of regional dialects, and greater geographic mobility have led to the demise of the rural counter-cultures and weakened regional politics. The decline in cleavage-based politics is probably one of the major causes of the increased electoral volatility of recent decades (Aardal 1999; Jenssen 1999).

As traditional cleavages have weakened – but not disappeared – new cleavages and associated issues have emerged. Gender politics, the conflict between the interests of the private and public sector (Knutsen 1986; Bjørklund 1999), Welfare State issues, and environmental concerns have joined the old set of cleavages. Moreover, questions relating to Norway's integration into the international economy have put pressure on the nation state and the national system of governance (Østerud 1998). International policy issues came to the fore in the EU referendums in 1972 and 1994, and were also reflected in the prominence of the immigration issue in electoral politics in the late 1980s and early 1990s.

How has the political system adapted to the changes that have transformed Norwegian society in this period? This is probably the most important question determining whether political disaffection has increased or not in the long term. It is also a question that is probably too broad to allow for a simple answer. In the following analysis I will offer answers that relate to more specific factors and to secular as well as cyclical change.

Disaffection: trends and explanations

The empirical analysis of the Norwegian case will be organized around three of the indicators that Torcal and Montero highlight in their Introduction to this volume: efficacy, trust in politicians, and confidence in representative institutions. My aims are to establish for all indicators whether the trend has evolved in a positive or negative direction, and to explain the patterns identified. While disaffection is an attitudinal concept, it may also be useful to incorporate relevant behavioural correlates. In the section on efficacy I discuss the trend in political participation since efficacy is expected to be positively associated with participation. If efficacy declines, participation may also decline, while a positive trend could lead to higher levels of political participation.

Political efficacy

Let us start by examining the trend in internal political efficacy. Has citizens' sense of political competence increased or decreased? The relevance of this question for disaffection is obvious. If more and more citizens feel that they have no opportunities to participate in politics or influence political decisions, they will become frustrated and dissatisfied. Such dissatisfactions may also spill over into citizens' attitudes towards elements of the wider political system such as politicians, parties, and institutions.

The Norwegian Election Studies include four efficacy questions. Unfortunately, only one of the items has been asked every year, while the other questions cover only parts of the period. The format of questions requires respondents to agree or disagree with four statements. The statements read as follows:

Voting: People like me can only vote, but we cannot do other things to influence politics.
Relevance: What's happening in politics is rarely of any importance to me.
Complexity: Politics is often so complex that ordinary citizens cannot understand what's going on.
Differences: It is difficult to see the important differences between the parties.

An efficacious respondent is one who disagrees with the statements. It is undoubtedly a weakness of the measurement of efficacy that all statements are asked in an agree–disagree format, and have the same direction.[2] The results of a principal component analysis of all political support items in the Norwegian Election Studies show that the items load on the same factor, but *Differences* has a lower loading than the other items (Listhaug 1989: Ch. 10). This is probably due to the fact that this item captures evaluations of how the parties have moved relative to each other, rather than the ability to identify differences between parties. If political efficacy is increasing we would expect that more voters will be able to appreciate the differences between parties. However, if real differences between parties are becoming more blurred, it will become more difficult to disagree with the statement. The two processes might thus operate in opposite directions.

Figure 9.1 presents the trend for these items. In general, the trend line creeps upwards with three items ending at a higher level than they started. Only *Differences* declines: 24 per cent disagreed in 1985 compared with 30 per cent in 1969. In the case of *Voting*, for which data are available for the longest period, in 2001, 52 per cent disagreed that voting is the only way to influence politics; this represented a major increase on the 34 per cent who disagreed with the statement in 1957. The rise in efficacious responses on *Voting* has been relatively consistent, only declining in 1969 and 1973. We also can see that *Complexity* is quite unstable across elections.

As noted in the Introduction, we would expect rising levels of education to contribute to an increase in efficacy. The link between education and efficacy is analysed in Table 9.1. The dependent variable is the item *Voting*, which has been asked on the occasion of all elections. Along with education, age, income, and gender are included in the multivariate model. Education makes a positive contribution to efficacy at all time points. Moreover, education is also the strongest predictor of efficacy. The impact of the other variables varies, but for most of the time income has a positive effect, while the effect of age is negative. In the elections from 1957 to 1985 women expressed a weaker sense of efficacy than men, but

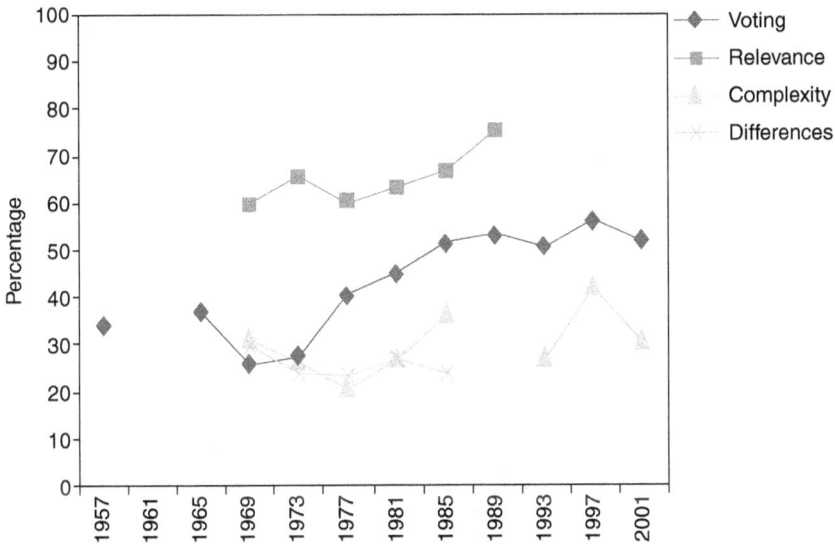

Figure 9.1 Internal political efficacy in Norway, 1957–2001 (sources: Norwegian Election Studies, 1957–2001).

for the four most recent elections the statistical difference between men and women has disappeared (and in 2001 the sign is reversed). The elimination of the gender gap in the sense of efficacy is just one of many examples of an area in which gender political equality has been achieved in the postwar period (Raaum 1995).

The trend for internal efficacy shows that Norwegians now see more opportunities for political participation than they did 40 years ago. Politics now goes beyond the mere act of voting, and citizens may have become more willing to contribute their political opinions and issue positions in exchanges and discussions with others. Whether this is actually the case can be tested through data from a small battery of questions designed to measure how open one should be about one's political views if this creates tensions and conflicts with those who take opposite positions. These questions were asked in the first election survey in 1957. Two of the items were replicated in 1965 and 1981, while another was only replicated in 1981. The format was identical to the efficacy items. Those who disagree with the statement are more likely to be open about politics, while those who agree see exchanges about politics as something that should be avoided in daily life. The questions were:

Disagreements: It would have been better if people stopped talking about the disagreements between the parties rather than what they agree about.

Table 9.1 Multivariate analysis of political efficacy in Norway, 1957–2001[a]

Variables	1957		1965		1969		1973		1977		1981		1985		1989		1993		1997		2001	
	b	Beta	b	Beta	b	Beta	b	Beta	b	Beta	b	Beta	b	Beta	b	Beta	b	Beta	b	Beta	b	Beta
Education	0.19	0.14**	0.10	0.19**	0.22	0.21**	0.16	0.16**	0.27	0.27**	0.27	0.27**	0.27	0.27**	0.24	0.25**	0.31	0.30**	0.26	0.26**	0.25	0.25**
Age	-0.01	-0.02	-0.02	-0.06*	-0.04	-0.07**	-0.05	-0.08**	-0.03	-0.05	-0.06	-0.10**	-0.06	-0.11**	-0.06	-0.11**	-0.07	-0.11**	-0.07	-0.12**	-0.01	-0.11**
Income	0.01	0.01	0.03	0.06*	0.12	0.10**	0.10	0.08*	0.15	0.10**	0.17	0.11**	0.15	0.11**	0.17	0.13**	0.10	0.08**	0.17	0.14**	0.11	0.09**
Gender	-0.19	-0.08**	-0.01	-0.10**	-0.33	-0.16**	-0.30	-0.15**	-0.27	-0.12**	-0.28	-0.13**	-0.16	-0.07**	-0.06	-0.03	-0.09	-0.04	-0.06	-0.03	0.03	0.02
Adjusted R²	0.03		0.07		0.11		0.08		0.13		0.14		0.14		0.13		0.15		0.13		0.11	
(N)	(1,097)		(1,501)		(1,318)		(1,080)		(1,526)		(1,428)		(1,799)		(1,873)		(1,912)		(1,845)		(1,793)	

Sources: Norwegian Election Studies, 1957–2001.

Note

a Political efficacy is coded from 1 = low to 4 = high; Education has four categories from low to high; Age has seven categories from low to high; Income has three categories from low to high; and Gender is coded, 1 = male, 2 = female. Levels of statistical significance are **$p < 0.01$ and *$p < 0.05$.

Private opinions: People should keep their political opinions to themselves; it always spells trouble if one publicizes one's
opinions.

Avoid discussions: When one meets people who support a party other
than one's own, it is almost always best not to talk
politics.

The trend lines in Figure 9.2 show that two items go up and one down,
implying that, on balance, people were more likely to be open about politics in 1981 than in 1957. Elsewhere (Listhaug 1989: 237–239) I carried
out a multivariate analysis similar to the one I performed for political efficacy, and found much the same results. Education has a positive impact
on openness in all three years. The effect of gender is strong in 1957 and
1965 (women are less likely to be open about politics than men); in 1981
men and women are statistically equal in this respect.

The rise in the levels of efficacy, and the tendency for citizens to
become more willing to engage in discussions with their fellow citizens,
lead us to expect an increase in forms of political participation that are
demanding of citizens' motivations and skills. We can test whether this is
actually the case using data from the World Values Surveys from the years
1982, 1990, and 1996. The levels of those reporting having taken part in
the various types of political action slowly increased over this period (see
Figure 9.3). In 1982, 55 per cent of respondents declared that they had
signed petitions, while in 1996 this figure rose to 65 per cent. The proportion participating in lawful demonstrations increased from

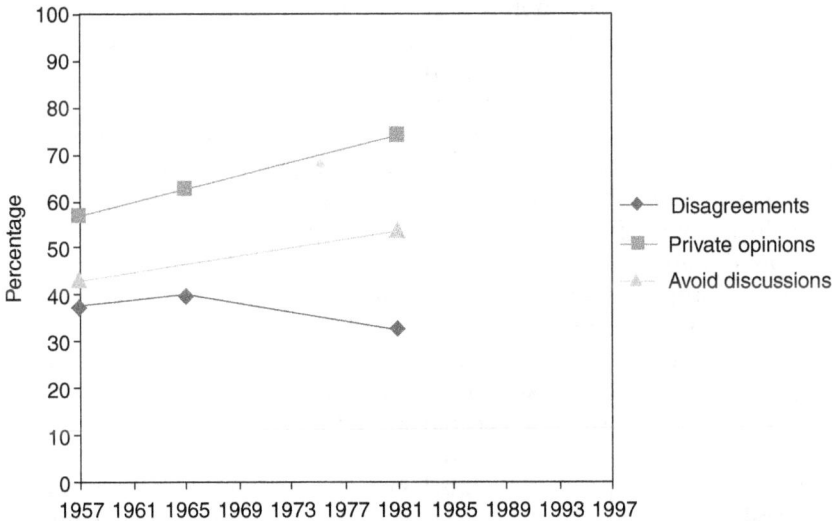

Figure 9.2 Political openness in Norway, 1957–1997 (sources: Norwegian Election
     Studies, 1957–1997).

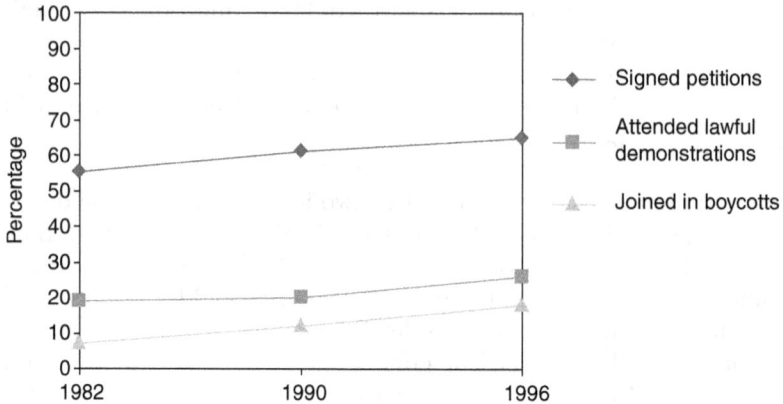

Figure 9.3 Political action: percentages of Norwegians who have participated in the various types of action, 1982, 1990, and 1996 (sources: World Values Surveys, 1982, 1990, and 1996).

19 per cent in 1981 to 26 per cent in 1996, while participation in boycotts went up from 7 per cent in 1982 to 18 per cent in 1996.[3]

The emergence of a more involved public is also supported by an analysis of election studies data (Listhaug and Grønflaten 2002). These data corroborate the increase in the proportion of the electorate who have signed petitions in the period 1985 to 1997. Even more significantly, citizens have also become more engaged in contacting elected representatives and in taking up issues and complaints through parties and organizations. This demonstrates that the increased activism embraces both old and new political channels.

The data from the World Values Survey and the election studies do not give any indication of which particular issue has triggered political action. From earlier research (Olsen and Sætren 1980) we know that the number of political action groups cover a quite diverse range of issues, from both new politics and traditional politics. We also know that the two referendums on European integration in 1972 and 1994 generated a wide variety of different types of political action, including participation in demonstrations and petitions (Gleditsch and Hellevik 1977; Jenssen, Pesonen, and Gilljam 1998). It is also likely that participation in the two referendum campaigns had a learning effect that strengthened the potential for political action over issues other than whether Norway should join the EU.

The increase in political action contrasts with the tendency seen for electoral participation: in the same period, there was a decline in voting at regular elections. Turnout at the three most recent parliamentary elections was below 80 per cent for the first time in nearly 30 years. Only around 59 per cent of the electorate voted in the last municipal elections in 2003, the lowest turnout in modern times.

The rising levels of efficacy should stimulate electoral participation as well as political action. However, the increase has been limited to political action, while election turnout has declined. This divergence could suggest that citizens perceive the political system as being less responsive to their demands and interests. As a result, we might expect disaffection with politicians and representative institutions to increase. Let us begin with trust in politicians.

Trust in politicians

Since 1973 Norwegian Election Studies have included three questions that tap generalized confidence in politicians. They are as follows:

Waste taxes: 'Do you think that those who govern waste a lot of money we pay in taxes, waste some of it, or that they waste very little of it?' 'Waste very little' and 'waste some' are coded as trust.

Politicians knowledgeable: 'Do you feel that almost all Norwegian politicians are smart people who usually know what they are doing, or do you think that many have very little knowledge about the questions they are handling?' 'Intelligent people' is coded as trust.

Politicians trusted: 'Do you think that most of our politicians can be trusted, that politicians by and large can be trusted, or that few Norwegian politicians can be trusted?' 'Most' and 'by and large' are coded as trust.

Figure 9.4 includes the distribution for trusting responses to these questions from 1973 to 1997. The relevant lines here are not the absolute levels of the items, but rather their evolution over time. The results are fairly easy to summarize. First of all, confidence in politicians rose from 1973 to 1977 and then remained roughly constant until 1985. Trust declined sharply in 1989, then edged upwards a bit in 1993 and 1997. In 2001 trust fell to the lowest level recorded in this time series.

Previous research on confidence in politicians in Norway has relied on an index of political cynicism constructed by combining the non-trusting responses to these items (Miller and Listhaug 1990, 1993, 1998). In contrast to what we found in the case of political efficacy, the pattern over time for cynicism is cyclical, suggesting that political and economic factors of a cyclical nature may contribute to the variations in levels of cynicism. A wide range of factors may account for these variations (Levi and Stoker

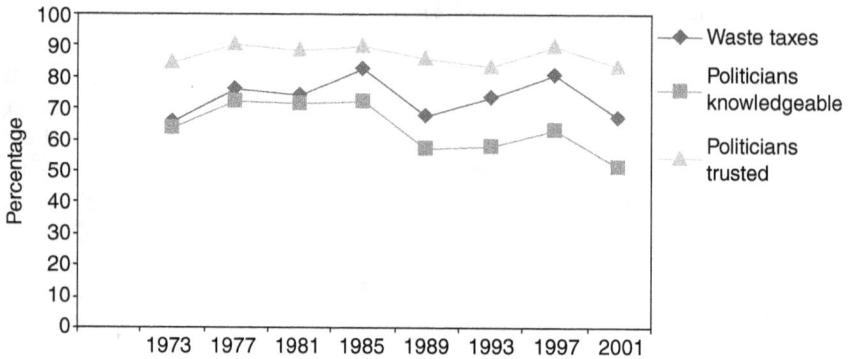

Figure 9.4 Confidence in politicians in Norway, 1973–2001 (sources: Norwegian Election Studies, 1973–2001).

2000). We focus here on three of them: party, policy issues, and evaluations of performance.

Let us begin with party. Two aspects of party are especially important: the shifts in power between government alternatives and party as a source of identification and involvement in politics. Previous research has demonstrated that confidence in politicians is influenced by who is in and who is out of power (Miller and Listhaug 1990; Listhaug 1995; Anderson and Guillory 1997; Anderson *et al.* 2004). Table 9.2 shows the relationship between vote and confidence in politicians for all elections between 1973 and 2001. The Percentages Difference Index (PDI) values in the table refer to the percentage differences of high confidence minus the percentage of low confidence on the cynicism index. High values indicate confidence. Two things are worth mentioning. First, note the expected relationship between winners and losers. This can be exemplified by reference to the confidence pattern in 1985 and 1993. In 1985, a government formed by the Conservatives, the Centre party, and the Christian People's Party was in power both before and after the election. As can be seen, voters for these parties show greater confidence than the voters for other parties. In 1993, Labour was in power both before and after the election. At the time of this election confidence in politicians was higher among Labour voters than among supporters of the other parties. The trust level for the Socialist Left Party was almost identical to the value for Labour. This can be explained by the fact that the Socialist Left normally backs Labour governments, and Socialist Left voters can be considered to be government supporters in 1993. Second, voters of the Progressive Party expressed the lowest levels of confidence in all elections. This party has never been in government and the other parties have tried to maintain their distance from the party. It is the nearest thing Norway has to a marginalized out-party.

Table 9.2 Confidence in politicians in Norway by party vote, 1973–2001[a]

Party vote	1973	1977	1981	1985	1989	1993	1997	2001
Socialist Left	34	46	46	46	47	46	69	37
Labour	44	71	69	55	50	48	61	49
Liberal	43	61	46	52	47	32	61	48
Christian People's	43	46	59	77	39	34	52	47
Centre	40	47	49	64	41	38	52	33
Conservative	17	36	38	66	33	35	44	24
Progressive	−10	13	21	47	4	18	23	8

Sources: Norwegian Election Studies, 1973–2001.

Note
a Entries are the Percentages Difference Index (PDI) values obtained by subtracting the percentages of low trust from the percentages of high trust on the cynicism index.

While shifts in the level of confidence in politicians among supporters of in-parties and out-parties do not normally affect the long-term evolution of the indicator, a change in partisan attachments could fuel either an increase or decline. We would expect strong attachments to parties (as measured by party identification or by membership) to boost citizens' confidence in politicians. In this respect, Figure 9.5 shows the development for party identification from 1965 to 2001. The proportion of Norwegian voters aged 25 and over identifying with a political party dropped from 72 per cent in 1965 to 63 per cent in 1969. In 1973 it remained at the same level (64 per cent), and then rose to 71 per cent in 1977 and 74 per cent in 1981. Since 1981 there has been a long-term decline, so that in 2001 only 43 per cent reported a sense of party identification. These findings for party identification are confirmed by the tendency for party membership. The series goes back to 1957 (see Figure 9.6), when 18 per cent of voters aged 25 and over reported that they belonged to a political party. This level did not change significantly over the next 25 years. Since 1981 (when 17 per cent said that they were members), party membership has declined continuously: in 2001 only 8 per cent of citizens belonged to a political party, a drop of 56 per cent over the 44-year period. This striking decline in attachment to parties has a negative impact on confidence in politicians because, as can be seen from Table 9.3, strength of party identification is positively associated with confidence; however, we can also see that the fall in confidence in politicians is largely independent of strength.

Trust is also influenced by the evolution of conflict on political issues. We find that those who hold issue positions opposed to current public policy tend to be less trusting than those whose positions are in line with public policy. Some of the most significant relationships are shown in Table 9.4. It is possible to identify the sources of citizens' lack of confidence in politicians (cynicism towards politicians) in a wide range of political issues: in the small opposition movement to the North Atlantic Treaty

Table 9.3 Confidence in politicians in Norway by strength of party identification, 1973–2001[a]

Party identification	1973	1977	1981	1985	1989	1993	2001
Independents	29	50	46	58	31	33	30
	(358)	(439)	(406)	(567)	(747)	(836)	(981)
Weak identifiers	29	54	55	57	37	37	33
	(294)	(469)	(469)	(515)	(632)	(578)	(345)
Strong identifiers	47	58	52	59	41	46	35
	(338)	(543)	(523)	(770)	(573)	(558)	(388)

Sources: Norwegian Election Studies, 1973–2001.

Note
a Entries are Percentages Difference Index (PDI) values obtained by subtracting the percentages of low trust from high trust on the cynicism index.

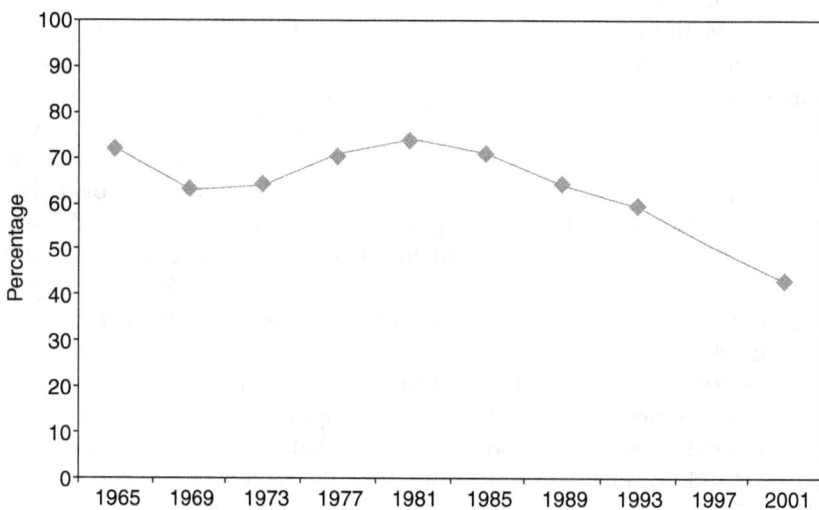

Figure 9.5 Party identification in Norway, 1965–1993 (electors aged 25 and over) (sources: Norwegian Election Studies, 1965–1993).

Organization (NATO) in the 1970s and 1980s, among those who were against the legalization of free choice abortion in the late 1970s and the 1980s, in the groups opposing aid to underdeveloped countries throughout the period, and for those who reject welfare benefits for immigrants. Interestingly, the position on the EU issue is not related to confidence in politicians. In 1973 this can be explained by the fact that the issue had already been resolved in the referendum; the government had no alternative but to follow the advice of the majority. This argument also holds for 1997: the 1994 referendum resulted in another *no* to membership. The

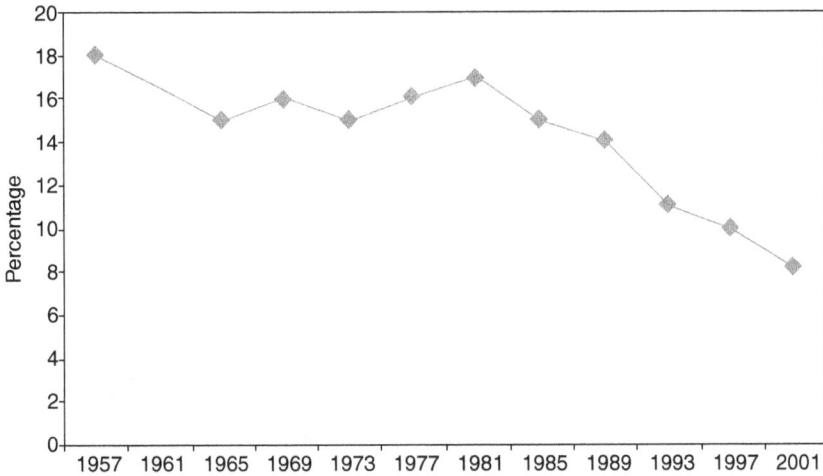

Figure 9.6 Party membership in Norway, 1957–1993 (citizens aged 25 and over) (sources: Norwegian Election Studies, 1957–1993).

government followed this advice, even though it had campaigned hard for a *yes* vote.

A static coefficient does not in itself demonstrate that an issue leads to an increase or decrease in confidence levels. In order to establish whether this is in fact the case we have to consider distribution as well as saliency. In this light, we will argue that the immigration issue very probably played a role both in the rise in cynicism towards politicians in 1989 and in the recovery of confidence later in the 1990s. Following an increase in the flow of non-Western immigrants into Norway during the second half of the 1980s, popular resentment towards immigrants increased. The majority position on this issue was also more restrictive than official policy. Moreover, this issue was highly affective and was linked to a number of Welfare State issues in a way that increased its potential to boost cynicism towards politicians. As a question which became popular at the time put it, why should immigrants receive the same Welfare State benefits as Norwegian citizens when immigrants had not paid taxes in Norway? The immigration issue remained important in 1993, when a strong majority favoured a more restrictive policy (Aardal and Valen 1995: Ch. 7). In 1997, restrictive policies were still supported by the majority, although the size of this had declined sharply (Aardal 1999).

Confidence in politicians is also affected by voters' assessment of the economy. Previous research has demonstrated a weak but consistent effect of evaluations of economic performance on trust (Listhaug 1989, 1995). As is clear from Table 9.5 (which gives the results of a regression model in

Table 9.4 Multivariate analysis of cynicism towards politicians in Norway by issues, 1973–1997[a]

Variables[b]	1973 b	1973 Beta	1977 b	1977 Beta	1981 b	1981 Beta	1985 b	1985 Beta	1989 b	1989 Beta	1993 b	1993 Beta	1997 b	1997 Beta
NATO membership	0.11	0.04	−0.17	−0.07*	−0.39	−0.14**	−0.42	−0.14**	−0.24	−0.15**	n.a.	n.a.	n.a.	n.a.
EC/EU membership	0.03	0.01	−0.02	−0.01	0.09	0.04	n.a.	n.a.	0.07	0.04	−0.08	−0.04	0.01	0.00
Aid to underdeveloped countries	0.27	0.19**	0.31	0.21**	0.33	0.21**	0.12	0.12	0.28	0.18**	0.29	0.18**	0.30	0.22**
Increase economic support for immigrants	n.a.	n.a.	n.a.	n.a.	n.a.	n.a.	n.a.	n.a.	0.08	0.08	0.05	0.09*	0.06	0.07**
Abortion	0.01	0.01	0.08	0.08*	0.10	0.09**	0.02	−0.02	0.07	0.06*	0.06	0.06	0.03	0.03
Age	0.05	0.08*	0.06	0.13**	0.04	0.08*	0.01	0.01	0.03	0.06	0.03	0.06	0.02	0.04
Education	0.06	0.07	0.07	0.09*	0.07	0.08*	−0.03	−0.03	−0.01	−0.01	−0.04	−0.05	−0.02	−0.02
Income	−0.01	−0.01	0.00	0.00	0.11	0.08**	−0.04	−0.04	−0.01	0.00	−0.11	−0.10**	−0.09	−0.09**
Adjusted R^2	0.05		0.07		0.07		0.04		0.07		0.08		0.08	
(N)	(654)		(955)		(965)		(1,297)		(1,130)		(1,479)		(1,670)	

Sources: Norwegian Election Studies, 1973–1997.

Note
a Levels of statistical significance are $**p < 0.01$ and $*p < 0.05$.
b The independent variables are coded as follows: NATO membership, 2 = For, 1 = Against; EC membership, 2 = For, 1 = Against; Aid to underdeveloped countries (1973 and 1977), 3 = Stop aid, 2 = Should continue but change, 1 = Should continue as today; (1981 and later), 3 = Reduce aid, 2 = As today, 1 = Increase; Increase economic support for immigrants, 1 = Agree strongly, 2 = Agree somewhat, 3 = Both agree and disagree, 4 = Disagree somewhat, 5 = Disagree strongly; Abortion, 4 = Never allowed, 3 = Medical reasons, 2 = Personal reasons, 1 = Free choice; Age, seven categories from low to high; Education, four categories from low to high; and Income, three categories from low to high. n.a., data not available.

which the index of cynicism towards politicians is the dependent variable and a number of economic indicators for each survey year form the independent variables), negative assessments of the main dimensions of economic evaluations – inflation, unemployment, and personal finances – are linked to cynicism. Evaluations can be retrospective or prospective, and they can be simple or mediated. Questions which measure mediated evaluations attribute responsibility for economic conditions to government, while simple evaluations do not. As in previous research, we find that negative assessments correlate with cynicism towards politicians, but that the impact of these evaluations is weak. It is difficult to compare the effects of evaluations across time since there is some disparity in the variables included in each survey. The 1985, 1989, and 1993 surveys include the most complete measurement of economic variables with the same set of questions asked on all three occasions. We noted above that there was a sharp drop in confidence from 1985 to 1989, and that confidence levels remained low in 1993. Is it likely that the economy played a role for this decline? In Table 9.5, the regression effects increase for some of the economic evaluations from 1985 to 1989 and 1993. This can be seen by comparing the size of the b coefficients and the associated significance levels (in 1985 none of the effects were significant). There is also a strong increase in negative evaluations from 1985 to 1989. Past personal finances, negative evaluations more than doubled (from 14 to 36 per cent), and future expectations of personal finances became more pessimistic (as negative assessments increased from 15 to 22 per cent) (data not shown). The rise in negative evaluations is especially important due to the well-known asymmetry in the impact of the economy on trust: negative assessments have a stronger impact than positive assessments (Listhaug 1995; Huseby 2000).

The analysis of issues and economic performance in the previous tables cannot be extended to 2001 owing to changes in format of questions. This is unfortunate as the sharp fall in confidence in politicians in 2001 needs explaining. Norway's economy performed well between 1997 and 2001, unemployment continuing to fall from its record levels in the first half of the 1990s. During the good times, Norway transferred huge amounts of money to the *oil fund* which is invested abroad. As a result, 2000–2001 was a period of rapid growth in the fund, its market value rising from NOK 386 billion to NOK 614 billion in just one year. Interests groups and some parties, especially the Progressive Party and the Socialist Left Party, called for more of the oil money to be spent on improving the Welfare State and education. The Progressives also wanted to cut taxes. The governing parties mainly defended the policy of establishing a fund abroad to avoid inflation and guarantee the pensions of the future generations. It is likely that the rapid increase in the oil fund fuelled some voters' sense of frustration with the country's economic performance. Why could Norway not enjoy the benefits of all the wealth being created? These assessments, in

Table 9.5 Multivariate analysis of cynicism towards politicians by evaluations of economic performance, 1973–1997[a]

Variables[b]	1973 b	1973 Beta	1977 b	1977 Beta	1981 b	1981 Beta	1985 b	1985 Beta	1989 b	1989 Beta	1993 b	1993 Beta	1997 b	1997 Beta
Past personal finances	n.a.		n.a.		n.a.		0.059	0.049	0.095	0.076**	0.090	0.072**	0.021	0.017
Future personal finances	0.251	0.156**	0.094	0.080**	0.028	0.022	0.054	0.046	0.108	0.087**	0.097	0.075**	0.053	0.044
Past personal unemployment	n.a.		n.a.		n.a.		0.070	0.058	0.064	0.056	0.076	0.073**	0.038	0.035
Future personal unemployment	0.222	0.130**	0.064	0.055	0.058	0.047	0.048	0.044	−0.030	−0.030	−0.047	−0.048	0.036	0.034
Past national economy	n.a.		n.a.		n.a.		0.055	0.047	0.059	0.057	0.084	0.075**	0.035	0.023
Past government performance on unemployment	n.a.		0.066	0.043	0.155	0.106**	−0.045	−0.039	0.216	0.150**	0.143	0.086**	n.a.	
Past government performance on inflation	n.a.		0.204	0.136**	0.059	0.040	−0.013	−0.010	0.013	0.008	0.047	0.026	n.a.	
Age	0.059	0.094**	0.034	0.075**	0.057	0.111**	0.008	0.017	−0.003	−0.005	0.020	0.035	0.024	0.047
Education	0.093	0.098**	0.033	0.046	0.037	0.047	−0.022	−0.030	−0.047	−0.052	−0.057	−0.063**	−0.039	−0.049
Income	0.005	0.004	0.014	0.013	0.047	0.035	−0.004	−0.004	0.043	0.035	−0.063	−0.057*	−0.062	−0.061*
R^2	0.059		0.045		0.028		0.021		0.051		0.058		0.020	
(N)	(895)		(1,152)		(1,058)		(1,205)		(1,373)		(1,470)		(1,662)	

Sources: Norwegian Election Studies, 1973–1997.

Notes

a Levels of statistical significance are **$p < 0.01$ and *$p < 0.05$.

b The *economic evaluation* variables are coded as 1 for positive evaluations, 2 for neutral evaluations, and 3 for negative evaluations; *Age* is coded in seven categories from low to high; *Education* is coded in four categories from low to high; and *Income* is coded in three categories from low to high. *n.a.*, data not available.

Table 9.6 Confidence in politicians in Norway by position on use of state revenues from oil, 2001

Items	Percentage (N)
Be restrictive with using the money	47 (434)
Undecided	33 (205)
Use more of the money	25 (1,282)

Source: Norwegian Election Study, 2001.

Note

a Entries are Percentages Difference Index (PDI) values obtained by subtracting the percentages of low trust from high trust on the cynicism index.

turn, could fuel political cynicism. Is there any support for the oil money hypothesis?

Table 9.6 offers a provisional answer. The Percentages Difference Index (PDI) value for the cynicism index is lowest for those who say that Norway should use more of the money, and highest for voters who take a restrictive position. Undecided voters fall between these groups. It is also important to note that two-thirds of voters say that Norway should use more of the oil money while less than a quarter support a restrictive position. In Table 9.7 the analysis is extended to include variables from the policy model and the performance model that we used earlier. The results for policy attitudes are similar to those for the previous year. The effects of performance evaluations of unemployment (which are the only economic items that are included in the 2001 survey) are weak, but in line with expectations. The effect of oil money frustrations hold up well in the multivariate model. Voters who want to use more of the oil money now have less confidence in politicians than voters who take a restrictive position on the use of Norway's oil wealth.

Confidence in institutions

Institutional disaffection is more serious than disaffection with politicians. Unpopular politicians can be replaced, but it is more difficult to repair institutional damage. With data from the World Values Survey we can now track confidence in nine institutions from 1982 to 1996. This was a period in which trust in politicians first declined and then recovered some of the lost ground. Was this pattern replicated in the case of the institutions? As well as looking at confidence over time, we will also compare the relative levels of support for public and private institutions. When judging public institutions it is useful to see how they perform on a relative scale, to find out whether government institutions fare better or worse than private institutions. Figure 9.7 presents the trend line for those expressing some confidence in the institutions. For public institutions, support for order

Table 9.7 Multivariate analysis of cynicism towards politicians in Norway by position on oil, issues and performance, 2001[a]

Items[b]	b	Beta
Use more of the state revenues from oil	0.23	0.12**
Past unemployment in the household	0.08	0.06*
Fear of personal unemployment in the future	0.06	0.05
EU membership	−0.01	−0.00
Against economic redistribution between rich and underdeveloped countries	0.10	0.12**
Restrictive towards immigration	0.06	0.16**
Abortion	0.01	0.01
Tax relief	0.05	0.06*
Age	−0.00	−0.01
Education	−0.04	−0.04
Income	−0.07	−0.06*
Adjusted R^2		0.10
(N)		(1,419)

Source: Norwegian Election Study, 2001.

Note
a Levels of statistical significance are **$p<0.01$ and *$p<0.05$.
b The independent variables are coded as follows: *State revenues from oil,* 1 = Against using state revenues from petroleum or undecided, 2 = Use more of the revenues; *Past unemployment in the household,* 1 = No unemployment, 2 = Had difficulties finding a job, 3 = Have been unemployed; *Fear of personal unemployment in the future,* 1 = No fear, 2 = Some fear, 3 = Fear of being unemployed; *EU membership,* 1 = Against, 2 = For; *More economic redistribution between rich and underdeveloped countries,* 1 = Agree strongly, 2 = Agree somewhat, 3 = Both agree and disagree, 4 = Disagree somewhat, 5 = Disagree strongly; *Restrictive towards immigration,* 0 = Less restrictive, 10 = More restrictive; *Abortion,* 1 = Free choice, 2 = Personal reasons, 3 = Medical reasons, 4 = Never allowed; *Tax relief,* 1 = Strongly disagree, 2 = Disagree somewhat, 3 = Both agree and disagree, 4 = Agree somewhat, 5 = Agree strongly; *Age,* seven categories from low to high; *Education,* four categories from low to high, and *Income,* three categories from low to high.

institutions (armed forces, legal system, police) is high and relatively stable. A partial exception is confidence in the legal system, which slid from 84 per cent in 1982 to 70 per cent in 1996. Norway has a Lutheran state Church, but this is increasingly independent from the government, and is not easily classified as either public or private. The Church enjoys notably less confidence than the other order institutions. After a drop in 1990, in 1996 confidence in the Church bounced back to a level slightly over that of 1982.

Parliament and the civil service both suffered a strong decline in confidence in 1990, but recovered much of the losses in 1996. So far the picture for government institutions looks pretty rosy. However, we should also consider how private institutions (the press, trade unions, and major companies) have fared. They show quite distinct trends. The press has the lowest confidence level; this sunk to a low of 33 per cent in 1996. In con-

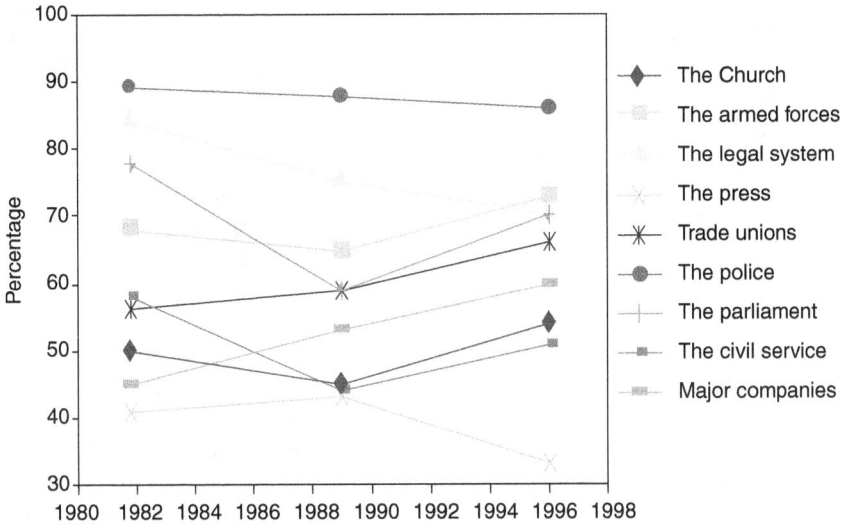

Figure 9.7 Confidence in institutions in Norway, 1982, 1990, and 1996 (percentages of confidence) (sources: World Values Surveys, 1982, 1990, and
1996).

trast, confidence in trade unions and major companies has increased. The
proportion of respondents expressing confidence in the unions rose from
56 per cent in 1982, to 59 per cent in 1990, and reached a high of 66 per
cent in 1996. The increase in confidence is even greater for major companies: 45 per cent, 53 per cent, and 60 per cent, respectively, for the
three time points. We can conclude that confidence in public institutions
holds up quite well, although the fact that the recovery of confidence in
parliament and the civil service between 1990 and 1996 did not take
support back to the levels of 1982, might be of some concern. Likewise,
the fact that the standing of the two major private institutions (labour and
business) improved more significantly than that of these public institutions might add to our unease.

Confidence in the parliament has fluctuated significantly, both in terms
of the decline in 1990 and the partial recovery between 1990 and 1996.
These shifts, and the pivotal role that parliament plays in the Norwegian
political system, highlight the need for an explanation.[4] The main variables in the model are the effect of winning or losing, political issues, economic performance evaluations, and the changing pattern of linkages
between citizens and parties.

Let us begin by examining the relationship between the in–out
mechanism in government and confidence in parliament. In countries
like Sweden, for instance, the incumbency effects of confidence in

politicians are remarkable (Listhaug 1995): supporters of the non-socialist parties expressed little confidence in their parties' ability to govern effectively. The negative evaluations probably originated from the partial failure of the coalition government in 1976–1982, and may help explain why the non-socialist victories in the elections of 1976 and 1979 – after years of social democratic governance – did not lead to an increase in political trust among bourgeois voters. This example may hold ramifications that go beyond the Swedish case. Coalition governments, especially of the minority variety, are inherently more unstable than majority governments. Following the breakdown of the majority government of the non-socialist parties in 1986, all Norwegian governments have had minorities in the *Storting*. The problems facing the formation of majority governments of both the Left and the Right could weaken the incumbency effect on support for the parliamentary institution, as a weak government will yield more power to the national assembly and as opposition parties can amend the proposals that the government puts before the *Storting*.

Is this the case in Norway? The hypothesis of a declining incumbency effect on confidence in parliament is not supported by the data. The effect does not get weaker over time. In the spring of 1982 the Conservative Party governed alone, but with parliamentary support from the agrarian Centre Party and the Christian People's Party. Some months after the survey data were collected these parties formally joined the government. If we include these two parties as in-parties with the Conservative Party, the distribution changes only marginally. This suggests that the voters for these parties already considered them part of the coalition.

Among the range of possible issues that could be used to account for changes in institutional confidence in Norway in the 1980s and 1990s, the immigration issue would rank high on most lists. The number of refugees and asylum seekers admitted into Norway increased rapidly in the late 1980s. By international standards the Norwegian government's immigration policies were restrictive. Nonetheless, public opinion became very hostile towards immigration. Neither the governing alternatives on the Right-Right or the Left-Left (Labour) was able to accommodate the electorate's anti-immigration sentiments. Beginning in the local elections of 1987, the right-wing Progressive Party received increased support partly as a result of its strong stand against immigration. It was also in 1987 that a noticeable drop in trust in politicians was first recorded in the election surveys (Aardal and Valen 1995).

The World Values Surveys (WVS) include relatively few questions on attitudes towards immigrants or foreigners. Two items referring to groups that one would not like to have as neighbours (social distance) show that the proportion of Norwegians that would not like to have immigrants as neighbours rose from 10 per cent in 1982 to 16 per cent in 1990, before dropping back to 10 per cent in 1996. The same trend can be seen for race: the proportion that did not want persons of a different race as neighbours went up from 9 to 12 per cent from 1982 to 1990, and then fell to 8 per cent in 1996. In response to a question asking if Norwegians should be given preferential access to scarce jobs, 59 per cent agreed with this statement in 1990 compared with only 41 per cent in 1996 (the question was not asked in 1982). In short, the WVS data show that anti-immigration feelings were stronger in 1990 than at the two other points in time.

The bivariate relationships between issue measures and confidence in parliament is easy to summarize (data not included). For social distance the relationship is zero in the three years. For work preference for Norwegians as opposed to immigrants, the relationship goes in the expected direction. Those who want to give preference to Norwegians in the labour market have less confidence in the *Storting* than those who are against doing so. This suggests that the immigration issue produces distrust only when it is linked to a current public policy. Labour market policy is something that is decided by government, while race and the immigration status of neighbours are not regulated by public policy. Negative sentiments on these two issues might not be politicized in such a way that channels frustrations back into the political process.

The Conservative government which came to power after the 1981 elections set out to transfer power from the government to markets. In 1986, the Labour government which took over after the collapse of the bourgeois coalition did not reverse this policy shift. The 'modernizers' among Norwegian social democrats agreed with the outgoing government that markets should be given a more prominent role in the economy – a policy that has been continued by subsequent Labour governments. The economic expansion that accompanied liberalization was cut short by the stock market crash of 1987. Some of the major private banks ran into trouble and had to be bailed out by the central bank. Moreover, unemployment began to rise, and by 1990 the standardized unemployment rate was above 5 per cent, a very high figure by Norwegian standards. Unemployment did not peak until 1993, but by 1996 was falling fast. Of the three time points of our surveys, 1990 is located in a period of economic problems, while by 1996 economic expansion was safely underway. To what extent did Norway's changing economic fortunes contribute to the variations seen in confidence in parliament? We have calculated mean values for satisfaction with household finances for the three years. Between 1982 and 1990 the average on the 1–10 scale fell by almost one point, from 7.52 to 6.67. From 1990 to 1996 the curve is almost flat. Confidence in parliament shows a statistically significant relationship with economic evaluations in all years (data not included).

Parties are key institutions in the Norwegian political system. Government is party government, elections are choices between party lists as there is little, if any, chance of getting elected if a candidate is not approved and nominated by a party organization, and citizen participation in political life is largely facilitated by parties. As for institutional disaffection, we would expect that citizens who feel close to parties will have greater confidence in political institutions than those who are not aligned with parties. Unfortunately, the question about party membership in the WVS has been slightly changed and cannot be used for detailed examinations of trends in membership levels. However, the wording of the question is close enough to serve as a functional equivalent for that variable for the three years.[5] If the decline in attachment to parties plays a role in explaining shifts in levels of confidence across time, we need to demonstrate that party members have greater confidence in parliament than those who are not members. This is also what we find in the bivariate case (data not included).

The bivariate analysis should not constitute the final word. Some of the independent variables will correlate in a way that makes it difficult to assign relative effects. We also need to include relevant demographic variables. Table 9.8 presents the results of a multivariate regression analysis. Party membership and economic satisfaction have a statistically significant influence in the expected direction for all years. The effect of winning is significant in 1990 and 1996, and has the correct sign in 1982. The variable measures support for job preference for Norwegians over immigrants (a question not asked in 1982) has the expected impact in 1990 and 1996.

The results presented in this section suggest that the increase in political disaffection in the late 1980s and early 1990s was not limited to confidence in politicians, but that core political institutions were also affected. It seems likely that both the decline in confidence in politicians and the weakening of confidence in parliament was affected by immigration issues, which increased the policy distance between government and the governed, and by the downturn of the economy, which created uncertainty about future job and income among citizens, all of which made Norway more difficult to govern.[6]

Democratic legitimacy: Norway compared with other countries

The analysis of the three indicators of political disaffection has produced a mixed pattern of trends. Norwegians feel more efficacious in the political sphere, which may have contributed to their increased levels of political action. Combined with the observed decline in conventional electoral participation, this could be interpreted as indicating an increase in political disaffection, although the increase in efficacy could also be seen as a positive trend. The level of *confidence* in politicians has moved in a cyclical pattern, with the level slightly lower at the end of the period than at the beginning. The evolution over time of confidence in political institutions is also cyclical, and the level is also lower at the end than at the start of the period for which data are available. As Torcal and Montero suggest in the Introduction to this volume, support for democratic principles may not be affected by an increase in political disaffection. Since the development of disaffection over time in Norway does not show any clear trend, it is not

Table 9.8 Multivariate analysis of confidence in parliament in Norway, 1982, 1990 and 1996[a]

Variables	1982		1990		1996	
	b	Beta	b	Beta	b	Beta
In-party	0.08	0.05	0.18**	0.11	0.16**	0.12
Social distance	-0.02	-0.02	-0.00	0.00	-0.04	-0.04
Work for Norwegians	n.a.	n.a.	-0.13**	-0.09	-0.08*	-0.06
Economic satisfaction	0.04**	0.13	0.02*	0.07	0.03**	0.10
Party member	0.13*	0.06	0.21**	0.10	0.15**	0.09
Age	0.07**	0.08	0.00	0.00	0.00	0.01
Gender	-0.05	-0.04	-0.05	-0.03	-0.09**	-0.08
Education	0.06	0.08	0.03	0.03	0.06*	0.08
R^2	0.05		0.04		0.06	
(N)	(1,051)		(1,239)		(1,127)	

Sources: World Values Surveys, 1982, 1990, and 1996.

Note

a Levels of statistical significance are $**p < 0.01$ and $*p < 0.05$; n.a., data not available.

b The coding of confidence is reversed such that 1 is low and 4 high. The independent variables are coded as follows: In-party, 1 = Vote for incumbent party, 0 = Otherwise; Social distance, 0 = Do not object to having immigrants or people of a different race as neighbours, 1 = Mentions one of these groups, 2 = Mentions both groups; Work for Norwegians, 1 = Agree with statement that if jobs are scarce priority should be given to Norwegians over immigrants, 0 = Disagree with the statement; Economic satisfaction, 1–10 scale: 1 = Satisfied, 10 = Dissatisfied; Party member, member of a political party, 1 = member, 0 = not a member; Age, 1 = 18–24, 2 = 25–44, 3 = 45–66, 4 = 67–79; Gender, 1 = male, 2 = female; Education, years of actual or planned schooling, 1 = 16 years, 2 = 17–20 years, 3 = 21+ years. Missing data are substituted by means.

possible to test if support for democratic principles is independent of political disaffection. In addition, we have no good time series data tapping into support for democratic principles. Therefore, in order to get a feel for the level of democratic legitimacy we have substituted comparisons over time with a comparison between Norway and seven other advanced democracies: Sweden, Finland, West Germany, Switzerland, Spain, Australia, and the United States. The data come from the 1995–1996 WVS, which was partly designed to study the state of global democracy. Table 9.9 compares two variables capturing support for principles: how good or bad it is to have a democratic system, and whether democracy is better than any other form of government.[7]

In all the countries selected very large majorities of respondents say that it is good to have a democratic system. Norway stands out as the country in which the largest group say it is a very good thing (70 per cent). Similarly, although in all the countries around 90 per cent agree that democracy is better than any other form of government, the proportion agreeing strongly is higher in Norway (73 per cent) than in the other countries. While we probably should not read too much into these variations in the degree of support, we can conclude that there is certainly very strong support for democratic principles in Norway. This conclusion is not surprising given the characteristics of Norway highlighted in the Introduction: Norway has a strong democratic tradition, is very rich, and suffers from limited internal conflicts.

Conclusion

Our analysis of political disaffection in Norway over a period of more than 40 years has produced a varied picture of trends. In line with some of the expectations suggested by Torcal and Montero in the Introduction to this volume, trends in political disaffection do not move in a single direction. While the overall level of disaffection may be relatively stable, each sub-dimension appears to follow a separate path. We find that internal political efficacy is edging upwards, indicating that citizens feel that they are becoming more politically competent. The increase in efficacy fits in well with the pattern of increasing political action. The rise in political action provides a contrast to the decline in electoral turnout, which has been falling for some time in the case of local elections, as well as in the last three *Storting* elections. Parties, meanwhile, have experienced a strong decline in membership and identification since the 1980s. This is by far the most dramatic pattern of change seen here.

While parties and electoral turnout have evolved in what at least in part seems to be a linear trend, disaffection with politicians and government institutions have moved much more cyclically. The low levels of confidence in politicians and in public institutions in the late 1980s and early 1990s are probably best explained by the economic downturn and the increase in policy distance between government and the governed in this

Table 9.9 Support for democratic principles in Norway and other advanced democracies, 1995–1996

Support for democracy	Norway	Sweden	Finland	West Germany	Switzerland	Spain	Australia	United States
Having a democratic system								
Very good	70	63	31	58	49	45	52	55
Good	27	33	46	38	44	50	36	36
Very bad	3	4	17	3	6	3	9	6
Bad	1	0	6	0	1	2	4	3
(N)	(1,108)	(978)	(912)	(995)	(1,098)	(1,140)	(1,969)	(1,452)
Democracy better than other form of government								
Agree strongly	73	69	44	49	43	40	33	49
Agree	22	25	41	45	48	53	54	43
Disagree	3	5	11	5	8	6	12	7
Disagree strongly	2	1	4	1	1	1	1	1
(N)	(1,111)	(958)	(892)	(996)	(1,102)	(1,110)	(1,938)	(1,460)

Sources: World Values Surveys, 1995–1996.

period. Trust and confidence in institutions regained much of the ground loss by the mid-1990s, but not quite enough to reach the peak levels of the 1980s. The further decline in confidence in politicians that we have seen in 2001 may paradoxically be a reflection of good times rather than bad. As Norway came out of the recession in the mid-1990s, the country was able to establish a reserve fund to be invested in foreign markets. The purpose of the oil fund was to avoid inflationary pressures in the Norwegian economy, and at the same time contribute to pensions for future generations. But the oil fund soon sparked a sense of frustration, as voters did not enjoy the cake that they could not eat. Our findings do suggest that these frustrations may help explain the drop in confidence levels in 2001, although we admit that we have not been able to provide conclusive evidence for the oil hypothesis.

This brief analysis of support for democratic principles demonstrates that Norway is in a favourable position when compared with other advanced democracies. The results for support for principles are corroborated by a major comparative study by Fuchs, Guidorossi, and Svensson (1995) that shows that Norway tops EU countries in terms of satisfaction with the way democracy operates. Some 86 per cent of Norwegians say they are satisfied with the working of democracy, compared with an average of 57 per cent of citizens in the EU-12 as a whole. Norway's strong position in comparative rankings of support for the political system is confirmed by other studies (Listhaug and Wiberg 1995; Klingemann 1999; Listhaug 1997b). While comparative assessments suggest that affection, not disaffection, most appropriately describes Norwegians' relationship with their polity, a partial exception must be made for parties. Confidence in political parties in Norway is more in line with what we find in other advanced democracies (Listhaug 1997b). In a recent major study of parties in Norway, two leading scholars conclude that 'as formal organizations, Norwegian parties are probably better off now than they have been for decades. They are richer, they have more local branches, more staff, and as many members as in the 1960s. But as socially integrated movements they are falling apart' (Strøm and Svåsand 1997: 354). It is obvious from the more recent data analysed in this chapter that the parties are also in trouble in terms of support in the mass public. The decline of cleavage-based politics and the overall economic growth and affluence might be the ultimate cause of this development. In any event, parties continue to provide citizens with a linkage to the broader political system. How they perform this function, and if they are able to stop the decline in membership and identification, could be decisive for the broader development of political disaffection in Norway.

Notes

* The chapter is in debt to joint work carried out with Arthur H. Miller. I would like to thank Lars Grønflaten, Stein Olav Gystad, and Roar Håskjold for research assistance. José Ramón Montero and Mariano Torcal gave valuable comments on the chapter. The data sets were made available by the Norwegian Social Science Data Services. Henry Valen and Bernt Aardal were the principal researchers in the Norwegian Election Studies. Valen and Listhaug were the principal researchers in the Norwegian Values Study.

1 See also their respective chapters included in this volume.

2 Some of the methodological issues related to the measurement of support are discussed in Listhaug (1989: Ch. 10).

3 The time frame for these questions is open, meaning that a person need only participate in a given form of action once in his/her lifetime to be recorded in the relevant category.

4 I have performed a detailed analysis for parliament as well as for the civil service in an earlier paper (Listhaug 1997b). I will adapt the main parts of the analysis for parliament in this section, but excluding all the tables, which can be consulted in the earlier paper. The main elements of the explanatory model for confidence in parliament should be the same as those used to explain trust in politicians.

5 In 1982 and 1990 the question asked was if the respondent belonged to political parties or groups. In 1996 the question referred to active or inactive members of political parties (both categories are counted as members).

6 It is unfortunate that we are not able to extend the analysis of the institutions to see if the new downturn in confidence in politicians at the turn of the millennium was accompanied by a negative shift in citizens' beliefs in institutions.

7 The questions were as follows: 'Having a democratic political system, would you say it is a very good, fairly good, fairly bad or very bad way of governing this country?' And, 'Democracy may have problems but it's better than any other form of government. Do you agree strongly, agree, disagree or disagree strongly?'

10 Italy, forty years of political disaffection

A longitudinal exploration*

Paolo Segatti

Italy appears to be the country *par excellence* in which to study negative attitudes towards politics for three reasons. First, while in many Western democracies a confidence gap between electors and political institutions appeared at the end of the 1960s, in Italy the existence of a low level of political consensus became apparent much earlier. At the end of the 1950s, Almond and Verba (1963) found that Italians scored very poorly in terms of civic culture and political integration. Building on the results of Almond and Verba's empirical work, in 1965 La Palombara employed three well-chosen words to define Italians' attitudes towards politics: alienation, fragmentation, and isolation. In doing so, he shaped a lasting image of Italian politics which has influenced generations of political science students.

Second, attitudes towards politics have continuously been more negative in Italy than elsewhere. In the 1950s, again according to Almond and Verba (1963), the level of system support in Italy was lower not only than in the United States, Great Britain, and Germany, but even than in Mexico. In the decades that followed, several studies drew the same conclusions (except, perhaps, for Mexico). Survey after survey, Italians have expressed low levels of trust in politicians and political institutions, while the *Eurobarometer* series indicates that, over the last 30 years, Italians have on average held more negative opinions of the way democracy operates in their country than all other Europeans.

Third, the Italian case stands out in terms of the relation which appears to exist between attitudes toward politics and actual political behaviour. For many years, Italian politics was simultaneously characterized by a very low level of system support and stable electoral behaviour. In the early 1990s, however, this paradoxical combination seemed to break down. That period saw a radical electoral realignment in Italy, the scale of which was and still is quite exceptional in the European political landscape. Within a couple of years all the governing parties disappeared, at the same time as new forces appeared on the political scene. Moreover, the 1994 election resulted in one of the most spectacular instances of turnover among the political class in Italian history. These tumultuous events inevitably raise a number of questions about the relation between the very low level of system support and the restructuring of the party system.[1]

The purpose of this chapter, however, is not to explore these questions. Rather, I will focus here on the reasons why, for such a protracted period, so many Italian citizens have felt that they are politically ineffective and that politicians do not respond to their opinions. Hence, the main objective of this chapter is to try to understand why low levels of political system support have become an idiosyncratic feature of Italian politics (Bardi and Pasquino 1995; Morlino and Tarchi 1996; Sabetti 2000; Sani and Segatti 2001). Several hypotheses will be tested against data for the period from 1959 to 2001. First, however, I will define and explain the concept of disaffection and the measures employed in this chapter. Then, evidence will be provided which reveals that even a serious syndrome of disaffection appears to be quite independent from other attitudes towards politics.

The concept of disaffection and how to measure it

Previous analyses of political support have tended to address a vast array of negative orientations, shifting in their focus from low satisfaction with government performance and negative attitudes toward democratic institutions to political disaffection. Disaffection usually appears to be a kind of residual category, made up of a whole variety of negative sentiments towards politics. In contrast with this approach, Torcal and Montero suggest that disaffection should be treated as an attitude in its own right. In the Introduction to this volume, they define political disaffection, following di Palma (1970), as 'the subjective feelings of powerlessness, cynicism and lack of confidence in the political process, politicians, and democratic institutions, but with no questioning of the political regime' (p. 30). Along with an emotional component, it can be seen that disaffection includes a cognitive one, that is, the belief that politics is distant, hard to understand, and self-referential. Moreover, political disaffection should be understood as distinct from belief in the illegitimacy of the democratic institutions, or even from feelings of disappointment with governmental performance. In short, political disaffection should be treated as a system of beliefs, charged with emotional feelings, that the body politic is not working in a responsive way either because citizens are incapable of, or are not interested in, making their voice heard, or because politicians and political institutions are deaf to people's political demands. Hence, as Torcal and Montero rightly stress, disaffection has an internal dimension related to political engagement as well as an external one related to institutional disaffection.

Moving on from conceptual to empirical issues, the most reliable indicators of political disaffection should include measures of political (dis)trust, lack of political interest (or low levels of political saliency), and finally indicators of political (in)efficacy. In this chapter, I will only discuss the last of these indicators, namely political (in)efficacy, for two reasons. First, over the last 40 years, several studies of Italian political attitudes have replicated some of the standard Michigan measures of political efficacy. In 1959, Almond and Verba (1963) asked a sample of Italians how they saw their role in the body politic and their evaluation of the responsiveness of the government and politicians to the people. The same indicators were replicated, with the same or similar format, in the 1968 and the 1972 Barnes and Sani surveys, in the 1975 Political Action Study, in the 1985 Four Nations Study, and in the 1990, 1996, and 2001 Italian National Election Studies (ITANES). (See the Appendix for the precise wording of the questions in each study.)[2] Second, in Italy there is evidence to suggest that the internal dimension of (in)efficacy is correlated with the external one, in contrast to what happens in other countries (Lane 1959a; Abramson 1983; Acock, Clarke, and Stewart 1985; Acock and Clarke 1990). When surveys provide more than two measures of (in)efficacy, principal component analysis shows that they in fact form a single factor.[3] Therefore, it can be argued that measures of political (in)efficacy are able to grasp the two dimensions of political disaffection stressed by Torcal and Montero, although they do not fully capture the sense of estrangement or alienation from politics that the concept of political disaffection implies and embraces.

Table 10.1 shows how four standard measures of political efficacy have evolved over the last 40 years. Three points should be highlighted. First, in each year the vast majority of Italians thought that politics is complicated, that they have no say in it, that politicians lose touch when elected, and that they are not interested in citizens' opinions but only with their votes. In the light of these data, one can only conclude that most Italians seem to feel comfortable defining themselves as politically incompetent or powerless. This is a surprising attitude, since it runs against the well-known psychological predisposition that obliges individuals to give the impression that they are socially competent in everyday social interactions, and in control of their environment. Apparently, Italians did (and do) not feel this type of pressure when invited to talk about politics. Moreover, the evolution of the figures over time clearly shows that political disaffection is a far from recent malaise in Italy. Quite the contrary, in most cases 'the picture in the Italians' head' of what politics is has long been rather bleak.

Second, even if the percentage of disaffected citizens always seems to have been extremely high, it does appear to have increased over time. Particularly large increases have been recorded with respect to answers given to the first and final two statements. In any event, however, these increases do not seem to be as large as those found in other democracies (Pharr and Putnam 2000; Norris 1999b; Nye *et al.* 1997). Third, there are also some significant variations between years. The percentage of disaffected citizens was higher in 1972 than in 1968, declined a little in 1975, dropped more sharply in 1996, and increased dramatically in 2001.

Table 10.1 Political inefficacy in Italy, 1959–2000

Political inefficacy	1959	1968	1972	1975	1985	1990	1996	2001
Politics is so complicated[a]	65	80	85	83	79	89	–	88
People like me have no say[a]	84	–	–	73	–	78	52	84
Politicians lose touch[a]	90	52	93	88	83	90	83	94
Politicians don't care[a]	–	67	77	81	81	83	–	88
Politically disaffected[b]	50	45	68	57	62	62	47	71

Sources: For 1959, Civic Culture; for 1968–1972, Barnes and Sani; for 1975, Political Action Survey; for 1985, Four Nation Study; and for 1990, 1996, and 2001, ITANES. See the Appendix for the precise wording of the questions.

Notes
a Percentages agreeing with the statement.
b Percentage of respondents agreeing with all the statements.

The figures shown in the bottom row of Table 10.1 refer to the percentage of respondents who in each year agreed with all the sentences. These would certainly seem to be highly disaffected citizens. It goes without saying that the figures can in no way be treated as an estimation of the level of disaffection in Italy over the period. Rather, they simply show the proportion of electors which in each year openly expressed a feeling of powerlessness with respect to politics, or openly expressed the opinion that politicians were not responsive to their political demands.[4] These data confirm some points revealed by the preceding analysis. The percentage of highly disaffected Italians has remained very high across time, never dropping below 45 per cent during these 40 years. Moreover, disaffection actually increased from 1972 to 1990. On the other hand, the variation in the figure for highly disaffected citizens is greater than for the responses to the various individual statements. In 1972 the proportion of highly disaffected respondents was more than 20 points higher than in 1968. It dropped a little in 1975, then remaining almost stable until 1990. In 1996 the percentage plummeted by 15 points from the 1990 level. However, the recovery did not last very long, as five years later the number of highly disaffected electors jumped again, reaching a staggering 71 per cent. This latest increase is confirmed by other studies. For instance, using similar indicators of political inefficacy, an IPSO–CRA–Nielsen survey found in spring 1999 that the percentage of highly disaffected respondents stood at over 69 per cent. In 2000 Sani (2000) designed a survey in which respondents were allowed to define what politics meant to them in their own words; he then compared the results with similar data from 1990 and found that the level of cynicism, rage, disillusion, and disgust was higher then than it had been ten years earlier.

Disaffection, illegitimacy, and dissatisfaction: three different political orientations

Our data set does not include, for the period in question, the full range of measures necessary to grasp the relations between disaffection, on the one hand, and illegitimacy and dissatisfaction, on the other (see also Gunther and Montero, in this volume). However, some scattered data from a few time points suffice to show that political disaffection does not correlate closely with the negative evaluations of regime legitimacy or satisfaction with government output. In two 1985 and 1996 surveys, respondents were asked to express a preference for one type of political regime in relation to others.[5] In both years the vast majority of those expressed a preference for democracy. Moreover, the percentage of those who preferred democracy was also higher than the proportion of highly disaffected citizens (75 per cent as opposed to 62 per cent in 1985, and 84 per cent compared with 47 in 1996). As can be seen from Table 10.2, even if the strength of the relation changed from 1985 to 1996, it is remarkable that in both

Table 10.2 Regime legitimacy and political disaffection in Italy, 1985 and 1996 (in percentages)

Regime legitimacy	1985		1996	
	Not or somewhat disaffected	Strongly disaffected	Not or somewhat disaffected	Strongly disaffected
Democracy is always preferable	83	70	84	83
Sometimes dictatorship is preferable	10	17	13	14
All the same	7	13	3	4
(N)	(711)	(1,104)	(1,109)	(1,008)

Source: See Table 10.1.

years the great majority (70 per cent in 1985, and 83 per cent in 1996) of disaffected citizens declared that democracy is better than other regimes.

As for satisfaction with government outputs, our data indicate that its relationship with disaffection not only tends to be weak, but also shows a variable sign. For instance, in 1975 the relation between disaffection and dissatisfaction was weak and negative. In other words, disaffected citizens were also a little less likely to be dissatisfied (odds ratio 0.73).[6] According to the ITANES study carried out in 1996, despite the then still recent political earthquake in Italy, the level of dissatisfaction with the way democracy was working was as high as usual. In fact, three out of four respondents declared themselves to be dissatisfied. It is worth noting, however, that the association between political dissatisfaction and political disaffection was still very weak, but positive (odds ratio 1.3). In other words, in 1996 disaffected citizens were also a little more likely to be dissatisfied.

In contrast, the measures of political efficacy do seem to be associated with attitudes towards political institutions and the party system. A large majority of Italians have always expressed a preference for a party system with a limited number of parties. In 1985 more than 80 per cent preferred a party system with no more than four parties. The likelihood that most of these respondents were also highly disaffected was strong (odds ratio 2.0), particularly for the best-educated (odds ratio 3.9). Moreover, a severe syndrome of disaffection appears to be strongly linked to negative feelings towards political parties' role in the polity. In 1985, disaffected respondents were three times more likely than those who were not disaffected to agree that parties divide people (odds ratio 3.4), more than twice as likely to agree that parties are useless (odds ratio 2.5), and almost three times more likely to state that parties are all alike (odds ratio 2.8). It should be noted, however, that disaffection has only a weak correlation with the factual (instrumental) opinion that parties do not defend interests (odds ratio 1.3), that parties are not the cornerstones of democracy (odds ratio 1.2), and that they do not constitute channels for participation (odds ratio 1.3). This means that disaffection is more closely tied to negative attitudes towards parties than to opinions as to their actual role in democracy (Torcal, Gunther, and Montero 2002; Linz 2002). In fact, according to the 1985 data, a large majority (83 per cent) of disaffected citizens displayed negative feelings towards politics. These sentiments include indifference (23 per cent), boredom (15 per cent), diffidence (15 per cent), irritation (19 per cent), and disgust (11 per cent).

In short, these data seem to suggest that in Italy, as in other countries, political disaffection should not be confused with discontent with specific government outputs or the perception of regime legitimacy. Rather, disaffected citizens seem to be more critical of the linkage between citizens and political institutions. Their criticism, moreover, seems to be based on a marriage between beliefs and strong feelings which is hard to break (Linz 1999; Klingemann 1999; Norris 1999b; Torcal *et al.* 2002).

We have very few data with which to measure the connection between political disaffection and support for the national community. Looking at the level of national pride found in *Eurobarometer* series, Italians feel just as much a part of their national community as citizens of other states do of theirs. *Eurobarometer* data on the level of national pride are also confirmed by other studies (Klingemann 1999; Segatti 1999; Diamanti and Segatti 1994). We suspect, however, that indicators of level of national pride alone do not allow us to grasp fully how Italians identify with their national community. Almond and Verba (1963) persuasively argued that Italians were proud of their history, art, way of life, and culture, but certainly not of their political institutions. The 1995 ISSP survey replicated Almond and Verba's indicators and very clearly showed that, 40 years later, Italians are still proud of being Italian on ethno-cultural rather than civic grounds (Segatti 1999). In short, one could argue that Italians are perfectly integrated into their nation, but not into their political community. That is, Italians think of themselves as Italians but not as Italian (political) citizens. What is missing is a full sense of the civic dimension of Italian nationhood. Why is this so? My tentative answer is that such a perception, or rather the absence of it, is somehow related to their political disaffection. In 1959, the association between disaffection and pride in the political and economic institutions was limited (odds ratio 0.67), but negative. In other words, disaffected Italians were proud of their nation less because of its political and economic achievements than for ethno-cultural reasons. There are good reasons to think that this situation has not changed significantly since then.

How to explain the Italian severe disaffection syndrome? Three sets of hypotheses

From the beginning, several hypotheses were put forward to try to account for the extent of political disaffection and the other negative orientations towards politics in Italy (Almond and Verba 1963; La Palombara 1965; di Palma 1970). Most interpretations operate within a general framework which incorporates three broad and overlapping types of causes: lack of individual resources because of the backwardness of Italian society; the persistence of culturally rooted criteria when evaluating political life; and the performance of government and political institutions.[7] However, each of these macro-factors conceals a cluster of different, but interrelated, factors that may affect disaffection as well as other political attitudes. In other words, we need to analyse in more detail which factor accounts for what.

The role of resources

Amongst the politically significant individual-level resources, education is believed to have a direct impact on feelings of political efficacy (Lane

1959a; Abramson 1983; Acock and Clarke 1990). Almond and Verba (1963) and La Palombara (1965) attributed the extent of negative feelings towards politics to Italians' low level of education in the 1950s. According to the 1961 census, in Italy more than 8 per cent of the population was illiterate, and 70 per cent of Italians had only completed elementary school. Over the past 40 years, Italian society has changed significantly in terms of its level of education. The ratio between the proportion of Italians educated to above secondary-school level in 1991 compared with 1961 was 4 to 1. The change was even greater among women, for whom the ratio was 5 to 1.

Given that more Italians have become more educated over the last few decades, one would expect the percentage of highly disaffected citizens to have declined somewhat in the same period. Our data, however, shows no evidence of this. We can conclude, therefore, that the composition effect of education (that is, the effect of the variation in the educational composition of the population over time) has been modest. It is still of interest, however, to find out exactly how modest it may have been.

The discrepancy between, on the one hand, the tendency for the percentage of highly disaffected citizens to remain high or to slightly increase in recent decades and, on the other, the steady increase in the educational levels in the same period could also be explained by the fact that over the last 40 years the direction of the main effect of education has changed. Some scholars claim that in the same period a similar change has taken place in many countries. They argue that over the last four decades the process of social modernization, in which rising education has been a major driving force, has changed the values system in many democracies (Inglehart 1977; Klingemann and Fuchs 1995b). In consequence, there has been an increase in political competence. People take more interest in politics, have become more politically aware, better informed, and more inclined to engage in new forms of participation (Inglehart 1990; Dalton 1996; Norris 1999b). Both citizens' attitudes and the new forms of political involvement are considered to be at odds with the 'church like' rituals of participation offered by traditional political institutions and political intermediaries. As a result, Pharr and Putnam (2000) and Dalton (2000b), among others, claim that, at the individual level, the sign of the relationships between education and political awareness and disaffection have changed. In the past, education and political awareness promoted system support, while now they are credited with widening the confidence gap. According to this thesis, most (or some) citizens now experience feelings of frustration with the way the political system operates. In other words, rather than becoming 'alienated or apathetic citizens' because they lack the resources necessary to be politically effective, they are more likely to become 'critical citizens' because they enjoy greater political competence. Italy experienced many of the structural social changes that are seen as responsible for these new political attitudes. Moreover, as we saw in Table 10.1, our data show that disaffection has increased a little since the 1970s.

In short, if Italian society has undergone the same process, then, it could be argued that, at the individual level, the relations between education and political awareness with disaffection should also have changed their direction, or, more probably, there should be signs of a weakening of the strength of the relation.

> Our first hypothesis (H1) states, first, that the size of the highly disaffected segment is only faintly influenced by the increase in the level of education within the population, and, second, that at individual level, the link between education and political awareness and disaffection has weakened, while, however, maintaining its negative sign.

The role of civic culture

Disaffection may be a consequence of how politics is evaluated.[8] For some, citizens' evaluation criteria are shaped by cultural orientations towards politics. This is the main argument of Almond and Verba (1963) and particularly La Palombara (1965), who argued that political disaffection cannot be attributed to Italy's democratic institutions or to the failure of its political class, but rather to an inherited cultural predisposition.

A cultural explanation of political disaffection offers some useful insights. For example, one strength of this approach is that it does not put all the blame on the politicians or the institutions. From this cultural perspective, citizens are not innocent observers of the misbehaviour of politicians or institutions; they are part of the same cultural game. La Palombara (1987) has also argued that disaffection and cynicism were traits that Italians were expected to display when performing their role as citizens in the 'Italian political spectacle'. One could argue that the line between the self-defined innocent observers and the supposedly guilty observed is much more blurred, since Italian citizens are prone to the same types of misbehaviour attributed to their politicians, particularly when they are involved in decision-making processes within the governing bodies of non-political institutions.[9]

The cultural explanation, however, is not without its own weaknesses. Civic culture is a broad term that covers many different things: inherited cognitive beliefs, value systems, and moral criteria, amongst others. Each of these dimensions may have different sources, ranging from intellectual traditions hegemonic in the society in question, in particular among the literate population, to collective memories of past political experiences. We know, for example, that in Italy negative experiences of political institutions date back far into the past. According to a leading Italian historian, after the glorious decade of the Italian *Risorgimento*, from 1870 onwards the public attitude towards politics was negative. More than a

century ago Italians denounced almost exactly the same features of politics as they do today. As Chabod (1990: 522) wrote,

> Cabinets were too often built up only to be changed after few weeks,
> and with them all the useless promises made and destroyed by careless
> politicians who seemed to care more about their personal ambitions,
> or passions or interests, than the common good. Parliament was
> blocked by unproductive discussions, barren debates caused by per-
> sonal greed ... and then, too much politics. Every single issue was
> brought on the field of political debates, fought by politicians and
> congressmen, with the consequence of getting the system to slow
> down as a whole.

It is interesting to note that opinions like these were widespread within
an electorate that accounted for just 2 per cent of the entire population.
Therefore, one of the side effects of the democratization process was that
similar considerations percolated down from the social elite to other strata.

Unfortunately, cultural effects are difficult to identify except through
carefully designed comparative research, which is not the object of this
chapter. Here, I will test two different aspects of the thesis that culture
matters. First, cultural effects are deemed to be characterized by intense
inertia because they are path dependent. If past negative political experiences can influence the way new generations make sense of politics, it is
because stock of ways of thinking and talking about politics are transmitted
almost intact over the years. In other words, we assume that culture has a
powerful effect on disaffection when a persistent cultural pattern prevails in
each birth cohort despite the fact that their members grew up at different
phases of political regimes, in dissimilar ideological climates, and in distinct
political circumstances. In terms of cohort analysis, a permanent cultural
predisposition would be indicated by a very small generational change
effect. Second, my argument that culture matters is based on a different line
of reasoning. Italian society is marked by profound and well-explored territorial cleavages. Amongst these, the dividing line between the central-
northern regions and the southern part of the country is considered
relevant in civic culture terms. The central-northern regions were the birth-
place of modern parties based on ideological mobilization, while the *Mezzogiorno* long remained characterized by patterns of behaviour by the political
class based on clientelistic linkages with voters (Putnam 1993). One could
reasonably expect that if cultural legacy matters, the feelings of powerlessness and the cynical beliefs that politicians are self-interested should be
more prevalent in the south than in central-northern Italy.

> Thus, our second hypothesis (H2) states that, if civic culture has a
> powerful impact on disaffection, then over the period considered in
> each generation there would be a similar proportion of highly disaf-

fected citizens, and also that the percentage of highly disaffected citizens should also be higher in the *Mezzogiorno* than in other parts of Italy.

The role of parties and ideologies

The third macro-level factor mentioned above is government performance. This is obviously a macro-variable that includes a vast array of different political and institutional dimensions. Some of these could have more effect on the level of dissatisfaction, while others may have a greater impact on political disaffection. Recently, Norris (1999b) has highlighted the importance of the workings of the party system. She suggests that the low level of political confidence found in Italy (and in Japan) is an effect of a party system in which there was no alternation for many years (see also Listhaugh 1995). Therefore one should also expect that negative feelings towards politics should be most intense and frequent among the electorates of the opposition parties, that is, the *Partito Comunista Italiano* (PCI) and the neofascist *Movimento Sociale Italiano* (MSI). Both parties remained in opposition from 1948 until the electoral earthquake of the early 1990s, when their direct heirs finally managed to enter government. Implicit in this thesis seems to be the idea that a severe disaffection syndrome may indeed affect the partisan choice. In particular, it is suggested that disaffection can easily turn into protest voting. I should note that this idea runs contrary to a well-known thesis developed by di Palma (1970). He discovered that disaffection was distributed almost equally among the electorates of all the different parties, regardless of their government position. Therefore he argued that disaffection could be connected less to protest than to apathy and, because of that, highly disaffected citizens were more likely to be non-voters than non-disaffected.

> Our third hypothesis (H3) follows di Palma's argument and predicts that highly disaffected citizens are spread fairly evenly throughout all parties, regardless of whether the party is in government or in opposition, and that they are more likely not to vote.

Parties represent, however, different worldviews, the contents of which often also encompass different visions of politics and political involvement. Accordingly, as well as controlling for any possible party system effect, our analysis should also control for ideology. There are in fact good grounds for doing so. Criticism of parties, parliament, and pluralistic politics was and is a common theme on the Italian right, and in particular among the heirs of the fascists, although it is true that fascism rejected pluralism rather than politics itself (Sani and Segatti 2001). On the other hand, socialist and communist ideologies have valued political involvement as a civic virtue. Although socialist and communist movements have often been highly critical of the way the political system operates, they promote a participatory conception of citizenship. Therefore one could expect that cynicism towards politics is more frequent among citizens who place themselves on the right of the ideological continuum than among electors with other ideological orientations.

Finally, ideology may influence political disaffection in another way. The perception that politics is not beyond citizens' reach, and that politicians are not always self-interested, may simply be more common among citizens with an ideological predisposition, regardless of the actual nature of this. In contrast, electors unable or unwilling to place themselves on the left–right continuum should be more likely to be highly disaffected.

> Thus, we could argue, as our fourth hypothesis (H4), first, that those who state that they are unable to place themselves on the left–right spectrum are more likely to be highly disaffected and, second, that those who are highly critical of politics also tend to self-locate on the extreme right of the ideological spectrum rather than on the extreme left. The prevailing orientation towards politics amongst those choosing other ideological positions remains an open question.

Testing the hypotheses

The impact of education and political awareness

Our first hypothesis (H1) maintains that education has a limited composition effect on the evolution over time of the percentage of disaffected citizens. In fact, the trend in disaffection is by no means one of linear decline, as it would be if education were the only factor responsible for any change. But what has the actual impact of education been over the years? In order to measure the education effect I have first regressed disaffection over time, and then included education as a control variable in the regression equation.

The data presented in Figure 10.1 show two lines.[10] Both indicate that the odds of a citizen being disaffected increased a little after 1959. However, disaffection appears to increase more when education is kept constant across time. This would mean that the increase in education over the last 40 years has actually helped reduce disaffection. However, the gap between the two lines only widened between 1975 and 1990, and even then it was small. When the model is adjusted for education, the odds ratio increases in 1975 from 1.3 to 1.7; in 1985 and 1990, from around 1.6 to 2.0; and in 2001 from 2.4 to 3.8. In short, education seems to work in the expected way, reducing disaffection, but its effects are to a large extent offset by other factors. One of these factors could be that, as some scholars claim, the structural effects of education have changed over the years, at least for a segment of respondents. Rather than being negatively

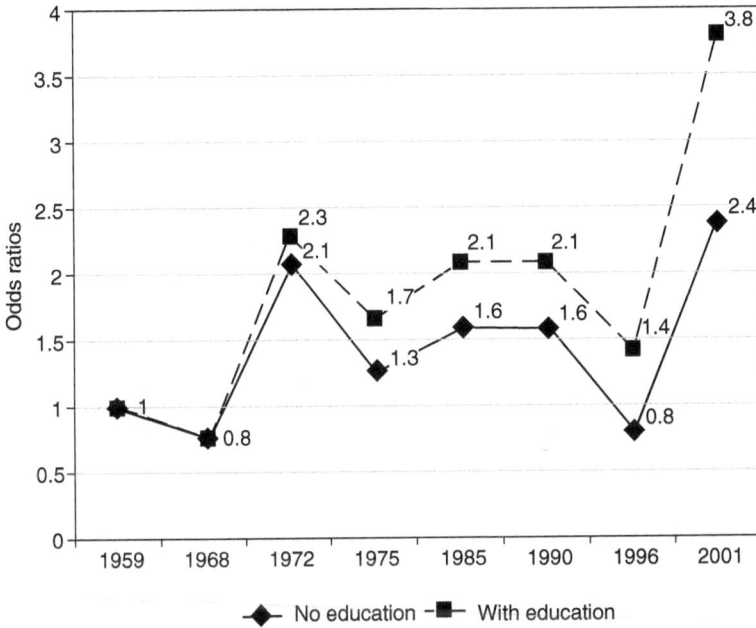

Figure 10.1 Impact of time on percentage of highly disaffected (before and after adjusting for education), 1959–2001 (sources: See Table 10.1).

associated with alienation, education might be positively related to a sense of frustration caused by some kind of imbalance between the way democracy works and the democratic ethos of a particular segment of the electorate.

The second part of hypothesis H1 states that the strength of the relationship between education and disaffection has weakened over the years. We tested this hypothesis by analysing how the odds ratios between education, political awareness, and disaffection have changed year-by-year.[11]

Figure 10.2 makes it clear that, except for 1996, there is no evidence of any change in the negative relation between education and disaffection. The odds ratios differences are indeed very small (some of them are not significant). Therefore, except in 1996, education reduced disaffection; for instance, a well-educated citizen was as likely to be as disaffected in 2001 as a well-educated one in 1959. The same conclusion would apply to the relation between political awareness and disaffection. Consequently, education, and its correlate, political awareness, do not seem to have changed their structural effect, as some scholars claim, at least in the case of the disaffection we measured.

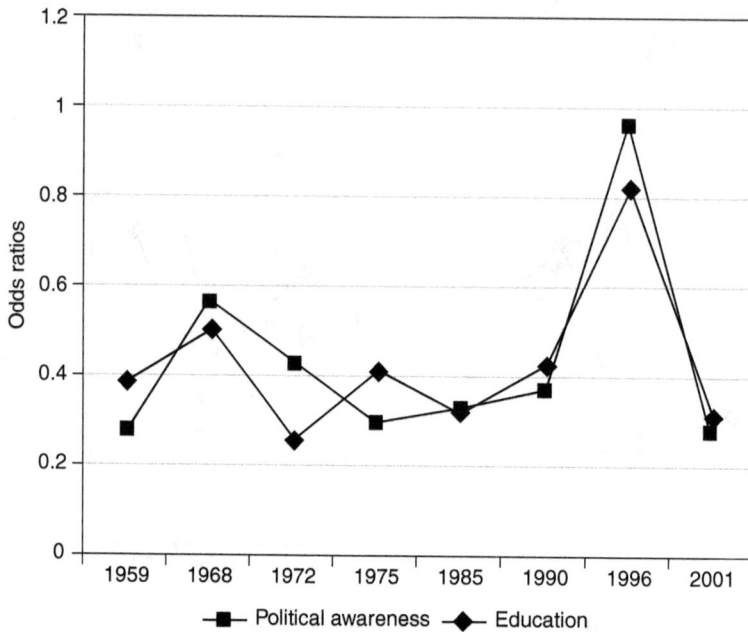

Figure 10.2 How likely it is to be well educated, politically aware, and highly disaffected, 1959–2001 (sources: see Table 10.1).

The cultural persistence of political disaffection through generations and across Italy

Generational change is usually held to be one of the most important vehicles of cultural change. As far as popular attitudes toward politics are concerned, one could assume that the experience of growing up in a working democracy, even if this is deeply divided into opposing camps, could promote the development of political attitudes which differ at least a little from those held by citizens who became adults in a non-democratic regime. Accordingly, new generations, born after the war, should be less likely to be highly disaffected than other birth cohorts, which grew up under fascism. If the difference were small, this would suggest that cultural inheritance is more influential than generational learning. Our second hypothesis (H2) claims that this is exactly what has happened in the case of the disaffection syndrome.

Figure 10.3 shows the percentage of highly disaffected citizens in different generations. It is easy to see that the gaps between the lines, which roughly indicate the impact of generational change, tend to be quite small. Whereas there are some differences between generations, they are not stable across time. For instance, individuals born before 1918 became more

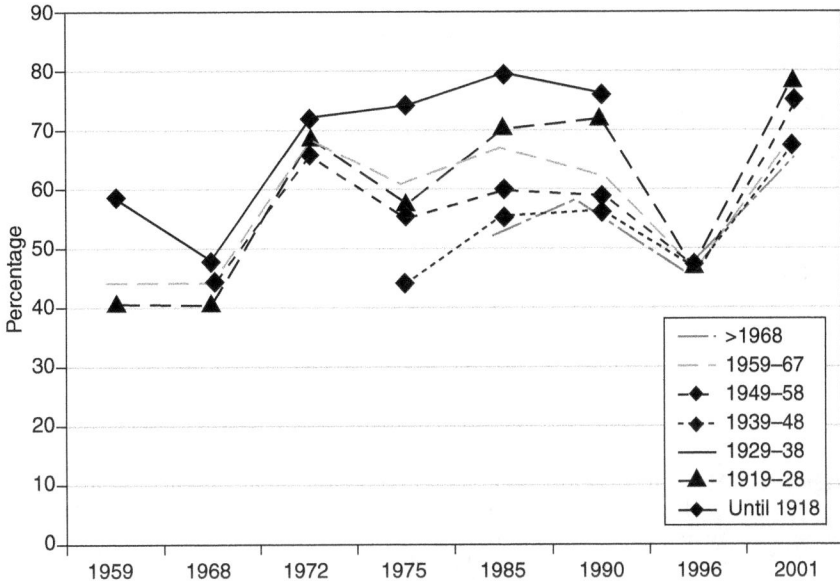

Figure 10.3 Highly disaffected by generations and year, 1959–2001 (sources: see Table 10.1).

disaffected in 1972 and subsequently remained at the same level. In the case of those who were born between 1949 and 1958, the percentage of highly disaffected citizens was quite low in 1975. In fact, this generation seems to have been the birth cohort that was least disaffected when it reached voting age. Nonetheless, this generation fell into line with the pattern of the other cohorts in the following years. Finally, time seems to be important. In 1972, 1996, and 2001, the percentage of highly disaffected citizens in each generation converged at the same level. These simultaneous shifts suggest a period effect, a question we shall return to below.

To what extent can some of the differences between generations be attributed to the fact that the internal composition of each generation varies in terms of its educational level? In order to assess the net effect of generation change, it is necessary to hold the effects of education, time, and the interaction between the last two factors constant over the years. In this respect, the data shown in Figure 10.4 are impressive.[12] They clearly indicate that, adjusting for control variables, the generation effect is almost null. The odds of each generation being disaffected are always 0.30 to 0.20 points less than the generation in the reference group (born before 1918). Thus hypothesis H2 (which stated that the transmission of a stock of negative cognitive schemata and feelings towards politics is largely independent of generational change) seems to be confirmed. Moreover,

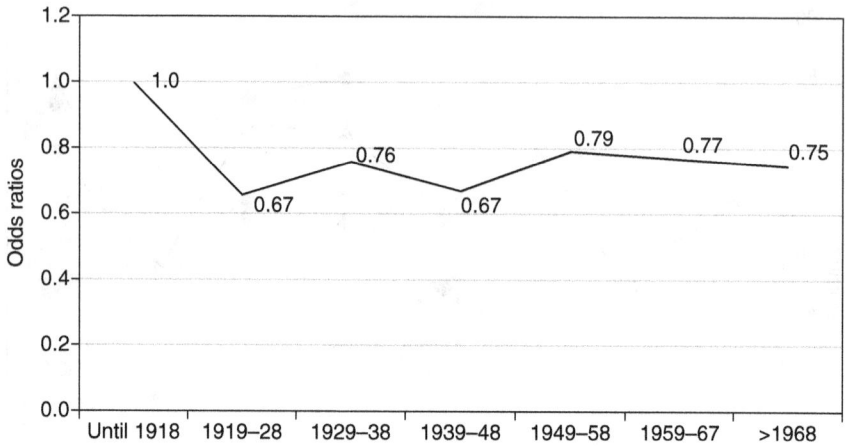

Figure 10.4 How different are the chances of being highly disaffected of several
birth cohorts from those of the generation born before 1918. For the
years 1959–2001, education and interaction between them are kept
constant (sources: see Table 10.1).

the very small differences between generations in terms of the percentage
of highly disaffected citizens suggest that the transmission of cultural patterns is highly institutionalized. That is, the cultural pattern has been
transmitted almost intact from generation to generation because each
new birth cohort learns how to make sense of its political experiences in a
culture in which native ways of thinking and of talking about politics were
so socially legitimized that they were taken for granted.

Finally, contrary to expectations, we discovered that, from 1968 to 2001,
the number of highly disaffected citizens in southern Italy was not much
higher than in other parts of the country (Table 10.3). It is true that, especially in the early years, political disaffection was higher in the *Mezzogiorno*
than elsewhere; but the differences have been less constant over the
period than we would expect in the light of the vast array of analyses that
claim that the attitude towards politics should be much less negative in the
Centre-North because politics in this part of Italy was more modern,
either because parties were able to build strong political identities capable
of empowering resourceless citizens or as a result of the legacy of strong
civic traditions. Thus, we can conclude that severe disaffection is not
simply a residue of pre-modern politics, or the mere effect of the (supposedly) typical absence of civic virtue in the *Mezzogiorno*. Rather, it would
appear to be as a nationwide political malaise, widespread throughout
Italy or, at least, which has expanded as democracy itself has became consolidated.

Table 10.3 Highly disaffected citizens in Italy by area of residence, 1968–2001 (in percentages)

Year	North-west	North-east (white area)	Red belt	Centre-Sardinia	South-Sicily	Italy
1968	37	45	37	49	54	45
1972	66	71	66	61	74	68
1975	51	60	50	49	69	57
1985	58	54	50	51	65	57
1990	59	80	55	64	61	62
1996	49	49	46	43	39	45
2001	71	70	68	68	75	71

Source: See Table 10.1.

Electoral and ideological choices, do they matter?

Hypothesis H3 maintains that severe disaffection is not systematically connected with voting for opposition parties but, if anything, to non-voting. Our data seem to bear out this hypothesis. As can be seen in the second column of Table 10.4, in 1968, 1996, and 2001 non-voters were likely to be highly disaffected. The odds ratio in these years is quite high. In contrast, disaffected citizens are not very likely to vote for opposition parties: the odds ratio of pooled surveys, from 1968 to 2001, is a modest 1.1. In some years, disaffected citizens did seem to be more likely to engage in protest. However, in others, as for example in 1975, they seem more likely to vote for one of the governing parties. Hence, our results do not support the thesis that voters whose party is excluded from power are more strongly inclined to be disaffected, even when their party is out of power for a long period, as was the case of the PCI and MSI.[13] Of course, some of these voters are disaffected, but the relationship does not seem as strong as the link between disaffection and withdrawal from participation.[14]

Hypothesis H4 also posited that politics could counteract severe disaffection syndrome by providing citizens with ideological identities. In fact, as Figure 10.5 shows, in each and every year from 1968 to 2001 citizens unwilling or unable to place themselves on the ideological spectrum were more likely than other respondents to be highly disaffected. On the other hand, Table 10.5 clearly indicates that severe disaffection is also widespread among those who are ideologically oriented. Can we conclude, therefore, that political disaffection is more prevalent on the right of the ideological continuum than on the left, as hypothesis H4 would lead us to expect?

The figures given in Table 10.5 show that this was in fact the case in 1975 and in 2001, and a little less so in 1985. However, the relation is far

Table 10.4 Vote for opposition parties, non-voting, and disaffection in Italy, 1968–2001[a]

Year	Vote for opposition parties	Non-voting behaviour
1968	1.6	1.8
1972	1.5	–
1975	0.6	–
1985	1.1	–
1990	1.1	–
1996	1.6	2.0
2001	0.6	2.4
Pooled average	1.1	–

Source: See Table 10.1.

Note
a Entries are odds ratios.

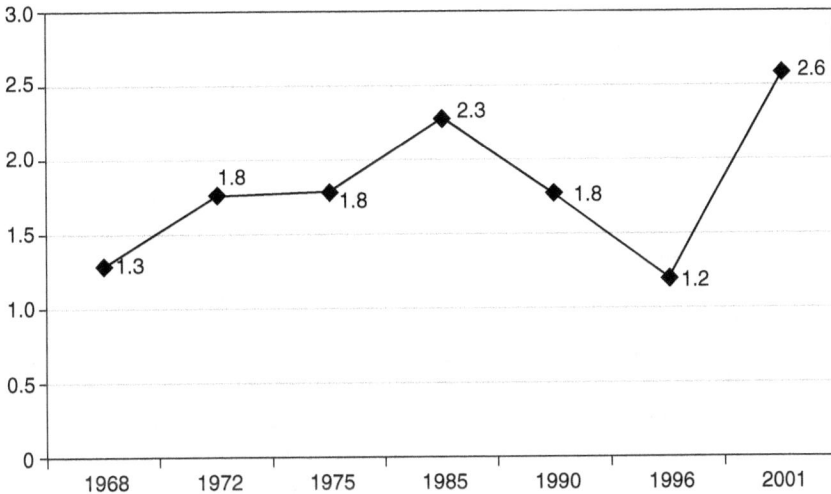

Figure 10.5 How likely it is to be unable to self-locate on the ideological continuum and highly disaffected, 1968–2001 (sources: see Table 10.1).

Table 10.5 Highly disaffected citizens in Italy by self-placement on the ideological continuum, 1968–2001 (in percentages)

Ideology	1968	1972	1975	1985	1990	1996	2001
Left	46	66	33	57	62	44	58
Centre-left	46	70	57	55	53	43	66
Centre	41	61	66	59	59	50	74
Centre-right	48	68	58	61	61	56	67
Right	43	70	56	65	62	41	73
Absolute differences between left–right	3	4	22	8	0	3	15
Eta^2	0.003	0.084	0.065	0.003	0.005	0.01	0.01

Sources: See Table 10.1.

from stable. In some years the differences between the extreme left and extreme right are quite modest. In others, the percentage of highly disaffected citizens was higher among those who placed themselves at the centre of the spectrum. In almost every year (except in 1975) a large plurality of citizens on the extreme left of the spectrum were highly disaffected. Last but not least, the *eta*^{2} in the final row of Table 10.5 indicates that every year (except 1972 and 1975) and in all the ideological segments there is considerable individual heterogeneity. Thus, we can conclude that severe disaffection is a syndrome with the potential to become endemic across the ideological spectrum. While in some years it may affect voters with certain ideological positions more than others, in other years it can spread to respondents with different ideological leanings. In other words, in Italy a severe level of disaffection has not been a fixed and stable component of a particular ideological orientation; rather it has coexisted with all of them.

In short, in Italy, as elsewhere, there is a pretty fair chance that the highly disaffected citizen is also a marginal citizen. That is, the disaffected are less educated, less politically competent, less ideologically motivated, and less inclined to electoral participation. However, this severe disaffection syndrome is far from being confined to this segment of the population. As we have seen from the extent of disaffection, some highly disaffected citizens are also well-educated and politically knowledgeable. When asked to place themselves on the ideological continuum, many disaffected Italians do, feeling free to mix their ideological identity with expressions of overt political cynicism. At election time, the persistently high rates of Italian electoral turnout over the last 40 years shows that the vast majority turns out to vote. A more sober conclusion of our analysis would be, therefore, that the persistently strong presence of severely disaffected Italians is only weakly explained by the factors we have analysed (lack of resources, lack of ideological commitment, and apathy). Certainly, all these factors increase the probability that citizens will feel politically ineffective, but it is hard to believe that they alone are responsible for such severe disaffection. In any case, they cannot explain why a serious syndrome of disaffection appears to be a cultural pattern transmitted from one generation to the next. As di Palma (1970) suggested years ago, in order to explain why disaffection has remained so widespread in Italy, we should look not only at the effects of the individual characteristics of the voters, but also at some peculiar features of the whole system of Italian political representation.

Disaffection as tacit and biased background knowledge

Pitkin (1967) has persuasively argued that political representation is not simply the descriptive or symbolic standing of a few for many, but it is rather the outcome of the interrelated acting of a few for many. From this perspective, representation requires deliberation through compromises between conflicting identities and interests about an agenda that changes across time and therefore it is different from the electoral platforms. It is quite obvious that many voters simply don't have either the political interest or sufficient information to judge how their representatives are actually acting for them. Political identities, party competition, and participation opportunities are, nonetheless, crucial in this respect, since they can provide the voters with cues, criteria of evaluation, judgemental short cuts, and personal empowerment to help them make the necessary judgement as to how their representatives are performing.

However, even though partisanship may help bridge the gap between how representatives are performing their role and the citizen's lack of cognitive resources, it does not resolve the problem. As a cognitive device, partisanship may in fact coexist with many electors' tendency to substitute factual cues on representative politics with fuzzy ways of thinking and emotionally charged ways of talking. This is most likely when electors can draw on a vast and long-lasting reservoir of popular Machiavellism created by centuries of negative experiences of previous non-elected elites. The risk of disaffection should then be considered inbuilt in any democratic country (Linz 1999). We also know that in recent years, the risk of sweeping disaffection has intensified because of a number of interconnected processes (the decline of partisanship, increasing role of the mass media as an intermediary between politicians and the electorate, and so on). In Italy, however, the evidence presented in this chapter shows that a severe disaffection syndrome is not just a longstanding threat from the past, since it still remains strong. Therefore, one could come to the conclusion that the Italian representative system has not only been incapable of checking disaffection, but that some of its peculiarities may even have contributed to intensify the disaffection syndrome.

In the postwar period, the Italian representative has shown some peculiar features at both the macro and elite level: public institutions unable to limit effectively politics and polarized competition between parties in the electoral context, accompanied by coalescent behaviour among them within institutions. The outcome of these features was a pervasive party system (*partitocrazia*), and a political class that skilfully combined its passion for ideological battles with the more prosaic exploitation of the extensive opportunities for particularistic behaviour provided by the scope of the political decision (di Palma 1970; Sartori 1976; Morlino 1991; Pizzorno 1993b; Cotta and Isernia 1996; della Porta 2000; Sani and Segatti 2001). All these features rapidly provided Italians with many opportunities to question the way their representation system operated, and to wonder about the honesty of their representatives. Moreover, in order to understand why so many Italians were and remain cynical about politics one should not only consider the way the political system actually operates, but also two cultural features of grass roots Italian partisanship.

First, the two major actors in postwar democratic consolidation, *Democrazia Cristiana* (DC) and the PCI, developed from two political families (Catholic and Socialist) that played a marginal role in both the state- and the nation-building processes. On the one hand, in the postwar period they successfully became embedded in the institutions and managed to create opportunities for participation for their voters. On the other, their mass partisanship maintained subcultural roots. In consequence, as di Palma (1970: 119) following Pizzorno (1966) notes, 'their political subcultures have acquired a double, if unstable, personality: they accepted the values and rules of the game at leadership level; they were isolated and partially disaffected subcultures among the rank and file'. There is some evidence of this pattern. In 1959 Almond and Verba (1963: 109; emphasis in the original) found that, in comparison with citizens of other countries, Italians were more prone to 'view the intensity of their commitment to their party as a rejection of the other parties as members of the *system* of parties, a rejection of the other parties as members of a system of interaction; also they regard their own party, not as an electoral contestant, but as a church or a "way of life"'. Over the period subcultural partisanship has weakened, and the social isolation between partisans diminished, but Italians remain ambivalent about the way partisan representation operates in democracy. For instance, Biorcio and Mannheimer (1995: 213) highlighted that, at the end of the 1980s, 'Italy stands out [in comparison with other European countries] for the high proportion ... of those [that] feel close to a political party but do not attribute to it any specific capacity to transmit social demands'. In other words, subcultural partisanship keeps alive feelings of political marginality that are a central component of the political disaffection syndrome.

Second, an ideological style of reasoning among the political class, coupled with the polarized multi-party competition (Putnam 1973; Sartori 1976), may have strengthened the ideological component of Italian political identities. According to Pizzorno (1993a), political identities with a strong ideological component are unlike other political identities, based on class, religion, or ethnicity. The latter can curb feelings of political marginality when the demands they give rise to are finally recognized by political institutions and integrated into party competition. In contrast, ideologically based political identities do not simply struggle for institutional recognition.[15] They tend to defend universalistic demands that are at odds with the idea that in a democracy each collective identity is simply a component of the political body. In other words, ideology-based political identities may raise expectations of what politics should deliver, but they do little to legitimize those compromises with other political groups which are a central feature of democratic life. Therefore, even if political identities alone may provide shortcuts which help voters to resolve their information costs and limit their feeling of marginality, ideologically shaped identities ultimately tend to convey a negative bias and sentiments of suspicion which operate against the everyday working of a representation system.

The negative aspect of these features of the Italian representation system, at both the macro and micro levels, could well be the severe disaffection we have identified. They could actually have widened the gap between what representatives do in their role and many electors' attempts to make sense of it. Subcultural legacies and ideologically based political identities might ultimately have generated cynicism not only with respect to the leaders of other groups, but, as an unexpected consequence, in relation to politicians in general. On the other hand, the vast scope of the political decisions often provided the political class with opportunities to develop their own personal agendas, as opposed to the platform they asked the electorate to vote for, as well as opportunities for irregular behaviour or misconduct. The consequence is that these behavioural patterns would have confirmed ancient prejudices about the self-referential behaviour of the elite.

In Italy, therefore, disaffection is influenced not only by individual-level factors, as the analyses above have shown, but may also stem from two system-level sources: the actual behaviour of parties and politicians, and cultural features of mass partisanship. While it is impossible to say which of these last two system-level factors have played a more important role in generating disaffection, we can say a little more about their role in having an impact on disaffection.

As we saw, in Italy, severe disaffection would appear to constitute something akin to what ethno-methodologists call 'tacit background knowledge', an emotionally loaded meaning system which, in the case of Italy, is distinguished by a strong bias against politics. 'Tacit background knowledge' is nothing like the complete truth; it is merely a common sense picture of reality. But it works, because it enables citizens to make sense of a world that is objectively complicated, and sometimes it may also be backed up by the real facts. It is influenced by inherited prejudices, but it can also be reinforced or (re)-activated by current negative experiences with politics. Therefore, disaffection seems to have a dual character. On the one hand, because it is shaped by inherited cultural bias (subcultural legacies and ideological political identities), it can be conceived as a predisposition which is exogenous to the current political context. On the other, it should also be understood as an endogenously primed-reaction to current political events and to the actual behaviour of political elites and parties.[16]

An analysis of the evolution of disaffection in Italy over the last 30 years testifies how both the two system-level factors shape phenomena. Once all individual-level sources of disaffection are kept constant, the disaffected percentage of the electorate should display, year after year, the following two patterns. First, since disaffected citizens are influenced by an exogenous cultural legacy through birth cohort transmission, we should find little variation in their number over the years. However, since political events also stoke disaffection, significant incidents or developments should have a visible influence across each birth cohort. In other words, their impact should occur as a period effect. Moreover, after major political events of this type, the percentage of highly disaffected should remain more or less stable for some years (as long as no other period effect occurs). Evidence for both phenomena (stability and period effect) can be found in our data.

Table 10.6 compares the coefficients of two models of a pooled logistic

Table 10.6 Disaffection change in Italy across the years (1968–2001) before and after controlling for education, generation, political awareness, and ideology[a]

	First model		Second model	
	b	s.e.	b	s.e.
Years				
1968	0		0	
1972	0.99	0.08	1.13	0.08
1975	0.49	0.08	0.92	0.08
1985	0.70	0.07	1.11	0.07
1990	0.70	0.07	1.04	0.08
1996	0.10*	0.08	0.51	0.10
2001	1.11	0.06	1.64	0.08
Education				
Elementary certificate or less			0	0
Middle school			−0.36	0.06
High school or more			−0.86	0.06
Cohort				
Born before 1918			0	0
1919–1928			−0.38	0.11
1929–1938			−0.26	0.10
1939–1948			−0.30	0.10
1949–1958			−0.28	0.08
1959–1968			−0.27	0.08
Born after 1968			−0.22	0.08
Political awareness			−0.57	0.05
Ideology				
Unable to self-locate			0	0
Left			−0.48	0.08
Centre-Left			−0.32	0.07
Centre			−0.24	0.06
Centre-Right			−0.15	0.08
Right			−0.32	0.10
Constant	−0.21	0.05	0.42	0.08
Improvement	Chi square 418.03 (DF6)		Chi square 1261.73 (DF20)	
(N)	(12,955)		(12,895)	

Source: See Table 10.1.

Note

a Entries are b coefficients and standard errors (*s.e.*). The dependent variable is the percentage of disaffected citizens. Independent variables are time in *years* (reference category = 1968); level of *education* (reference category = elementary certificate or less); birth *cohort* (reference category = born before 1918); *political awareness* (see note); and *ideology* measured through self-placement on left–right scale (reference category = unable to self locate). Level of significance is *$p<0.05$; the remaining coefficients are significant at 0.01 or less.

regression in which the percentage of disaffected citizens has been regressed with time (indexed in years), first without and then while keeping constant the impacts of education levels, political awareness, birth cohorts, and self-location on the left–right continuum. As we can see, there are large differences between the two models. Before the control variables are included in the model, the year logit parameter is floating. As the individual-level disaffection factors are taken into account, a strong variation (a period effect) occurs in 1972, 1996, and 2001.[17] Between 1972 and 1990, the coefficients appear to be almost stable.[18] The parameters of the control variable confirm what we already know about the effect of individual-level sources of disaffection. The higher the citizens' level of educational and political awareness, the less likely they are to be disaffected. A similar effect occurs with ideology. Sharing an ideological point of view helps to reduce the chance of disaffection in comparison to the reference group (those unable to place themselves on the ideological continuum).[19] Finally, in each birth cohort the level of disaffection appears to be almost the same (in comparison to the oldest generation).

Why were 1972, 1996, and 2001 such important years? In 1972, the Italian party system was in the midst of political turmoil. The 1972 elections were the first to be called before the end of the five-year legal deadline. The centre-left coalition, at that time comprising the DC and *Partito Socialista Italiano* (PSI) plus other minor parties, was in complete disarray, and all the parties were internally and externally divided over different coalition strategies. Moreover, beyond the *Palazzo* (a key term used to refer to the pinnacle of the political and economic elites), numerous protest movements were taking to the streets. Equally, the 1996 elections came at the end of a period characterized by dramatic political change, but in a different direction. Many studies of the 1992–1996 period maintain that at that time the institutional change and the new party system were welcomed by many voters, who saw them as offering a way out of the profound sense of disillusion with the old political class, deeply and widely involved in an extended web of corruption (Diamanti and Mannheimer 1994; Corbetta and Parisi 1997; Segatti 1997). The drop in disaffection seen in the 1996 data could reflect these popular expectations of a new beginning. On the other hand, the dramatic increase of political disaffection in 2001, which is also suggested by other surveys, could be interpreted as an indication of renewed frustration provoked by the political stalemate resulting from the failure of the institutional transition (Sani 1999; ITANES 2001). Therefore, disaffection may be affected by major political events. However, the impact of such events, which would influence all generations, reinforces or weakens a culturally shaped common wisdom as to what politics is or is not believed to be.

Conclusion

There are three main conclusions to be drawn. First, for over 40 years political disaffection was, or has been, more likely among marginal citizens (the poorly educated, those with less political awareness, and the less ideologically motivated). Moreover, in Italy disaffection tends to correlate with apathy. Second, lack of individual resources is not the only factor explaining why so many Italians were and are disaffected from politics. As di Palma (1970) showed more than 30 years ago, and as our data very clearly confirm, in addition to the individual resources factor, disaffection is likely to be affected by a more general systemic factor. This factor may be related to both the actual working of the political system and to the subjective, culturally shaped, evaluations of politics. Our analysis shows that these two systemic elements have an impact on disaffection in different ways. Over the past 30 years, once individual factors are held constant, the percentage of disaffected citizens has remained almost constant because disaffection has been transmitted from one generation to another. On the other hand, the percentage of disaffected citizens has changed dramatically when major political events (such as scandals, or political turmoil, or opportunities for a new beginning) threw the actual working of political systems into question. Therefore, our third conclusion is that political disaffection is both a culturally rooted predisposition and a response to current events. To put this another way, the analysis of 40 years of disaffection in Italy demonstrates that this attitude can change, but also that inverting its negative sign could be as difficult as blowing in the wind.

Appendix: survey questions on political efficacy in Italian surveys, 1959–1996

1959

1 *Politics so complicated*
   'Some people say that politics and government are so complicated that the average man cannot really understand what is going on. In general, do you agree or disagree with that?'
2 *Lose touch*
   'All candidates sound good in their speeches but you can never tell what they will do after they are elected'.
3 *Non-influence*
   'People like me don't have any say over what the government does'.
      1. Agree
      3. Depends
      5. Disagree

1968

1   *Politics so complicated*
    'Politics and government sometimes seem so complicated that people like me can't really understand what's going on'.

2   *Lose touch*
    'In general, the deputies we elect quickly lose touch with the people'.

3   *Don't care*
    'I don't think the government cares much about what people like me think'.
    1. Agree
    2. Disagree
    8. Don't know
    0. No answer

1972

1   *Politics so complicated*
    'Politics and government sometimes seem so complicated that people like me can't really understand what's going on'.

2   *Accomplishments*
    'Politicians talk a lot but accomplish little'.

3   *Don't care*
    'I don't think the government cares much about what people like me think'.
    1. Agree
    2. Disagree
    8. Don't know
    0. No answer

1975

1   *Politics so complicated*
    'Sometimes politics and government seem so complicated that a person like me cannot really understand what is going on'.

2   *Lose touch*
    'Generally speaking, those we elect to parliament lose touch with the people pretty quickly'.

3   *Don't care*
    'I don't think that public officials care much about what people like me think'.

4   *No influence*
    'People like me have no say over what the government does'.
    1. Agree strongly
    2. Agree

3. Disagree
4. Disagree strongly

1985

1   *Politics so complicated*
    'Politics is so complicated that people like me can't really understand what's going on'.
2   *Personal interest*
    'Those in power, always pursue their personal interests'.
3   *Don't care*
    'Politicians do not care much about what people like me think'.
    1. Agree strongly
    2. Agree
    3. Disagree
    4. Disagree strongly
    8. Don't know
    9. No answer

1990

1   *Politics so complicated*
    'Sometimes, politics is so complicated that people like me can't really understand what's going on'.
2   *Lose touch*
    'In general, people we elect to parliament quickly lose touch with the people'.
3   *Don't care*
    'I don't think that politicians care much about what people like me think'.
4   *No influence*
    'People like me have no say over what government does'.
    4. Agree strongly
    3. Agree
    2. Disagree
    1. Disagree strongly
    9. No answer

1996

2   *Lose touch*
    'In general, people we elect to parliament quickly lose contact with the people'.
4   *No influence*
    'People like me have no say over what the government does'.

4. Agree strongly

3. Agree

2. Disagree

1. Disagree strongly

9. No answer

Notes

* This chapter draws on research from a larger project on Italian electoral change being carried out by Paolo Bellucci, Marco Maraffi, and the author. I have benefited from many comments and suggestions from Roberto Biorcio, Jean Blondel, Arturo Parisi, Gianfranco Pasquino, Maurizio Pisati, Alessandro Pizzorno, Giacomo Sani, and Hans Schadee. I am also grateful for the comments of the participants at the seminar on Political Disaffection held in Santiago de Compostela in October 2000 and from the suggestions by the editors of this volume, Mariano Torcal and José Ramón Montero. I have done all possible to avoid misinterpreting their words; any remaining errors are mine alone.

1 Preliminary responses to these questions can be found in Sani and Segatti (2001), Mastropaolo (2000), Segatti, Bellucci, and Maraffi (1999), and Morlino and Tarchi (1996).

2 I combined data from all eight surveys in a single matrix in order to perform a pooled cross-section time series analysis, identifying how disaffection, at the individual level, has changed over 40 years according to some predictors. Some caveats are in order. It should be noted that simply using almost the same indicators, although helpful, does not solve all the comparability problems. Although if information is rare, it is easy to imagine that the seven surveys were not all conducted with the same design, the same sampling criteria, and in the same political circumstances. Some of them, however, have this useful peculiarity. The 1968 and 1972 surveys are both post-electoral and were conducted by the same team and the same polling agency, presumably with the same design and interviewing procedures. The same is partly true of others, such as those of 1990, 1996, and 2001, which were carried out by almost the same team using the same measures, but with a slightly different sampling design and in different political circumstances: after a second-order election in 1990 and after a highly debated parliamentary election in 1996 and 2001.

3 This is the case in 1968, 1972, 1975, 1985, 1990, and 2001. The variance explained by the single factor ranges from 40 per cent in 1990 to 52 per cent in 1985. A confirmatory principal component, multisample analysis, performed on the 1975 and 1990 surveys, confirms that the model which fits the data best includes only one latent factor and not two (data not shown). Besides, the parameters of the coefficients were the same in both years. I would like to thank H. Schadee for his help with this analysis.

4 The proportion of highly disaffected citizens is calculated only from the interviewees who responded to all the questions; missing data are excluded. It should be noted that from 1959 to 1972 the percentage of missing data varied between about 30 and 25 per cent of the entire sample. In the following surveys the segment was much lower (between about 2 and 5 per cent). Respondents who fail to express their opinion of politics are likely to be disaffected. On the other hand, they could be also simply reticent. Because it is impossible to disentangle the two attitudes, we have preferred to consider in

the analysis only those respondents who openly expressed their feelings towards politics.

5 The question allowed for three responses (democracy always better, dictatorship sometimes, all the same).

6 The odds ratio is a measure of association between two dichotomous variables. It is based on the ratio between the odds of the variables categories. Its range runs from zero to positive infinity. An odds ratio of 1 means that the two variables are unrelated. Values of less that 1 mean a negative association; values over 1 signify a positive relation (see Bohrnstedt and Knoke 1994).

7 Pharr and Putnam (2000) trace the decline in political confidence that has occurred in many countries over the last few decades from a similar perspective, incorporating into their analysis, along with these three macro-factors, the role of information.

8 Disaffection may also depend on the picture citizens have of politics as a result of their exposure to information. Recently, television has been credited with spreading popular cynicism towards politics. Norris (2000), however, found no evidence of this in her comparative analysis. Moreover, the Italian case shows widespread disaffection even before television dominated political communication. On the other hand, della Porta (2000) found that in the 1980s, at the aggregate level, the number of cases of corruption in the press and the percentages of those interviewed dissatisfied with democracy both increased. Given the lack of systematic data for the period as a whole, the link between information and disaffection is not explored here.

9 It would be worth comparing the behaviour of some university professors in academic governing bodies with the behaviour of some politicians in their own sphere. It is highly probable that in both cases we would discover poor behaviour, and that it is difficult to say who is the pupil and who the teacher.

10 Entries in Figure 10.1 are odds ratios of each year estimated through two pooled logistic regression models; in both cases the dependent variable is a disaffection index, while in one case time (indexed as survey years) is the only independent variable, the other also includes education level (indexed in three categories: primary, secondary, and higher). The time reference category is 1959.

11 We constructed the index of political awareness by including in the same category all the respondents who in each survey self-reported higher than average political interest and showed higher than average levels of political knowledge.

12 Entries in Figure 10.4 are odds ratios estimated through a pooled logistic regression model in which the usual disaffection index is the dependent variable, while birth cohort, time, education, and interaction between them constitute the independent variables. The reference group in the model is the birth cohort born before 1918.

13 We present data on non-voting for only three points in time because some surveys did not feature a direct question on turnout. Moreover, even those surveys that did include a non-voting question tend to underestimate the real level of non-voting because many respondents do not self-report such behaviour. As a proxy for voting behaviour in some years we used intention to vote or, in post-electoral surveys, recall of voting. The category of governing parties was made up, from 1968 to 1990, of voters for the *Democrazia Cristiana* (DC), *Partito Socialista Italiano* (PSI), *Partito Socialista Democratico Italiano* (PSDI), and *Partito Liberale Italiano* (PLI), while voters for the *Partito Comunista Italiano* (PCI) and *Movimiento Sociale Italiano* (MSI) were categorized in the opposition. In 1996 we included in the governing parties category voters for the *Ulivo* coalition, and in the opposition parties voters for *Casa delle Lebertà*, and vice versa in 2001.

14 We are convinced that the strength of the relationship between disaffection

and non-voting is underestimated because Italians are not inclined to declare their non-voting behaviour in survey interviews.

15 Pizzorno (1993a) argues that a theory of conflict should distinguish between three types of conflict, each with a different basis: interest, identity, and ideology. Ideology-shaped conflict has a more universalistic (populistic) bias, which de facto makes it impossible to achieve and stabilize recognition.

16 Jackman and Miller (1998) argue that in the social capital debate there are two approaches to social and political trust. One treats trust as an endogenous component of social and political interaction, shaped by learning experiences with social and political institutions. The other treats trust as a politico-cultural dimension, exogenous to actual political experiences. While they also argue that attempts to combine the two approaches are 'unproductive', I think they are partly mistaken. As the Italian case shows, political disaffection is shaped by a strong cultural bias, but in particular circumstances this bias can be disproved or confirmed according to the political context.

17 As can also be seen from Figure 10.3.

18 There are, of course, some differences. The 1975 coefficient is different to its 1972 equivalent, but the difference is small.

19 The effect seems to be stronger among those who place themselves on the extreme left. I also applied a different logistic model in order to identify the difference among those that self-locate on different points of the continuum in comparison with those that self-place on the centre. I found that the logit coefficients of the different ideological orientations were not significant, except for those on the extreme left. Again, however, the differences were small.

Part V

Consequences: participation, protest, and information

11 Does protest signify disaffection?

Demonstrators in a postindustrial democracy[1]

Pippa Norris, Stefaan Walgrave, and Peter Van Aelst

Large numbers of studies have drawn attention to rising levels of political protest, whether understood as the spread of 'demonstration democracy' (Etzioni 1971), the growth of the 'protest society' (Pross 1992), an expression of 'global civic society' (Kaldor 2000) or, more popularly in contemporary newspaper headlines, as the emergence of the so-called 'Genoa generation'. This phenomenon raises important questions about the causes and consequences of these developments, and in particular about *who* demonstrates, the focus of this chapter. Understanding this issue highlights familiar methodological challenges regarding the extent to which *ad hoc* and irregular protest activities can be measured through traditional survey techniques or event (content) analysis (Rucht, Koopmans, and Neidhardt 1999). In a bid to examine these developments, the first section summarizes alternative theories commonly used in the literature to explain and interpret demonstration activism, contrasting disaffection, resource-based, and contextual accounts. Today, are most demonstrators disaffected radicals? Are they conventional participants using protest simply as another option or strategic resource, just like any other such as election campaigns or community organizing? Or do demonstrations provide a meeting place that can bring together both radicals and moderates, depending on the particular contextual issue, political actors, and cultural frame? In the second section we describe the sources of evidence used to evaluate these interpretations. The study draws on three main sources of survey evidence. (i) We compare the 1973–1976 baseline Political Action study with successive waves of the World Values Survey 1981–2001 to establish cross-national trends in the extent of protest activity. (ii) The chapter then focuses on Belgium, chosen as a postindustrial society exemplifying the rise of protest politics, where we analyse the 1999 Flanders-Belgium general election study to provide a representative cross-section of the electorate. Lastly (iii) we use a unique series of surveys of protesters who took part in seven different demonstrations in Belgium. The third section examines the evolution of the relevant trends since the mid-1970s, revealing the substantial rise in protest activism in many countries, while the fourth analyses who demonstrates in Belgium by comparing the social background and attitudinal characteristics of party members, civic joiners, and demonstrators. The fifth section offers a similar analysis of participants in different types of demonstration in Belgium. The conclusion summarizes the major findings and considers their implications for our understanding of the rise of demonstration activism and the challenges this poses to contemporary representative democracy.

Theoretical framework

The literature seeking to explain protest politics is divided between macro- and micro-level approaches, each belonging to a distinct scientific tradition and scholarly domain. The macro approach, grounded in historical sociology, comparative politics, and political institutions, can be traced back to Barrington Moore's *Social Origins of Dictatorship and Democracy* (1966). Macro accounts, which are closely related to mainstream social movement theory, seek to explain outbreaks of protest, the mobilization of collective action, and the process of 'contentious politics' as a systemic phenomenon.[2] Alternative, micro accounts focus on individual-level political behaviour. Drawing on social psychology, political behaviour, and sociology, they originated with Almond and Verba's *The Civic Culture* (1963). Micro accounts study the specific characteristics, social background, and attitudinal orientations that lead some individuals to engage in protest activism while others stand passively on the sidelines (Klandermans 1995). Within the micro-level perspective, the main explanations have emphasized the role of disaffected radicalism, conventional strategic resources, and contextual factors.

Disaffected radicalism

Perhaps the most common explanation for the growth of protest politics, and the main source of popular concern about this, is the claim that growing political disaffection and alienation has generated this phenomenon. Early social movements scholars like Gustave Le Bon (1895) stressed the dangers of collective action. In the mid-1970s the widely influential Trilateral report *The Crisis of Democracy* by Crozier, Huntington, and Watanuki (1975) presented the May 1968 street uprisings and their subsequent reverberations as a serious threat to the stability of the Trilateral democracies. Protest politics, the authors suggested, challenged established sources of authority, and this phenomenon was generated by the rise of a more critical and autonomous media, the spread of post-materialist values among the younger generation, the development of an adversarial intellectual class, and, in particular, by the way that the demands on government were understood to be intensifying, while the capacity of the state to meet these demands appeared to be stagnating. Along related lines, Ted Robert Gurr's seminal work (1970) interpreted violent acts as an expression of discontent with conventional channels of representative democracy and the search for alternative ways to challenge the regime, including through riots damaging property or people or non-violent direct action such as blocking traffic or occupations. In his view, protest represents an avenue for channelling and expressing deep-rooted feelings of frustration, anger, and alienation, not just with particular political leaders or public policy issues, but also with the political process and system themselves. Studies have interpreted the upsurge in protest politics in the United States and Western Europe as an expression of disaffection with conventional channels of political participation and mobilization in representative government, as well as symbolizing lack of trust and confidence in political institutions (Nye 1997; Tolchin 1996).

Yet the claim that disaffection with the political system motivates protest activism receives little, if any, support from the available systematic empirical analyses of survey data. For example, the original 8-nation Political Action study failed to establish a significant association between protest potential and feelings of 'external efficacy', or beliefs in the responsiveness of the political system (see Farah, Barnes, and Heunis 1979). In the follow-up study, Thomassen (1990) compared political attitudes in the Netherlands and West Germany and confirmed that support for the political regime was unrelated to protest potential (see also Dalton 2002; Koopman 1996; Van Aelst, Walgrave and Decoster 1999). In the 1960s, Parkin (1968) criticized mass society approaches and found that people who were willing to protest in the British Campaign for Nuclear Disarmament (CND) were more, not less, likely to be engaged in conventional forms of political activism. More recently, Dalton (1993) examined whether willingness to protest was stronger among the alienated and deprived in the United States, Britain, Germany, and France. His research, which drew on data from the 1990–1991 World Values Survey, concluded that there was no support for this notion.

The available empirical evidence, therefore, throws considerable doubt on the claim that disaffection motivates protest. Nevertheless, there are many reasons why this issue is worth exploring further with alternative sources of data. First, previous empirical studies have often limited themselves to examining 'protest *potential*', although critics have long suggested that this represents an unsatisfactory indicator of actual protest behaviour. Survey items may prompt answers that are regarded as socially acceptable, or just tap a more general orientation towards the political system (such as approval of freedom of association or tolerance of dissent) (see Barnes *et al.* 1979; Rootes 1981). Surveys usually prove more successful when tapping attitudes and values rather than actual behaviour, and they are generally more reliable when measuring routine and repetitive actions (such as 'How often do you attend church?') than occasional acts. Unfortunately hypothetical questions (such as 'Might you ever demonstrate or join a boycott?') may well prove a poor predictor of actual behaviour (Topf 1995). In contrast, random surveys conducted among demonstrators who are *actually engaged* in these events should provide far more reliable indicators of the real profile of protestors. Many previous studies have also adopted a fairly limited measure of system support, focusing on a single dimension, rather than using a more complete battery of items monitoring political interest, external and internal efficacy, satisfaction with democracy, confidence in government, and civic activism. If system support is multidimensional, as argued elsewhere (Norris 1999b), then many indicators need to be compared. Here it will be shown that, given the substantial growth in protest politics in postindustrial societies since the 1970s, older studies also need to be updated in order to verify whether their findings still hold among the current protest population. Finally, despite the lack of systematic support from empirical studies, popular commentators commonly interpret protest events in different countries as expressions of political disaffection symbolizing serious challenges to authority. Such a popular interpretation has been offered on numerous occasions in mainstream popular culture and journalism, and applied to events ranging from peaceful demonstrations (exemplified by the 'Million Mom March'), through direct action such as European fuel blockades, the anti-poll tax movement in the United Kingdom, the anti-globalization and anti-World Trade Organization (WTO) protest in Genoa, the May Day riots in the City of London, the anti-Chávez street mobilizations in Venezuela, and most recently, the anti-Iraq War demonstrations, which drew an estimated eight million people onto the streets worldwide in mid-February 2003. The sheer pervasiveness and tenacity of this interpretation in popular culture makes it worth exploring further.

Conventional strategic resources

An alternative perspective suggests that the interpretation of demonstrators as disaffected radicals only reflects popular stereotypes common in the framing of social movements during the 1960s, when American news media focused on hippies and Black Panther radicals and the European press conveyed images of 1968 violent revolutionaries in Paris, London, and Berlin. Scholars claim that such images no longer reflect patterns of protest participation in the contemporary world, because the demonstration population has gradually 'normalized' over the years to become mainstream, heterogeneous, and conventional in both attitudes and social characteristics (Van Aelst and Walgrave 2001). This account builds on the theories of societal modernization developed by Ronald Inglehart (1977, 1990, 1997b) and Russell Dalton (1993, 2000a, 2002). Inglehart maintains that societal modernization involves the shift from agrarian to industrial, and then postindustrial societies. The process of modernization is associated with multiple complex developments in the workforce, home, and public sphere. The social and economic shifts characterizing postindustrial societies include, among others, the emergence of a highly educated, skilled and specialized workforce; rising living standards and greater leisure time; the expansion and fragmentation of mass media channels, technologies, and markets; and the growth of multilevel governance with power shifting away from the nation state towards global and local levels. The most important consequences of these developments for political participation, these theorists suggest, is that secular trends in secondary and higher education, in leisure hours, and in mass communications in postindustrial societies have generated far more cognitively informed, skilled, and demanding citizens. Such citizens, it is argued, come to use political protest as another strategic resource for civic expression, whether relating to environmental protection, jobs, or welfare.

Yet there are some important differences within this strategic-resource perspective, which have been discussed fully elsewhere (see Norris 2002: Ch. 10). For example, Bennett (1998: 741–761) suggests that, as in a zero-sum game, societal modernization leads to the decline of traditional activities such as voting and party membership, and a simultaneous increase in newer forms of more demanding activities (exemplified by involvement in new social movements and referendum campaigns) or to the development of alternative 'lifestyle politics'. Other accounts see the rise of protest politics as essentially supplementing, rather than replacing, traditional channels of political expression and mobilization in representative democracies (Norris 2002). From this perspective, rather than regarding demonstrations as a distinct type of radical activism, many mainstream activists will turn strategically to whichever alternative form or mode of political organizing they feel will be most effective at the time, whether campaigning through parties and elections, working through traditional interest group organizations such as trade unions and civic associations, joining social movements, using consumers power to support or boycott manufacturers, or publicizing their concerns on the streets. Other authors suggest that protest activism has become more conventional over time as less repressive policing of these activities has lowered the barrier for mainstream mass participation (della Porta and Reiter 1998; della Porta 1995).

Contextual factors

Another alternative theory suggests that the social groups which demonstrate, and their underlying attitudinal motivations, depend critically on the specific context of the event in question. This is defined by the issues at stake, the political actors, coalition partners, mobilization processes, and cultural frames surrounding each demonstration. In this view, attempts to generalize about 'demonstrations' or 'demonstrators' are fundamentally mistaken, resulting in a category mistake if this label is used to lump together disparate events that need to be carefully disentangled into a typology of events. In this argument, some protests will indeed bring together multiple disaffected groups challenging authority, by violent means if necessary, perhaps exemplified by the street action attempting to bring about the downfall of the Hugo Chávez regime in Venezuela, the May Day anti-capitalist protestors damaging property in the City of London, or the anti-Ramos demonstrations in the Philippines. By contrast, other conventional mainstream groups can adopt public protest as just one strategy out of a repertoire available to publicize their issue or cause. Certain heterogeneous coalitions provide a meeting place for both radicals and moderates: for example, the anti-globalization protests in Genoa brought together various mainstream charities like Oxfam and Christian Aid, as well as radicals like British Drop the Debt protestors and the German *Freie Arbeiterinnen* Union. Some demonstrations attract young people, others the elderly. Some protests mobilize blue-collar workers, others middle class professionals, or even employers.[3] Some draw highly educated protesters, while others are largely made up of low-skilled workers.

From this contextual perspective, there is little about the activity of protest politics *per se* that predicts the attitudes or social background of participants. This may seem a relatively uncontroversial, perhaps even tautological, claim, unless the diversity of the protest population is explicitly contrasted with resource-based interpretations predicting a systematic bias in the protest population towards the middle-class and university-educated. If protest politics is commonly used by all major sectors of society, not just the well resourced and cognitively skilled, the rise of such activism will not necessarily exacerbate, and indeed may even reduce, existing social inequalities in public life.

One approach to understanding these contextual factors draws on the classic distinction made in social movement theory between 'traditional' interest groups, exemplified by trade unions and churches, and 'new' social movements such as environmentalists and women's groups (McAdam, McCarthy, and Zald 1996; Dalton and Kuechler 1990; Offe 1985; Melucci 1996). Most demonstrations are organized rather than being spontaneous.[4] Since traditional interest groups differ from new social movements in terms of their core issues, constituencies, and relationships with the State, it is reasonable to expect to find differences among the demonstrators they mobilize. The classic ideological distinction between issues on the left and right of the ideological spectrum can also be expected to give rise to significant differences among different types of demonstrations, for example those concerned with pay and working conditions organized by trade unions and professional associations, and others focused on anti-immigrant sentiments mobilized by far right parties. If protest activity is essentially contextual, as this perspective maintains, then such differences should be apparent if we compare different types of demonstration events.

Data methods and hypotheses

What social and attitudinal differences could we expect to find among party members, civic joiners, and demonstrators, based on these theories? The testable propositions examined in this study are formally summarized in Table 11.5. What kind of demonstrators would each theory predict?

Disaffection hypotheses

If the disaffection interpretation is correct, we hypothesize (H1.1) that, all other things being equal, compared with party members and civic joiners, *demonstration activists will display low levels of system support*, as measured by satisfaction with the performance of democracy, confidence in government, and external political efficacy (belief in the responsiveness of the political system). Moreover, disaffection theories also suggest that we should find important differences in political behaviour, as demonstrators form a distinctive group which turns to protests out of frustration with traditional democratic channels of political expression and mobilization, such as electoral or interest group politics. This leads to the second hypothesis (H1.2), namely that, all other things being equal, compared with party members and civic joiners, *demonstrators will show low levels of traditional political participation*, as measured by active membership of civic associations, labour, business, or professional associations, and political parties. Moreover, according to this thesis, activists will come disproportionately from the ranks of extremists and radicals, who feel alienated from mainstream moderate parties and policies. This suggests our third hypothesis (H1.3), namely that we expect that *demonstrators will cluster to the far right or far left of the ideological spectrum*, well removed from the median voter. Lastly, by implication, we might expect this group of activists to come disproportionately from among the poor and dispossessed, who may have the most legitimate cause to feel that their interests are neglected by the established political system. The fourth hypothesis (H1.4) is, therefore, that *demonstrators will display a distinctive socio-economic profile compared with party members and civic joiners*, as they will be drawn disproportionately from among working-class, less educated, and lower-status sectors.

Strategic resource hypotheses

Alternatively, if strategic resource theories are correct, then they too would generate certain testable propositions about the characteristics of demonstrators. In particular, a series of books by Verba and colleagues, as well as many subsequent studies, have established that certain standard social and attitudinal characteristics are commonly associated with traditional forms of political participation such as campaigning and community activism (Verba and Nie 1972; Verba, Nie, and Kim 1978; Verba,

Schlozman, and Brady 1995). If demonstrations have now become conventional, then similar characteristics can be expected to help predict participation in demonstrations as well. Again we can compare our three groups: party members, civic joiners, and demonstrators. First, in terms of political attitudes, if strategic resource theories are correct, then (H2.1) we would *expect to find greater similarities than differences between the motivational attitudes of demonstrators, party members, and civic joiners*, for example in terms of levels of political interest, internal efficacy (the belief that people can effect politics and the policy-making process), and external efficacy. In terms of behaviour, if demonstrations supplement rather than replace other modes of activism, (H2.2) *demonstrators should also be active in traditional forms of political participation*, as members of civic associations and political parties. Third, if demonstrations have become mainstream politics, we would expect demonstrators not to be on the far left or right. Therefore we could hypothesize that demonstrators will not show extremist political preferences and will (H2.3) *display similar political preferences on the ideological spectrum* to civic joiners and party members. Lastly, the characteristics of education, socio-economic status, and age usually help predict party membership and associational activism. If the protest population has normalized then these characteristics should also help identify demonstrators as well. We therefore hypothesize that (H2.4) *demonstrators will share the social characteristics of other types of activists*, and more particularly, that they will have higher than average educational qualifications and socio-economic occupational status, and will be drawn mainly from among the middle-aged and male population. Some support for this latter proposition comes from Marsh and Kaase's (1979) analysis of the 1973–1976 Political Action Study. They found that in the past protest potential was more common among men than women, as well as among the highly educated, both characteristics of participants in traditional activities. At the same time, Marsh and Kasse noted two important areas of contrast between conventional and unconventional activists. On the one hand, they found that in the 1970s protest potential was strongest among the younger generation, not the middle-aged. They also identified a middle-class bias among traditional or conventional activists, but somewhat mixed indicators of the propensity to protest by socio-economic status and income. All these characteristics need re-examining in the light of the contradictory expectations generated by the rival theories examined here, as well as the immense social and political changes that have taken place over the last few decades.

Contextual theory hypothesis

The contextual theory's central claim is that the type of event matters, and that demonstrations cannot, therefore, all be lumped together in the same category. From this perspective, demonstrations vary greatly, as do the social and attitudinal characteristics of their participants. 'Old' and 'new' social movements, for example, as well as right-wing and left-wing issues, may bring different kinds of people onto the streets. The greater the differentiation between demonstrations, the more the contextual theory is corroborated. The core hypotheses derived from this account are straightforward. First (H3.1), *support for the political system will vary significantly among participants in different types of demonstration, rather than being uniform across the demonstration population.* More specifically, some demonstrations may bring together anti-state radicals with low levels of system support, while others will attract those trusting in government. In addition, given what we know from many previous studies of activism in interest group and new social movements, as a secondary hypothesis we expect (H3.2) that *the social characteristics of demonstrators will also vary significantly by the type of event.* In particular, we expect that 'New Left' demonstrations are likely to mobilize younger, highly educated, more female, and middle-class activists; in contrast, we anticipate that 'Old Left' events may attract more working-class, older, and male participants, while 'New Right' demonstrations can be expected to mobilize less educated, male participants. These hypotheses can be explored by comparing the social and political characteristics of participants attending different demonstration events.

In order to examine these issues, the study draws on three sources of survey evidence: (i) trend data tracing the rise of protest activism and drawn from the Political Action Survey and the World Values Survey; (ii) the general election survey of a representative cross-section of the Belgian electorate; and lastly (iii) the Van Aelst and Walgrave survey of a random sample of Belgian demonstration participants.

(i) The Political Action Study and World Values Survey

Longitudinal evidence of trends in protest activism comes from comparing the eight nations included in the original Political Action survey conducted by Barnes and Kaase in 1973–1976; these are Britain, West Germany, the Netherlands, Austria, the United States, Italy, Switzerland, and Finland (Marsh 1977; Barnes *et al.* 1979). In order to update the trends we can compare evidence on these same countries from successive waves of the World Values Survey that replicated the items measuring experience of protest politics.[5]

(ii) The 1999 General Election Study of Flanders-Belgium

To further explore developments, this case study focuses on Belgium, chosen as an established democracy exemplifying the rise of protest politics. Belgium boasts the highest proportion of demonstrators of any country in our comparative data, as well as the sharpest rise in demonstration activism since the early 1980s.[6] To assess the distribution and characteristics of political activism in the general population, we have analysed data from the 1999 General Election Study of Flanders-Belgium. This cross-sectional face-to-face survey with a supplementary mail-back questionnaire is representative of the Flanders electorate, as a total of 2,099 respondents were interviewed, with a response rate of 74 per cent.[7]

The work of Verba and his colleagues in the early 1970s originally distinguished between four conventional modes of political participation: voting, campaign activism, community organizing, and particularized contacting activity (Verba, Nie, and Kim 1971, 1978; Verba and Nie 1972; Verba, Schlozman, and Brady 1995). Barnes *et al.* (1979) later added a battery of protest items to the standard survey items, to measure protest activism ('have done') and protest potential ('would do'). The distribution of the available evidence on activism from the 1999 Belgian general election study is shown in Figure 11.1. As can be seen, the type of activities mentioned ranges from voting, which is almost universal, to more unorthodox forms of protest such as refusing to pay taxes and damaging property. In this study, we focus on comparing the attitudes and behaviour of three groups of activists: party members, civic joiners, and demonstration activists.

Party membership is understood to be one of the most important standard indicators of traditional or conventional political participation, especially in Western European mass-branch parties. It is also an issue which has given rise to considerable concern about declining membership rolls weakening linkages between citizens and the State (Mair 2001). Belgium in particular is widely considered to be a so-called 'partitocracy', in which mass-membership parties permeate society and politics (De Winter, della Porta, and Deschouwer 1996; Walgrave, Caals, and Suetens 2003). The survey estimates suggest that overall some 11 per cent of Belgians report belonging to a political party or political association. This is a higher estimate than that obtained from official party records (7 per cent), but differences between these sources are not uncommon, as both measures suffer from limitations (see Norris 2002: Ch. 6). The inclusion of 'association' in the survey item may account for some of the difference, along with the fact that the survey included self-reported 'passive' members (7 per cent) as well as 'active' members (4 per cent).

Civic joiners are strongly emphasized in Putnam's (1993, 2000, 2002b) thesis about the crucial importance of social capital for community organizing and political participation. We define this group as being made up of those citizens who currently belong, as active or passive members, to any of nine different types of voluntary association and community organization, including sports clubs, charitable groups, religious-affiliated societies, the environmental movement, and cultural groups, excluding membership of political parties. The list includes both traditional interest groups as well as new social movements. We elaborated a summary scale of how many civic organizations people belong to and weighted this according to whether the respondents reported being active (2) or passive members (1) of each

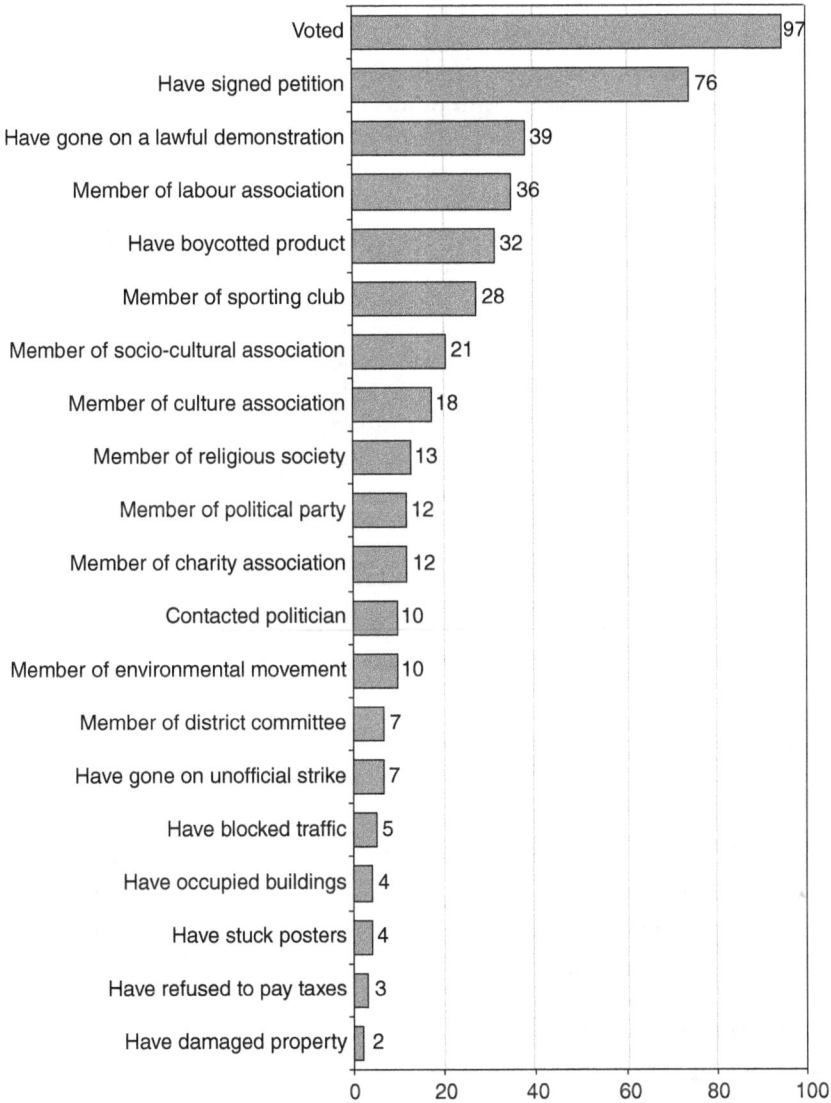

Figure 11.1 Frequency of political and civic activism in Flandes-Belgium, 1999 (in percentages). 'Membership' includes both 'active' and 'passive' categories (source: 1999 General Election Study of Flanders-Belgium).

organization. The full list of organizations is provided in Figure 11.1, which shows the distribution of memberships, ranging from those like labour and professional associations and sports clubs, which are the most popular, down to environmental groups and district committees that are minority interests.

Demonstration activists are defined as those who report actually taking part in a series of 13 different types of demonstrations, listed with their distributions in Figure 11.2. These range from demonstrations about working conditions, that proved most popular, involving one-fifth of the Belgian electorate, compared with others that attracted only small minorities, such as women's issues and agriculture. The list includes both traditional bread-and-butter welfare issues exemplified by working conditions and jobs, as well as 'newer' post-materialist concerns like the environment and anti-racism. One common limitation of the existing literature is that it usually focuses on protest potential, but this has proved a poor indicator of what activities people actually participate in. As Topf (1995) argues, responses can best be understood as what citizens think they ought to do, rather than what they actually will do (see also Barnes *et al.* 1979; Rootes 1981). As we have already noted, this is because surveys are generally better at tapping attitudes and values rather than actual behaviour; and they are usually more reliable at reporting repetitive rather than occa-

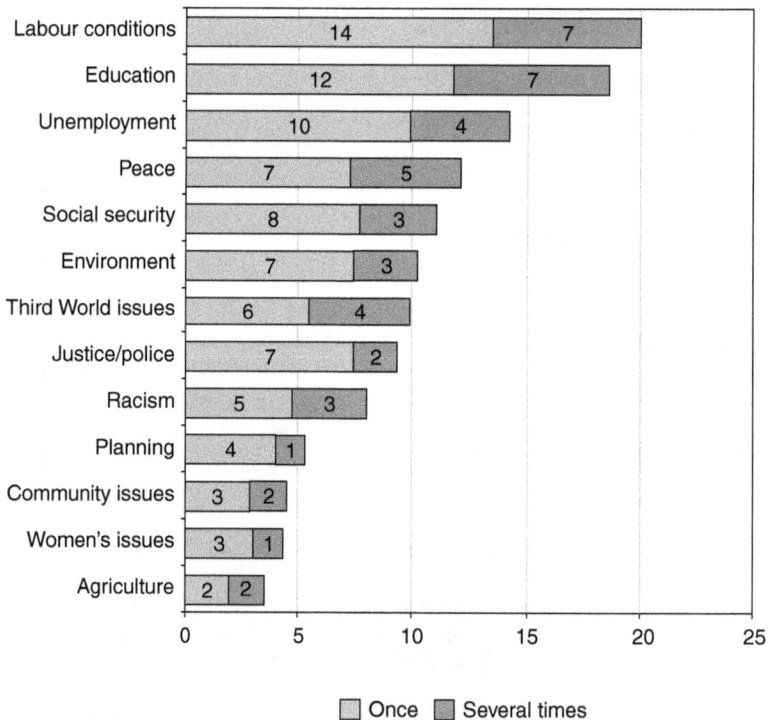

Figure 11.2 Issue focus of demonstration activism in Belgium, 1999 (in percentages). The question asked was 'Have you demonstrated about...?'; the percentages include those responding 'only once' or 'several times' (source: 1999 General Election Study of Flanders-Belgium).

sional actions. Given these considerations, this study focuses on whether people say they actually have demonstrated, taken as the most accurate and reliable indicator of behaviour, and excludes those acts that people say they might do, that is, protest potential.

(iii) The Van Aelst and Walgrave survey of demonstration activists

To explore the characteristics of the protest population in more depth, and to test the claim that context matters, we have used a unique series of face-to-face and postal surveys of demonstration participants in Belgium conducted by Van Aelst and Walgrave (2001) from 1998 to 2001. Here we will briefly outline the methodology, sampling frame, and fieldwork.

In terms of the selection of demonstration events, the seven demonstrations in Belgium were chosen on the basis of their expected popularity. In this way, the surveys covered most of the largest demonstrations held in Brussels from 1998 to 2001. A relatively small anti-drugs demonstration was also surveyed, to broaden the issue diversity of the demonstrations. The demonstrations were staged by the 'White Movement' (protesting against the failings of the judicial system in the Dutroux case of child abuse and murder), the anti-racist movement, the anti-globalization movement, white-collar unions (nurses and teachers), general unions, and political parties supporting the movement against drugs. It can be seen that the events were organized by typical traditional interest groups and political parties as well as by 'new' social movements.

The events were classified on theoretical grounds into four major categories reflecting the type of organizer and the location of the issue on the ideological spectrum: 'New Left' demonstrations (anti-globalization and anti-racism), 'Old Left' demonstrations (social security, non-profit sector, and education), 'New-mixed' demonstrations (White March), and 'New Right' demonstrations (anti-drugs). The latter categorization might appear particularly problematic, as opposition to drugs cannot automatically be considered to be an issue of the 'New Right', which in Western Europe is normally associated with anti-immigrant movements and neo-Nazi events. Nevertheless, the anti-drugs demonstration was classified as a 'New' gathering because the participants displayed overwhelming sympathy for the Flemish-Belgian extreme right-wing party, *Vlaams Blok*. No less than 70 per cent of all anti-drugs demonstrators voted for the *Vlaams Blok*, and 84 per cent of the party members among the demonstrators belonged to that same extreme Right party. Ongoing research, currently in the data-collection phase and which applies the same methodology to other protest events such as the anti-Iraq War demonstrations, will allow us to explore the implications of this typology more fully.

The survey covers a targeted-sample of demonstrators selected randomly who were engaged in seven different events, involving a total of 2,448 respondents (see Table 11.1). Interviewing participants at protest demonstrations is not a common research technique; in this context, Favre, Fillieule, and Mayer (1997) have even referred to 'a strange gap in the sociology of mobilizations'. To the best of our knowledge, few studies have used this approach. The most elaborate is the work of the French research team made up of Favre, Mayer, and Fillieule, who developed a method designed to give all participants an equal opportunity of being interviewed. Their method was refined further in this research. The survey process used in this study to establish a targeted-sample survey of demonstration participants selected randomly involved two steps. First, fieldwork supervisors counted the rows of participants, selecting every nth row, to ensure that the same number of rows was skipped throughout. Then a dozen interviewers selected every nth person in that row and distributed questionnaires to these individuals during the actual protest march.

The selected participants were asked to complete the questionnaire at home and to mail it back. The questionnaires had a common core, including the participants' profile, the mobilization context, and the political attitudes and values of the demonstrator, with a few specific items adapted slightly to each demonstration. In addition to the mail survey, a random sample of other demonstrators was interviewed in person before the start of the demonstration. As the crowd gathered before the departure of the demonstration it was divided into sectors, and the interviewers each randomly selected a fixed number of respondents in 'their' sector. These (shorter) face-to-face interviews were used as a cross-check in order to see how far the responses to the mail survey generated a representative random sample of demonstrators. Confidence in the surveys' reliability is strengthened by the fact that hardly anyone refused a face-to-face interview, and by the absence of significant differences between the two types of interviews. The overall response rate for the postal survey was more than 40 per cent, which is satisfactory for an anonymous survey without any reminders, which also boosts our confidence in the procedure.

Surveys of demonstrations raise important questions about reliability and the representativeness of sampling procedures. Two kinds of representativeness are at stake here: the selection of the particular events and then the selection of the random sample of respondents and the response rate within each event. With respect to the first point, the selected demonstrations cannot be considered to constitute a perfectly representative sample of all demonstrations in Belgium; the study lacks the typical student and farmers' protests, and we only focused on larger demonstrations in the capital. Yet, big demonstrations in Brussels account for a large majority of protest events and of Belgian demonstrators. The incidence of farmers' and students' protests is unevenly spread over time, with sudden and successive peaks and troughs, but they are not continuously present (Van Aelst and Walgrave 1999). Moreover, analysis of the 1999 General Election Study shows that the type of issues that we selected, including working conditions, education, social security, and racism, roughly

Table 11.1 Seven demonstrations dataset, Belgium, 1998–2001

Classification	New Mixed	New Left	Old Left	Old Left	Old Left	New Right	New Left
Demonstration	Second White March	Anti-racism	Non-profit sector	Social security	Education	Anti-drugs	Anti-globalization
Date	15 Feb. 1998	22 March 1998	26 March 1998	11 Sept. 1998	17 May 2000	30 Sept. 2001	14 Dec. 2001
Aim	Expressing solidarity with all sort of victims + discontent about judicial system	Demanding equal rights for immigrants + stop extreme right	For higher wages and more staff in hospitals and non-profit organizations	For higher social allowances and pensions	Teachers demanding higher wages and more staff in schools	Against the government's liberal drug policy + solidarity with parents of addicts	Against neo-liberal globalization + for another Europe
Organizers[a]							
Unions	–	+	++	++	++	–	–
Social organizations	–	++	–	+	–	–	++
Political parties	–	+	–	–	–	+	+
Others	Families of victims	–	–	–	–	Parents of drug addicts	–
Estimated number of participants[b]	25,000–30,000	7,000–15,000	12,000–20,000	30,000	10,000–18,000	2,000–3,000	12,500–25,000
Postal questionnaires							
Distributed	270	700	700	730	635	622	1,000
Completed	123	337	254	256	299	365	378
Response rate (%)	45.5	48.1	36.3	35.1	47.1	58.7	37.8
Face-to-face interviews	0	125	120	99	92	0	0

Source: Peter Van Aelst and Stefaan Walgrave survey of seven demonstrations dataset in Belgium (1998–2001).

Notes

a ++ = primary organizer; + = supporting organization.

b The first figure is the official estimate of the police, the second is the highest estimate mentioned in the national press.

reflected the distribution of issues among the general public who demonstrated in Flanders-Belgium in the 1990s (see Figure 11.2). In addition, longitudinal analysis of demonstration events in Belgium from the 1950s onwards reveals that the balance of themes covered in the dataset reflects the bulk of the Belgian demonstrations during the post-war era (Van Aelst and Walgrave 1999). The protests analysed in the survey do constitute, therefore, a fairly satisfactory reflection of these events in Belgium and they provide sufficient evidence to explore the issues raised in this study.

Concerning the demonstrators who responded within a demonstration, three potentially problematic issues should be mentioned. First, if the demonstration is large and fairly static, and if all the streets become congested with people, it becomes difficult for the interviewers to cover the whole of the march since they are also immobile. Second, it is impossible to get a good sample of respondents in violent and/or irregular demonstrations, although these kinds of protest events usually involve relatively few people. Third, in some exceptional cases extremist groups of demonstrators *within* a peaceful event refuse to accept the questionnaires. This was the case when surveying the anti-globalization demonstration on 14 December 2001; a small group of 'blackbox' demonstrators also refused to accept the postal questionnaire. Again, however, this attitude is rare, and demonstrators, like many other types of political activist, are usually highly collaborative.

Trends in protest activism

Despite cyclical theories, emphasizing the unpredictability and contextuality of contentious politics, the available systematic evidence suggests that protest politics has intensified, and dramatically, in many countries during the late twentieth century. Data are available from content (event) analysis of media coverage (Rucht 1998) and official statistics monitoring the number of protests and demonstrations (della Porta and Reiter 1998; Fillieule 1997; Van Aelst and Walgrave 1999), as well as from cross-national surveys. All these provide alternative estimates of the level of citizen involvement in protest politics. Surveys show that political acts such as petitioning, consumer boycotts, and demonstrations have become far more common since the mid-1970s, especially among the public in affluent postindustrial societies (Norris 2002: Ch. 10). The most striking finding in Table 11.2 is the consistency of the trends in the Political Action countries (highlighted in italics in the table) over the last 25 years. The rise in demonstration activism is evident across all eight nations, although it varies in strength, with the Netherlands, Italy, and West Germany as leaders, and Britain and Finland as laggards.

The original Political Action countries were all established democracies and affluent postindustrial societies. Do we also find comparable

Table 11.2 Rise in demonstration activism: proportion who have demonstrated by country, mid-1970s to date[a]

Country	Mid-1970s	Early 1980s	Early 1990s	1999 to 2001	Difference early 1980s−2001
Belgium		13	21	39	+26
Netherlands	7	12	25	32	+20
Sweden		15	22	35	+20
France		26	31	38	+12
Denmark		18	27	28	+10
Ireland		12	16	21	+9
South Korea[b]		5	19	14	+9
Italy	19	25	34	33	+8
United States	12	12	15	20	+8
Norway[b]		19	19	26	+7
South Africa		6	13	13	+7
West Germany	9	14	20	20	+6
Iceland		14	23	20	+6
Canada		13	21	19	+6
Australia[b]		12		18	+6
Britain	6	10	14	13	+3
Japan		7	9	10	+3
Northern Ireland		18	18	20	+2
Spain		22	21	24	+2
Mexico		8	20	10	+2
Finland	6	14	12	14	0
Argentina		19	16	13	−6
Switzerland	8			16	
Austria	7		10	16	
Mean	9	14	20	21	+7

Sources: For the mid-1970s, Barnes *et al.* (1979); for the other three columns, the World Values Surveys.

Notes

a The question was as follows: 'Now I'd like you to look at this card. I'm going to read out some different forms of political action that people can take, and I'd like you to tell me, for each one, whether you have actually done any of these things, whether you might do it, or would never, under any circumstances, do it'. In this table figures are the percentages of those who 'have actually attended lawful demonstration'. Data are unavailable for blank entries.

b Latest available data is for 1995–1997.

developments in other countries, and are similar trends evident from a shorter chronological perspective? Table 11.2 shows experience of demonstrating from the early-1980s to 2000 in some two dozen societies for which evidence from the World Values Survey is available for both points in time. It confirms that the rise in protest politics is a phenomenon which is by no means confined to postindustrial societies or established democracies. Experience of demonstrations has become more common in most nations, with particularly marked increases in some of the smaller consensus democracies, including Belgium, the Netherlands, and Sweden. According to successive waves of the World Values Surveys, 14 per cent of citizens attended legal demonstrations in Belgium in 1981, 23 per cent in 1990, but a remarkable 39 per cent in 2000, when this figure is corroborated independently by other sources.[8] Estimates based on the World Values Survey suggest that demonstrating (experienced by 16 per cent of the public overall) has become more widespread today than many traditional forms of political participation such as active party membership (5 per cent) or active trade union membership (5 per cent).

The characteristics of demonstrators

The rise in protest activity in Belgium encouraged us to focus on activists in this country, and particularly on the social and attitudinal characteristics of demonstrators compared with party members and civic joiners. The analytical model in Table 11.3 includes many of the factors that are typically used in existing studies of political participation to predict activism. In terms of participants' social background, the profile confirms that age continues to prove significant, with participation in parties and in civic associations increasing as people enter middle age, before tapering off slightly among the elderly. Among demonstrators, the sign remains negative, indicating that protest activity remains more popular among the younger generation than for their parents or grandparents. But this is the *only* social factor that proves significant in explaining demonstration activism. Gender helps to predict civic membership, with women slightly more likely to join than men. As shown elsewhere (Inglehart and Norris 2003), gendered patterns of membership are highly dependent on the type of civic organization, since some remain predominantly male (such as sports clubs) while others are predominately female (such as charitable work), reflecting well-established gender roles. However, gender is no longer important in distinguishing either party membership or demonstration activism. Education is important in predicting party membership but the impact is negative, suggesting that Belgian parties of the Left enjoy more success in organizing the working class than the parties of the Right do among the middle or upper classes.[9] Patterns of education are strong predictors of many types of political participation in the United States, but their influence varies cross-nationally, depending upon the ability of parties to mobilize their social support. By contrast, class proves to be strongly related to joining civic groups such as cultural and religious organizations, which remain, as expected, very middle-class in background. Yet, most importantly, social class fails to predict participation in demonstrations, confirming what Barnes *et al.* (1979) first found three decades ago. Therefore the way that socio-economic status influences patterns of participation is by no means simple. While it has no effect on demonstration activism, civic associations constitute a more middle-class channel of participation in Belgium, while party membership is a more working-class route. This suggests that if, as Dalton (2000a) suggests, demonstrations are gradually displacing traditional modes of engagement such as parties and groups, this will not necessarily generate greater social inequality in political activism. Finally religiosity is negatively associated with party membership but positively linked to civic joining. Comparing the three types of activists and their social background variables, it becomes clear that, of all the groups, demonstrators most closely resemble the electorate as a whole.

Turning to the motivational attitudes of activists, the common denominator across all types of engagement concerns political interest, a simple 5-point scale that nonetheless proves strong and significant in helping to explain party membership, civic joiners, and demonstrators. Similar results are found with alternative standard indicators of political interest (not shown here), such as the frequency of political discussion or the propensity to follow the news in the media. Internal efficacy, meaning how confident people are that they have sufficient skills and knowledge to participate in politics, was strongly related to civic joining, but proved unrelated to the other forms of activism.[10]

The different predictions made by the disaffection and the strategic resource theories, however, are in sharpest contrast when it comes to system support. While disaffection theories predict that demonstrators will be particularly unhappy about government and dissatisfied with democracy, strategic resource theories suggest that they will not differ sharply from other forms of activists in these regards. If system support is a multidimensional orientation, as argued elsewhere (Norris 1999b), then it would be important to compare a variety of indicators, including external political efficacy, confidence in government, and satisfaction with democracy. The results in Table 11.3 show that all the system support indicators fail to predict demonstration activism: people who take to the streets to defend their cause cannot be regarded as particularly critical of the political system, whether in terms of satisfaction with how democracy works in Belgium, how far government and politicians are responsive to their needs and concerns, or how far they trust government. While the Crozier *et al.* (1975) thesis may appear plausible to many popular commentators, this study in fact found no systematic evidence for these claims, thereby confirming the previous behavioural literature.

Two other important findings about motivational attitudes are worth noting. In terms of their ideological self-placement on a 10-point scale, demonstrators are drawn disproportionately from the Left. It may well be that in Belgium groups on the Left have been particularly successful at using these tactics to mobilize their supporters, including in the labour and environmental movements, as well as teachers and welfare professionals, or it could be that left-wing citizens are more willing to engage in this form of political expression. But, on the Left of the political spectrum,

Table 11.3 Predictors of party, civic, and demonstration activism in Belgium, 1999[a]

Predictors	Party members				Civic joiners				Demonstrators			
	B	s.e.	St. Beta	Sig.	B	s.e.	St. Beta	Sig.	B	s.e.	St. Beta	Sig.
Social structure												
Age	0.003	0.001	0.13	***	0.015	0.003	0.11	***	-0.013	0.004	-0.09	***
Male sex	0.025	0.014	0.04		-0.346	0.094	-0.08	***	0.146	0.100	0.04	
Education	-0.018	0.008	-0.07	**	0.272	0.050	0.15	***	-0.060	0.053	-0.05	
Social class	0.001	0.003	-0.01		0.030	0.023	0.03		0.001	0.024	0.01	
Religiosity	-0.003	0.002	-0.03		0.014	0.011	0.03		-0.011	0.014	-0.03	
Motivational attitudes												
Political interest	0.067	0.008	0.20	***	0.110	0.054	0.05	*	0.311	0.059	0.16	***
Internal efficacy	-0.005	0.002	-0.05	*	0.103	0.011	0.22	***	0.016	0.016	0.03	
Social trust	0.003	0.008	0.01		0.165	0.051	0.07	***	0.101	0.054	0.05	
Left–right self-placement	0.001	0.003	0.01		-0.020	0.023	-0.02		-0.182	0.024	-0.17	***
System support												
External efficacy	-0.004	0.001	-0.09	***	-0.024	0.010	-0.07	**	-0.017	0.010	-0.05	
Democratic satisfaction	-0.002	0.009	-0.01		0.050	0.061	0.02		-0.017	0.066	-0.01	
Confidence in government	0.011	0.009	0.03		-0.083	0.061	-0.03		-0.078	0.066	-0.03	
Political behaviour												
Civic activism	0.016	0.003	0.11	***	0.667	0.149	0.10	***	0.155	0.021	0.16	***
Party member									0.414	0.159	0.06	**
Trade union member	0.041	0.011	0.09	***	0.383	0.071	0.12	***	0.369	0.071	0.12	***
Constant	-0.06				-1.36				1.8			
Adjusted R^2	0.11				0.15				0.15			

Source: 1999 General Election Study of Flanders-Belgium.

Note

a The coefficients represent unstandardized betas (B), standard errors (s.e.), standardized betas (St. Beta), and significance (Sig.) in ordinary least squares regression analysis models predicting party membership, civic joiners, and demonstration activists as the dependent variables. Levels of significance are ***$p < 0.001$; **$p < 0.01$; and *$p < 0.05$. The variables were entered in the order of the table. *Party members* includes both active and passive members. *Civic joiners* is a summary index of active and passive membership of a series of eight voluntary organizations and community associations such as sports, cultural, charity, environmental, and religious groups (excluding party and labour organization membership). And *Demonstrators* is a summary index of reported active participation in any of 13 types of demonstrations (for the list see Figure 11.2). Collinearity statistics were checked for the tolerance of all variables. Number of cases was 1,637. See Appendix 11.1 for coding details of all the items.

demonstrators were not found disproportionately on the Far Left, as the anti-state account would expect; rather they were concentrated on the Centre Left. Other evidence about political behaviour also supports the strategic resource thesis: people who demonstrate are significantly more, not less, likely to be civic joiners, party members, and members of labour, business, or professional associations. Demonstrations can therefore be seen as constituting another way for people to connect with public life, joining with others to express their concerns about racism, globalization, or jobs. As such, this does not mean that demonstrations replace or even threaten traditional associational life, as some fear. Rather demonstration activism complements it; the main reason, social capital theories suggest, is that the social ties forged in groups such as community associations and unions create the social networks and bonds that may encourage people to participate in demonstrations (McAdam 1988). In this respect, it seems likely that there is a 'pull'-factor at work: if people go on a protest march it is partly because they are asked to by their workmates, neighbours, friends, and colleagues, complementing the 'push'-factors derived from self-motivated political interest. This suggests that the specific mobilization context in which a demonstration takes place may play an important role in bringing people to these events.

Variations by type of demonstration

The evidence analysed until now supports the strategic resource approach. But so far we have not directly considered the third explanation, the claim that context matters, implying that important differences exist among participants in the various types of demonstrations. If correct, then we may need to distinguish between radical and middle-of-the-road protests, as well as between blue-collar marches about bread-and-butter issues like pay and jobs, and more middle-class events concerning anti-racism or anti-globalization. One difficulty about examining the contextual thesis is that in the past we have often lacked sufficient evidence to be able to compare and contrast the participants in different types of protest event. The Van Aelst and Walgrave survey of a random sample of participants in seven separate demonstrations held in Belgium from 1998 to 2001 is well suited to this purpose. This section focuses on running similar models to those that we have already examined, since the demonstration surveys contain functionally equivalent items, analysing and comparing the results in each of the separate demonstrations as the units of analysis. The binominal logistic regression models contrast participation in each of the selected types of demonstrations as dummy (1/0) variables compared with the weighted pooled sample of all other demonstrators, as the reference category. The results can therefore be understood to show how far the characteristics of participants in each of the various demonstrations differ to those of all demonstrators in the pooled sample. Using the theoretical classification of the demonstration into the categories of *New Left* (anti-globalization and anti-racism), *New Right* (anti-drugs), *Old Left* (social security, non-profit sector, and education), and *Mixed* (White March), we ran the models predicting participation in each of the various types of demonstration. The results are presented in Table 11.4.

The claim that the characteristics of demonstrators vary systematically among these different types of events receives some support from the analysis. In terms of social background, as expected, compared with other demonstrators, New Left demonstrators are usually younger, well-educated, and middle class. In contrast, Old Left demonstrations attract a more working-class constituency, while New Right events bring older groups onto the streets. The most plausible reason for these differences concerns the type of issue and type of organizers. For example, some Old Left demonstrations deliberately targeted and mobilized a specific professional group such as teachers or nurses engaged in conflict over wages or working conditions. The education demonstration, for example, drew many highly educated teachers, above all those working in Christian schools. The least distinct social profile was found in the White March, which appealed to no particular group in society, and which managed to get a heterogeneous mass public onto the streets of Brussels.

The comparison of motivational attitudes shows that political ideology plays an important role in that, as expected, New Left and New Right events draw participants with different ideological profiles. There are also some contrasts with respect to political interest, this being higher than average among New Left demonstrators, and lower than average on the Old Left. This could be related to the contrasts in educational background that we have already noted, since education has often been found to be strongly associated with interest (Verba, Schlozman, and Brady 1995).

In terms of system support, however, the main contrast is that Old Left demonstrators expressed higher than average satisfaction with democracy, while the opposite pattern was evident among New Right participants. What is clear, however, is that across all indicators there is no consistent difference among groups in terms of their level of system support, and there is little evidence of anti-state radicalism.[11] Democratic satisfaction does vary, but external efficacy and political confidence hardly serve to distinguish the demonstrations from each other. Not only are demonstrators as a group generally not disaffected about government and democracy, as we showed earlier, but none of the seven individual demonstrations, and not even the anti-globalization protest, was packed with anti-state radicals. People who take to the streets in Belgium do not generally consider government and politicians to be unresponsive to their needs and concerns, nor do they deeply distrust government.[12]

Lastly, the measures of political behaviour also produced important differences, which are probably best explained in terms of the characteristics

Table 11.4 Predictors of demonstrations in Belgium by type of event, 1998–2001[a]

Predictors	New Left (Anti-globalization and anti-racism)		Old Left (Non-profit sector, social security and education)		New Right (Anti-drugs)		New Mixed (Second White March)	
	Beta	Sig.	Beta	Sig.	Beta	Sig.	Beta	Sig.
Social structure								
Age	**-0.038**	***	0.001		**0.046**	***	**0.011**	*
Male sex	0.255		-0.171		0.082		-0.029	
Education	**0.244**	*	-0.177		-0.090		-0.021	
Social class	**0.192**	*	**-0.171**	*	0.071		**0.115**	*
Religiosity	-0.338		0.315		0.362			
Motivational attitudes								
Political interest	**0.482**	***	**-0.603**	***	-0.128			
Internal efficacy	0.100		-0.128		0.012			
Left–right scale	**-1.460**	***	0.073		**2.127**	***	**-0.238**	***
System support								
External efficacy	0.004		-0.019		-0.007			
Democratic satisfaction	-0.262		**0.856**	***	**-0.727**	**	**-0.238**	***
Confidence in government	0.87		0.038		-0.043			
Political behaviour								
Trade union membership	**-1.264**	***	**3.349**	***	**-3.879**	***	-0.096	
Party membership	**-0.643**	**	-0.127		**0.979**	**	**-0.372**	*
Civic activism	**0.446**	*	-0.324		0.017		**-1.131**	***
Percentage correct	84.9		83.1		94.2		77.6	
Adjusted R^2	0.57		0.59		0.84		0.20	
(N)	(1,199)		(1,199)		(1,199)		(1,373)	

Source: Peter Van Aelst and Stefaan Walgrave survey of seven demonstrations dataset in Belgium (1998–2001).

Note

a The coefficients represent non-standardized Betas and their significance (Sig.) in binominal logistic regression analysis models predicting participation in one type of demonstration (versus the pooled sample of the other six demonstrations) as the dependent variables. Levels of significance are ***$p < 0.001$ **$p < 0.01$ *$p < 0.05$. The variables were entered in the order of the table. Collinearity statistics were checked for the tolerance of all variables. See Appendix 11.2 for coding details of all the items. The data are weighted so that every demonstration has an equal number of respondents in the analysis. This weighting procedure did not make much difference, except for the White March (New Mixed), where the initial N was small, and some variables became significant after weighting.

of the event organizers. Unions strongly mobilize supporters for Old Left events, but we find fewer than average union members at New Left and New Right events. Parties also seem to have played an important role in getting their supporters to New Right marches, while civic associations fulfilled this function in New Left events. The one 'New Mixed' (White March) demonstration in our sample, a mass protest against the failings of the judiciary in a case of child abduction and murder, differs from the types of other demonstration on a number of variables, but the adjusted R^2 of its model is much lower. The White March attracted a rather heterogeneous constituency. As discussed elsewhere, this kind of internally diverse demonstrations may have become more frequent recently (Van Aelst and Walgrave 2001; Walgrave and Verhulst 2002).

Conclusions

Establishing the root causes of rising levels of protest politics is important, not just for its own sake, but also because of the insights this can provide into its consequences for democratic stability and the legitimacy of elected governments. If the anti-state theory is correct, in that protests represent a forewarning of deep-seated public disaffection with traditional channels of civic engagement and political participation, and if demonstrations are on the increase, then this phenomenon could indeed pose a major challenge to the legitimacy of representative democracy. If, however, demonstrations are seen as just one more legitimate and increasingly conventional channel of expression, drawn from a varied repertoire of alternative actions including involvement in election campaigns, traditional interest groups, and community organizations, bringing together concerned citizens, then the attitudes and values that these acts make manifest could be regarded as far healthier for the state of democracy. And if, depending on the particular context, demonstrators can be both radical or mainstream, anti-state or pro-state, involving both excluded minorities and privileged elites, then this also provides important insights into their potential for both challenging and strengthening democracy.

Table 11.5 recapitulates the core hypotheses more formally and also summarizes the key findings of this analysis. The results of the analysis of the Belgian general electorate suggest that overall the anti-state theory of Crozier, Huntington, and Waknuki (1975), while popular among media commentators and contemporary observers, and often voiced by political leaders, fails to find support from the evidence. Today demonstrations have become conventional in Belgian politics, as almost four out of ten Belgians have participated in these events at some time in their lives. Comparison of the frequency of all types of political acts revealed that voting is by far the most ubiquitous (mainly because it is compulsory). But signing a petition is the second most common type of act, followed by experience of having demonstrated. Many indicators reveal that Belgian demonstra-

Table 11.5 Formal statement of hypotheses and summary of findings

Explanations		Hypotheses: all other things being equal, compared with party members and civic joiners, demonstrators will:	Findings
Anti-state theories			
	(H1.1)	Display low levels of system support such as trust in government.	False
	(H1.2)	Fail to engage in traditional channels of political activism.	False
	(H1.3)	Cluster to the far right or far left of the ideological spectrum.	False
	(H1.4)	Be drawn disproportionately from working-class, less educated, and lower-status sectors.	False
Strategic resource theories			
	(H2.1)	Display similar motivational attitudes in terms of political interest.	True
	(H2.2)	Belong to traditional civic associations.	True
	(H2.3)	Display similar political preferences within the ideological spectrum.	True
	(H2.4)	Be drawn disproportionately from the educated, middle class, male, and middle-aged.	Mixed
Contextual thesis			
	(H3.1)	Support for the political system will vary significantly among demonstrators according to the type of event.	Mixed
	(H3.2)	The social characteristics of demonstrators will vary according to the type of event.	True

tors are as supportive of the political system as other citizens are, while they are more willing to join civic groups, an indicator of traditional activism. They are not drawn disproportionately from the poorer sections of society. Indeed, demonstrations as a channel of participation cut across conventional divisions of class, education, and gender, drawing disparate groups onto the streets, while, at the same time, there remains a bias towards the younger generation as opposed to the middle aged. Demonstrators are not anti-state radicals who belong to socially marginal groups or who despise conventional forms of political participation. By contrast, they are more similar to the Belgian population as a whole than civic joiners and party members are.

Yet analysis of a range of demonstrations reveals that context does matter. Treating all demonstrations as equivalent phenomena is a category mistake. The social characteristics, systems support, motivational attitudes, and the political behaviour of demonstrators varies by type of event. The analysis confirms that anti-state radicalism is not demonstrators' dominant motive, nor is it behind the prevailing types of demonstration in Belgium. But the strategic resource perspective has its flaws too. Some demonstrations mobilize educated middle-class professionals, but others bring workers or students onto the streets. The specific issues, organization, and mobilization processes involved, in short, the context of a specific demonstration, do make a considerable difference. This supports the contextual account, in that it points towards the importance of specific issues, organizations, and mobilization processes in explaining demonstration activity and contrasts between events. Probably a large part of the solution of the 'who demonstrates?' puzzle lies precisely in these mobilization contexts. Who do people attend demonstrations with? How are they informed and persuaded to participate? An important task for future research in this field would be to provide greater understanding of these issues.

In general, therefore, popular concern that demonstrations are undermining representative democracy, by displacing conventional channels with radical and extremist politics, even violent tactics, due to political disaffection, seems misplaced. Clearly some demonstrations do result in destruction or damage to property and even illegal acts. But on balance demonstrations appear to be a growing channel of political expression used for the legitimate articulation of demands in a democratic state, and a form of activism that has evolved and expanded over the years to supplement and compliment existing organizations in civic society. In cases such as the massive, worldwide anti-war demonstrations against American and British actions over Iraq, where most citizens are largely powerless to affect decisions through the usual channels of representative democracy within their own countries, mass demonstrations and non-violent civil disobedience may appear to be the only legitimate and effective channels of political expression. Far from threatening or even challenging democracy, demonstrations have become today one of the major channels of public voice.

Appendix 11.1 Coding and measurement for the 1999 General Election Study of Flanders-Belgium

Variables	Coding and measurement
Social background	
Age	Years old (Age)
Gender	Male 1, Female 0 (R2)
Education	5-categories from lower 1 to higher 5 (Educ5)
Class	5-categories from unskilled workers (1) to executives-professionals (5) (EGP05)
Religiosity	Intensity of religious beliefs (R27)
Political attitudes	
Political interest	(R53) 'Some people are very interested in politics. Others are not interested at all. Are you very interested in politics, or are you not at all interested?'
External efficacy	(R79_1 to R79_9) 'There's no sense in voting; the parties do what they want to do anyway'. 'Parties are only interested in my vote, not in my opinion'. 'If people like me let the politicians know what we think, then they will take our opinions into account'. 'Politicians have never learned to listen to people like me'. 'Most politicians promise a lot, but don't do anything'. 'As soon as they are elected, politicians think they are better than people like me'. 'Most of our politicians are competent people who know what they are doing'. 'At the current time, there is no politician I would trust'. (8 Agree/disagree scales)
Internal efficacy	(RS17_1 to RS17_4) 'I consider myself to be sufficiently capable to participate in politics'. 'I feel that I have a good understanding of the major issues in Belgium'. 'I'm as capable as anyone else of maintaining a political commitment'. 'I feel that I'm more informed about politics and government than most people'. 'People like me have influence on the government'. (5 Agree/disagree scales)
Democratic satisfaction	(R78) 'Are you, generally speaking, very satisfied, more or less satisfied, more or less dissatisfied or very dissatisfied with the functioning of democracy in Belgium?'
Confidence in government	(R113_11) 'Now I am going to read you a list of institutions. Could you tell me, for each of these institutions, whether you trust them a lot or a little? . . . The Government'.
Social trust	(R30_10) 'Today, most people can still be trusted'. (Agree/disagree scales)
Left–right self-placement	(R31) 'In politics, people sometimes talk about "left" and "right". Card No. 11 defines this situation: 0 stands for someone whose views are entirely to the "left"; 10 for someone whose views are more or less to the "right". Of course, there are intermediary positions to the degree that one's views are more or less to the "left" or to the "right". When you think about your own ideas on this, where would you place yourself on this scale?'
Political behaviour	
Civic activism	(RS26_1 to RS26_9) 'Are you at the moment a member of the following kinds of organization? For each association, are you an active member (i.e. participated during the last year [1999] in at least one activity), a passive member (coded 1), an ex-member or not a member (coded 0)?'
Member of labour association	R26.10. Same question as above: trade union, association of small businessmen or professional association?
Party member	R26.6. Same question as above: political association/party?

Source: The 1999 General Election Study of Flanders-Belgium.

Appendix 11.2 Coding and measurement for the seven demonstrations dataset, Belgium, 1998–2001

Variables	Coding and measurement
Social background	
Age	Years old (Age)
Gender	Male 1, Female 0
Education	5-categories from lower 1 to higher 5
Religiosity	2-categories: Believer 1 (Christian, Catholic, Protestant and Other), Non-believer 2 (non-believer, free-thinker)
Political attitudes	
Political interest	'Some people are very interested in politics. Others are not interested at all. Are you very interested in politics, or are you not at all interested?'
Internal efficacy	'People like me have influence on the government/For people like me, politics is far too complicated, you have to be an expert to understand it'. (2 Agree/disagree scales)
External efficacy	'There's no sense in voting; the parties do what they want to do anyway/Parties are only interested in my vote, not in my opinion/Most politicians promise a lot, but don't do anything/Most of our politicians are competent people who know what they are doing'. (4 Agree/disagree scales)
Democratic satisfaction	'Are you, generally speaking, very satisfied, more or less satisfied, more or less dissatisfied or very dissatisfied with the functioning of democracy in Belgium?'
Confidence in government	'Now I am going to read you a list of institutions. Could you tell me, for each of these institutions, whether you trust them a lot or a little?' (Sum of confidence in the government, the parliament and political parties)
Left–right position (constructed)	While the classical left–right scale was absent in the questionnaire we constructed this scale on the basis of the voting behaviour of the respondents. Each party was placed on this scale on the basis of their average score in the general election study. For example, voters of the Green Party in the election study had an average score of 3.8 on the left–right self-placement scale (0 = extreme-left; 10 = extreme-right; see Appendix 11.1). So we gave all Green voters in our demonstration surveys the same score. As a result, the range of score is rather limited in comparison with the left–right self-placement scale used in the election study.
Political behaviour	
Union membership	'Are you member of a union?' Non-member = 0; member = 1
Party membership	'Are you member of a political party?' Non-member = 0; member = 1
Civic activism	'Are you an active member (i.e. during the last year), have you participated in the activities or meetings of any club, association or society?' Non-member = 0; member = 1.

Source: Peter Van Aelst and Stefaan Walgrave seven demonstrations dataset in Belgium.

Notes

1 This chapter is a (much) more detailed and extended version of an article that has been published in *Comparative Politics* (January 2005).
2 See, for example, McAdam, McCarthy, and Zald (1996); Tarrow (1992); Kriesi *et al.* (1995); Kriesi, della Porta, and Rucht (1998); della Porta and Diani (1999). For a review and synthesis of the literature see Aminzade *et al.* (2001).
3 The demonstration held by French employers against the introduction of the 35-hour week appears to confirm this view. On 4 October 1999, two large employers' organizations mobilized approximately 25,000 'bosses' for a sit-in in the French capital (*Le Monde*, 5 October 1999).
4 In France, for example, Fillieule (1997) observed less than 7 per cent 'spontaneous' demonstrations in the 1980s.
5 It should be noted that not every nation was included in every wave of the WVS survey, so the average figures across all eight nations are presented here, but further examination suggests that this process did not influence the substantive findings.
6 This sharp rise in demonstration activity in Belgium is confirmed by detailed protest event analysis, on the basis of media coverage and police records, from the 1950s onwards. In contrast with widely extended views in Belgium about the roaring sixties characterized by unequalled protest activities, it was the 1990s which registered most demonstrators; see Van Aelst and Walgrave (1999).
7 We are most grateful to the principal investigators Jaak Billiet and Marc Swyngedouw, of the Interuniversity Centre for Political Opinion Research, sponsored by the Federal Services for Technical, Cultural and Scientific Affairs (ISPO) at the Department of Sociology of the University of Leuven, for access to the 1999 General Election Study of Flanders-Belgium.
8 This latter estimate was confirmed by the 1999 General Election Study of Flanders-Belgium, which found that 39 per cent of citizens reported having participated in a demonstration.
9 The official membership figures of the Flemish parties reveals that the right-wing parties claim *more* members than the left-wing parties, in contrast to what we expected on the basis of the 1999 General Election Study of Flanders-Belgium.
10 Hierarchical modelling, with the variables entered as social and attitudinal blocks, revealed that internal efficacy was probably strongly related to education, as the effect of education on civic joining drops considerably when internal efficacy is added to the model.
11 It should be noted that, when surveying the anti-globalization demonstration on 14 December 2001, a small group of about 200 'black box' demonstrators refused to accept our postal questionnaire. Our sample of anti-globalization demonstrators is, therefore, probably rather less representative than that of other groups, a factor which could underestimate their anti-state radicalism.
12 However, a simple bivariate comparison of the surveyed demonstrators with the total population (in the 1999 General Election Study of Flanders-Belgium) shows that satisfaction with democracy is lower among demonstrators (30 per cent) than among the total population (57 per cent). In the General Election Study, though, democratic satisfaction was no significant predictor of demonstration participation. Perhaps this difference could be attributed to a context effect of surveying people during or just after a demonstration, when they are excited and maybe rather 'angry', and therefore more dissatisfied.

12 Political participation, information, and accountability

Some consequences of political disaffection in new democracies

Mariano Torcal and Ignacio Lago

Although political disaffection is a widely discussed and well documented phenomenon in contemporary democracies, its consequences for the functioning and performance of democratic institutions have hardly been studied. Most research on this topic focuses on the determinants of political disaffection, with the result that there is still a major gap in the literature when it comes to the analysis of the effects of disaffection on individuals' role as citizens.

The literature on the behavioural consequences of political disaffection tends to present a rather contradictory picture. The confidence gap was originally seen in an entirely negative light, and identified as one of the major fault lines in contemporary representative democracies (Huntington 1968; Crozier, Huntington, and Watanuki 1975; Offe 1984; Habermas 1985). However, a number of more recent studies have highlighted the more positive consequences that the growing numbers of critical citizens may have for the transformation and evolution of democratic institutions and the relationship between citizens and their representatives (Dalton 1988, 1999; Kaase and Newton 1995; Klingemann and Fuchs 1995a; Norris 1999d). The main purpose of this chapter is precisely to investigate some of the ways political disaffection widens the gap between citizens and representatives in new democracies. In particular, we will analyse the impact of political disaffection on conventional and non-conventional political participation and information acquisition and processing. We will argue that political disaffection in new democracies (1) has a dominant and strong 'demobilizing effect', thereby contributing to the widespread estrangement of citizens from politics; and (2) produces uninformed citizens, preventing them from using the political environment as an informational crutch or shortcut (i.e. the amounts of informational clues provided by the environment that enable even poorly informed citizens to make competent political judgements) (Lupia 2000).

The impact of political disaffection on political participation

Contrary to the claims made by some of the classic studies of the topic (Milbrath 1977), political participation is a multidimensional phenomenon (Verba and Nie 1972; Verba, Nie, and Kim 1978; Marsh 1977; Kaase and Marsh 1979; Marsh 1991). This implies that each type of participation requires, among other things, different degrees of initiative, commitment, information, and assessment of the different goals on the part of the citizens. The multidimensionality of participation has a number of other implications. First, certain dimensions or types of participation might require different resources, motivations, cooperation, and incentives. Second, we may find citizens who concentrate on only certain types of political action. In this sense, we must certainly recognize the existence of different types of citizenship depending on individuals' preferred form of participation. At the same time, the presence of distinct dimensions of participation also means there may be a set of factors that influence the distinct dimensions of participation in different ways. Many scholars have shown that people who do not have confidence in institutions, who feel left out of politics, or are incapable of understanding it, will be reluctant to participate in the democratic process, producing general apathy.[1] But it is equally possible that political disaffection could encourage citizens to seek alternative ways of expressing their political opinions and their frustration with the functioning and performance of existing democratic institutions (Barnes *et al.* 1979; Dalton 1988, 1999). In Gamson's (1968: 48) view, it is the combined effect of low levels of political trust and high political efficacy which produces 'the optimum combination for mobilization'. Hence, according to this literature (Craig and Maggiotto 1982; Sigelman and Feldman 1983; Craig and Wald 1985; Wolfsfeld 1986), an attitudinal cluster of perceptions that political institutions are unresponsive provides the strongest motivation for unconventional behaviour, at the same time discouraging more traditional forms of political action. Some of these attitudes constitute the driving force that may be transforming the nature of the relationship between citizens and the state in representative democracies (Dalton 1988; Fuchs and Klingemann 1995; Nye, Zelikow and King 1997; Norris 1999d).

Do the different dimensions of political disaffection (institutional disaffection and political disengagement) have the same mobilizing effect on citizens in new democracies? Here we argue that political disaffection in new democracies does have the same effects on both conventional and non-conventional political participation, reducing the incentives to participate in both. Political disaffection in new democracies has a very dominant and strong 'demobilizing effect', reducing participation or the propensity to participate to the mere act of voting (and delegation), and undermining the accountability of representatives between elections. In order to substantiate this argument, we defined two models of political participation in the new democracies to analyse the available data: one model for conventional participation and one for non-conventional participation.

In order to test the effect of political disaffection on participation, we have estimated and discussed a regression model for conventional and non-conventional participation. The model includes information on individual social and economic resources (the basic socio-demographic variables), indicators of political discontent such as evaluations of the economy in general, and the individual's economic situation (*Overall economic situation* and *Personal economic situation*), and finally satisfaction with the functioning of democracy (*Satisfaction with democratic functioning*) and democratic support (*Support for democracy*). Two variables have been included to measure the two dimensions of political disaffection: first, an index constructed by combining confidence in institutions and external political efficacy for institutional disaffection (*Institutional affection*) and, second, an index of internal political efficacy for political disengagement (*Political engagement*).[2] We have also included a variable combining external political inefficacy and internal political efficacy; the purpose of this is to test the hypothesis that the perception that the political institutions are unresponsive, combined with an individual sense of political capability, might provide, as suggested above, the strongest motivation for unconventional behaviour while at the same time discouraging more traditional forms of political action (*Gamson's hypothesis*).[3] We have also included ideology in order to control for the effects of current political competition and exclusion.

Model 1, which estimates conventional participation,[4] is as follows:

$$Y_{\text{conventional participation}j} = \beta_{0j}\alpha_j + \beta_{1j} \text{ Overall economic situation}_j + \beta_{2j} \text{ Personal economic situation}_j + \beta_{3j} \text{ Ideology}_j + \beta_{4j} \text{ Satisfaction with democratic functioning}_j + \beta_{5j} \text{ Support for democracy}_j + \beta_{6j} \text{ Institutional affection} + \beta_{7j} \text{ Political engagement}_j + \beta_{8j} \text{ Gamson's hypothesis}_j + \beta_{9j} \text{ Education}_j + \beta_{10j} \text{ Gender}_j + \beta_{11j} \text{ Age}_j + \beta_{12j} \text{ Income}_j + e$$

In order to test the mobilizing effects of political disaffection on non-conventional participation, we have added two additional variables for the model of non-conventional participation:

1   Conventional participation (*Conventional*).
2   The interaction between not using the conventional activities of participation and institutional disaffection (*Conventional × institutional disaffection*). This variable is intended to tap the attitudes of those citizens who, rejecting conventional modes of participation, turn to non-conventional forms due to their institutional disaffection.[5]

Model 2, which estimates non-conventional participation,[6] is as follows:

$$Y_{\text{non-conventional participation}j} = \beta_{0j}\alpha_j + \beta_{1j} \text{ Overall economic situation}_j + \beta_{2j} \text{ Per-}$$

sonal economic situation$_j$ + β_{3j} Ideology$_j$ + β_{4j} Satisfaction with demo-cratic functioning$_j$ + β_{5j} Support for democracy$_j$ + β_{6j} Institutional affection + β_{7j} Political engagement$_j$ + β_{8j} Gamson's hypothesis$_j$ + β_{9j} Education$_j$ + β_{10j} Gender$_j$ + β_{11j} Age$_j$ + β_{12j} Income$_j$ + β_{13j} Conventional$_j$ + β_{14j} No participation in Conventional $\times$ Institutional disaffection + e

If political disaffection constitutes a starting point for democratic innovation, an alternative source of political control, and a new instrument for the expression of citizens' preferences, we should find the following:

a Neither dimension of political affection should be related to conventional participation; hence, in model 1, $\beta_{6j} = 0$ and $\beta_{7j} = 0$.

b Gamson's index (of the externally disaffected and internally efficacious) should be negatively related to conventional participation; therefore, in model 1, $\beta_{8j} < 0$.

c Both dimensions of political affection should be negatively related to non-conventional participation; that is, the disaffected should be those promoting this kind of non-formal participation; therefore, in model 2, $\beta_{6j} < 0$ and $\beta_{7j} < 0$.

d Gamson's index should have a positive relationship with non-conventional participation; therefore, in model 2, $\beta_{8j} > 0$.

e Conventional participation should not be related, or should be negatively related, to non-conventional participation; therefore, in model 2, $\beta_{13j} \leq 0$.

f The interaction of dummy conventional participation and institutional affection should be negatively related to non-conventional participation; therefore, in model 2, $\beta_{14j} < 0$.

If the preceding discussion of the different consequences of political disaffection in new democracies is correct and offers an explanation for the widening gap between citizens, the institutions, and political authorities, a general lack of participation, weaker expression of political preferences, and the more limited political accountability of authorities between elections, thereby creating a more elitist, less participatory democracy, we should expect the following:

g Both dimensions of political affection should have a positive relationship with conventional participation; therefore, in model 1, $\beta_{6j} > 0$ and $\beta_{7j} > 0$.

h Gamson's index (of the externally disaffected with the internally efficacious) should have a positive or non-existent relationship with conventional participation; therefore, in model 1, $\beta_{8j} \geq 0$.

i Institutional affection and political engagement should have a positive relationship with non-conventional participation; that is, the affected should be those promoting this kind of non-formal participation; therefore, in model 2, $\beta_{6j} > 0$ and $\beta_{7j} > 0$.

j   Gamson's index should have a negative or non-existent relationship with non-conventional participation; therefore, in model 2, $\beta_{8j} \leq 0$.

k   Conventional participation should be positively related to non-conventional participation; therefore, in model 2, $\beta_{13j} > 0$.

l   The interaction of dummy conventional participation and institutional affection should be positively or not related to non-conventional participation; therefore, in model 2, $\beta_{14j} \geq 0$.

Before estimating the model, we should point out that this obviously does not capture important contextual variables for political participation. However, our primary objective is not to develop a complete model to account for political participation in these countries. Rather we merely wish to explore the nature of the influence of political disaffection for conventional and non-conventional participation, after controlling for the usual set of significant individual-level variables typically included in the literature. Furthermore, the fact that the model does not include contextual national-level variables in individual-level analyses by country should not be considered to reveal a problem of under-specification.[7] Contextual national-level variables are constant within each country and only provide information to explain the differences in the levels among countries, which is not our main concern here.

Moreover, as we have shown above, the political attitudes under analysis here (particularly those relating to political disaffection) do tell us much of interest about the political context in the past. As discussed in the Introduction to this volume, this means that, although political attitudes are reflections of individual characteristics, they are shaped by a cultural legacy of past political events. Most models of political participation try to include in their explanations current contextual political factors, but political attitudes may also incorporate information about past political events. This point is important because most current models of political participation assign politics a residual role when they include only current contextual political features; politics is generally thought to explain only what is left after sociological and individual attitudinal attributes have been taken into account. By considering and stating more clearly the effects of the 'politics of the past' on attitudes we may be better able to overcome this 'residual status' of politics in models explaining political participation.

Table 12.1 contains the results of the estimation of the models in which conventional participation is the dependent variable in eight new democracies.[8] The results show that political disaffection, together with socioeconomic resources, is in general a strong predictor of conventional participation. However, the coefficients of political disaffection have a positive sign (the greater the affection, the greater the use of conventional mechanisms). This confirms hypothesis (g) instead of (a), and shows that political disaffection reinforces the political inequality produced by individual resources. This holds true for institutional affection as well as for political engagement. Even Gamson's hypothesis is not confirmed; hypothesis (b) is rejected for all the countries except Chile, where the combination of external inefficacy and political engagement produces a rejection of conventional forms of participation. In the remaining countries, hypothesis (h) is confirmed; that is to say, this attitudinal combination of politically engaged but discontent citizens does not produce a negative reaction against conventional participation, but rather has a positive effect even in Peru and Greece.

Table 12.2 shows the results of the estimation of model 2 for non-conventional participation in the same group of new democracies. In this case, the major predictors are the individual resource variables (especially education and age), ideology (possibly because leftist respondents resort to this kind of participation more frequently), and conventional participation. However, the effect of the political affection variables in the different countries is either positive and significant, or non-existent. Furthermore, this positive relationship between political affection and this type of participation intensifies when the conventional participation variable, which, as we saw above, is strongly related to these attitudes, is eliminated from the model (data not shown). In this case, the model confirms hypothesis (i) rather than (c), indicating that political affection also has a positive relation with non-conventional participation. This leads us to conclude that political disaffection is in part responsible for the lack of *both* types of political participation in these societies, reinforcing the political inequality resulting directly from the significant differences in individual socio-economic resources that exist in these societies. Furthermore, with the weak and anecdotal exception of Spain, Gamson's hypothesis is not confirmed for this dimension of political disaffection; in other words, the combination of disaffected but politically engaged citizens does not lead to an increase in non-conventional participation. Hypothesis (d) is not confirmed for new democracies. Instead, hypothesis (j) is verified: this attitudinal combination does not have any effect on non-conventional participation in the eight new democracies analysed here.

These results contrast with the effect of political disaffection on political participation in more traditional democracies. According to the dominant interpretation in the literature, political disaffection in old democracies has a mobilizing effect that stimulates non-conventional forms of participation, resulting in greater control, alternative ways of expressing political preferences, democratic and institutional innovation, political accountability beyond pure democratic delegation, and more responsive leadership. In fact, the best predictor of non-conventional participation in new democracies is conventional participation, since the two are linked by a positive relationship, confirming hypothesis (e) instead of (k). The use of non-conventional forms of participation in new

Table 12.1 Models to explain conventional political participation in eight new democracies[a]

Variable	Argentina	Brazil	Chile	Greece	Peru	Portugal	Spain	Uruguay
Overall economic situation								
Personal economic situation								−0.07*
Ideology	−0.15***						−0.15***	−0.15***
Satisfaction with democratic functioning								
Support for democracy	0.18***	0.19***	0.07*	0.11***	0.13***	0.13***	0.10***	
Institutional affection	0.14**		0.27***	0.26***		0.20***	0.11***	0.15***
Political engagement							0.31***	0.18***
Gamson's hypothesis			−0.16***	0.09***	0.13**			
Education	0.16***	0.10*	0.14***	0.16***	0.15***			0.18***
Gender	0.17***			0.10***	0.14***			0.17***
Age	0.08**			0.08***		0.14***	0.07**	0.07*
Income		−0.11**				0.12**		
Constant (coefficient)	0.25***	0.27***	0.12**	0.58***	0.25***	0.10	0.51***	0.26***
R^2	0.16	0.12	0.12	0.10	0.08	0.10	0.18	0.17
(N)	(638)	(548)	(837)	(594)	(735)	(537)	(699)	(768)

Sources: 2002 CSES Portuguese Study; 2002 Spanish and Greek surveys of Values Systems of the Citizens and Socio-Economic Conditions – Challenges from Democratization for the EU-Enlargement, and *Latinobarometer* 1995.

Note

a Only statiscally significant beta coefficients are shown. Levels of statistical significance are ***$p<0.001$; **$p>0.05$; *$p<0.1$.

Table 12.2 Models to explain non-conventional political participation in eight new democracies[a]

Variables	Argentina	Brazil	Chile	Greece	Peru	Portugal	Spain	Uruguay
Overall economic situation	-0.11**	0.09**			-0.09**		-0.07**	-0.21***
Personal economic situation	-0.20**							
Ideology	-0.10***	-0.07*	-0.14***	-0.08**	-0.06*		-0.13***	-0.06*
Satisfaction with democratic functioning			-0.11***					
Support for democracy				-0.10***				-0.10***
Institutional affection				0.09*	0.12***			0.13***
Political engagement				0.15*				
Gamson's hypothesis							0.07*	
Education		0.19***	0.09***			0.24***		0.07*
Gender								0.06**
Age	-0.10***							
Income				0.14***	0.11***		0.10***	
Conventional participation	0.29***	0.23***	0.29***	0.44***	0.31***	0.22***	0.57***	0.29***
No participation in conventional forms of institutional disaffection						0.15*		
Constant (coefficient)	0.45***	0.45***	0.35***	1.57***	0.33***	0.42***	0.38***	0.46***
R^2	0.25	0.19	0.22	0.34	0.16	0.13	0.44	0.31
(N)	(606)	(525)	(829)	(594)	(734)	(530)	(696)	(764)

Source: See Table 12.1.

Note

a Only statistically significant beta coefficients are shown. Levels of statistical significance are ***$p < 0.001$; **$p < 0.05$; *$p < 0.1$.

democracies is not a response to a lack of satisfaction with current conventional politics, but rather the result of decades of political exclusion of many generations of citizens in the past, reflected in high levels of political disaffection (see Torcal in this volume). Even the effect of political disaffection among the citizens that do not use conventional forms of participation is very revealing. The relationship is only significant in Portugal. This means that in only one country does institutional disaffection among conventional non-participants increase the probability of their using non-conventional forms of participation (hypothesis [e]). In all the other countries analysed here there is no effect (hypothesis [l]).

It is also important to note that support for democracy has no impact on political participation in the new democracies under study. The only exceptions are Uruguay and Greece, as their negative signs indicate that they go in the other direction; that is to say, decrease the level of participation in non-conventional forms. Nor does political discontent have any significant effect. There is only a weak relationship between non-conventional participation and satisfaction with the functioning of democracy in Argentina, Chile, and Uruguay. That is, people tend to use fewer non-conventional forms of participation when they are more satisfied with the functioning of democracy, but there is no effect on conventional forms. This shows, again, that satisfaction with the functioning of democracy is in fact a measure of satisfaction with the incumbent authorities (Gunther and Montero in this volume; Linde and Ekman 2003) and that people tend to participate less through alternative forms when they are satisfied with the current authorities, since there are fewer incentives. It seems, therefore, that democratic support and political discontent do not substantially affect political participation, a basic aspect of the nature of the relationship between citizens and their representatives. Of all the attitudes of political support, only the two dimensions of political disaffection have any impact on citizens' individual decisions on participation in new democracies.

To conclude, our analysis has revealed the important role of political disaffection in explaining the low levels of conventional and non-conventional political participation found in new democracies. Contrary to what seems to be the case in more established democracies, political disaffection discourages all kinds of political participation and, therefore, appears to be *the* crucial factor shaping the nature of the relationship between citizens and incumbent authorities. In fact, political disaffection is widening the already significant gap between citizens and representatives. While traditional democracies are aiming for a more inclusive and more participatory republican democratic polity (Dalton 1988, 1999; Kaase and Newton 1995; Nye, Zelikow, and King 1997; Norris 1999d), new democracies have taken another path, one leading towards a more elitist and less participatory democracy. This difference in the nature of democracy is in part due to the distinct effect that political disaffection has on new democracies, which may be linked to the distinctive nature of political disaffection in these countries.

The impact of political disaffection on information acquisition and processing

In our second empirical analysis, we present a comparative revision of how information is acquired and processed in new democracies characterized by widespread political disaffection. We focus on the role of the political environment in serving as an informational crutch or shortcut that assists citizens when they are making political judgements (i.e. the environment helps citizens think and behave as they would if not slowed by the difficulties inherent in evaluating information) (Lupia 2000: 3). In other words, we examine whether, as hypothesized in the more established democracies, in new democracies too the environment may promote responsible citizens when they are disaffected.

The literature on voting behaviour and/or public opinion hinges on three diverging conceptions of citizens in democratic societies, conceptions which differ in accordance with their implicit assumptions about citizens' political capacity (that is to say, the public's level of knowledge, understanding, and interest in political matters) (Dalton and Wattenberg 1993; Jones 2001: Ch. 3).

First, much of the early literature on voting behaviour, drawn largely from sociology and social psychology, viewed voters as pawns of social location or their limited cognitive makeups. For the sociologists of the Columbia school, the causes of voting behaviour were to be found in groups: the vote was dictated by one's social position (Lazarsfeld, Berelson, and Gaudet 1944). For social psychologists of the Michigan school, the focal point was the mediating role of long-term psychological predispositions, particularly party identification, in guiding citizens' actions (Campbell *et al.* 1960). However, probably the most striking finding of this body of literature was the contrast that exists between the classic image of the democratic citizen and the actual nature of the electorate. The public's political sophistication falls well short of the theoretical ideal: voters are unable to organize and understand the political world around them, and therefore rely on a more educated and informed politicized elite to tell them what to do in the voting booth.

A second conception of the democratic voter, which may loosely be labelled as *economic*, is diametrically opposed to this pessimistic vision. Born in the field of economics and first imported into political science by Downs (1957) in his *An Economic Theory of Democracy*, this perspective asserts that individuals are instrumentally rational: they act in accord with their preferences for final outcomes and their beliefs about the effectiveness of the choice of actions open to them. Downs (1957) highlighted the existence of costs (in time, energy, or opportunity) attached to the acquisition and analysis of political information, and also underlined that rational voters will choose to invest in acquiring information only insofar as the information promises a return. Given the infinitesimal probability that they may influence the outcome of elections, and hence reap rewards from their actions, the result is 'rational ignorance'. Hence, this school of thought holds voters to be just as uninformed as the literature discussed above, even if the reasons have changed significantly. Their lack of knowledge is not as a result of their being cognitively crippled; rather, they are rationally ignorant because they have very low incentives for informing themselves. In short, they develop simplified ways of using attitudinal factors, such as issue opinions and candidate evaluations, as a basis for their voting decisions (Dalton and Wattenberg 1993: 197).

Finally, a new perspective on voters in democratic societies has emerged since the early 1990s. In this, rather than being prisoners of group identifications and almost unchanging or permanent attitudes, voters are active decision-makers who respond to the dynamic of politics, policies, and external events (Jones 2001: 80). However, contrary to what most of the modern economics and political science literature suggests, individuals are not fully adaptable to the current environment in their decision-making activities. Because of human cognitive and emotional architecture, people must adapt not just to the objective circumstances in which they find themselves, but also to their own inner cognitive and emotive constitutions. They are, in sum, boundedly rational (Simon 1996).

In this way, six decades of survey research carried out in the wake of Lazarsfeld, Berelson, and Gaudet's *The People's Choice* have convincingly demonstrated how little attention citizens pay to politics, how rarely they think about even major issues, and how often they have failed to work through a consistent position on them (see, for example, Luskin 1987). For instance, voters cannot recall basic political facts (delli Carpini and Keeter 1991), do not have a solid understanding of ideological abstractions (Converse 1964), and fail to recognize the names of their elected representatives (Montero and Gunther 1994; Neuman 1986). However, this limited information need not prevent people from making reasoned choices or decisions based on accurate predictions about the consequences of a given decision (Lupia and McCubbins 1998: 18). Given that encyclopaedic knowledge is beyond their reach, the public may however muddle through by relying on a variety of sensible and mostly adaptive shortcuts. Thus, heuristics are judgemental shortcuts, efficient ways to organize and simplify political choices; efficient, that is, in the double sense of requiring relatively little information to execute, yet yielding dependable answers even to complex problems of choice (Sniderman, Brody, and Tetlock 1991: 19). The numerous possible heuristics include opinion leaders (Berelson, Lazarsfeld and McPhee 1954), party identification (Downs 1957), campaign events (Popkin 1991), costly action (Lupia

1992), the media (Iyengar and Kinder 1987), interpersonal influence (Beck, Greene, and Huckfeldt 2002), social relations (Huckfeldt 2001), or the political environment (Kuklinski *et al.* 2001).[9]

But, in order to avoid a black-box explanation, in which the link between input and output, or between *explanans* and *explanandum*, is assumed to be devoid of structure or, at least, whatever structure there may be is considered to be of no inherent interest (Hedström and Swedberg 1998: 9), it is essential to establish the causal mechanisms that make a shortcut persuasive. We need a theory that, in addition to showing that people can use shortcuts, explains when and how people choose from among the many shortcuts that political settings offer, as well as enabling us to understand when shortcuts are, or are not, effective substitutes for detailed information. Otherwise, 'the most serious risk is that ... every correlation between independent and dependent variable [is] taken as evidence of a new judgmental shortcut' (Sniderman, Brudy, and Tetluck 1991: 70). Such a theory has recently been put forward by Lupia and McCubbins (1998: Chs 1 to 4) and Lupia (2000, 2002). Integrating both psychological and rational insights, this theory linking limited information and reasoned choice builds on two well-established premises from the cognitive and social sciences. First, learning is active and goal-oriented: people only pay attention to certain types of stimuli and ignore most others. Second, individuals systematically connect current observations of their physical world to physical or emotional feedback from experience. In other words, people attribute meaning to new or relevant objects by connecting them with objects, events, or people that they have encountered in the past. The interaction between these two principles allows individuals to make reasoned choices in a wide range of complex circumstances with limited information: they pay attention and connect the information they attend to in ways that are likely to minimize costly mistakes.

People who want to make reasoned choices need knowledge (that is, they must be able to predict the consequences of their actions). They have two possible ways of obtaining such knowledge: they can obtain it from personal experience or from what other people say, write, or do. However, in many political situations only this second option is available, since politics generates problems that are unfamiliar to people. Under what conditions can individuals obtain knowledge from others? According to Lupia and McCubbins (1998: 40), learning from others requires persuasion or one person's successful attempt to change the beliefs of another. Persuasion occurs only if the principal or the person who learns or is persuaded (1) is initially uncertain about which alternative is better for him/her, (2) believes that the speaker or the person who teaches may have the knowledge he/she desires, and (3) believes that the speaker has an incentive to reveal what he/she knows (Huckfeldt 2001; Popkin 1991). If just one of these conditions is not met, then persuasion cannot take place.

This model has a number of important implications. First, all statements are not equally informative. Second, concepts such as reputation, party, or ideology are useful heuristics only if they convey information about knowledge and trust. In other words, a speaker's personal attributes are only a useful indicator when there is a strong correlation between them and the factors underlying the conditions for persuasion. Third, all speakers are not equally persuasive: a person's ability to persuade is related to how he/she is perceived by others. Finally, although the principal's personal attributes are not contemplated in the model, all principals are not equally susceptible to be persuaded. According to Zaller (1992: Ch. 3), individual responses to political information depend on two axioms. First, the greater a person's level of cognitive engagement with an issue, the more likely they are to be exposed to and to comprehend political messages relating to that issue. Second, people tend to resist arguments that are inconsistent with their political predispositions, but they do so only to the extent that they possess the contextual information necessary to perceive a relationship between the message and their predispositions. Consequently, when one person attempts to learn from another, enlightenment or an increase in the ability to make an accurate prediction about the consequences of a given action only takes place if (1) the speaker is persuasive, (2) only the speaker possesses the knowledge the principal needs, and (3) the speaker has incentives to reveal what he/she knows.

As we already know, the empirical evidence provided by the political-heuristic school has validated this theory connecting limited information and reasoned choice. The political environment requires people to make simple judgements, and generally facilitates reliable cues to help citizens perform them. However, as recent experimental analyses have shown, this information from the environment is not sufficient to enable poorly informed individuals to make competent political judgements (Kuklinski *et al.* 2001). The environment can either promote or fail to promote political judgement, depending on its capacity to induce citizens to take their tasks seriously, invest effort, and withstand the psychological burden of responsible decision-making. Thus, motivation or attention has an important effect on decision-making in an intermediate range of the information diagnostic value: when the environment provides some cues about the need for trade-offs but does not explicitly and fully spell out the feasible options. Without such informational cues, enhanced motivation makes no differences; without the ambiguity, it is not needed (Kuklinski *et al.* 2001: 411).

In what follows we test the capacity of this theory of information acquisition and processing to explain the national economic evaluations in four new democracies: Chile, Greece, Spain, and Uruguay. We argue that, in contrast to the situation in more established democracies, political disaffection in new democracies prevents citizens from using the political environment as an informational support. Since political disaffection leads to lower engagement in the *res publica* and therefore a less participatory democracy, we will demonstrate that it is not so easy for the environment to offset the logic of collective action and encourage responsible citizens. Moreover, this negative effect is exacerbated if we take into account that citizens in new democracies cannot draw on knowledge of actions and outcomes of democratic institutions from their own personal experience. On the other hand, this empirical analysis allows us to replace findings that come from survey experiments with inferences about real-world effects.

In order to test this impact of political disaffection on information acquisition and processing, we have adopted a two-stage procedure. First, we have estimated the extent to which a model based on knowledge and shortcuts can account for the amount of information individuals possess on the (perceived) situation of the national economy. Second, we have divided the sample of citizens into three groups according to their level of political disaffection, and then we re-estimated the regression model. Our main hypothesis is that if political disaffection operates as expected, the model or the information sources should work worse when individuals are disaffected. And since political behaviour depends to a large extent on the (perceived) economic situation and, moreover, the economic information is extensively covered by the mass media, the dependent variable comprises standard measures of *national economic evaluations* with three response categories. The corresponding survey questions ask individuals to describe the current economic situation. Responses have been coded so that they range from 'bad' or 'very bad', 'worse' to 'good' or 'very good'. 'Neither good nor bad' is the intermediate category. Given that these economic evaluations constitute an ordered categorical variable, ordered probit analysis is a more appropriate method than linear regression, since it does not impose the assumption that all adjacent responses are quantitatively equidistant from each other (Long 1997: Ch. 5).

Here again two variables have been created to measure the two dimensions of political disaffection. On the one hand, we have created a proxy for *institutional disaffection* in the form of an index based exclusively on external political efficacy, since there are no data available on confidence in institutions. The index is composed of two items: agreement or disagreement with the statements 'people like me do not have any influence over what the government does', and 'politicians do not care much about what people like me think'. Responses to these questions have been coded as 1 when the individual agrees with the proposition and 0 when he/she does not. The scale has a potential minimum of 0 (not political disaffection) and a maximum of 2 (strong political disaffection). On the other hand, *political disengagement* has been proxied through an index based on internal political efficacy and subjective political interest. This index comprises two items: agreement or disagreement with the statement 'generally, politics seems so complicated that people like me cannot understand what is happening' and individuals' stated level of interest in politics. The former again has two possible values (1, agreement; 0 no agreement), while the latter ranges from 0 (very) to 3 (not at all). Intermediate values assigned are 1 (somewhat) and 2 (little). Political interest has been transformed into a 1-point scale by multiplying by one-half. As a result, each component of the index carries equal weight. The scale has a potential minimum of 0 (not political disengagement) and a maximum of 2 (political disengagement). With these variables, and as can be seen in Table 12.3, Greece and Spain, on the one hand, and Chile and Spain, on the other, show the highest levels of institutional disaffection and political disengagement, respectively. On the contrary, in Uruguay political disaffection does not seem to be a very significant variable.

The sources of information acquisition and processing are operationalized through the following independent variables. *Political knowledge* is a 4-point scale of information (where 0 is the potential minimum and 4 the potential maximum) based on neutral factual knowledge about politics (such as 'Do you remember the name of the Minister of the Economy?' or 'Do you remember the name of the President of the Senate?'); *self-placement on a left–right ideological scale* goes from 1 (left) to 10 (right); *long time residency in a community*, or the number of years living in the same building; *age* (measured in years); *civil status* (1, married/living together; 0, not married); *level of education* (0, no studies at all; 1, primary education; 2, secondary education; 3, university education); *work* (1 when an individual works, 0 otherwise); respondent's *economic situation* (0, bad or very bad; 1, nor good nor bad; 2, good or very good); *media consumption* is an index with two items: the frequency with which the respondent follows politics through newspapers and television (both coded 0–4: 4, every day or almost every day; 3, three or four days per week; 2, one or two days per week; 1, less frequently, and 0, never or almost never). This scale has a potential minimum of 0 and maximum of 8. Finally, *political discussion* is the frequency with which the respondent discusses or talks about politics with friends (0, never or rarely; 1, sometimes; 2, often).

Very briefly, the literature suggests that the causal mechanisms operating behind these variables are as follows. Long-term residents in a community have better contextual knowledge with which to evaluate the local impact of politics. Education and age generate knowledge that is useful in processing information. Married people enjoy economies of scale, so to speak, in information acquisition. Personal contacts, either at work or through social networks, provide inexpensive information. Ideology and personal experience may act as default sources of information. Finally, media consumption is the main source of information for *active* citizens.

The model of information acquisition and processing about the current economic situation in the different countries is as follows:

Table 12.3 Summary statistics for political disaffection in four countries

Country	Institutional disaffection					Political disengagement				
	Mean	Standard deviation	Minimum	Maximum	(N)	Mean	Standard deviation	Minimum	Maximum	(N)
Spain	1.32	0.77	0	2	(1,445)	1.31	0.57	0	2	(1,443)
Greece	1.34	0.75	0	2	(933)	1.12	0.62	0	2	(950)
Chile	1.28	0.77	0	2	(1,295)	1.39	0.55	0	2	(1,293)
Uruguay	1.17	0.79	0	2	(1,967)	1.15	0.63	0	2	(2,987)

Source: See Table 12.1.

Table 12.4 Summary statistics for the explanatory variables in four countries (aggregated pool)

Variable	Mean	Standard deviation	Minimum	Maximum	(N)
Political knowledge	1.32	1.23	0	4	(4,724)
Ideology	5.18	2.29	1	10	(4,411)
Years living in a community	19.02	15.37	0	88	(3,362)
Age	44.55	17.51	18	93	(4,690)
Civil status	0.63	0.48	0	1	(4,723)
Education	1.66	0.96	0	3	(4,695)
Work	0.51	0.50	0	1	(4,710)
Personal economic situation	0.97	0.69	0	2	(4,699)
Media consumption	5.01	2.22	0	8	(4,664)
Political discussion	0.74	0.71	0	2	(4,708)

Source: See Table 12.1.

$$Y_{\text{National economic evaluations}j} = \beta_{0j}\alpha_j + \beta_{1j} \text{ Political knowledge}_j + \beta_{2j} \text{ Ideology}_j + \beta_{3j}\text{Age}_j + \beta_{4j}\text{Married}_j + \beta_{5j}\text{Education}_j + \beta_{6j}\text{Work}_j + \beta_{7j} \text{ Personal economic situation}_j + \beta_{8j}\text{Media consumption}_j + \beta_{9j}\text{Political discussion}_j + e$$

If political disaffection makes it harder for citizens to use the political environment as an informational crutch, then we would expect to find the following:

a   The capacity to explain how individuals acquire information should be negatively related to the spread of political disaffection. Therefore, the fit or the Pseudo R^2 of the model (and the magnitude and statistical significance of the regression coefficients) should be greater in the sub-sample of citizens who are not, or only weakly politically disaffected, than among other respondents.

b   The greatest differences in the fit or the Pseudo R^2 among sub-samples of citizens should be observed in democracies that display the highest levels of political disaffection. Therefore, the most significant differences should appear in Greece on the *institutional disaffection* dimension and in Chile with respect to the *political disengagement* dimension. In contrast, the least significant differences should be found in Uruguay, on the one hand, and Greece and Uruguay, on the other.

In Tables 12.5 to 12.8 we show the full ordered probit results for the estimation of the model for the different samples in each country. Most of the variables are of the sign we would expect from our theoretical analysis, many are statistically significant, and the chi-squared statistics of the overall models fit refutes the null hypothesis that national economic evalu-

Table 12.5 Ordered probit models of national economic evaluations in Greece, 1996[a]

Explanatory variable	General model	Institutional disaffection			Political disengagement		
		Low	Medium	High	Low	Medium	High
Political knowledge	0.17*** (0.05)	0.14 (0.14)	−0.36*** (0.10)	0.06 (0.07)	0.15* (0.10)	0.16* (0.09)	0.18** (0.73)
Ideology	−0.12*** (0.20)	−0.16*** (0.06)	−0.18*** (0.04)	−0.09*** (0.29)	−0.17*** (0.04)	−0.09** (0.04)	−0.13*** (0.03)
Years living in a community	0.01** (0.00)	0.02** (0.01)	0.01*** (0.01)	0.00 (0.00)	0.01** (0.01)	0.00 (0.01)	0.01 (0.01)
Age	−0.00 (0.00)	0.01 (0.01)	0.01 (0.01)	−0.00 (0.01)	−0.00 (0.01)	−0.00 (0.01)	0.00 (0.01)
Civil status	−0.11 (0.11)	0.24 (0.25)	0.28 (0.22)	−0.35*** (0.16)	−0.08 (0.19)	−0.16 (0.22)	−0.04 (0.18)
Education							
Primary	0.15 (0.21)	−0.86 (0.91)	0.51 (0.58)	0.07 (0.26)	1.54** (0.73)	−0.21 (0.41)	−0.02 (0.30)
Secondary	−0.16 (0.22)	−1.15 (0.90)	0.17 (0.58)	−0.23 (0.28)	1.37* (0.73)	−0.54 (0.44)	−0.49 (0.32)
University	−0.14 (0.25)	−1.35 (0.91)	0.06 (0.62)	−0.08 (0.33)	1.25* (0.74)	−0.41 (0.47)	−0.70* (0.39)
Work	0.00 (0.94)	−0.07 (0.25)	−0.04 (0.18)	−0.14 (0.14)	−0.15 (0.18)	0.25 (0.19)	−0.10 (0.15)
Personal economic situation							
Nor bad nor good	0.93*** (0.11)	1.98*** (0.50)	1.41*** (0.24)	0.57*** (0.15)	1.30*** (0.25)	0.87*** (0.22)	0.81*** (0.17)
Good or very good	1.42*** (0.14)	3.19*** (0.54)	1.61*** (0.28)	0.88*** (0.21)	1.76*** (0.28)	1.35*** (0.30)	1.37*** (0.22)
Media consumption	−0.00 (0.02)	−0.10 (0.06)	0.07 (0.05)	−0.03 (0.03)	−0.02 (0.05)	−0.04 (0.05)	0.02 (0.04)
Political discussion	−0.04 (0.07)	−0.05 (0.17)	−0.02 (0.13)	−0.10 (0.10)	−0.05 (0.13)	−0.27* (0.14)	−0.02 (0.12)
Cut 1	0.61* (0.34)	0.29 (1.02)	2.36*** (0.86)	−0.29 (0.49)	1.90* (0.86)	−0.31 (0.72)	0.71 (0.55)
Cut 2	2.16*** (0.35)	2.35*** (1.04)	4.15*** (0.88)	1.18*** (0.50)	3.39*** (0.87)	1.46*** (0.73)	2.30*** (0.57)
LR chi²	172.66***	68.77***	92.30***	37.33***	79.49***	33.45***	61.89***
Pseudo R^2	0.13	0.25	0.22	0.06	0.16	0.10	0.12
(N)	(807)	(138)	(251)	(398)	(252)	(208)	(347)

Source: See Table 12.1.

Note

a Standard error of parameter estimates are in parentheses. Levels of statistical significance are ***$p < 0.001$; **$p < 0.5$; *$p < 0.10$.

Table 12.6 Ordered probit models of national economic evaluations in Chile, 1993[a]

Explanatory variable	General model	Institutional disaffection			Political disengagement		
		Low	*Medium*	*High*	*Low*	*Medium*	*High*
Political knowledge	0.19*** (0.38)	0.28*** (0.09)	0.20*** (0.07)	0.16*** (0.06)	0.17 (0.11)	0.14* (0.08)	0.19*** (0.05)
Ideology	0.02 (0.02)	-0.02 (0.04)	0.05 (0.03)	0.01 (0.02)	-0.01 (0.04)	0.07* (0.04)	0.00 (0.02)
Years living in a community	–	–	–	–	–	–	–
Age	0.00 (0.00)	-0.00 (0.01)	0.01 (0.00)	0.00 (0.00)	0.00 (0.01)	0.01 (0.01)	-0.00 (0.00)
Civil status	-0.05 (0.07)	0.22 (0.17)	-0.13 (0.14)	-0.10 (0.10)	-0.05 (0.21)	-0.03 (0.17)	-0.06 (0.09)
Education							
Primary	-0.04 (0.14)	0.15 (0.34)	0.02 (0.27)	-0.14 (0.18)	0.08 (0.67)	-0.22 (0.43)	-0.00 (0.15)
Secondary	0.18* (0.10)	0.36 (0.27)	0.45** (0.20)	0.00 (0.14)	0.69* (0.38)	0.30 (0.32)	0.09 (0.12)
University	0.17 (0.13)	0.22 (0.30)	0.42* (0.23)	-0.01 (0.18)	0.48 (0.40)	0.33 (0.34)	0.09 (0.16)
Work	0.02 (0.07)	0.01 (0.17)	-0.01 (0.13)	0.08 (0.11)	-0.27 (0.22)	0.21 (0.17)	0.02 (0.09)
Personal economic situation							
Nor bad nor good	0.86*** (0.10)	0.56* (0.30)	1.39*** (0.21)	0.67*** (0.13)	1.74*** (0.40)	0.83*** (0.27)	0.79*** (0.12)
Good or very good	1.90*** (0.13)	2.10*** (0.34)	2.34*** (0.25)	1.55*** (0.17)	2.62*** (0.43)	1.85*** (0.31)	1.84*** (0.15)
Media consumption	0.03* (0.02)	-0.05 (0.05)	0.01 (0.03)	0.04* (0.02)	0.04 (0.06)	0.01 (0.04)	0.02 (0.02)
Political discussion	0.13** (0.06)	0.33** (0.14)	0.04 (0.11)	0.11 (0.09)	-0.39** (0.17)	0.26* (0.15)	0.12 (0.08)
Cut 1	0.39** (0.19)	-0.12 (0.52)	0.96*** (0.36)	0.19 (0.26)	0.55 (0.70)	0.80 (0.52)	0.09 (0.023)
Cut 2	2.48*** (0.20)	2.06*** (0.55)	3.34*** (0.40)	2.17*** (0.28)	2.33*** (0.73)	3.10*** (0.55)	2.29*** (0.24)
LR chi^2	445.10***	125.92***	181.27***	139.90***	69.28***	84.50***	234.94***
Pseudo R^2	0.19	0.28	0.24	0.13	0.22	0.19	0.16
(N)	(1,222)	(242)	(410)	(565)	(172)	(257)	(793)

Source: See Table 12.1.

Note

a Standard error of parameter estimates are in parentheses. Levels of statistical significance are ***$p < 0.001$; **$p < 0.5$; *$p < 0.10$.

Table 12.7 Ordered probit models of national economic evaluations in Spain, 1993^a

Explanatory variable	General model	Institutional disaffection			Political disengagement		
		Low	Medium	High	Low	Medium	High
Political knowledge	-0.04 (0.03)	0.04 (0.06)	-0.09** (0.05)	-0.05 (0.04)	-0.05 (0.07)	-0.01 (0.05)	-0.08** (0.40)
Ideology	-0.09*** (0.02)	-0.09* (0.04)	-0.12*** (0.03)	-0.07*** (0.02)	-0.15*** (0.04)	-0.11*** (0.03)	-0.06* (0.22) **
Years of living in a community	-0.00 (0.00)	-0.01 (0.01)	-0.00 (0.01)	-0.00 (0.00)	0.00 (0.01)	-0.00 (0.01)	-0.00 (0.00)
Age	0.00 (0.00)	0.00 (0.00)	0.01** (0.00)	-0.00 (0.00)	0.00 (0.00)	0.01 (0.01)	0.00 (0.00)
Civil status	-0.07 (0.08)	-0.11 (0.19)	-0.18 (0.13)	-0.01 (0.12)	-0.07 (0.19)	-0.08 (0.16)	-0.09 (0.11)
Education							
Primary	-0.35*** (0.10)	-0.50** (0.24)	-0.59*** (0.19)	-0.18 (0.15)	-0.29 (0.33)	-0.55*** (0.25)	-0.31** (0.12)
Secondary	-0.49* (0.12)	-0.78*** (0.30)	-0.44*** (0.22)	-0.40** (0.17)	-0.80** (0.36)	-0.43 (0.27)	-0.44*** (0.15)
University	-0.57*** (0.16)	-0.95*** (0.37)	-0.29 (0.27)	-0.69*** (0.24)	-0.52 (0.38)	-0.64*** (0.33)	-0.79*** (0.26)
Work	-0.13** (0.08)	-0.50*** (0.19)	-0.23* (0.14)	0.08 (0.11)	-0.05 (0.18)	0.02 (0.15)	-0.29*** (0.11)
Personal economic situation							
Nor bad nor good	0.67*** (0.09)	0.78*** (0.24)	0.52*** (0.15)	0.71*** (0.13)	1.00*** (0.24)	0.70*** (0.19)	0.59*** (0.11)
Good or very good	1.32*** (0.11)	1.50*** (0.28)	1.16*** (0.18)	1.29*** (0.16)	1.59*** (0.27)	1.27*** (0.22)	1.27*** (0.15)
Media consumption	-0.04* (0.06)	-0.08* (0.05)	0.00 (0.03)	-0.06* (0.02)	-0.03 (0.05)	-0.07* (0.04)	-0.04** (0.02)
Political discussion	0.04 (0.06)	0.06 (0.14)	0.09 (0.11)	-0.02 (0.09)	-0.02 (0.15)	-0.09 (0.13)	0.11 (0.09)
Cut 1	-0.23 (0.19)	-0.91* (0.47)	-0.08 (0.34)	-0.03 (0.27)	-0.26 (0.58)	-0.21 (0.41)	-0.27 (0.25)
Cut 2	1.38*** (0.19)	0.93*** (0.48)	1.63*** (0.36)	1.49*** (0.28)	1.34*** (0.58)	1.47*** (0.42)	1.32*** (0.25)
LR chi²	245.82***	67.55***	103.10***	99.35***	66.92***	67.17***	135.28***
Pseudo R²	0.11	0.15	0.14	0.09	0.15	0.12	0.11
(N)	(1,347)	(246)	(428)	(673)	(261)	(347)	(739)

Source: See Table 12.1.

Note

a Standard error of parameter estimates are in parentheses. Levels of statistical significance are ***$p < 0.001$; **$p < 0.5$; *$p < 0.10$.

Table 12.8 Ordered probit models of national economic evaluations in Uruguay, 1994

Explanatory variable	General model	Institutional disaffection			Political disengagement		
		Low	*Medium*	*High*	*Low*	*Medium*	*High*
Political knowledge	0.05 (0.06)	0.14 (0.12)	0.12 (0.12)	-0.17 (0.11)	0.11 (0.10)	-0.01 (0.12)	-0.06 (0.12)
Ideology	0.10*** (0.02)	0.13*** (0.04)	0.15*** (0.03)	0.05 (0.03)	0.19*** (0.04)	0.10** (0.04)	0.05 (0.03)
Years living in a community	-0.01* (0.00)	-0.00 (0.01)	-0.01** (0.01)	-0.01 (0.01)	-0.01* (0.01)	-0.00 (0.01)	-0.01* (0.00)
Age	0.01** (0.00)	-0.00 (0.01)	0.01* (0.01)	0.01*** (0.01)	0.01* (0.01)	0.01 (0.01)	0.01 (0.00)
Civil status	-0.11 (0.09)	0.16 (0.19)	-0.17 (0.15)	-0.23* (0.14)	0.01 (0.17)	-0.07 (0.18)	-0.29** (0.13)
Education							
Primary	-0.20 (0.15)	0.52 (0.42)	-0.56** (0.27)	-0.18 (0.21)	1.32*** (0.67)	-0.21 (0.33)	-0.38** (0.19)
Secondary	-0.22 (0.15)	0.10 (0.40)	-0.59** (0.26)	0.03 (0.22)	1.16* (0.66)	-0.15 (0.32)	-0.40** (0.20)
University	-0.29* (0.18)	0.06 (0.43)	-0.54* (0.31)	-0.22 (0.29)	1.07 (0.67)	-0.27 (0.37)	0.27 (0.28)
Work	-0.02 (0.09)	-0.19 (0.19)	0.03 (0.16)	0.09 (0.15)	0.03 (0.17)	-0.12 (0.19)	0.02 (0.14)
Personal economic situation							
Nor bad nor good	0.65*** (0.11)	0.44* (0.24)	0.68*** (0.19)	0.72*** (0.17)	0.67*** (0.22)	0.50** (0.24)	0.73*** (0.15)
Good or very good	1.54*** (0.13)	1.52*** (0.28)	1.34*** (0.22)	1.79*** (0.22)	1.54*** (0.25)	1.02** (0.28)	1.98*** (0.21)
Media consumption	0.02 (0.03)	-0.07 (0.06)	0.07* (0.04)	0.01 (0.04)	-0.03 (0.05)	0.06 (0.05)	0.02 (0.04)
Political discussion	-0.12 (0.06)	0.03 (0.15)	-0.04 (0.11)	-0.33*** (0.10)	-0.18 (0.12)	0.04 (0.13)	-0.18 (0.11)
Cut 1	1.23*** (0.27)	1.11* (0.60)	1.47*** (0.46)	1.10*** (0.43)	3.00*** (0.79)	1.70*** (0.56)	0.60* (0.38)
Cut 2	2.79*** (0.28)	2.63*** (0.63)	3.08*** (0.49)	2.76*** (0.45)	4.36*** (0.81)	3.08*** (0.59)	2.52*** (0.40)
LR chi²	213.72***	59.24***	81.90***	98.16***	86.67***	39.66***	119.32***
Pseudo R^2	0.13	0.17	0.15	0.16	0.18	0.10	0.17
(N)	(860)	(198)	(295)	(346)	(267)	(205)	(388)

Source: See Table 12.1.

Note

a Standard error of parameter estimates are in parentheses. Levels of statistical significance are ***$p < 0.001$; **$p < 0.5$; *$p < 0.10$.

ations are purely random. However, the important result to focus on for our purposes is the fit of the different models. As was hypothesized, political disaffection does hamper the use of the political environment as an informational shortcut. According to our estimates, first, the Pseudo R^2 is always higher for the sub-sample of not or weakly politically disaffected individuals than for the remaining sub-samples. In other words, the acquisition of information responds much better to the predictions of the theory we have sketched when citizens are *not* politically disaffected. Second, the greatest and smallest differences in the fit of the model in the sub-samples of individuals are found for those countries in which *more* and *less* citizens are politically disaffected, respectively. On the one hand, the differences in the Pseudo R^2 are particularly important in Greece on the dimension of institutional disaffection and in Chile for the dimension of political disengagement: 0.19 and 0.06, respectively. On the contrary, these differences are negligible in Uruguay: 0.01 in both dimensions. Spain lies somewhere between these two extremes: the Pseudo R^2 is 0.06 and 0.04 higher in the sample of not disaffected individuals on each one of the two dimensions. In short, this analysis reveals that the greater the level of political disaffection in a country, the less is the capacity of our theoretical model to explain how individuals acquire information.

On the basis of our empirical analysis we can assert that the environment's alleged capacity to mitigate the logic of collective action and encourage responsible citizenship is undermined when in contexts of widespread political disaffection. Although our measures of the two dimensions of political disaffection could well be improved upon, the empirical evidence we have provided gives reasonable support to this thesis. Since elections can only guarantee that governments are representative when citizens have sufficient information to select their preferred policies or policy-bearing politicians, or to hold governments responsible for the results of their past actions (Manin, Przeworski, and Stokes 1999: Ch. 1), democracies are less representative when political disaffection develops.

Conclusions

We have highlighted the consequences of political disaffection for the functioning and performance of democratic institutions in new democracies. The perspective defended here is that variations in political disaffection are crucial when it comes to explaining both conventional and non-conventional political participation and information acquisition and processing. The theoretical justification for this general proposition comes from (some) of the classics on the topic. Given that political disaffection results in reduced engagement in the *res publica*, the most plausible expectation is that people who are disaffected have a weaker propensity to participate in politics and, moreover, less political awareness.

Although we lack a totally satisfactory measure of political disaffection, the findings of the analyses presented here strongly support our hypothesis. In particular, we find, that, contrary to what happens in more traditional democracies, political disaffection in new democracies discourages any kind of political participation: the two different dimensions of political disaffection (institutional disaffection and political disengagement) have a significant demobilizing effect on both conventional and non-conventional political participation. On the other hand, and contrary again to what occurs in more traditional democracies, political disaffection in new democracies prevents citizens from using the political environment as an informational support. When political disaffection becomes widespread, individuals can hardly make reasoned choices on the basis of informational shortcuts. The main conclusion to be drawn from our empirical analysis is that political disaffection widens the gap between citizens and representatives and thus makes democratic governments less representative and accountable.

Notes

1 As di Palma (1970: 30) claims, 'people tend to participate in politics if they are not disaffected from the political system ... I expect participation to be sustained by the belief that the political system, or at least some of its strategic institutions are open and accessible to the individual. Also, participation does not flourish unless people feel that the polity is not a remote entity, but rather something that is present and important in their daily lives, and unless they are closely identified with and committed to it'. For similar conclusions, see Parry, Moyser, and Day (1992).

2 Political interest is another powerful predictor of political participation, as well as a dimension of political disengagement. However, we have decided to exclude it from the model because of its behavioural component.

3 In order to create the double condition of these variables (external inefficacy and internal efficacy), we have created an interactive variable with two dummy variables. For external inefficacy, the variable contains values 1 for those who agree with the external efficacy statement and 0 for those who disagree; for the internal efficacy, the variable contains values 0 for those who agree with the internal efficacy statement and 1 for those who disagree. Therefore, when this interactive variable is equal to 1, the respondent feels critical with the responsiveness of the system and, at the same time, politically competent; for the rest of the combinations, the value of this variable is equal to 0.

4 The dependent variables for conventional participation are, for Latin America, trying to convince others of my own political opinions, contacting or asking an official representative or politician, and working for a political party (variables p64b to p64e of the 1995 *Latinobarometer*); for Spain and Greece, contacting a politician, working for a political party, and going to a party rally (2002 Values Systems of the Citizens and Socio-Economic Conditions – Challenges from Democratization for the EU-Enlargement survey); and, finally, for Portugal, trying to persuade friends during the campaign, attending a meeting or helping during the campaign, contacting or asking an official representative (variables p19, p19b, and p33a of the Comparative Study of Electoral Systems [CSES] 2002 Portuguese study). As all these questions in all the surveys contain quite similar

response categories, we were able to recode the answers in the following order: 1, 'I will never do so'; 2, 'I might do so'; and 3, 'yes, I have done so'. We have created an average participation index ranging from 0 to 1 from all these items.

5 We first created a dummy variable for conventional participation with values 1 when $x \leq -1S$; and 0 when $x > \bar{x} - 1S$. We then multiplied this dummy variable by the institutional disaffection index. This variable has value 0 for those who use some conventional mechanisms and the values of the institutional disaffection index for those who do not.

6 This dependent variable for non-conventional participation was created as follows. We first constructed a participation index from the following activities: participating in demonstrations, blocking traffic, and occupying buildings or factories (variables p65a, p65b, and p65d of the 1995 *Latinobarometer*); and blocking traffic, occupying buildings or factories, participating in actions and opinion movements, and signing petitions (variables p63_1, p63_4, p63_6, and p63_7 of the CSES 2002 Portuguese study); signing a petition, participating in demonstrations, boycotting products, and participating in a strike (variables p24E, p24F, p24G, and p24H of 2002 Values Systems of the Citizens and Socio-Economic Conditions – Challenges from Democratization for the EU-Enlargement survey). All these questions contain quite similar response categories so we were able to recode the answers as follows: 1, 'I will never do so'; 2, 'I might do so'; and 3, 'yes, I have done so'. Only the Portuguese data are dummy variables with values 1, 'yes, I have done so'; 2, 'I have not done so'. We have created an average participation index from all these items from 0 to 1. These variables also measure the potential for participation as an attitudinal predisposition to participate and participation itself, so they are impossible to disentangle, and our dependent variable is an index comprising both. Therefore, we gave a value of 0 to the potential participants. For Latin America, respondents are asked about the frequency with which they participate in the activity.

7 Furthermore, under-specification substantially supports our conclusions and parameters, given that the most relevant variables in the discussion are significant and robust.

8 The Latin American data include a question not found in other surveys on democracy's capacity to resolve problems (p22 in the 1995 *Latinobarometer*). For the Latin American data, we have also used a socio-economic status variable instead of income.

9 Nevertheless, shortcuts do not completely solve the democratic problem of misinformed citizens for at least four reasons (Kinder 1998: 176). First, although citizens may be willing to rely on the opinions of experts, it should not be presumed that these experts always get things right or that citizens always know and understand what experts say. Second, as Althaus (1998), Bartels (1996), Duch *et al.* (2000), or Hetherington (1996) demonstrate, (1) poorly informed voters do not always behave as if they were fully informed, and (2) this 'noise' does not essentially cancel out in aggregate. Third, shortcuts have little to say about inequalities in information. Finally, when shortcuts are taken, they do not always lead to the right place.

Part VI
Conclusions

13 Some basic conclusions about political disaffection in contemporary democracies

José Ramón Montero and Mariano Torcal

In the Introduction to this volume, we set out to analyse a cluster of attitudes that are often lumped together as political support, but which, we argued, should be instead treated as both conceptually and empirically distinct. Following di Palma (1970: 30), we labelled as *political disaffection* a set of attitudes whose common denominators are a distrustful perception of politics as well as a chronic detachment from democratic institutions and political authorities. We also discussed that political disaffection contains two basic dimensions: institutional disaffection and political disengagement, or disaffection *tout court*. Both dimensions are related to a number of specific symptoms, including feelings of personal inefficacy, cynicism and distrust, lack of confidence in the major political institutions, the beliefs that political elites are unresponsive and the political system is unaccountable, and a general sense of estrangement from politics and the political system. This volume has attempted to answer some questions related to these attitudes by analysing a wide range of contemporary democracies either with comparative studies or with longitudinal case studies. In this concluding chapter, we will revise some discussions and systematize some empirical evidence presented by the contributors to this volume.

Democratic support, disaffection, and discontent

Various authors in this volume have discussed the question of the autonomy of democratic support, political disaffection, and political discontent. In the first part of his chapter, Claus Offe has highlighted the theoretical relevance of the distinction drawn among these three concepts. For him, widespread apathy and withdrawal from politics must be conceived as the normal *modus operandi* of current representative democracies, which at the same time also enjoy more than considerable levels of democratic support. Richard Gunther and José Ramón Montero's contribution in Chapter 3 stands out, in the sense that it is the only chapter to focus exclusively on the empirical distinction between political disaffection, political discontent, and democratic support. Their comparative analysis of a number of countries belonging to three different regions presents clear evidence that such attitudes are both conceptually and empirically distinct, forming three different attitudinal dimensions. Using some of the indicators proposed by the editors and incorporated into the Comparative National Election Project on which they base their study, Gunther and Montero have revealed the same latent structure of these three dimensions in the vast majority of their cases (Bulgaria, Chile, Greece, Hungary, Spain, and Uruguay). Although Mariano Torcal's chapter on political disaffection in new democracies has mainly focused on explaining its presence in a larger set of countries, his comparative analysis has enabled him to demonstrate the distinctive character of political disaffection vis-à-vis the other two concepts. While not actually focusing fully on this issue, the chapters by Ola Listhaug and Jan van Deth have also explicitly or implicitly referred to the different nature of some of these dimensions. In his empirical analysis of 14 European countries, van Deth has clearly found that political disaffection and political discontent need to be distinguished. As he concludes, 'feelings of political disaffection might be too far away from concepts like disloyalty and alienation to uncover real threats'. Neither has Listhaug, examining his single-case study of Norway, found any relationship between political disaffection and democratic support.

Moreover, the empirical evidence presented in these chapters confirms from still another perspective that contemporary democracies might not be in the middle of a 'legitimacy crisis' (Kaase and Newton 1995). But the data also point to the presence of an important and enduring number of 'disaffected democrats' or 'critical democrats', two convergent types of citizens characterized by an interplay of diffuse support for democratic ideals, on the one hand, and critical attitudes toward democratic practice, on the other (Klingemann 1999; Norris 1999a; Pharr and Putnam 2000; Torcal 2002c, 2003). We do not know much about who these citizens are and about their social profiles. But there is abundant empirical information about their changing relationships with the public sphere, their increasing critical assessments of key political institutions, and their more sceptical orientations toward political authorities. On the other hand, it is also true that the development of these aforementioned attitudes throughout new and old democracies does not apparently follow a clear trend. In fact, the chapters dealing directly or indirectly with the evolution of political disaffection point to the absence of distinctive trends. As van Deth states at the end of his chapter, 'it is clear that profound feelings of political disaffection are not widely spread among citizens of European democracies...'. In the same vein, Listhaug's longitudinal analysis of the Norwegian case suggests the existence more of cyclical processes of increasing and declining levels of political disaffection than positive, irreversible trends.

New democracies, however, present a different picture. In a substantial number of them, citizens' critical and disaffected attitudes toward the main elements of the democratic polity are still very prominent and have not experienced a significant change, even many years after the successful completion of the democratic transition. As Torcal has demonstrated, while political disaffection may not be a defining feature of third- and fourth-wave democracies, large numbers of disaffected citizens are definitively a permanent ingredient of the new political landscape.

Explaining political disaffection: culturalist versus rational-culturalist factors

The research concerned with the origins and evolution of political disaffection is fully linked to the theoretical discussion about the character of political attitudes being cultural (exogenous to the political system) or rational (endogenous to the political system). As we already stated in the introductory chapter, this debate is centred on two main paradigms for studying political attitudes: the traditional-culturalist and the rational-culturalist. The traditional-culturalist model contends that attitudes change slowly because they are rooted, so to speak, in the personality of citizens and therefore depend on long-term processes of socialization that reproduce them over time. Rational-culturalists, on the other hand, believe that, whatever their actual content, cultural attitudes can change quickly through rational adaptation and even adult learning, as a result of political or economic events, actual assessments, institutional performance, or different institutional settings (see Lane 1992; Whitefield and Evans 1999; Mishler and Rose 2001).

We have defended that cultural and rational arguments aiming to explain different levels of political disaffection may not necessarily be antithetical. In this volume we have taken these two arguments as complementary, rather than rival, explanations. Attitudes are more or less stable depending on their interaction with both long- and short-term factors, whose relative relevance is essentially an empirical question. Among the long-term factors, some contributors to this volume have reached novel conclusions about the effects of social trust and social connectedness on political disaffection; whereas others have been looking at cross-national political, and particularly institutional, factors to account for individual and cross-national variations in levels of political disaffection.

Social capital, social connectedness, and political disaffection

In searching for the factors that account for the evolution and different levels of disaffection, some chapters in this volume have paid particular attention to the role of social capital. Although their conclusions in this respect differ, they coincide in highlighting two important points. First, the relationship between social capital and political disaffection is not strong at the individual level, and more importantly, it is also not uniform among countries. Second, the effect of social trust and existing social networks on political disaffection basically depends on the interaction between political factors and these basic elements of social capital; in other words, the relationship between social capital and political disaffection is contingent upon the political context. In Chapter 6, for instance, Geoffrey Evans and Natalia Letki show that there is a positive relationship between social capital and disaffection in some Eastern and Central European countries: the more trusting the citizens, the fewer of them participate in politics or trust political institutions and politicians. They attribute this finding to the particular political context of these new democracies. In fact, social trust is higher precisely in those societies with a non-democratic past. And this is not a deterministic argument, since networks of social trust are developed to compensate for environments where, as Evans and Letki summarize, 'a government fails to provide adequately for its population, where cynicism with respect to the political system is prevalent, where the economy is in disarray ... In other words, the causal relation is exactly the opposite of that assumed in Putnam's theory of social capital and its effects on political systems ... [T]rust does not influence politics, politics influence trust'. More importantly, this relationship is not only reversed but it is also conditioned by long-term contextual factors that are, in the case of these countries, related to the nature of the former non-democratic regimes, which has exacerbated the dysfunctional nature of politics.

In Chapter 4, Kenneth Newton shows that the relationship between political disaffection and social trust is negative, albeit at the aggregate level, while no relationship is observed at the individual level.[1] Newton attributes the lack of relationship at the individual level to the fact that individual social trust is rooted in the social conditions of political life, while political disaffection is for him mainly a function of how well the political system is performing in general. But social capital is a social and collective property, not individual or personal. And both, therefore, depend on the political context, or to be more precise, on the nature of the democratic regime in place; on this point, Newton's findings coincide with Evans and Letki's. This is why the highest levels of social trust seem to be related to the lowest levels of political disaffection, as found in countries such as Norway, Finland, Sweden, and Denmark; and the lowest levels of social trust are found in countries such as Brazil, Peru, Colombia, Macedonia, and Venezuela, which of course display the highest levels of political disaffection. As Newton claims in his chapter, building a democracy with an effective and efficient government in those countries where social institutions are rather precarious, or where attitudes of social trust and cooperation are particularly weak and unevenly distributed, is a much more difficult task.

Alongside these contributions to the debate on social capital, van Deth attempts in Chapter 5 to measure the effect of membership in a series of associations and organizations on attitudes of political engagement. He concludes that this relationship is positive: membership in associations and organizations tends to be positively related to subjective political interest, with the exception of religious organizations. The relationship is however more ambiguous with political saliency and satisfaction with democracy. Furthermore, participation in voluntary associations has very few implications for the representation of interest, mainly because basic political orientations between members and non-members of most associations are almost indistinguishable. This should be considered good news for the consequences of social capital. The only exceptions are human rights associations and political parties, whose members tend to opt for more extreme positions. Therefore, not all organizations generate social capital, and hence, nor do they all have a positive impact on the attitudes of political disaffection. As van Deth emphasizes, and recalling Eliasoph's (1998) observations, 'face-to-face contact in clubs and organizations implies the avoidance of political topics and the "evaporation of politics" from public life'; but it does not produce negative attitudes toward politics. In these conditions, the 'dark side' of social capital hardly surfaces.

In summary, all of these contributions coincide on the fact that the relationship between social capital and political disaffection varies according to the political context and, moreover, interacts with political factors.[2] Once again, politics matter. And this reasoning directly connects with the approaches being defended by those who explicitly reject any variant of purely macro-sociological and/or cultural variables for explaining variations in political disaffection.[3]

The shaping role of politics and institutions

Among the factors explaining political disaffection, all the contributors have highlighted the decisive role of politics and institutions. With this common denominator, two different approaches exist. The first seeks to analyse the impact of specific short-term political events. In Chapter 9, Listhaug shows how his indicators of disaffection in Norway evolve through political parties' dealings with particular issues such as immigration, as well as with questions linked to the repeated absence of specific parties in government. In Chapter 8, Pedro Magalhães points to the same direction. As he convincingly demonstrates, institutional confidence in the parliament, one of the indicators of political disaffection, seems to be somewhat linked to short-term changes within Western European countries. Contrary to the alleged existence of a secular cross-national decline in civic attitudes that is repeatedly argued by the culturalists, Magalhães connects levels of disaffection with institutional performance and support for incumbent parties.

Thus, variations on political disaffection may depend on the democratic political process itself. Another essential element of this political process consists of the rules and procedures through which public affairs are being conducted. As Offe argues in Chapter 2, withdrawal from political life may simply be the result of a long-term process of accumulated frustrations with these rules and procedures. On the other hand, the impact of politics and institutions on disaffection is not confined to these certain political events taking place in the present. We believe it should also include the influence of political processes that have taken place in a more or less distant past. As Torcal discusses in Chapter 7, most studies of political disaffection focus on established democracies, and attempt to explain the origin and presence of attitudes toward politics in countries that have been enjoying democratic institutions for 50 years or more. Their citizens have thus accumulated a considerable *democratic experience.* But citizens in new democracies obviously have a much more recent and fragile experience with democracy, one that would enable them to assess the functioning, achievements, and performance of their newly established democratic institutions with only a limited temporal perspective. More importantly, their only baseline for evaluating the institutions and practices of political processes is often linked to pseudo- or anti-democratic experiences in their countries' recent past, to histories replete with irregular democratic memories, and/or to discourses directly attacking both the foundations and the components of democratic life. It is hardly surprising, therefore, that these previous political experiences have a negative influence on citizens' evaluations of the current democratic institutions, or on their confidence in them. Whereas citizens of most new democracies are continually influenced by these negative past references, in older democracies, by contrast, this baseline is usually not as salient and its socializing impact is much smaller. One remarkable exception is that of Italy, as Paolo Segatti shows in Chapter 10. As a second-wave democracy, the strength of a negative past seems to be also reflected in Italy today in the high levels of political disaffection among its citizens. The politics of the past has an accumulative impact on current attitudes toward politics and democracy, whether in a positive or a negative sense.

In line with this same argument, Magalhães has complemented his findings on short-term effects in explaining individual variations in confidence in the parliament with others emphasizing longer periods. For him, confidence stems from the belief that political institutions are expected to act positively to each and every citizen in a manner that is reasonably equal, fair, and just, and not act negatively in an arbitrary, harmful, or discriminatory manner. And this belief is mainly, for most institutions and in most countries, fostered by long-term and continuous operation of institutional rules that allow (or not) congruence between citizens' preferences and those of the rulers, as well as rulers' accountability before citizens. As Magalhães put it, institutional confidence becomes in this way 'an element of political culture that can be subsumed neither into the legitimacy afforded to the political regime as a whole nor into specific support for political actors and authorities ... [C]onfidence stems from citizens' expectations of whether or not institutions are likely to act in voters' interests, beliefs that are fostered by long-term ongoing operation of institutional rules...'.

In short, advocates of the rational-culturalist approach are on the right track when they state that politics and institutions play a crucial role in shaping political attitudes. But we additionally believe that politics, institutions, and memories of the past also matter. In fact, we do not see any inherent incompatibility between these two approaches. In both of them politics matter, in both political attitudes are malleable by political events, and both share the otherwise obvious premise that similar factors might cause differentiated effects according to somewhat different political pasts. Furthermore, the cluster of political attitudes for a distinctive set of citizens only really makes sense in the political context in which they have originated and developed collectively; in the end, culture is more than a mere aggregation of individual attitudes and beliefs. The coexistence of high levels of democratic support and political disaffection in some new democracies, for instance, only makes sense if we take into account the political context and circumstances in which these attitudes were formed. The much sought-after 'attitudinal coherence' of citizens lies in a country's political history and not, as it is often suggested, in its convergence with any ideal theoretical model of citizenship. This also means that there is no single model of political culture, nor is there any set of political attitudes that, by definition, better suits a particular democratic regime's stability and functioning.

Consequences of political disaffection

As it is also often stated, the nature of citizen–government relations in the more traditional democracies is currently undergoing a process of change. Among many other factors, it is allegedly the result of citizens' alienation from politics, their increasing mistrust of political institutions, governments, and leaders, and their devastating criticisms of political parties and other central components of political representation. All this is reported to entail beneficial consequences for the polity in terms of a significant increase in non-conventional participation as well as in greater political control of political authorities (see for example, Abramson 1983; Klingemann and Fuchs 1995b; Orren 1997; Blendon *et al.* 1997; Norris 1999d; and Putnam, Pharr, and Dalton 2000).

But some chapters in this volume are a bit more pessimistic about the consequences of political disaffection. For instance, Pippa Norris, Stefaan Walgrave, and Peter Van Aelst question in Chapter 11, based on data collected in Belgium with innovative survey techniques, whether political disaffection might be contributing to increased levels of accountability in political authorities or increased mobilization through motivating non-conventional political involvement. In fact, they empirically find, after comparing party members and civic joiners, that demonstrators are similar to the Belgian population and that there is little evidence that Belgian demonstrators are disaffected radicals. More specifically, Mariano Torcal and Ignacio Lago also empirically reveal in Chapter 12 that, in many new democracies in Southern Europe and the American Southern Cone, disaffection leads to widespread estrangement from politics and public affairs, and that this consequence deepens the breach between citizens and politicians still further. This same argument is implicitly addressed also by Evans and Letki when they analyse some of the indicators of participation.

These findings are difficult to exaggerate. Disaffection may increase the elitist (aristocratic) facets of many contemporary democracies (Manin 1997), particularly new democracies. As Gunther and Montero have demonstrated, political disaffection might be directly or indirectly conducive to a reinforcing combination of lack of information and involvement for the average voter. As Torcal and Lago have shown in their chapter, disaffected citizens are more likely to take short-cuts when voting, but at the same time they are the least informed about the issues and the parties' positions. Therefore, it is hardly surprising that, as they underline, democracies with the highest levels of political disaffection are also those with strikingly low levels of political accountability. As Offe concludes, political disaffection may affect the nature of the relationship between elites and citizens in a very negative way, as it creates 'space and opportunities that might be exploited by anti-liberal and/or anti-democratic political entrepreneurs and their populist projects'. While disaffected democrats might not challenge the democratic order, their un-information, un-involvement, and estrangement from the public sphere do have a lasting impact on the mechanisms of democratic accountability.

Notes

1 But see note 4 of Newton's chapter for some cautionary remarks based on different survey data and using different survey techniques, which apparently reveal a strong relationship between social trust and political confidence at the individual level.
2 For similar and complementary arguments, see, among others, Streeck (1992), della Porta (2000), King (2000), Newton and Norris (2000), Hardin (2002), and Farrell and Knight (2003).
3 See, for instance, Evans and Whitefield (1995), Whitefield and Evans (1999), and Katzenstein (2000).

References

Aardal, B. (1999) *Velgere i 90-årene.* Oslo: NKS-forlaget.

Aardal, B. and Valen, H. (1995) *Konflikt og opinion.* Oslo: NKS-forlaget.

Abramson, P. (1983) *Political Attitudes in America: Formation and Change.* San Francisco: W. H. Freeman.

Ackerman, B. and Fishkin, J. (2004) *Deliberation Day.* New Haven: Yale University Press.

Acock, A. *et al.* (1985) 'A New Model for Old Measures: A Covariance Structure Analysis of Political Efficacy', *Journal of Politics* 47 (4): 1062–1084.

Acock, A. and Clarke, H. (1990) 'Alternative Measures of Political Efficacy: Models and Means', *Quality and Quantity* 24: 87–105.

Alesina, A. and Wacziarg, R. (2000) 'The Economics of Civic Trust', in S. J. Pharr and R. D. Putnam (eds) *Disaffected Democracies: What's Troubling the Trilateral Countries.* Princeton, NJ: Princeton University Press.

Allport, G. W. (1961) *Pattern and Growth in Personality.* New York: Holt, Rinehart and Winston.

Almond, G. A. and Verba, S. (1963) *The Civic Culture. Political Attitudes and Democracy in Five Nations.* Princeton, NJ: Princeton University Press.

Althaus, S. (1998) 'Information Effects in Collective Preferences', *American Political Science Review* 92: 545–558.

Altman, D. and Pérez-Liñán, A. (2002) 'Assessing the Quality of Democracy: Freedom, Competitiveness and Participation in Eighteen Latin American Countries', *Democratization* 9 (2): 85–100.

Aminzade, R. *et al.* (2001) *Silence and Voice in the Study of Contentious Politics.* New York: Cambridge University Press.

An interview with Robert Putnam about America's collapsing civic life (1995) Available at: http://muse.jhu.edu/demo/journal_of_democracy/v006/putnam.interview.html, on line.

Anderson, C. J. (1995) *Blaming The Government: Citizens and The Economy in Five European Democracies.* New York: M.E. Sharpe.

—— (1998a) 'Parties, Party Systems and Satisfaction with Democratic Performance in the New Europe', in R. Hofferbert (ed.) *Parties and Democracy: Party Structure and Party Performance in Old and New Democracies.* Oxford: Blackwell.

—— (1998b) 'Political Satisfaction in Old and New Democracies', Institute for European Studies Working Paper 98.4. Ithaca: Cornell University.

Anderson, C. J. and Guillory, C. A. (1997) 'Political Institutions and Satisfaction with Democracy: A Cross-National Analysis of Consensus and Majoritarian Systems', *American Political Science Review* 91 (1): 66–88.

Anderson, C. J. and Lo Tempio, A. (2002) 'Winning, Losing, and Political Trust in America', *British Journal of Political Science* 32 (2): 335–351.

Anderson, C. J. and Tverdova, Y. V. (2003) 'Corruption, Political Allegiances, and Attitudes Toward Government in Contemporary Democracies', *American Journal of Political Science* 47 (1): 91–109.

Anderson, C. J. *et al.* (2004) *Losers' Consent: Elections and Democratic Legitimacy.* Oxford: Oxford University Press.

Arnold, D. (1990) *The Logic of Congressional Action.* New Haven, CT: Yale University Press.

Arrow, K. (1972) 'Gifts and Exchanges', *Philosophy and Public Affairs* 1 (Summer): 343–362.

Bacalhau, M. (1995) *Atitudes, Opiniones e Comportamientos Políticos dos Portugueses: 1973–1993.* Lisbon: FLAD.

Baier, A. (1986) 'Trust and antitrust', *Ethics* 96 (January): 231–260.

Banducci, S. A. *et al.* (1999) 'Proportional Representation and Attitudes about Politics: Results from New Zealand', *Electoral Studies* 18 (4): 533–555.

Banks, A. S. and Muller, T. C. (1995) *Political Handbook of the World: 1994–95. Government and Intergovernmental Organizations as of August 1, 1994.* New York: McGraw-Hill.

Barber, B. (1983) *The Logic and Limits of Trust.* New Brunswick, NJ: Rutgers University Press.

Bardi, L. and Pasquino, G. (1995) 'Politicizzati e alienati', in A. Parisi and H. Schadee (eds) *Sulla Soglia del Cambiamento.* Bologna: Il Mulino.

Barnes, S. H. and Kaase, M. (eds) (1979) *Political Action. Mass Participation in Five Western Democracies.* Beverly Hills, CA: Sage.

Barry, B. (1970) *Sociologists, Economists and Democracy.* London: Collier-Macmillan.

Bartels, L. M. (1996) 'Uninformed Votes: Information Effects in Presidential Elections', *American Journal of Political Science* 40: 194–230.

Beck, P. A. *et al.* (2002) 'The Social Calculus of Voting: Interpersonal, Media, and Organizational Influences on Presidential Choices', *American Political Science Review* 96: 57–73.

Beem, C. (1999) *The Necessity of Politics. Reclaiming American Public Life.* Chicago: Chicago University Press.

Beer, S. H. (1990) 'The British Legislature and the Problem of Mobilizing Consent', in P. Norton (ed.) *Legislatures.* Oxford: Oxford University Press.

Bellah, R. *et al.* (1985) *Habits of the Heart.* Berkeley: University of California Press.

Bennett, W. L. (1998) 'The Uncivic Culture: Communication, Identity and the Rise of Lifestyle Politics', *PS Political Science and Politics* 31: 741–761.

Berelson, B. R. *et al.* (1954) *Voting.* Chicago: University of Chicago Press.

Biorcio, R. and Mannheimer, R. (1995) 'Relationship between Citizenship and Political Parties', in H.-D. Klingemann and D. Fuchs (eds) *Citizens and the State.* Oxford: Oxford University Press.

Bjørklund, T. (1999) 'Public versus Private Sector: A New Division of Voting Behavior', in H. M. Narud and T. Aalberg (eds) *Challenges to Representative Democracy: Parties, Voters and Public Opinion.* Bergen: Fagbokforlaget.

Blendon, R. *et al.* (1997) 'Changing Attitudes in America', in J. Nye Jr. *et al.* (eds) *Why Americans Mistrust Government.* Cambridge: Harvard University Press.

Bohrnstedt, G. W. and Knoke, D. (1994) *Statistics for Social Data Analysis.* Itasca, Ill: F.E. Peacock Publishers.

Boix, C. and Posner, D. N. (1998) 'Social Capital: Explaining Its Origins and Effects on Governmental Performance', *British Journal of Political Science* 28: 686–693.

Bollen, K. (1993) 'Liberal Democracy: Validity and Method Factors in Cross-National Measures', *American Journal of Political Science* 37 (4): 1207–1230.

Brady, H. E. *et al.* (1995) 'Beyond SES: A Resource Model of Political Participation', *American Political Science Review* 89: 271–294.

Braithwaite, V. and Levi, M. (eds) (1998) *Trust and Governance*. New York: Russell Sage Foundation.

Brehm, J. and Rahn, W. (1997) 'Individual-Level Evidence for the Causes and Consequences of Social Capital', *American Journal of Political Science* 41 (3): 999–1023.

Bruneau, T. C. (1984a) 'Continuity and Change in Portuguese Politics: Ten Years After the Revolution of 25 April 1974', *West European Politics* 7: 72–83.

—— (1984b) 'Popular Support for Democracy in Postrevolutionary Portugal: Results from a Survey', in L. S. Graham and D. L. Wheeler (eds) in *Search of Modern Portugal. The Revolution and Its Consequences*. Madison: University of Wisconsin.

Bruneau, T. C. and Bacalhau, M. (1978) *Os Portugueses e a Política Quatro Anos Depois do 25 de Abril*. Lisbon: Meseta.

Bruneau, T. C. and Macleod, A. (1986) *Parties in Contemporary Portugal. Parties and the Consolidation of Democracy*. Boulder: Lynne Rienner.

Bruszt, L. (1998) 'The Politics of Patience: Support of Capitalism', in S. H. Barnes and J. Simon (eds) *The Postcommunist Citizen*. Budapest: Erasmus Foundation and Institute for Political Studies.

Campbell, A. *et al.* (1954) *The Voter Decides*. Evanston, Ill: Row Peterson.

—— (1960) *The American Voter*. New York: Cambridge University Press.

—— (1999) *Tuning In, Tuning Out Revisited: Proceedings of the 95th Annual Meeting of the American Political Science Association*. Atlanta.

Canache, G. *et al.* (2001) 'Meaning and Measurement in Cross-National Research on Satisfaction with Democracy', *Public Opinion Quarterly* 65: 506–528.

Cattell, R. B. (1965) *The Scientific Analysis of Personality*. Baltimore: Penguin Books.

Chabod, F. (1990) *Storia della Politica Estera Italiana dal 1870 al 1896*. Bari: Laterza.

Citrin, J. (1974) 'Comment: The Political Relevance of Trust in Government', *American Political Science Review* 68 (3): 973–988.

Citrin, J. *et al.* (1975) 'Personal and Political Sources of Political Alienation', *British Journal of Political Science* 5: 1–31.

Clarke, H. D. (1992) *Citizens and Community: Political Support in Representative Democracy*. Cambridge: Cambridge University Press.

Clarke, H. D. and Acock, A. C. (1989) 'National Elections and Political Attitudes: The Case of Political Efficacy', *British Journal of Political Science* 19 (3): 551–562.

Clarke, H. D. and Kornberg, A. (1989) 'Public Relations to Economic Performance and Political Support in Contemporary Liberal Democracies', in H. D. Clarke *et al.* (eds) *Economic Decline and Political Change: Canada, Great Britain, the United States*. Pittsburg: University of Pittsburg Press.

Clarke, H. D. *et al.* (1993) 'The Political Economy of Attitudes Toward Polity and Society in Western Democracies', *Journal of Politics* 55: 998–1021.

Coleman, J. S. (1988) 'Social Capital in the Creation of Human Capital', *American Journal of Sociology* 94: 95–120.

—— (1990) *Foundations of Social Theory*. Cambridge, Mass.: The Belknap Press of Harvard University Press.

Converse, P. E. (1964) 'The Nature of Belief System in Mass Publics', in D. E. Apter (ed.) *Ideology and Discontent.* New York: Free Press.

—— (1969) 'Of Time and Partisan Stability', *Comparative Political Studies* 2: 139–171.

Corbetta, P. and Parisi, A. M. L. (eds) (1997) *A domanda risponde. Il cambiamento di voto degli italliani nelle elezione del 1994 e 1996.* Bologna: Il Mulino.

Cotta, M. and Isernia, P. (1996) *Il Gigante dal Piede d'Argilla.* Bologna: Il Mulino.

Couto, R. A. and Guthrie, C. S. (1999) *Making Democracy Work Better. Mediating Structures, Social Capital, and the Democratic Prospect.* Chapel Hill: University of North Carolina Press.

Craig, S. C. (1993) *The Malevolent Leaders: Popular Discontent in America.* Boulder, CO: Westview Press.

Craig, S. C. and Maggioto, M. A. (1982) 'Measuring Political Efficacy', *Political Methodology* 8: 85–109.

Craig, S. C. and Wald, K. D. (1985) 'Whose Ox to Gore? A Comment on the Relationship Between Political Discontent and Political Violence', *The Western Political Quarterly* 30 (4): 625–662.

Crozier, M. *et al.* (1975) *The Crisis of Democracy: Report on the Governability of Democracies to the Trilateral Commission.* New York: New York University Press.

Curtis, J. E. *et al.* (1992) 'Voluntary Association Membership in Fifteen Countries: A Comparative Analysis', *American Sociological Review* 57 (2): 139–152.

Cusack, T. R. (1997) 'On the Road to Weimar? The Political Economy of Popular Satisfaction with Government and Regime Performance', *Germany Discussion Papers FSI 97-303.* Berlin: Wissenschaftszentrum fur Sozialforschung.

—— (1999) 'The Shaping of Popular Satisfaction with Government and Regime in Germany', *British Journal of Political Science* 29: 641–672.

Dahl, R. A. (1971) *Polyarchy.* New Haven: Yale University Press.

—— (1992) 'The Problem of Civic Competence', *Journal of Democracy* 3: 45–59.

Dalton, R. J. (1988) *Citizen Politics in Western Democracies. Public Opinion and Political Parties in the United States, Great Britain, West Germany, and France.* Chatham, NJ: Chatham House.

—— (1993) 'Citizens, Protest and Democracy' a special issue of *The Annals of Political and Social Sciences.*

—— (1996) 'Citizens and Democracy: Public Opinion and Political Parties', in *Advanced Western Democracies.* Chatham, NJ: Chatham House.

—— (1999) 'Political Support in Advanced Industrial Democracies', in P. Norris (ed.) *Critical Citizens: Global Support for Democratic Governance.* Oxford: Oxford University Press.

—— (2000a) 'Citizen Attitudes and Political Behavior', *Comparative Political Studies* 33 (6–7): 912–940.

—— (2000b) 'Value Change and Democracy', in S. J. Pharr and R. D. Putnam (eds) *Disaffected Democracies: What's Troubling the Trilateral Countries.* Princeton, NJ: Princeton University Press.

—— (2002) *Citizen Politics.* Chatham, NJ: Chatham House.

—— (2004) Democratic Challenges, Democratic Choices. The Erosion of Political Support in Advanced Industrial Democracies. Oxford: Oxford University Press.

Dalton, R. J. and Kuechler, M. (1990) *Challenging the Political Order. New Social and Political Movements in Western Democracies.* Cambridge: Polity Press.

Dalton, R. J. and Wattenberg, M. P. (1993) 'The Not So Simple Act of Voting', in

A. Finifter (ed.) *Political Science. The State of the Discipline II.* Washington, D.C.: American Political Science Association.

De Winter, L. *et al.* (1996) 'Comparing Similar Countries: Italy and Belgium', *Res Publica* 38: 215–235.

Delhey, J. and Newton, K. (2003) 'Who Trusts: The Origins of Social Trust in Seven Nations', *European Societies* 5 (2): 93–137.

della Porta, D. (1995) *Social Movements, Political Violence and the State. A Comparative Analysis of Italy and Germany.* Cambridge: Cambridge University Press.

—— (2000) 'Social Capital, Beliefs in Government, and Political Corruption', in S. Pharr and R. Putnam (eds) *Disaffected Democracies.* Princeton: Princeton University Press, pp. 202–228.

della Porta, D. and Diani, M. (1999) *Social Movements.* Oxford: Blackwell.

della Porta, D. and Reiter, H. (eds) (1998) *Policing Protest: The Control of Mass Demonstrations in Western Democracies.* Minneapolis: University of Minneapolis Press.

delli Carpini, M. X. and Keeter, S. (1991) 'Stability and Change in the US Public's Knowledge of Politics', *Public Opinion Quarterly* 55: 583–612.

Deutsch, K. W. (1961) 'Social Mobilization and Political Development', *American Political Science Review* 55: 493–514.

di Palma, G. (1970) *Apathy and Participation. Mass Politics in Western Societies.* New York: The Free Press.

Diamanti, I. and Mannheimer, R. (1994) *Milano a Roma.* Roma: Donzelli.

Diamanti, I. and Segatti, P. (1994) *Orgogliosi di essere italiani*, in *liMes*, 4: 15–36.

Diamond, L. (1999) *Developing Democracy: Toward Consolidation.* Baltimore: The Johns Hopkins University Press.

Díaz-Salazar, R. (1993) 'La Transición Religiosa en España', in R. Díaz-Salazar and S. Giner (eds) *Religión y Sociedad.* Madrid: Centro de Investigaciones Sociológicas.

Dimitras, P. E. (1987) 'Changes in Public Attitudes', in K. Featherstone and D. K. Katsoudas (eds) *Political Change in Greece: Before and After the Colonels.* London: Croom Helm.

Dogan, M. (1995) 'Testing the Concepts of Legitimacy and Trust', in H. E. Chehabi and A. Stepan (eds) *Politics, Society and Democracy: Comparative Studies. Essays in Honor of Juan J. Linz.* Boulder, CO: Westview Press.

—— (1997) 'Erosion of Confidence in Advanced Democracies', *Studies in Comparative International Development* 32: 3–29.

Döring, H. (1992) 'Higher Education and Confidence in Institutions: A Secondary Analysis of the "European Values Survey" 1981–83', *West European Politics* 15: 126–146.

—— (1995) 'Time as a Scarse Resource: Government Control of the Agenda', in H. Döring (ed.) *Parliaments and Majority Rule in Western Europe.* Frankfurt: Campus.

Downs, A. (1957) *An Economic Theory of Democracy.* New York: Harper and Row Publishers.

Duch, R. M. *et al* (2000) 'Heterogeneity in Perceptions of National Economic Conditions', *American Journal of Political Science* 44: 635–652.

Easton, D. (1965) *A Systems Analysis of Political Life.* Chicago: The University of Chicago Press.

—— (1975) 'A Re-Assessment of the Concept of Political Support', *British Journal of Political Science* 4: 435–457.

Eckstein, H. (1961) *A Theory of Stable Democracy*. Princeton: Princeton University Press.

—— (1988) 'A Culturalist Theory of Political Change', *American Political Science Review* 82: 789–804.

Edwards, B. and Foley, M. W. (2001) 'Civil Society and Social Capital: A Primer', in B. Edwards *et al.* (eds) *Beyond Tocqueville. Civil Society and the Social Capital Debate in Comparative Perspective*. Hanover, NH: University Press of New England.

Eliasoph, N. (1998) *Avoiding Politics. How Americans Produce Apathy in Everyday Life*. Cambridge: Cambridge University Press.

Elster, J. (1993) *Political Psychology*. Cambridge: Cambridge University Press.

—— (1994) 'Constitutional Courts and Central Banks: Suicide Prevention or Suicide Pact?', *East European Constitutional Review* 3: 66–78.

Erikson, E. H. (1950) *Childhood and Society*. New York: Norton.

Ester, P. *et al.* (eds) (1983) *The Individualizing Society. Value Change in Europe and North America*. Tilburg: Tilburg University Press.

Etzioni, A. (1971) *Demonstration Democracy*. New York: Gordon and Breach.

Eurobarometer Trends 1974–1993 (1994) Luxembourg: European Commission, EU Office for Official Publication.

Evans, G. (ed.) (1999) *The End of Class Politics? Class Voting in Comparative Context*. Oxford: Oxford University Press.

Evans, G. (2000) 'The Continued Significance of Class Voting', *Annual Review of Political Science* 3: 401–417.

Evans, G. and Heath, A. (1995) 'The Measurement of Left–right and Libertarian-authoritarian Values: A Comparison of Balanced and Unbalanced Scales', *Quality and Quantity* 29: 191–206.

Evans, G. and Whitefield, S. (1995) 'The Politics and Economics of Democratic Commitment: Support for Democracy in Transition Societies', *British Journal of Political Science* 25: 485–514.

Farah, B. G. *et al.* (1979) 'Political Dissatisfaction', in S. H. Barnes *et al. Political Action: Mass Participation in Five Western Democracies*. Beverly Hills, CA: Sage.

Farrell, H. and Knight, J. (2003) 'Trust, Institutions and Institutional Evolution: Industrial Districts and the Social Capital Hypothesis', *Politics and Society* 31 (4): 537–556.

Favre, P. *et al.* (1997) 'La fin d'une étrange lacune de la sociologie des mobilisations: l'étude par sondage des manifestants: fondaments théoriques et solutions techniques', *Revue Française de Science Politique* 47: 3–28.

Fillieule, O. (1997) *Strategies de la Rue. Les Manifestations en France*. Paris: Presses de la Fondation Nationale des Sciences Politiques.

Finkel, S. *et al.* (1989) 'Economic Crisis, Incumbent Performance and Regime Support: A Comparison of Longitudinal Data from West Germany and Costa Rica'. *British Journal of Political Science* 19: 329–351.

Fiorina, M. P. (1999) 'Extreme Voice: A Dark Side of Civic Engagement', in T. Skocpol and M. P. Fiorina (eds) *Civic Engagement in American Democracy*. Washington, D.C.: Brookings Institution Press.

Foley, M. W. and Edwards, B. (1996) 'The Paradox of Civil Society', *Journal of Democracy* 7: 38–52.

Foweraker, J. and Krznaric, R. (2000) 'Measuring Liberal Democratic Performance: An Empirical and Conceptual Critique', *Political Studies* 48: 759–787.

Franz, G. (1986) 'Economic Aspirations, Well-Being and Political Support in

Recession and Boom Periods: The Case of West Germany', *European Journal of Political Research* 14: 97–112.

Freedom House (1985, 1992–1993, and 1996) *Freedom in the World. The Annual Survey of Political Rights and Civil Liberties.* New York: The Freedom House.

Fuchs, D. and Klingemann, H.-D. (1995) 'Citizens and the State: A Changing Relationship', in H.-D. Klingemann and D. Fuchs (eds) *Citizens and the State.* Oxford: Oxford University Press.

Fuchs, D. and Roller, E. (1998) 'Cultural Conditions of Transition to Liberal Democracy in Central and Eastern Europe', in S. H. Barnes and J. Simon (eds) *The Postcommunist Citizen.* Budapest: Erasmus Foundation and Institute for Political Studies.

Fuchs, D. *et al.* (1995) 'Support for the Democratic System', in H.-D. Klingemann and D. Fuchs (eds) *Citizens and the State.* Oxford: Oxford University Press.

Fukuyama, F. (1995) *Trust: The Social Virtues and the Creation of Prosperity.* New York: Free Press.

—— (1999) *The Great Disruption. Human Nature and the Reconstruction of Social Order.* London: Profile Books.

Gabriel, O. W. (1995) 'Political Efficacy and Trust', in J. W. van Deth and E. Scarbrough (eds) *The Impact of Values.* Oxford: Oxford University Press.

Gabriel, O. W. and van Deth, J. W. (1995) 'Political Interest', in J. W. van Deth and E. Scarbrough (eds) *The Impact of Values.* Oxford: Oxford University Press.

Gallagher, M. (1991) 'Proportionality, disproportionality, and electoral systems', *Electoral Studies* 10 (1): 33–51.

Gambetta, D. (1988) *Trust: Making and Breaking Social Relations.* Oxford: Oxford University Press.

Gamson, W. A. (1968) *Power and Discontent.* Homewood, IL: The Dorsey Press.

Gibson, J. L. (2000) 'Changes in Russian Attitudes Toward Democratic and Economic Reform: Results from a 1996–2000 Panel Survey'. Paper presented at the Annual Meeting of the American Political Science Association. Washington, D.C.

—— (2001) 'Social Networks, Civil Society, and the Prospects for Consolidating Russia's Democratic Transition', *American Journal of Political Science* 45: 51–68.

Giddens, A. (1990) *The Consequences of Modernity.* Cambridge: Polity Press.

Gleditsch, N. P. and Hellevik, O. (1977) *Kampen om EF.* Oslo: Pax.

Greeley, A. (2001) 'Coleman Revisited: Religious Structures as a Source of Social Capital', in B. Edwards *et al.* (eds) *Beyond Tocqueville. Civil Society and the Social Capital Debate in Comparative Perspective.* NH: University Press of New England.

Gunther, R. and Montero, J. R. (2000) *Political Legitimacy in New Democracies.* Studies in Public Policy Number 341. Glasgow: Centre for the Study of Public Policy, University of Strathclyde.

Gunther, R. and Mughan, A. (2000) *Democracy and the Media: A Comparative Perspective.* Cambridge: Cambridge University Press.

Gunther, R. *et al.* (2003) 'Democracy and Intermediation: Some Attitudinal and Behavioral Dimensions'. Presented at the Comparative National Election Project II Conference, 4–7 September 2003. Columbus, OH.

Gunther, R. *et al.* (forthcoming) 'Democracy and Intermediation: Some Attitudinal and Behavioral Dimensions', in R. Gunther *et al.* (eds) *Political Intermediation in Old and New Democracies: Eastern Europe, Latin America, Southern Europe, and Asia in a Comparative Perspective.*

Gurr, T. R. (1970) *Why Men Rebel.* Princeton, NJ: Princeton University Press.

Habermas, J. (1985) *Legitimation Crisis.* Boston: Beacon Press.

Hall, P. A. (1999) 'Social Capital in Britain', *British Journal of Political Science* 29: 417–461.

Hall, P. A. and Taylor, R. C. (1996) 'Political Science and the Three New Institutionalisms', *Political Studies* 44: 936–957.

Hardin, R. (1991) 'Trusting Persons, Trusting Institutions', in R. J. Zeckhauser (ed.) *The Strategy of Choice.* Cambridge, Mass.: MIT Press.

—— (1993) 'The Street-Level Epistemology of Trust', *Politics and Society* 21 (December): 505–529.

—— (1996) 'Trustworthiness', *Ethics* 107 (October): 26–42.

—— (1998) 'Trust in Government', in V. Braithwaite and M. Levi (eds) *Trust and Governance.* New York: Russell Sage, pp. 9–27.

—— (1999) 'Do We Want Trust in Government?', in M. E. Warren (ed.) *Democracy and Trust.* Cambridge: Cambridge University Press, pp. 22–41.

—— (2000) 'The Public Trust', in S. J. Pharr and R. D. Putnam (eds) *Disaffected Democracies: What's Troubling the Trilateral Democracies.* Princeton: Princeton University Press, pp. 31–51.

—— (2002) *Trust and Trustworthiness.* New York: Russell Sage Foundation.

Haug, S. (1997) *Soziales Kapital. Ein kritischer Überblick über den aktuellen Forschungsstand.* Mannheim: Mannheimer Zentrum für Europäische Sozialforschung. Working paper 15.

Heath, A. F. *et al.* (1994) 'The Measurement of Core Beliefs and Values: The Development of Balanced Socialist/Laissez-Faire and Libertarian/Authoritarian Scales', *British Journal of Political Science* 24: 115–132.

Hedström, P. and Swedberg, R. (1998) 'Social Mechanisms. An Introductory Essay', in P. Hedström and R. Swedberg (eds) *Social Mechanisms. An Analytical Approach to Social Theory.* Cambridge: Cambridge University Press.

Hellman, J. S. (1998) 'Winners Take All: The Politics of Partial Reform in Postcommunist Transitions', *World Politics* 50: 203–234.

Hertz, J. (1978) 'Legitimacy: Can We Retrieve it?' *Comparative Politics* 10: 317–343.

Hetherington, M. J. (1996) 'The Media's Role in Forming Voters' Retrospective Economic Evaluations in 1992', *American Journal of Political Science* 40: 372–395.

—— (1998) 'The Political Relevance of Political Trust', *American Political Science Review* 92 (4): 791–808.

Heywood, P. M. (2002) 'Political Corruption, Democracy and Governance in Spain'. Paper presented at the Annual Meeting of the American Political Science Association, 29 August to 1 September 2002. Boston.

Hibbing, J. R. and Theiss-Morse, E. (1995) *Congress as a Public Enemy: Public Attitudes Toward American Political Institutions.* New York: Cambridge University Press.

Hofferbert, R. I. and Klingemann, H.-D. (1999) 'Remembering the Bad Old Days: Human Rights, Economic Conditions, and Democratic Performance in Transitional Regimes', *European Journal of Political Research* 36: 155–174.

—— (2001) 'Democracy and its Discontents in Post-Wall Germany', *International Political Science Review* 22: 363–378.

Holmberg, S. (1996) 'Policy Congruence Compared', in W. Miller *et al.* (eds) *Political Representation in Western Democracies.* Ann Arbor: University of Michigan Press.

—— (1999) 'Down and Down We Go: Political Trust in Sweden', in P. Norris (ed.) *Critical Citizens: Global Support for Democratic Governance.* Oxford: Oxford University Press, pp. 103–122.

Holmes, S. (1995) 'Constitutionalism', in S. M. Lipset (ed.) *The Encyclopaedia of Democracy*. London: Routledge.

Hooghe, M. (1999) 'Voluntary Associations and Social Capital. An Empirical, Survey-Based Test of the Putnam Hypothesis'. Paper presented at the Annual Meeting of the American Political Science Association, 2–5 September 1999. Atlanta.

Huber, J. D. and Powell Jr., G. B. (1996) 'Congruence between Citizens and Policy-makers in Two Visions of Liberal Democracy', *World Politics* 49 (3): 291–326.

Huckfeldt, R. (2001) 'The Social Communication of Political Expertise', *American Journal of Political Science* 45: 425–438.

Human Development Report (1999) New York: Oxford University Press.

Human Development Report (2000) New York: Oxford University Press.

Hunneus, C. and Maldonado, L. (2003) 'Demócratas y nostálgicos. Los apoyos a la democracia en Chile', *Revista Española de Investigaciones Sociológicas* 103: 9–49.

Huntington, S. P. (1968) *Political Order in Changing Societies*. New Haven: Yale University Press.

—— (1991) *The Third Wave. Democratization in the Late Twentieth Century*. Norman: University of Oklahoma Press.

Huseby, B. (2000) *Government Performance and Political Support*. Dr. polit.-dissertation in political science. Trondheim: The Norwegian University of Science and Technology.

Inglehart, R. (1977) *The Silent Revolution: Changing Values and Political Styles among Western Publics*. Princeton, NJ: Princeton University Press.

—— (1990) *Culture Shift in Advanced Industrial Society*. Princeton: Princeton University Press.

—— (1997a) 'Postmaterialist Values and the Erosion of Institutional Authority', in J. S. Nye, Jr., P. D. Zelikow, and D. C. King (eds) *Why People Don't Trust Government*. Cambridge, MA: Harvard University Press.

—— (1997b) *Modernization and Postmodernization: Cultural, Economic and Political Change in 43 Societies*. Princeton: Princeton University Press.

—— (1999a) 'Postmodernization Erodes Respect for Authority, but Increases Support for Democracy', in P. Norris (ed.) *Critical Citizens: Global Support for Democratic Governance*. Oxford: Oxford University Press.

—— (1999b) 'Trust, Well-Being and Democracy', in M. E. Warren (ed.) *Democracy and Trust*. Cambridge: Cambridge University Press, pp. 88–120.

Inglehart, R. and Norris, P. (2003) *Rising Tide: Gender Equality and Cultural Change Around the World*. New York: Cambridge University Press.

ITANES (2001) *Perché ha Vinto il Centro-Destra?* Bologna: Il Mulino.

Iyengar, S. and Kinder, D. R. (1987) *News That Matters: Television and American Opinion*. Chicago: University of Chicago Press.

Jackman, R. W. and Miller, R. A. (1996a) 'A Renaissance of Political Culture?', *American Journal of Political Science* 40 (3): 632–659.

—— (1996b) 'The Poverty of Political Culture?', *American Journal of Political Science* 40 (3): 697–716.

—— (1998) 'Social Capital and Politics', *Annual Review of Political Science* 1: 47–73.

Jagodzinski, W. and Manabe, K. (2004) 'How to Measure Interpersonal Trust? A Comparison of Two Different Measures', *ZA-Information* 55: 85–97.

Jenssen, A. T. (1999) 'All That is Solid Melts into Air: Party Identification in Norway', *Scandinavian Political Studies* 22: 1–27.

Jenssen, A. *et al.* (eds) (1998) *To Join or Not to Join?* Oslo: Universitetsforlaget.

Jones, B. D. (2001) *Politics and the Architecture of Choice. Bounded Rationality and Governance.* Chicago: University of Chicago Press.

Kaase, M. (1988) 'Political Alienation and Protest', in M. Dogan (ed.) *Comparing Pluralist Democracies: Strains on Legitimacy.* Boulder: Westview Press.

—— (1999) 'Interpersonal Trust, Political Trust and Non-institutionalised Political Participation in Western Europe', *West European Politics* 22 (3): 1–23.

Kaase, M. and Marsh, A. (1979) 'Measuring Political Action', in S. H. Barnes *et al.* (eds) *Political Action. Mass Participation in Five Western Democracies.* Beverly Hills, CA: Sage.

Kaase, M. and Newton, K. (1995) *Beliefs in Government.* Oxford: Oxford University Press.

Kaldor, M. (2000) ' "Civilising" globalisation? The Implications of the "Battle in Seattle" ', *Millennium Journal of International Studies* 29 (1): 105–121.

Katzenstein, P. (2000) 'Confidence, Trust, International Relations, and Lessons from Smaller Democracies', in S. J. Pharr and R. D. Putnam (eds) *Disaffected Democracies: What's Troubling the Trilateral Countries.* Princeton, NJ: Princeton University Press.

Kavanagh, D. (1997) 'Crisis of confidence: the case of Britain'. *Studies in Comparative International Development* 32 (3): 30–41.

Keane, J. (1998) *Civil Society: Old Images, New Visions.* Cambridge: Polity Press.

Kiewiet, R. and McCubbins, M. (1991) *The Logic of Delegation: Congressional Parties and the Appropriation Process.* Chicago: University of Chicago Press.

Kinder, D. R (1998) 'Communication and Opinion', *Annual Review of Political Science* 1: 167–197.

King, A. (2000) 'Distrust of Government: Explaining American Exceptionalism', in S. J. Pharr and R. D. Putnam (eds) *Disaffected Democracies: What's Troubling the Trilateral Countries?* Princeton: Princeton University Press.

Klandermans, B. (1995) *The Social Psychology of Protest.* Oxford: Blackwell.

Klingemann, H.-D. (1999) 'Mapping Political Support in the 1990s: A Global Analysis', in P. Norris (ed.) *Critical Citizens: Global Support for Democratic Governance.* Oxford: Oxford University Press.

Klingemann, H.-D. and Fuchs, D. (1990) 'The Left–Right Schema', in M. K. Jennings *et al.* (eds) *Continuities in Political Action. A Longitudinal Study of Political Orientations in Three Western Democracies.* Berlin: Walter de Gruyter.

—— (eds) (1995a) *Citizens and the State.* Oxford: Oxford University Press.

—— (1995b) 'Citizens and the State: A Changing Relationship?', in H.-D. Klingemann and D. Fuchs (eds) *Citizens and the State.* Oxford: Oxford University Press.

Knack, S. and Keefer, P. (1997) 'Does Social Capital Have an Economic Payoff? A Cross-Country Investigation', *The Quarterly Journal of Economics* 62: 1251–1288.

Knutsen, O. (1986) 'Offentlige Ansatte: Mulige årsaker til Partipolitisk Særpreg', *Norsk Statsvitenskapelig Tidsskrift* 4 (2): 21–44.

Koole, R. and Katz, R. S. (eds) (2000) 'Political Data in 1999', special issue of the *European Journal of Political Research* 38 (7).

Koopman, R. (1996) 'New Social Movements and Changes in Political Participation in Western Europe', *West European Politics* 19 (1): 28–50.

Kornberg, A. and Clarke, H. D. (1992) *Citizens and Community: Political Support in a Representative Democracy.* Cambridge: Cambridge University Press.

Kotowitz, Y. (1987) 'Moral Hazard', in P. Newman *et al.* (eds) *The New Palgrave: A Dictionary of Economics.* London: Macmillan.

Kriesi, H. *et al.* (eds) (1995) *New Social Movements in Western Europe: A Comparative Analysis.* MN: University of Minnesota Press.

Kriesi, H. *et al.* (eds) (1998) *Social Movements in a Globalizing World.* London: Macmillan.

Kuklinski, J. S. *et al.* (2001) 'The Political Environment and Citizen Competence', *American Journal of Political Science* 45: 410–424.

La Due Lake, R. and Huckfeldt, R. (1998) 'Social Capital, Social Networks, and Political Participation', *Political Psychology* 19: 567–584.

La Palombara, J. (1965) 'Italy, Fragmentation, Isolation and Alienation', in G. A. Almond and L. W. Pye (eds) *Political Culture and Political Development.* Princeton: Princeton University Press.

—— (1987) *A Democracy Italian Style.* New Haven: Yale University Press.

Laakso, M. and Taagapera, R. (1979) 'Effective Number of Parties: A Measure with Application to West Europe', *Comparative Political Studies* 12: 3–27.

Lagos, M. (1997) 'Latin America's Smiling Mask', *Journal of Democracy* 8: 125–135.

—— (2003) 'Support for and Satisfaction with Democracy', *International Journal of Public Opinion Research* 15 (4): 471–487.

Laitin, D. (1988) 'Political Culture and Political Preferences', *American Political Science Review* 82: 589–593.

Lane, R. E. (1959a) *Political Life.* New York: Free Press.

—— (1959b) *Why and How People Get Involved in Politics.* New York: The Free Press.

Lane, R. (1992) 'Political Culture. Residual Category or General Theory?', *Comparative Political Studies* 25: 362–387.

Latinobarometer (1995) *Latinobarómetro. Opinión pública latinoamericana,* Santiago de Chile: Corporación Latinobarómetro.

Latinobarometer (1996) *Latinobarómetro. Opinión pública latinoamericana,* Santiago de Chile: Corporación Latinobarómetro.

Latinobarometer (2002) *Latinobarómetro. Opinión pública latinoamericana,* Santiago de Chile: Corporación Latinobarómetro.

Lazarsfeld, P. *et al.* (1994) *The People's Choice.* New York: Cambridge University Press.

Le Bon, G. (1895) *Psychologie des foules.* Paris.

Ledeneva, A. V. (1998) *Russia's Economy of Favours: Blat, Networking and Informal Exchange.* New York: Cambridge University Press.

Lerner, D. (1958) *The Passing of Traditional Society: Modernizing the Middle East.* Glencoe: Free Press.

Letki, N. (2005) 'Socialization for Participation? Trust, Membership and Democratization in East-Central Europe', *Political Research Quarterly* 57 (4): 665–679.

Letki, N. and Evans, G. (2005) 'Endogenizing Social Trust: Democratization in East-Central Europe', *British Journal of Political Science* 35: 515–529.

Levi, M. (1993) 'Making Democracy Work: A Review', *Comparative Political Studies* 26 (3): 375–379.

—— (1996) 'Social and Unsocial Capital: a Review Essay of Robert Putnam's Making Democracy Work', *Politics and Society* 24: 45–55.

Levi, M. and Stoker, L. (2000) 'Political Trust and Trustworthiness', *Annual Review of Political Science* 3: 475–508.

Lijphart, A. (1989) 'The Structure of Inference', in G. Almond and S. Verba (eds) *The Civic Culture Revisited,* 2nd edn. Newbury Park: Sage.

—— (1999) *Patterns of Democracy: Government Forms and Performance in Thirty-Six Countries.* New Haven, CT: Yale University Press.

Linde, J. and Ekman, J. (2003) 'Satisfaction With Democracy: A Note on a Frequently Used Indicator in Comparative Politics', *European Journal of Political Research* 42 (3): 391–408.

Linz, J. J. (1978) 'Crisis, Breakdown and Reequilibration', in J. J. Linz and A. Stepan (eds) *The Breakdown of Democratic Regimes*. Baltimore: Johns Hopkins University Press.

—— (1988) 'Legitimacy of Democracy and the Socioeconomic System', in M. Dogan (ed.) *Comparing Pluralist Democracies*. Boulder: Westview Press.

—— (1999) 'Some Thoughts on Democracy and Public Opinion Research'. Manuscript.

—— (2002) 'Parties in Contemporary Democracies: Problems and Paradoxes', Manuscript.

Linz, J. J. and Stepan, A. (1996) *Problems of Democratic Transition and Consolidation: Southern Europe, South America, and Post-Communist Europe*. Baltimore: Johns Hopkins University Press.

Lipset, S. M. (1959) 'Some Social Requisites of Democracy: Economic Development and Political Development', *American Political Science Review* 53: 69–105.

—— (1994) 'The Social Requisites of Democracy Revisited', *American Sociological Review* 59 (1): 1–22.

Lipset, S. M. and Schneider, W. (1983) *The Confidence Gap: Business, Labor and Governments in the Public Mind*. New York: Free Press.

Listhaug, O. (1989) *Citizens, Parties and Norwegian Electoral Politics 1957–1985: An Empirical Study*. Trondheim: Tapir.

—— (1995) 'The Dynamics of Trust in Politicians', in H.-D. Klingemann and D. Fuchs (eds) *Citizens and the State*. Oxford: Oxford University Press.

—— (1997a) 'The Decline of Class Voting', in K. Strøm and L. Svåsand (eds) *Challenges to Political Parties: The Case of Norway*. Ann Arbor: University of Michigan Press.

—— (1997b) Confidence in Political Institutions: Norway 1982–1996. Paper presented at Harvard University, 13–14 November 1997.

Listhaug, O. and Grønflaten, L. (2002) Trends in Political Involvement and Activism in Norway. Conference on *Rethinking Democracy in Scotland and Scandinavia*, 24–25 May 2002. Aberdeen: Ardoe House Hotel.

Listhaug, O. and Wiberg, M. (1995) 'Confidence in Political and Private Institutions', in H.-D. Klingemann and D. Fuchs (eds) *Citizens and the State*. Oxford: Oxford University Press, pp. 298–322.

Loewenberg, G. (1971) 'The Influence of Parliamentary Behavior on Regime Stability', *Comparative Politics* 3: 170–195.

Long, S. J. (1997) *Regression Models for Categorical and Limited Dependent Variables*. Thousands Oaks: Sage.

Luhmann, N. (1979) *Trust and Power*. Chichester: John Wiley & Sons.

Lupia, A. (1992) 'Busy Voters, Agenda Control and the Power of Information', *American Political Science Review* 86: 390–404.

—— (2000) 'Institutions as Informational Crutches: Experimental Evidence from Laboratory and Field'. Presented at the annual meeting of the Midwest Political Science Association, 30 March to 2 April 2000. Chicago, IL.

—— (2001) 'Delegation of Power (Agency Theory)', in N. J. Smelser and P. B. Baltes (eds) *International Encyclopedia of the Social and Behavioral Sciences*. Oxford: Pergamon.

—— (2002) 'Who Can Persuade Whom? Implications from the Nexus of Psychology and Rational Choice Theory', in J. H. Kuklinski (ed.) *Thinking about Political Psychology.* New York: Cambridge University Press.

Lupia, A. and McCubbins, M. D. (1998) *The Democratic Dilemma. Can Citizens Learn What They Need To Know?* New York: Cambridge University Press.

Luskin, R. C. (1987) 'Measuring Political Sophistication', *American Journal of Political Science* 31: 856–899.

McAdam, D. (1988) 'Micromobilisation Contexts and the Recruitment to Activism', in B. Klandermans *et al.* (eds) *From Structure to Action.* Greenwich, CT: JAI-Press, pp. 125–154.

McAdam, D. *et al.* (eds) (1996) *Comparative Perspectives on Social Movements.* New York: Cambridge University Press.

McAllister, I. (1999) 'The Economic Performance of Governments', in P. Norris (ed.) *Critical Citizens: Global Support for Democratic Governance.* Oxford: Oxford University Press.

Magalhães, P. C. (2005) 'Disaffected Democrats: Political Attitudes and Political Action in Portugal', *West European Politics* 28: 973–991.

Maier, C. S. (1994) 'Democracy and its Discontents', *Foreign Affairs* (July/August): 48–64.

Mainwaring, S. (1999) 'Democratic Survivability in Latin America', in H. Handelman and M. Tessler (eds) *Democracy and Its Limits.* Notre Dame, IN: Notre Dame University Press.

Mainwaring, S. and Pérez-Liñán, A. (2000) 'Modernization and Democracy in Latin America'. Unpublished manuscript, Kellogg Institute for International Studies, University of Notre Dame.

Mair, P. (2001) 'Party Membership in Twenty European Democracies 1980–2000', *Party Politics* 7 (1): 5–22.

Majone, G. (1999) 'The Regulatory State and Its Legitimacy Problems', *West European Politics* 22 (1): 1–24.

Maletz, D. J. (2005) 'Tocqueville on Mores and the Preservation of Republics', *American Journal of Political Science* 49 (1): 1–15.

Manin, B. (1997) *The Principles of Representative Government.* Cambridge: Cambridge University Press.

Manin, B. *et al.* (1999) 'Elections and Representation', in A. Przeworski *et al.* (eds) *Democracy, Accountability, and Representation.* Cambridge: Cambridge University Press.

Maravall, J. M. (1984) *La Política de la Transición.* Madrid: Taurus.

—— (1997) *Regimes, Politics and Markets: Democratization and Economic Change in Southern and Eastern Europe.* Oxford: Oxford University Press.

Marsh, A. (1977) *Protest and Political Consciousness.* Beverly Hill, CA: Sage.

—— (1991) *Political Action in Europe and USA.* London: Macmillan.

Marsh, A. and Kaase, M. (1979) 'Background of Political Action', in S. H. Barnes *et al* (eds) *Political Action: Mass Participation in Five Western Democracies.* Beverly Hills, CA: Sage.

Martín, I. (2000) 'Political Interest in Eastern and Western Europe', Unpublished manuscript.

Martin, J. *et al.* (1993) 'Development of a Short Quiz to Measure Political Knowledge', in *CREST* Working Paper No. 21.

Mason, W. *et al.* (1985) 'On the Dimensions of Political Alienation in America', in N. Tuma (ed.) *Sociological Methodology.* San Francisco: Jossey-Bass, pp. 111–151.

Mastropaolo, A. (2000) *Antipolitica. All'origine della Crisi Italiana.* Napoli: L'Ancora.

Melich, A. (1999) *Eurobarometer 51.0: The Elderly and Domestic Violence, March–May 1999* [Computer file]. Brussels: INRA (Europe).

Melucci, A. (1996) *Challenging Codes: Collective Action in the Information Age.* Cambridge: Cambridge University Press.

Mendrinou, M. and Nicolacopoulos, I. (1997) 'Interests, Parties and Discontent in the Public Mind: Sympathy Scores for Greek Parties and Interest Groups'. Paper presented for the European Consortium for Political Research (ECPR) Congress. Berne, Switzerland.

Merkl, P. H. (1988) 'Comparing Legitimacy and Values Among Advanced Democratic Countries', in M. Dogan (ed.) *Comparing Pluralist Democracies.* Boulder, CO: Westview Press.

Meseguer, C. (1998) 'Sentimientos antipartidistas en el Cono Sur: un estudio exploratorio', *Latinoamérica Hoy* 18 (March): 99–111.

Milbrath, L. (1977) *Political Participation. How and Why Do People Get Involved in Politics?* 2nd edn. Chicago: Rand McNally.

Milbrath, L. and Goel, M. L. (1977) *Political Participation.* Chicago: Rand McNally.

Miller, A. H. (1974) 'Political Issues and Trust in Government: 1964–1970', *American Political Science Review* 68: 951–972.

Miller, A. H. and Listhaug, O. (1990) 'Political Parties and Confidence in Government: A Comparison of Norway, Sweden and the United States', *British Journal of Political Science* 20: 357–386.

—— (1993) 'Ideology and Political Alienation', *Scandinavian Political Studies* 16: 167–192.

—— (1998) 'Policy Preferences and Political Trust: A Comparison of Norway, Sweden and the United States', *Scandinavian Political Studies* 21: 161–187.

—— (1999) 'Political Performance and Institutional Trust', in P. Norris (ed.) *Critical Citizens: Global Support for Democratic Governance.* Oxford: Oxford University Press.

Miller, W. E. *et al.* (1980) *American National Election Studies Data Sourcebook 1952–1978.* Cambridge, Mass.: Harvard University Press.

Mishler, W. E. and Rose, R. (1994) 'Support for Parliaments and Regimes in the Transition Toward Democracy in Eastern Europe', *Legislative Studies Quarterly* 19 (1): 5–33.

—— (1996) 'Trajectories of Fear and Hope: Support for Democracy in Post-Communist Europe', *Comparative Political Studies* 28 (4): 553–581.

—— (1997) 'Trust, Distrust, and Skepticism: Popular Evaluations of Civil and Political Institutions in Post-Communist Societies', *Journal of Politics* 59 (2): 418–451.

—— (1999) 'Five Years After the Fall: Trajectories of Support for Democracy in Post-Communist Europe', in P. Norris (ed.) *Critical Citizens: Global Support for Democratic Governance.* Oxford: Oxford University Press.

—— (2001) 'What Are the Origins of Political Trust? Testing Institutional and Cultural Theories in Post-Communist Societies', *Comparative Political Studies* 34 (1): 30–62.

Misztal, B. A. (1996) *Trust in Modern Societies.* Oxford: Blackwell.

Montero, J. R. (1994) 'Religiosidad y voto en España', *Revista de Estudios Políticos* 83: 77–111.

Montero, J. R. and Gunther, R. (1994) 'Sistemas "Cerrados" y Listas "Abiertas": Sobre Algunas Propuestas de Reforma del Sistema Electoral en España', in J. R.

Montero *et al.* (eds) *La reforma del Sistema Electoral Español.* Madrid: Cuadernos del Centro de Estudios Constitucionales.

Montero, J. R. and Torcal, M. (1990) 'Voters and Citizens in a New Democracy: Some Trend Data on Political Attitudes in Spain', *International Journal of Public Opinion Research* 2: 116–140.

Montero, J. R. and Torcal, M. (1992) 'Patterns of Political Participation', in A. Almarcha (ed.) *Spain and EC Membership Evaluated.* London: Printer Publishers Ltd.

Montero, J. R. *et al.* (1997a) *Democracy in Spain: Legitimacy, Discontent, and Disaffection.* Madrid: Instituto Juan March, Working Paper 100.

Montero, J. R. *et al.* (1997b) 'Democracy in Spain: Legitimacy, Discontent, and Dissatisfaction', *Studies in Comparative International Development* 32 (3): 124–160.

Morales, L. (2001) 'Associational Membership and Social Capital in Comparative Perspective: The Problems of Measurement'. Annual Meeting of the American Political Science Association, 30 August to 2 September 2001. San Francisco, CA.

—— (2004) 'Institutions, Mobilization, and Political Participation: Political Membership in Western Countries'. Madrid: Instituto Juan March, PhD dissertation.

Morales, L. and Geurts, P. (forthcoming) 'Associational Involvement', in J. van Deth *et al.* (eds) *Citizenship and Involvement in Europe.*

Morán, M. L. and Benedicto, J. (1995) *La Cultura Política de los Españoles. Un Ensayo de Reinterpretación.* Madrid: Centro de Investigaciones Sociológicas.

Morlino, L. (1991) 'La Relazione Tra Gruppi e Partiti', in Id. (ed.) *Costruire la Democrazia, Gruppi e Partiti in Italia.* Bologna: Il Mulino.

—— (1998) *Democracy Between Consolidation and Crisis: Parties, Groups and Citizens in Southern Europe.* Oxford: Oxford University Press.

Morlino, L. and Montero, J. R. (1995) 'Legitimacy and Democracy in Southern Europe', in R. Gunther *et al.* (eds) *The Politics of Democratic Consolidation: Southern Europe in Comparative Perspective.* Baltimore: The Johns Hopkins University Press.

Morlino, L. and Tarchi, M. (1996) 'The Dissatisfied Society: The Roots of Political Change in Italy', *European Journal of Political Research* 30: 41–63.

Muller, E. N. and Jukam, T. O. (1977) 'On the Meaning of Political Support', *American Political Science Review* 71: 1561–1595.

Muller, E. N. and Seligson, M. A. (1994) 'Civic Culture and Democracy: The Question of Causal Relationships', *American Political Science Review* 88: 635–652.

Nadeau, R. *et al.* (2000) 'Elections and Satisfaction with Democracy'. Paper presented at the Annual Meeting of the American Political Science Association. Washington, D.C.

Need, A. and Evans, G. (2001) 'Analyzing patterns of religious participation in post-communist Eastern Europe', *British Journal of Sociology* 52 (2): 229–248.

Neuman, W. R. (1986) *The Paradox of Mass Politics: Knowledge and Opinion in the American Electorate.* Cambridge MA: Harvard University Press.

Newton, K. (1997) 'Social Capital and Democracy', *American Behavioral Scientist* 40: 575–586.

—— (1999a) 'Social Capital and Democracy in Modern Europe', in J. van Deth *et al.* (eds) *Social Capital and European Democracy.* London: Routledge, pp. 3–24.

—— (1999b) 'Social and Political Trust in Established Democracies', in P. Norris (ed.) *Critical Citizens: Global Support for Democratic Governance.* Oxford: Oxford University Press, pp. 169–187.

—— (2001) 'Trust, Social Capital, Civil Society, and Democracy', *International Political Science Review* 22 (2): 201–214.

Newton, K. and Norris, P. (2000) 'Confidence in Public Institutions: Faith, Culture, or Performance', in S. J. Pharr and R. D. Putnam (eds) *Disaffected Democracies: What's Troubling the Trilateral Countries.* Princeton, NJ: Princeton University Press.

Nie, N. H. and Andersen, K. (1974) 'Mass Belief Systems Revisited: Political Change and Attitude Structure', *Journal of Politics* 36: 540–591.

Nie, N. H. and Stehlik-Barry, K. (1996) *Education and Democratic Citizenship in America.* Chicago: University of Chicago Press.

Nie, N. H. *et al.* (1969) 'Social Structure and Political Participation: Developmental Relationships', *American Political Science Review* 63 (2): 361–378 (Part 1) and 63 (4): 808–832 (Part 2).

Nordsieck, W. (2003) *Parties and Elections in Europe.* Available HTTP: http://www.parties-and-elections.de/indexe.html, on line.

Norris, P. (ed.) (1999a) *Critical Citizens: Global Support for Democratic Governance.* Oxford: Oxford University Press.

—— (1999b) 'Introduction: The Growth of Critical Citizens?', in P. Norris (ed.) *Critical Citizens: Global Support for Democratic Governance.* Oxford: Oxford University Press.

—— (1999c) 'Institutional Explanations for Political Support', in P. Norris (ed.) *Critical Citizens: Global Support for Democratic Governance.* Oxford: Oxford University Press.

—— (1999d) 'Conclusions: The Growth of Critical Citizens and Its Consequences', in P. Norris (ed.) *Critical Citizens: Global Support for Democratic Governance.* Oxford: Oxford University Press.

—— (2000) 'The Impact of Television on Civic Malaise', in S. Pharr and R. Putnam (eds) *Disaffected Democracies.* Princeton: Princeton University Press.

—— (2002) *Democratic Phoenix: Reinventing Political Activism.* New York: Cambridge University Press.

Nye Jr., J. S. (1997) 'Introduction: The Decline of Confidence in Government', in J. S. Nye Jr. *et al.* (eds) *Why People Don't Trust Government.* Cambridge: Harvard University Press.

Nye Jr., J. S. and Zelikow, P. D. (1997) 'Conclusion: Reflections, Conjectures and Puzzles', in J. S. Nye Jr. *et al. Why People Don't Trust Government.* Cambridge, MA: Harvard University Press.

Nye Jr., J. S. *et al.* (1997) *Why People Don't Trust Government.* Cambridge, MA: Harvard University Press.

O'Connor, J. (1973) *The Fiscal Crisis of the State.* New York: St. Martin's Press.

O'Donnell, G. A. (1973) *Modernization and Bureaucratic-Authoritarianism.* Berkeley, CA: Institute of International Studies, University of California.

OECD (Organization for Economic Cooperation and Development). *Historical Statistics.* Paris: OECD, several years.

Offe, C. (1984) *Contradictions of the Welfare State.* Cambridge: MIT.

—— (1985) 'New Social Movements Challenging the Boundaries of Institutional Politics', *Social Research* 52: 818–868.

—— (1999) 'How Can we Trust our Fellow Citizens?' in M. E. Warren (ed.) *Democracy and Trust.* Cambridge: Cambridge University Press.

Offe, C. and Preuss, U. K. (1991) 'Democracy and Moral Resources', in D. Held (ed.) *Political Theory Today.* Cambridge: Polity.

Olsen, J. P. and Sætren, H. (1980) *Aksjoner og demokrati.* Bergen: Universitetsforlaget.

Orren, G. (1997) 'Fall from Grace: The Public's Loss of Faith in the Government', in J. S. Nye *et al.* (eds) *Why People Don't Trust Government.* Cambridge, MA: Harvard University Press.

Østerud, Ø. (1998) 'Makt og demokrati hinsides grenser?', in Øyvind Østerud *et al.* (eds) *Mot en ny maktutredning.* Oslo: Ad Notam Gyldendal.

Ostrom, E. (1990) *Governing the Commons: The Evolution of Institutions for Collective Action.* New York: Cambridge University Press.

Packenham, R. (1970) 'Legislatures and Political Development', in A. Kornberg and L. D. Musolf (eds) *Legislatures in Developmental Perspective.* Durham: Duke University Press.

Parisot, L. (1988) 'Attitudes About the Media: A Five-Country Comparison', *Public Opinion* 10.

Parkin, F. (1968) *Middle Class Radicalism.* Manchester: Manchester University Press.

Parry, G. *et al.* (1992) *Political Participation and Democracy in Britain.* Cambridge: Cambridge University Press.

Pateman, C. (1971) 'Political Culture, Political Structure and Political Change', *British Journal of Political Science* 1: 291–305.

Patterson, S. C. and Mughan, A. (2001) 'Fundamentals of Institutional Design: The Functions and Powers of Parliamentary Second Chambers', *Journal of Legislative Studies* 7 (1): 39–60.

Paxton, P. (1999) 'Is Social Capital Declining in the United States? A Multiple Indicator Assessment', *American Journal of Sociology* 105 (1): 88–127.

—— (2002) 'Social Capital and Democracy: An Inter-dependent Relationship', *American Sociological Review* 67: 254–277.

Persson, T. *et al.* (1997) 'Separation of Powers and Accountability', *Quarterly Journal of Economics* 112: 1163–1202.

Pharr, S. J. (2000) ' "Officials" Misconduct and Public Distrust: Japan and the Trilateral Democracies', in S. J. Pharr and R. D. Putnam (eds) *Disaffected Democracies. What's Troubling the Trilateral Countries.* Princeton, NJ: Princeton University Press, pp. 173–201.

Pharr, S. and Putnam, R. (eds) (2000) *Disaffected Democracies: What's Troubling the Trilateral Countries?* Princeton, NJ: Princeton University Press.

Pharr, S. J. *et al.* (2000a) 'Introduction: What's Troubling The Trilateral Democracies?', in S. Pharr and R. Putnam (eds) *Disaffected Democracies.* Princeton, NJ: Princeton University Press, pp. 3–27.

—— (2000b) 'A Quarter-Century of Declining Confidence', *Journal of Democracy* 11 (2): 5–25.

Pitkin, H. (1967) *The Concept of Representation.* Berkeley: University of California Press.

Pizzorno, A. (1966) 'Introduzione allo Studio della Partecipazione Politica', *Quaderni di Sociología*: 3–4, now published in A. Pizzorno (ed.) *Le Radici della Politica Assoluta.* Milano: Feltrinelli.

—— (1993a) 'Come Pensare il Conflitto', in A. Pizzorno (ed.) *Le Radici della Politica Assoluta.* Milano: Feltrinelli.

—— (1993b) 'Le Difficoltà del Consociativismo', in A. Pizzorno (ed.) *Le Radici della Politica Assoluta.* Milano: Feltrinelli.

Popkin, S. L. (1991) *The Reasoning Voter. Communication and Persuasion in Presidential Campaigns.* Chicago: University of Chicago Press.

Powell Jr., G. B. (2000) *Elections as Instruments of Democracy: Majoritarian and Proportional Visions.* New Haven, CT: Yale University Press.

Pross, H. (1992) *Protestgessellschaft.* Munchen: Artemis and Winkler.

Przeworski, A. (1991) *Democracy and the Market.* Cambridge: Cambridge University Press.

Przeworski, A. and Limongi, F. (1997) 'Modernization. Theories and Facts', *World Politics* 49: 155–183.

Przeworski, A. *et al.* (1995) *Sustainable Democracy.* Cambridge: Cambridge University Press.

Przeworski, A. *et al.* (1996) 'What Makes Democracies Endure?', *Journal of Democracy* 7: 39–55.

Putnam, R. D. (1973) *The Beliefs of Politicians: Ideology, Conflict, and Democracy in Britain and Italy.* New Haven: Yale University Press.

—— (1993) *Making Democracy Work: Civic Traditions in Modern Italy.* Princeton, NJ: Princeton University Press.

—— (1995a) 'Bowling Alone: America's Declining Social Capital', *Journal of Democracy* 6 (1): 65–78.

—— (1995b) 'Tuning In, Tuning Out: The Strange Disappearance of Social Capital in America', *Political Science and Politics* 28 (4): 664–683.

—— (2000) *Bowling Alone. The Collapse and Revival of American Community.* New York: Simon and Schuster.

—— (2002a) *Democracies in Flux: Social Capital in Contemporary Society.* Oxford: Oxford University Press.

—— (ed.) (2002b) *The Dynamics of Social Capital.* Oxford: Oxford University Press.

Putnam, R. D. *et al.* (2000) 'Introduction: What's Troubling the Trilateral Democracies?', in S. J. Pharr and R. D. Putnam (eds) *Disaffected Democracies: What's Troubling the Trilateral Countries.* Princeton, NJ: Princeton University Press.

Raaum, N. (1995) *Kjønn og politikk.* Oslo: Tano.

Ranney, A. (1983) *Channels of Power: The Impact of Television on American Politics.* New York: Basic Books.

Remmer, K. L. (1996) 'The Sustainability of Political Democracy: Lessons from South America', *Comparative Political Studies* 29: 611–634.

Ringdal, K. and Hines, K. (1995) 'Patterns in Class Voting in Norway 1957–1989: Decline or Trendless Fluctuations?', *Acta Sociologica* 38: 33–51.

Rootes, C. A. (1981) 'On the Future of Protest Politics in Western Democracies', *European Journal of Political Research* 9 (4): 421–432.

Rose, R. (1984) *Understanding Big Government.* London: Sage.

—— (1989) *Politics in England. Change and Persistence.* London: Macmillan.

—— (1992) 'Escaping From Absolute Dissatisfaction: A Trial and Error Model of Change in Eastern Europe', *Journal of Theoretical Politics* 4: 371–393.

—— (1998) *Getting Things Done with Social Capital. New Russia Barometer VII,* Studies in Public Policy. Centre for the Study of Public Policy, University of Strathclyde.

—— (1999) *What Does Social Capital Add to Individual Welfare? An Empirical Analysis of Russia,* Studies in Public Policy, Centre for the Study of Public Policy. University of Strathclyde.

Rose, R. and Mishler, W. (1996) 'Testing the Churchill Hypothesis: Popular Support for Democracy and its Alternatives', *Journal of Public Policy* 16: 29–58.

Rose, R. *et al.* (1997) *Getting Real. Social Capital in Post-Communist Societies,* Studies in Public Policy. Centre for the Study of Public Policy, University of Strathclyde.

—— (1998) *Democracy and its Alternatives: Understanding Post-Communist Societies*. Baltimore: The Johns Hopkins University Press.

Rose-Ackerman, S. (2001) 'Trust and Honesty in Post-Socialist Societies', *KYKLOS* 54: 415–444.

—— (2005) *From Elections to Democracy. Building Accountable Government in Hungary and Poland*. Cambridge: Cambridge University Press.

Rosenberg, M. (1956) 'Misanthropy and Political Ideology', *American Sociological Review* 21: 690–695.

—— (1957) 'Misanthropy and Attitudes Towards International Affairs', *Journal of Conflict Resolution* 4 (4): 340–345.

Rosenblum, N. L. (1998) *Membership and Morals. The Personal Uses of Pluralism in America*. Princeton, NJ: Princeton University Press.

Rothstein, B. (2002) 'Sweden. Social Capital in the Social Democratic State', in R. Putnam (ed.) *Democracies in Flux: The Evolution of Social Capital in Contemporary Society*. New York: Oxford University Press.

Rothstein, B. and Stolle, D. (2003) 'Social Capital, Impartiality, and the Welfare State: An Institutional Approach', in M. Hooghe and D. Stolle (eds) *Generating Social Capital: Civil Society and Institutions in Comparative Perspective*. Basingstoke: Palgrave.

Rucht, D. (1998) 'The Structure and Culture of Collective Protest in Germany Since 1950', in D. Meyer (ed.) *The Social Movement Society*. New York: Rowman & Littlefield.

Rucht, D. *et al.* (eds) (1999) *Acts of Dissent: New Developments in the Study of Protest*. New York: Rowman & Littlefield.

Sabetti, F. (2000) *The Search For Good Government*. Montreal: McGill-Queen's University Press.

Salzberger, E. M. (1993) 'A Positive Analysis of the Doctrine of Separation of Powers, or: Why Do We Have an Independent Judiciary?', *International Review of Law and Economics* 13 (4): 349–379.

Sani, G. (1999) 'L'elettore Assente', *Political Trends* 8: 33–44.

—— (2000) 'Non Ho Parole', *Political Trends* 10: 22–31.

Sani, G. and Segatti, P. (1990) 'Mutamento Culturale e Politica di Massa', in V. Cesareo (ed.) *La Cultura dell'Italia Contemporanea*. Torino: Edizioni della Fondazione Agnelli.

—— (2001) 'Antiparty Politics and the Restructuring of the Italian Party System', in N. Diamadouros and R. Gunther (eds) *Parties, Politics and Democracies in the New Southern Democracies*. Baltimore: The Johns Hopkins University Press.

Sartori, G. (1976) *Parties and Party System: A Framework for Analysis*. Cambridge: Cambridge University Press.

—— (1998) *Homo Videns: La Sociedad Teledirigida*. Madrid: Taurus.

Scharpf, F. W. (2000) 'Democratic Legitimacy under Conditions of Regulatory Competition. Why Europe Differs from the United States', Instituto Juan March: Estudios 2000/145.

Schattschneider, E. E. (1960) *The Semisovereign People. A Realist's View of Democracy in America*. Hinsdale: The Dryden Press.

Schlozman, K. L. *et al.* (1999) 'Civic Participation and the Equality Problem', in T. Skocpol and M. P. Fiorina (eds) *Civic Engagement in American Democracy*. Washington, D.C.: Brookings Institution Press.

Schmitt, H. (1983) 'Party Government in Public Opinion: A European Cross-National Comparison', *European Journal of Political Research* 11: 353–375.

Schmitter, P. C. (1995) 'More Liberal, Preliberal, or Postliberal?', *Journal of Democracy* 6 (1): 15–22.

Schudson, M. (1998) *The Good Citizen. A History of American Civic Life.* Cambridge, Mass.: Harvard University Press.

Schuller, T. *et al.* (2000) 'Social Capital: A Review and Critique', in S. Baron (eds) *Social Capital: Critical Perspectives.* Oxford: Oxford University Press.

Segatti, P. (1997) 'Un Centro Instabile Eppure Fermo: Mutamento e Continuità Nelle Elezioni Politiche del 1994 e del 1996', in A. Parisi and P. Corbetta (eds) *A Domanda Risponde.* Bologna: Il Mulino, pp. 215–260.

—— (1999) 'Quale Idea di Nazione Hanno gli Italiani? Alcune Riflessioni Sull'idea di Nazione in Prospettiva Comparata', in G. Bettin (ed.) *Giovani e Democrazia in Europa.* Padova: Cedam, pp. 451–483.

Segatti, P. *et al.* (1999) 'Stable Voters in Unstable Party Environment. Continuity and Change in Italian Electoral Behavior'. Working paper. Madrid: Juan March Institute.

Seligman, A. B. (1997) *The Problem of Trust.* Princeton: Princeton University Press.

Seligson, M. A. (2002) 'The Impact of Corruption on Regime Legitimacy: A Comparative Study of Four Latin American Countries', *Journal of Politics* 64 (2): 408–433.

Shin, Doh C. and Wells, J. (2001) 'Testing the Churchill Notion of Democracy as a Lesser Evil in Post-Communist Europe', *Central European Political Science Review* 2: 6–24.

Shklar, J. N. (1991) *American Citizenship. The Quest for Inclusion.* Cambridge, Mass.: Harvard University Press.

Shugart, M. S. and Carey, J. M. (1992) *Presidents and Assemblies: Constitutional Design and Electoral Dynamics.* New York: Cambridge University Press.

Sides, J. (1999) 'It Takes Two: The Reciprocal Relationship Between Social Capital and Democracy'. Annual Meetings of the American Political Science Association, Atlanta 2–5 September 1999.

Siegel, S. (1956) *Nonparametric Statistics for the Behavioral Sciences.* Tokyo: McGraw-Hill.

Sigelman, L. and Feldman, S. (1983) 'Efficacy, Mistrust, and Political Mobilization. A Cross-National Analysis', *Comparative Political Studies* 16 (1): 118–143.

Simmel, G. (1950) *The Sociology of Georg Simmel.* Translated and edited by Kurt Wolff. Glencoe, Ill.: The Free Press.

Simon, H. A. (1996) *The Science of the Artificial,* 3rd edn. Cambridge: MIT Press.

Sniderman, P. M. *et al.* (1991) *Reasoning and Choice. Explorations in Political Psychology.* New York: Cambridge University Press.

Stiglitz, J. E. (1987) 'Principal and Agent', in P. Newman *et al.* (eds) *The New Palgrave: A Dictionary of Economics.* London: Macmillan.

Stokes, S. C. (1995) *Cultures in Conflict. Social Movements and the State in Peru.* Berkeley, CA: University of California Press.

Stolle, D. (1998) 'Bowling Together, Bowling Alone: The Development of Generalized Trust in Voluntary Associations', *Political Psychology* 19: 497–525.

Stolle, D. and Rochon, T. R. (1998) 'Are All Associations Alike?', *American Behavioral Scientist* 42: 47–65.

Streeck, W. (1992) *Social Institutions and Economic Performance: Studies of Industrial Relations in Advanced Capitalist Economies.* London: Sage.

Strøm, K. (1990) *Minority Government and Majority Rule.* Cambridge: Cambridge University Press.

—— (1998) 'Parliamentary Committees in European Democracies', in L. D. Longley and R. H. Davidson (eds) *The New Roles of Parliamentary Committees.* London: Frank Cass.

—— (2000) 'Delegation and Accountability in Parliamentary Democracies', *European Journal of Political Research* 37 (3): 261–289.

—— (2002) 'Parliamentary Democracy as Delegation and Accountability', *ESRC Research Seminar on Modelling Political Accountability: The Principal-Agent Model.* School of Management, University of East Anglia.

Strøm, K. and Svåsand, L. (1997) 'Conclusion: The Limits of Entrepreneurship', in K. Strøm and L. Svåsand (eds) *Challenges to Political Parties: The Case of Norway.* Ann Arbor: University of Michigan Press.

Tarrow, S. (1992) *Power in Movement.* Cambridge: Cambridge University Press.

Thelen, K. and Steinmo, S. (1992) 'Historical Institutionalism in Comparative Politics', in S. Steinmo *et al.* (eds) *Structuring Politics. Historical Institutionalism in Comparative Analysis.* Cambridge: Cambridge University Press, pp. 1–32.

Thomassen, J. (1990) 'Economic Crisis, Dissatisfaction and Protest', in M. Kent Jennings *et al.* (eds) *Continuities in Political Action.* Berlin: Walter de Gruyter.

Thomassen, J. and van Deth, J. (1998) 'Political Involvement and Democratic Attitudes', in S. H. Barnes and J. Simon (eds) *The Postcommunist Citizen.* Budapest: Erasmus Foundation and IPS of HAS.

Tironi, E. and Agüero, F. (1999) 'Sobrevivirá el Actual Paisaje Político Chileno?', *Estudios Políticos* 74: 151–169.

Tocqueville, A. de (1961) *Democracy in America,* 2 vols, transl. by H. Reeve. New York: Schocken.

Tóka, G. (1995) 'Political Support in East-Central Europe', in H.-D. Klingemann and D. Fuchs (eds) *Citizens and the State.* Oxford: Oxford University Press.

Tolchin, S. J. (1996) *The Angry American: How Voter Rage is Changing the Nation.* Boulder, CO: Westview Press.

Topf, R. (1995) 'Beyond Electoral Participation', in H.-D. Klingemann and D. Fuchs (eds) *Citizens and the State.* Oxford: Oxford University Press.

Torcal, M. (2001) 'La Desafección en las Nuevas Democracias del Sur de Europa y Latinoamérica', *Instituciones y Desarrollo* 8–9 (May): 229–280.

—— (2002a) *Disaffected but Democrats. The Origin and Consequences of the Dimensions of Political Support in New Latin American and Southern European Democracies.* Madrid: unpublished manuscript.

—— (2002b) 'Institutional Disaffection and Democratic History in New Democracies', *Central European Political Science Review* 10: 40–77.

—— (2002c) 'Political Disaffection in New Democracies: Spain in Comparative Perspective'. PhD dissertation, Ohio State University.

—— (2003) 'Political Disaffection and Democratization History in New Democracies', Kellogg Working Paper Series no. 308. Notre Dame: University of Notre Dame.

Torcal, M. and Brusattin, L. (2003) 'The Dimensions of Political Support in Comparative Perspective'. Conference 'Democratic Values in New Democracies'. Barcelona, Spain, May 22–25.

Torcal, M. and Mainwaring, S. (2003) 'The Political Recrafting of Social Bases of Party Competition: Chile, 1973–1995', *British Journal of Political Science* 33: 55–84.

Torcal, M. *et al.* (2002) 'Antiparty Sentiments in Southern Europe', in R. Gunther *et al.* (eds) *Political Parties: Old Concepts and New Challenges.* Oxford: Oxford University Press.

Tsebelis, G. (2000) 'Veto Players and Institutional Analysis', *Governance* 13 (4): 441–474.

—— (2002) *Veto Players: How Political Institutions Work.* Princeton, NJ: Princeton University Press.

Turner, F. C. and Martz, J. D. (1998) 'Institutional Confidence and Democratic Consolidation in Latin America', *Studies in Comparative International Development* 47: 65–84.

Twight, C. (1991) 'From Claiming Credit to Avoiding Blame: The Evolution of Congressional Strategy for Asbestos Management', *Journal of Public Policy* 11 (2): 153–186.

—— (1994) 'Political Transaction-Cost Manipulation: An Integrating Theory', *Journal of Theoretical Politics* 6 (2): 189–216.

Uslaner, E. M. (2002) *The Moral Foundations of Trust.* Cambridge: Cambridge University Press.

Valen, H. (1981) *Valg og Politikk.* Oslo: NKS-forlaget.

Van Aelst, P. and Walgrave, S. (1999) 'De stille revolutie op straat. Betogen in België in de jaren '90', *Res Publica* 41: 41–64.

—— (2001) 'Who is that (Wo)man in the Street? From the Normalization of Protest to the Normalization of the Protester', *European Journal of Political Research* 39: 461–486.

Van Aelst, P. *et al.* (1999) 'Politiek Wantrouwen en Protest. Over Het Democratisch Kapitaal van Belgische Betogers', *Tijdschrift voor Sociologie* 20: 441–470.

van Deth, J. W. (1990) 'Interest in Politics', in M. K. Jennings *et al.* (eds) *Continuities in Political Action. A Longitudinal Study of Political Orientations in Three Western Democracies.* Berlin: Walter de Gruyter.

—— (1996) 'Voluntary Associations and Political Participation', in O. W. Gabriel and J. W. Falter (eds) *Wahlen und Politische Einstellungen in Westlichen Demokratien.* Frankfurt: Peter Lang Verlag, pp. 389–411.

—— (1997) 'Introduction: Social Involvement and Democratic Politics', in J. W. van Deth (ed.) *Private Groups and Public Life. Social Participation, Voluntary Associations and Political Involvement in Representative Democracies.* London: Routledge.

—— (2000) 'Interesting but Irrelevant. Social Capital and the Saliency of Politics in Western Europe', *European Journal of Political Research* 37: 115–147.

van Deth, J. W. and Kreuter, F. (1998) 'Membership of Voluntary Associations', in J. W. van Deth (ed.) *Comparative Politics. The Problem of Equivalence.* London: Routledge.

van Deth, J. W. *et al.* (eds) (1999) *Social Capital and European Democracy.* London: Routledge.

Vassilev, R. (2004) 'Economic Performance and Regime Legitimacy in Post-Communist Bulgaria', *Political Studies Association* 24 (2): 113–121.

Verba, S. and Nie, N. H. (1972) *Participation in America. Political Democracy and Social Equality.* New York: Harper and Row.

Verba, S. *et al.* (1971) *The Modes of Democratic Participation: A Cross-National Analysis.* Beverly Hills, CA: Sage.

—— (1978) *Participation and Political Equality: A Seven-Nation Comparison.* New York: Cambridge University Press.

—— (1995) *Voice and Equality. Civic Voluntarism in American Politics.* Cambridge, MA.: Harvard University Press.

Walgrave, S. and Verhulst, J. (2002) 'The Making of the (Issues of the) Vlaams Blok. On the Contribution of the News Media to the Electoral Success of the Belgian Extreme-Right Party'. Paper presented at the APSA Annual Meeting, August–September, 2002. Boston, MA.

Walgrave, S. *et al.* (2003) 'Ministerial Cabinets and Partitocracy. A Career Pattern Study of Ministerial Cabinet Members in Belgium'. *PSW paper*, University of Antwerp (4).

Warren, M. E. (1993) 'Can Participatory Democracy Produce Better Selves? Psychological Dimensions of Habermas's Discursive Model of Democracy', *Political Psychology* 14 (2): 209–234.

—— (ed.) (1999a) *Democracy and Trust.* Cambridge, Cambridge University Press.

—— (1999b) 'Civil Society and Good Governance', Manuscript to be published as part of the *U.S. Civil Society Project.* Washington: Georgetown University.

Weatherford, M. S. (1987) 'How Does Government Performance Influence Political Support?', *Political Behavior* 9: 5–28.

—— (1992) 'Measuring Political Legitimacy', *American Political Science Review* 86: 149–166.

Weil, F. D. (1989) 'The Structure and Sources of Legitimation in Western Democracies: a Consolidated Model Tested with Time-Series Data in Six Countries Since World War II', *American Sociological Review* 54: 682–706.

Weisberg, J. (1996) *Defense of Government: The Fall and Rise of Public Trust.* New York: Scribner.

Wessels, B. (1997) 'Organizing Capacity of Societies and Modernity', in J. W. van Deth (ed.) *Private Groups and Public Life. Social Participation, Voluntary Associations and Political Involvement in Representative Democracies.* London: Routledge.

Whitefield, S. and Evans, G. A. (1994) 'The Russian Election of 1993: Public Opinion and the Transition Experience', *Post-Soviet Affairs (formerly Soviet Economy)* 10: 38–60.

—— (1999) 'Political Culture Versus Rational Choice: Explaining Responses to Transition in the Czech Republic and Slovakia', *British Journal of Political Science* 29: 129–155.

Wildavsky, A. (1987) 'Choosing Preferences by Constructing Institutions: A Cultural Theory of Preference Formation', *American Political Science Review* 81: 3–21.

Wolfsfeld, G. (1986) 'Political Action Repertoires. The Role of Efficacy', *Comparative Political Studies* 19: 104–129.

Zaller, J. R. (1992) *The Nature and Origins of Mass Opinion.* Cambridge: Cambridge University Press.

Zmerli, S. *et al.* (forthcoming) 'Trust in People, Confidence in Political Institutions, and Satisfaction with Democracy', in J. van Deth *et al.* (eds) *Citizenship and Involvement in Europe.*

Index

eBooks – at www.eBookstore.tandf.co.uk

A library at your fingertips!

eBooks are electronic versions of printed books. You can store them on your PC/laptop or browse them online.

They have advantages for anyone needing rapid access to a wide variety of published, copyright information.

eBooks can help your research by enabling you to bookmark chapters, annotate text and use instant searches to find specific words or phrases. Several eBook files would fit on even a small laptop or PDA.

NEW: Save money by eSubscribing: cheap, online access to any eBook for as long as you need it.

Annual subscription packages

We now offer special low-cost bulk subscriptions to packages of eBooks in certain subject areas. These are available to libraries or to individuals.

For more information please contact webmaster.ebooks@tandf.co.uk

We're continually developing the eBook concept, so keep up to date by visiting the website.

www.eBookstore.tandf.co.uk

eBooks – at www.eBookstore.tandf.co.uk

A library at your fingertips!

eBooks are electronic versions of printed books. You can store them on your PC/laptop or browse them online.

They have advantages for anyone needing rapid access to a wide variety of published, copyright information.

eBooks can help your research by enabling you to bookmark chapters, annotate text and use instant searches to find specific words or phrases. Several eBook files would fit on even a small laptop or PDA.

NEW: Save money by eSubscribing: cheap, online access to any eBook for as long as you need it.

Annual subscription packages

We now offer special low-cost bulk subscriptions to packages of eBooks in certain subject areas. These are available to libraries or to individuals.

For more information please contact webmaster.ebooks@tandf.co.uk

We're continually developing the eBook concept, so keep up to date by visiting the website.

www.eBookstore.tandf.co.uk

For Product Safety Concerns and Information please contact our EU
representative GPSR@taylorandfrancis.com
Taylor & Francis Verlag GmbH, Kaufingerstraße 24, 80331 München, Germany

www.ingramcontent.com/pod-product-compliance
Lightning Source LLC
Chambersburg PA
CBHW071352290326
41932CB00045B/1517